AMERICAN CITIZEN

The Civil War Writings of Captain George A. Brooks,
46th Pennsylvania Volunteer Infantry

BENJAMIN E. MYERS

Mechanicsburg, PA USA

Published by Sunbury Press, Inc.
Mechanicsburg, Pennsylvania

www.sunburypress.com

For information about special discounts for bulk purchases, please contact Sunbury Press Orders Dept. at (855) 338-8359 or orders@sunburypress.com.

To request one of our authors for speaking engagements or book signings, please contact Sunbury Press Publicity Dept. at publicity@sunburypress.com.

ISBN: 978-1-62006-130-5 (Trade paperback)

Library of Congress Control Number: Application in Process

FIRST SUNBURY PRESS EDITION: July 2019

Product of the United States of America
0 1 1 2 3 5 8 13 21 34 55

Set in Bookman Old Style
Designed by Crystal Devine
Cover by Terry Kennedy
Edited by Erika Hodges

Continue the Enlightenment!

MOVE WITH US "on to Richmond," and aid our noble leader in reducing the stronghold of rebellion, till, like the ancient temple of Jerusalem, "not one stone shall be left standing upon another." True, it will cost immense amounts of treasure and blood; many noble lives will be sacrificed, but the great principles of liberty must be perpetuated; our government, in all its original purity, must be preserved. Let Pennsylvanians then rally around the old standard, support our noble Governor in the pledges he has made in behalf of the State of which he is justly proud, respond promptly to his call, and before the festive days of Christmas make the annual round you will have returned to your homes with the consciousness of having performed a sacred duty, and earned the glorious title of an "American citizen."

— Captain George A. Brooks. July 22, 1862

Contents

———◆———

————⟩◆⟨————

CAPTAIN GEORGE A. BROOKS started this book over one-hundred and fifty years ago. It is only through the strange twists of time and, perhaps, a little luck, that I am here to finish it. My role in Brooks' story started in the early 2000s when I was in my teens. My great, great aunt, then in her mid-nineties but still sharp as a tack, spent about a year living with my family. With a budding interest in history and the Civil War, the conversation often turned to stories of her youth, which included her grandfather, Elias Boyer, who is my great, great, great grandfather. He had died when she was only a year old, but her parents passed down a few stories of his life, including his service in the Civil War with the 46th Pennsylvania Infantry, Company D.

According to the family stories, Elias permanently damaged his feet on hard marches and lost the tip of a finger at Gettysburg. After the war, he went on "a trip" every year, and though no one knew or remembered the destination, my aunt was certain it had to do with the war. He was secretive in that way, and whatever else happened to him as a soldier, he didn't speak of it to anyone but his son-in-law. Both took the stories to their graves. Despite the lack of information, it was clear the war had left a lifelong scar.

Though the war never left him, Elias lived a full life running hotels in Harrisburg, Pennsylvania. He married and named his firstborn son Brooks Boyer, a name inspired by the first Captain he served under in Company D: George A. Brooks. Elias was an active member of his community, and hosted reunions for fellow veterans. An early 1900s photo shows him surrounded by family with his hand resting on his wife's shoulder and a content look upon his face. When he passed away in 1910, his wife followed him only a few days later from natural causes.

I found Elias' life interesting, and the more I learned about the details of his service, the more I wondered who he was. How had he come back from the horrors he had seen and lived a good and seemingly happy life? I wanted to learn more about the pieces of his life, like the name of his son, Brooks. George A. Brooks must

The author's great, great, great, grandfather, Elias
Boyer, enlisted in Company D of the 46th Pennsylvania
Volunteer Infantry in September of 1861 and served
through all four years of the war. (Source: Boyer Family
Collection.)

have meant something to Elias. What followed were years of research—in archives and libraries, walking through the peaceful,
modern calm of the hellacious battlefields Brooks once traversed,
searching for names etched in stone in the cemetery where he
once took his morning walks, and, of course, hunched over a
computer transcribing the flourishes and scrawls of his writings.

I could not have told the story of George Brooks' life without
the help of many others. My original research assistants were my
parents, who encouraged me to continue my search throughout
my teenage years. They drove me to countless libraries, cemeter-
ies, and battlefields in search of the past and my mom is still the

best copy editor anyone could ask for. I couldn't even estimate how many times she has read each chapter in all of their incarnations. Glenn Shepard traveled with me to Chapel Hill to photograph Brooks' diary and to several battlefields where Brooks fought. George Skotch offered me some mapping advice early on, and Ken Frew and David Buchannon at the Historical Society of Dauphin County helped me early in the stages of research. David Via at the Harrisburg Cemetery took me directly to Brooks' grave the first time I visited and pulled records about 46th Pennsylvania soldiers buried there. At the Chesapeake and Ohio Canal National Historical Park, Karen Gray kindly helped me locate information about Dam No. 6, and Mac Elser welcomed me into his home in Hancock, Maryland, to discuss the 46th's time there during the winter of 1862. Kelly Ford hiked to Dam No. 6 with me and provided copious knowledge on all things Civil War, which proved especially useful when translating Brooks' letters and diary. Jason Wilson at the PA Capitol Preservation Committee showed me the 46th Pennsylvania's flags on several occasions, including as a teenager, which helped inspire me to tell the tale of those who had once carried those battered colors. Joe Bordonaro helped with proofreading and fact checking. Most recently, George C. Bradley has graciously shared his vast amount of knowledge about the regiment with me, which has greatly added to the detail of some sections of my writings. Alissa Scheller helped with maps, editing, and also deserves some credit for listening to me babble about the Civil War. George Brooks' descendants graciously shared photographs and correspondence with me, welcoming and enabling me to tell the story of their ancestor.

As the years have passed and I have learned more about George Brooks, something unexpected happened. I got to know him just a little, in a way that spanned many, many years, and entwined me with his story. I have met people and experienced places that I never would have if I hadn't set out to get an idea of who he was, and, in turn, who my great, great, great grandfather was. In that way, George Brooks' story still continues. I am very grateful to be able to tell the portion of the story that he lived, and I hope that I have done it justice.

O N JANUARY 1ST, 1862, Captain George A. Brooks sat down at a boarding house in Frederick, Maryland, and recorded the activities of a mostly uneventful Wednesday. Unbeknownst to him, the coming year would have a momentous effect on not only his country, but the world. The rebellion of the southern United States had started almost a year prior and, although the war was expected to last only a few months, by early 1862 no progress toward reconciliation had been made. As the year progressed, Union commanders continually erred while Confederate leaders maneuvered fewer troops to near victory on several occasions. Hanging in the balance was the survival of the only true republic—the only experiment of government for and by the people. Should American freedom fall, so too would the hopes of new freedom held by citizens of other countries, some of whom, like the French, had recently lost their own contests to establish a republican government. Many viewed America's war as the ultimate showdown "between the forces of *popular* versus *hereditary* sovereignty, *democracy* versus *aristocracy*," and "*free* versus *slave* labor."[1]

Throughout 1862, America seemed nearly lost at times. Without the staunch resistance of northern citizens turned soldiers, the south's rebellion would have succeeded, and our modern country and world would be a very different place. Caught in the middle of a struggle of ideals, George Brooks dutifully entered a daily record during 1862 and created a firsthand account of this crucial time period in American—and world—history.

Brooks' regiment, the 46th Pennsylvania Volunteer Infantry, doesn't often find itself highlighted in modern histories. This is probably in part due to the fact that a regimental history was never created by the survivors of the regiment. It might also have something to do with the politicking of generals during the war, who brought favorable press coverage to some organizations and

---

1. Doyle, Don H. *The cause of all nations: An international history of the American Civil War.* Basic Books, 2014. 7-10.

not others, or because the regiment lacked vast financial backing. Whatever the reasons for the glossing over of its role, the 46th Pennsylvania played a key part in the defense of the Union and experienced some of the war's most savage fighting. George Brooks' accounts of the regiment's experiences during 1861 and 1862 offer a first-person narrative of some of the war's most famous campaigns against one of its most famous Generals, Stonewall Jackson, from the Shenandoah Valley to Second Manassas and Antietam.

Most of Brooks' known writings are included in this book. The majority of his accounts of military significance come from his 1862 diary, in which he wrote almost every day. The diary is held at the University of North Carolina at Chapel Hill, and is accessible to the public. My research also uncovered regular submissions he made to his local newspaper, Harrisburg's *Pennsylvania Daily Telegraph*, many of which he signed simply "SOLDIER." These articles were often polished and more complete versions of his diary entries, and so in some instances, the best account was selected and the duplicate account of lesser quality excluded. To fill in details Brooks failed to document, other first-hand accounts for the regiment or brigade were employed. To provide big-picture context with the benefit of modern historical understanding, many fine histories of the war were referenced, and I encourage the curious reader to browse the bibliography.

Thanks to over eighty letters Brooks wrote to his wife before and during the war that are still in the collection of his descendants, this book also includes the details of his personal life. Especially in his pre-war letters with his wife, Brooks offers a glimpse at not only the martial, economic, and political climate leading up to the war, but also who he was as a person ("a little wild," he tells us at one point). Although some parts of his correspondence, especially in the first two chapters, might seem unrelated or out of context, they often offer the most candid expressions of his personality.

Masthead of the Pennsylvania Daily Telegraph.

The scope of the letters paired with Brooks' diary and newspaper articles offers an incredibly full view of his life between 1858 and 1862. The personal details found in the letters (which were not located until recently) completely changed some of my assumptions about his life before and during the war. He didn't march off as a hero in the eyes of his family, in fact, his father-in-law told him he wished he would never come home. He had failed in his profession as a printer and struggled to find work, and so, as a result of an economic slump in the late 1850s, soldiering was the first steady job he had had in several years. He struggled with declaring himself a true Christian, even though I'm sure the majority of Christians today would view his faith as unquestionable. He recounts the struggles of his life with clarity in his letters, but pairs them with his optimism and sense of humor. I hope you, the reader, will find yourself chuckling or rolling your eyes at his antics. The Civil War, though of monumental consequence to American history, is often explained in the dehumanized terms of regiments, armies, and casualty counts. Within lies a very personal glimpse at the life of one soldier, whose hopes, dreams, and imperfections are not so different than those of us who live today.

CHAPTER ONE

Take the World Easily

December 1834–May 1859

----··◆·◆··----

FIVE DECADES AFTER the United States of America had declared its independence, the 1830s were a time of rapid expansion. Technology saw the introduction of the first American-built steam locomotive, the commercial wheat reaper, the telegraph, and the commercial sewing machine. Trade benefited from the creation of canals throughout the northeast that linked centers of industry and trade. Settlers moved into territories west of the Mississippi and established the Oregon Trail, pushing Native Americans in their wake.

The Federal government wielded more power than ever before and used its strength to squash uprisings of both Native Americans and slaves. A popular president with the people, Andrew Jackson pushed for a smaller government and paid off US debts, but when warranted he also used a firm fist. When South Carolina rejected legislation that would tax imported goods that they could not produce, Jackson threatened military intervention. South Carolina backed down, but the incident showed that the south's cotton- and slave-bound economy was beginning to clash with the free labor manufacturing economy of the north.

It was into this political and economic climate that George A. Brooks was born on December 31st, 1834. Unfortunately, many of the earlier details of his life are lost to time, although it's likely that he was born in Huntingdon County or Lancaster County, Pennsylvania. His mother died prior to 1842, and in December of that year his father, Samuel Brooks, Esq., married Mary Brooks of Cumberland County, Pennsylvania.[1] Mary raised George as her

---

1. Historical Society of Pennsylvania; Historic Pennsylvania Church and Town Records; Reel: 401.

own, and later in life he remarked, "she has been very good to me, so much so that I scarcely feel the loss of my own dear mother." Mary and Samuel welcomed a daughter, Anna, in 1846.

By 1850 Samuel had established the family in Columbia, Lancaster County, Pennsylvania. Samuel worked as a clerk and was elected Justice of the Peace.[2] Columbia was a small city of about 4,000 residents along the Susquehanna River and offered one of the only bridge crossings in the region. In 1833, the completion of the Pennsylvania Canal linked Columbia, at its southernmost point, with the communities reaching forty miles north, including the capital city of Harrisburg. As canal and later rail construction connected central Pennsylvania with the rest of the state, Columbia became a hub of commerce and also served as a stop on the Underground Railroad.

George remained in school well into his teens and received a good education. In 1856, he gained another half-sister, Mattie. Shortly thereafter, George's parents and sisters relocated about one hundred miles northwest to the small town of Coalmont in Huntingdon County, Pennsylvania. With the financial help of his parents, George parted ways with his family and moved to Harrisburg where he opened a bookbindery at 64 Market Street.[3]

While starting his business in Harrisburg, Brooks became acquainted with a fellow printer and publisher, Theodore Franklin Scheffer. Scheffer, a native of Germany, made his own ink and electrotypes, and was one of the first printers to use color inks in his publications. He printed a variety of genres in both German and English.[4]

Brooks' smaller operation took on private jobs, along with printing blank books for the local government.[5] In 1858 he expanded and published his first book, "The Annals of Harrisburg," which received favorable reviews and is still known by local historians.[6]

Brooks involved himself in the social circles of the city, attending Zion Lutheran Church where he taught Sunday School,

2. Year: 1850; Census Place: Columbia, Lancaster, Pennsylvania; Roll: M432_787; Page: 212B; Image: 426.

3. George Brooks personal correspondence with Emily Scheffer Brooks. May, 1859. The first advert for Brooks' Bindery appears in *The Columbia Spy Newspaper* on March 13, 1858, indicating he had relocated to Harrisburg by this time.

4. Kelker, Luther Reily. *History of Dauphin County, Pennsylvania: With Genealogical Memoirs.* Higginson Book Company, 1907. 351.

5. *Pennsylvania Daily Telegraph.* August 27, 1859.

6. Morgan, George Hallenbrooke. *Annals, Comprising Memoirs, Incidents and Statistics of Harrisburg: From the Period of Its First Settlement.* GA Brooks, 1858.

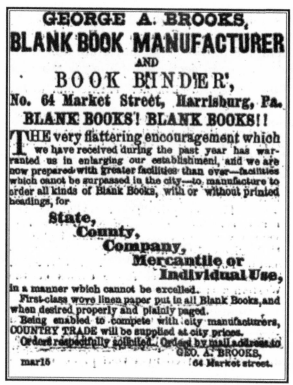

An advertisement for George Brooks' book bindery in Harrisburg. (Source: Pennsylvania Daily Telegraph [Harrisburg, PA], August 27, 1859.)

playing flute in the local harmonic group, spending time with friends, and attending parties where he would admit he could be "a little wild." He spent time with his closest friend, Lew Mill Hyers, and two friends he held as sisters, Mary and Tullie.[7]

Sometime in 1858, a friend introduced George to the eldest daughter of fellow publisher Theodore Scheffer, Emily.[8] Brooks immediately expressed interest in Emily and began visiting the Scheffer's family home. Despite having a healthy professional relationship with George, Scheffer reacted badly to George's interest in his daughter. His dissatisfaction turned into resentment and a near hatred that would, in time, threaten Brooks' business and social standing.

---

7. George Brooks personal correspondence with Emily Scheffer Brooks. October, 1858. Brooks Family Collection. Correspondence of Reverend Hay, February 13, 1860.
8. Ibid. April 23, 1859.

For the remainder of 1858 and the early months of 1859, Brooks maintained a steady correspondence with Emily. At times, Scheffer attempted to end their courtship, and they were forced to write one another in secret.[9] Although it proved to be a difficult courtship, George and Emily exchanged frequent and candid messages.

Throughout their correspondence in 1858 and the tensions that arose at home, the political climate of the United States continued to worsen. Years before, when both George and Emily were teenagers, rapid land annexation that included Texas, California, and most of the modern day western United States had forced the country to acknowledge the question of slavery and whether it should be allowed in newly established states. The presidential election of 1860 loomed on the horizon, and debates between candidates Stephen A. Douglas, who supported allowing new states to choose to permit slavery, and Abraham Lincoln, who believed new states should not be allowed to have slavery at all, highlighted a national divide.

In the following letters, printed for the most part in their original language, format, and content, George speaks of the concerns and joys of his life in Harrisburg. He struggles to prove his sincerity for Emily and win her affections. Despite his strong relationship with the Church and God, he expresses his uncertainty of declaring himself a true Christian. He worries of his financial standing, and the success of his business. Yet despite his concerns of everyday life, he also writes paragraphs of humor, poetic introspection, and an unending love for his friends, family, and the world around him.

October, 1858

[Emily,]

What a couple Lib and Mary Boyer are. If ever woman was "sick" after a man they are after Lew, and I am sorry his good sense and judgment has not enabled him to discern it. In fact several times I have had a notion to write to Lew and plainly tell him what I think, but then on reflection it is "none of my business." And yet Lib and Mary set themselves up as models,

---

9. Various personal correspondences between George Brooks and Emily Scheffer Brooks, 1858 through 1859. Brooks Family Collection.

primps of perfection, but I honestly believe they seeming will yet succeed—they will yet lay their fingers on him and perhaps quarrel over the spoils. Mary Hummel is worth a hundred of them as a <u>woman</u>, and yet Lew could not get her, much as she admires him as a friend. I was astonished that the staid, sober, party should go to such a place as Stallabach's and dance all night and not return until 6 o'clock next morning. Surely Emily, the one who informed you must be mistaken, at any rate keep quiet and say nothing about it.

You may thank your "queer daddy" that he never permitted you to go on such excursions, because a young lady is never any better off and frequently worse and sometimes her character is badly discouraged, sometimes beyond reparation. You may have thought it hard, at that time, but are you any worse for it now. I think not. Besides you are better able to guide your George who has tasted all those fleeting pleasures and may sometimes be a little wild. You can curb him.

I will send you my speech tomorrow. It will be published in one of the morning daily papers of this city, together with Mr. Duff's reply etc. I will send you several copies.

But Emily I must close. I have again written you a long letter and expect tomorrow morn to receive your Sunday letter. <u>Write daily</u>.

Love to all my friends, pop, mom, Theo, Frank etc[10]

Kind regards to ladies and gents and reserve for your own dear self the faithful devotion of

Your own
George

———••◦••———

January 1, 1859
Harrisburg, Saturday morn

Emily,

In truth you are a good kind hearted soul, for so readily and candidly responding to my note of yesterday, and I sincerely assure you that the "glad tidings" which it bore and the earnest sympathy which you so frankly expressed did me more good than all the medicine I have taken. It was not <u>too</u> long, and how often it was read I shall not tell you, but <u>will</u> tell you, that <u>I now know you better</u>. Purer, holier feelings than those of friendship

---

10. Brooks is referring to Emily's mother, father, and brothers, Theodore Jr. and Franklin.

shall hereafter prompt me to <u>confide in you</u>, and how greatly will you add to my happiness by placing implicit <u>confidence</u> in <u>me</u>. I know how you are situated and keenly feel how much it tends to mar our pleasures, but Emily henceforth I <u>shall not mind</u> [your father]. One must expect in traveling through life to meet with some difficulties, and I have concluded to meet mine, especially those which <u>he</u> throws in my way, as philosophically as possible "Every cloud has silver lining" and every sorrow which <u>we</u> now experience is but the forerunner of future happiness. But Emily do not think <u>he</u> has <u>forsaken</u> you. A father cannot forget the love he bears for a child. He is proud of you, and had hoped to see you do better than by encouraging <u>me</u>. I am sorry that I should cause you so much suffering, but Emily I speak in all candor. If I wrong him, you, I know will forgive me. But come what may the promise of Christmas night shall not be broken.[11]

. . . Emily, I do pray. I believe more in prayer than anything else, and try in my thoughtless way to do good, but there are so many stumbling blocks in my path to discourage an open profession, so many professed Christians with whom one is called into association by church membership, that rather than be like them, and be a hypocrite too, I cannot now conscientiously now join church and will not do so until my conscience approves it. Most gladly would I, and if you can convince me, do so. This may be sad news to you but tis better that I should be <u>frank</u> than <u>pretended</u> [sic], and I trust it will not change your feelings towards me.

I am better today, and shall if tis a fine afternoon take a walk out in the air, as far as the Brady house, as through the <u>persistent</u> kindness of Mr. and Mrs. Cunkle, <u>who would not let me go</u>. I have not been <u>very</u> far from the building.[12] Now remember your letter was not <u>too</u> long, and did not tire my patience. <u>My promise is kept again</u>. I have much more to tell you. [You] will be tired when you get this [but], if not inconvenient, a word or two would not be amiss to look at this evening. Otherwise I shall wait until Sunday eve

Truly Yours

George

---

11. Brooks often remarks on the Christmas Night Promise, but never directly restates it. It is always mentioned in the context of Emily's trust for him.
12. The Cunkle's were a family with whom George boarded.

———————◆•◉•◆———————

January 4
Tuesday afternoon

Emilie,[13]

In answer to your question, I would say "<u>I am very well</u>." My throat does not trouble me and the only remnant of my sickness is a very sore mouth. The next time I hope to have <u>somebody</u> to take care of me.

No excuses for abruptness as I well know the cause but do not by any means forget that "something of importance," as I am anxious to hear it when I come on Wednesday evening. Though long a coming it will be the sweeter when it comes, as deferred hope, crowned at last, brings a two-fold happiness. And do you not remember the conversation of Christmas night? Did I think it were so easily forgotten I should not have excited your curiosity by recurrency to it. But I do not think you <u>really</u> forget it, and shall perhaps on Wednesday eve may remind you of it. As to my kindness, "oh, never never mention it." Much more would have cheerfully been done for your sake, and I was amply repaid in your confidence.

In regard to your father I shall have nothing more to say. When he treats me the same as he did ere I committed the <u>unpardonable sin</u> of crossing his threshold, at the invitation of his daughter, then will I respect him and not until then. He sat within three feet of me last night, but didn't speak.

Now one thing I should like to know, that is, your reasons for exacting the "<u>promise</u>" you have from me, of course I always comply with it, but have you no confidence in me? If you trust me at all why not trust me all the time. I am sure I do not require it of you, but implicitly submit to your judgment. Can you not do the same to me?

But Emilie I am in a hurry so you will excuse this hasty note. I know it may not be as long as you wished, but expect better. Let me hear from you if convenient. Hoping you are occasionally given a random thought [of] me. I remain

Ever Yours
George

---

13. Brooks would alternate the spelling of Emily's name, interchanging Emilie and Emily

———————•◦•◦•———————

Mid-January
Friday morn

Emilie,

I commenced writing to you last night but was prevented from finishing by the arrival of "Lew" when we chatted pleasantly until 11 o'clock and then went home, at an hour when you were enjoying the pleasure of "balmy slumbers soft repose," and perhaps, would it were so, sweetly dreaming of <u>somebody</u>. Could you have heard some of our conversation I know you would have laughed heartily, for when two old familiar friends, like we are, and bachelors too, at that, get together, you may rest assured matters in general are pretty thoroughly discussed and <u>sometimes</u> our own fate, prospects etc, etc, etc, receive particular attention. But you didn't hear and I won't tell.

Emily, won't you forgive my little joke of yesterday? How I should have laughed to have seen you receive it, ever at the risk of having my ears boxed.

How sadly I miss Mary Hynicka. Truly, she is a good sweet girl, and Tillie and her have been as sisters to me. I have looked upon them as such and have lavished upon them a brother's love. Indeed Mrs. Hasler's old homestead has been a <u>home</u> to me. But the best of friends must part, the many pleasant evenings with Mary, Tillie, Lew and I have passed together will come no more. Soon Tillie will also go, but the ties which bound us shall never be broken, their memory will ever be sacredly and fondly cherished, and we know or at least hope we shall never be forgotten.

Your good friend Maggie is also gone, and therefore you can, from sympathy, more keenly appreciate my feelings. I myself value her friendship and felt sorry to see her leave.

But while losing the company of those who are so dear to me, am I not happy in having the society of one in whom I can confide and trust, who will confide and trust in me, and be unto me perhaps more than a sister. I know you do not forget me, and sincerely hope you never shall. Tell <u>me</u> your troubles, confide them to my keeping but wish not for "death" to relieve you. Tis true "sorrow treadeth upon the heels of joy" but there is no sorrow that is not tinged with joy, "Hope on, hope ever." Look not to the past, but fix thy gaze upon the future, place thy trust in God, and you shall yet be happy, <u>very</u> happy. On Wednesday evening

I wish you to tell me what you speak of in your note. In regard to going away, I would advise you not to. In truth, a due regard for my own pleasure would oppose such an idea. Why what would I do? I should be lost. <u>You shall not go</u>.

Don't send me any more bad penned notes or I shall box <u>your</u> ears. I can scarcely read it now.

Well, I have hastily scribbled you another long letter, and must now go to breakfast. Think of me occasionally through this day and I will safely surely be visible tonight about 7 o'clock. Until then, Emily, adieu

Very Truly
Your George

February
Monday evening

Emilie,

Truly you have well fulfilled your promise and have fairly earned my warmest and most sincere thanks. "Frank" brought [your letter] to me when at work this morning and in giving it to me. Mary Bush saw him when she at once suspected from whence it came. It makes but little difference, however.

Glad am I to know that George is the first one to whom you confide your troubles and pleasure, and most willingly will he share them.[14] I am fully satisfied to entrust you with mine, that is what few I have, but remember Emily I take the world easily, have few troubles and make more.

No, indeed. I shan't tell you of [Lew and my] conversation. "Bachelors" have secrets too, and must enjoy their lives of single blessedness as best they can. Perhaps <u>someday</u> I will tell you, but until then you may box my ears whenever I refuse.

Any arrangement you may make in regard to "our correspondence" will suit me, only so it is a safe one. <u>Suit</u> yourself and it will suit me. Now, what do you propose?[15]

. . . No, Emily, I do not think you are really so trivial, and in all candor allow me to say I do not like sedate people. I am not <u>very</u> sedate myself, and do not by any means want you, in order to satisfy <u>folks</u>, become as sedate as an old maid. Do not by any

---

14. Brooks referred to himself in third person at times.
15. Emily's father wouldn't allow George and Emily to correspond, so they did so in secret.

means. If you do, I shall tease you until you change, and you know I _can_ tease.

Emily, you are welcome to share of that love which I have bestowed on our dear friends <u>Mary and Tillie</u>, and can if you will fill the void which their departure will leave in my heart. You know I am without a sister, and until I had one who would become nearer than a sister to me, they of course were my confidants. I respect, esteem and even <u>love</u> them as a brother, and I know never thought of aught else, then truly should I not be proud to own them. You know me, how many kindnesses I have received from them, kindnesses which nothing can ever repay. Emily, you can promote my happiness if you will, and I hope you will cheerfully comply. More anon, on this. Don't call all Georges mischievous, surely I am an exception.

Pretty idea, truly "you go to the city." Of course did you go I would come and see you as often as business and funds would permit, but you will not deprive me of your company in that way, no indeed you shan't go.

If you go to Columbia [Pennsylvania] I will come down and stay over Sunday as I promised, but don't go to the city. Why what would I do. I surely would be lost. It is six o'clock. If you can read it excuse this hasty scrawl. I had scarcely time to quit work. No more but expect an answer.

Truly yours,
George

———— ·•●•· ————

February
Thursday Evening

Emilie,

Arose very early and took a ramble to enjoy the fragrance of the cool, bracing air, and admire the bright and beauteous scenery of nature. Oh, Emily, I love to stroll, when free from the cares of the world one can drink in as it were, the splendors which cluster around and adorn country life. When we can meditate upon the changes and sorrows which so often mar our happiness, and hopefully muse upon anticipated pleasures. Truly it was a glorious morning, so beautiful, all gayety and sunshine and while the remembrance of the kind encouraging words you had given me at our parting on yesterday evening filled my mind, I was indeed happy, but how much <u>happier</u> would I have been could you have been with me. I hope the day is not far distant when we shall share each other's' joy and sorrows—when free from the jealous cares of an over cautious father you can look to <u>me</u> for sympathy and consolation in <u>all</u> your troubles. On my return I passed the "Harris Mansion" and thought of the intended wedding <u>which you might get me an invitation to</u>. It is rather an antiquated, rough looking house to spend the honeymoon in, but 'tis better to <u>love</u> in that than to <u>fight</u> in a better <u>one</u>. How glad was I on coming to the store to find that Frank had not only the note I had not received but another one in waiting for me, and I need not tell you the eagerness and pleasure with which I read them.

I wonder what makes your father suspect we correspond? <u>Surely he must</u> be <u>greatly mistaken</u> to suppose such innocent souls as we would be guilty of the <u>grievous</u> sin of corresponding without his knowledge or consent. But for your sake dear Emily I shall write less frequently and be more cautious sending, lest he may find it out. I should be sorry, very sorry, to cause you any more trouble than I have already done, but rest assured you shall not be forgotten, that I will often constantly think of you, and when I do write, shall endeavor to make them longer and better, so that in hours of loneliness, if there is anything cheering in them you can peruse them and give a thought to George. You do not know how sadly I shall miss the frequent visits of your cheering and little musings, but I will patiently bear, with the confident hope that it will not long be so. Why should we hide <u>our</u> feelings and mask <u>our</u> pleasures simply to minister to the whimsical ideas of one who thinks as truly I am unworthy of his daughter. He cannot always have you at home or else I am sadly in error. Emily why do you say you have no friends that no one cares for you? Surely has not George given you reason to know better? Has not my actions convinced or at least given you room to think more than my lips have, as yet, breathed?

Why do you ask my forgiveness for the tears you shed on Wednesday evening? It is not wrong to give way to our feelings in thinking over the past and though sorry to see you weep, I was also glad, and as to your letters, I did not for a moment suppose you were in earnest, and am very happy to know you have not forgotten their contents. I sincerely trust no one will disturb us on next Wednesday evening for I always anticipate so much pleasure in spending it with you alone, and although I do not think I am a very selfish mortal yet I do not like intruders to <u>accidentally</u> "pop in."

You cannot fill the place of Mary and Tullie? They receive a brotherly love, but you can fill a nearer and place share a more sacred affection, be to me more than a sister, and make me truly happy. Will you give me a candid, truthful answer? Emily, I have given you many things to answer. You can write me a long, long letter and for George's sake let it contain "good news." I am obliged for giving my love to Maggie, and shall faithfully keep the secret of her "Clinton" safe, I am glad you trusted me. "Lew" has just dropped in, this after 10 o'clock, and consequently I shall finish and give it to Frank in the morning. I cannot direct it tonight for fear Lew might see to whom I write. So goodnight and pleasant dreams. Truly Yours, George

"Lew" says judging from a casual glance I must be writing to somebody I like.

[Continued] Friday morning 7 o'clock

Good Morning Emily

Have just returned from an hours ramble through the cemetery and will now finish my long, tiresome letter to you.[16] You doubtless know I am a great walker, indeed I do love morning walkins [sic], and it does one good to occasionally visit along the "silent city of the dead" to muse and meditate with the remembrance of man's mortality strewn around you as thickly as the "autumnal leaves which strew the brooks of Vallombrosa."[17] Reverend Hay called to see me yesterday. Had a good long conversation with him, and honestly wish I could make up my mind [about being a Christian]. In fact he called more particularly to see Frank and just gave me a pop visit.

Well now, dear Emily, isn't this long enough? Have not I for once written you a long letter and won't you give me one such in return? Now I shall anxiously look for one by Saturday at least. I hope it may not rain tonight though it now looks like it.

Hoping this may reach you safely and knowing you will have fun endeavoring to read it all. I remain until I hear or we meet

Yours faithfully

George

---

16. Brooks liked to take walks through Mount Kalma Cemetery. Today it is referred to as the Harrisburg Cemetery.
17. From Paradise Lost by John Milton.

March, 1859
Wednesday morn

Emily,

Think you have forgotten me! No, dear friend, no such thought for a moment entered my mind. I knew the confidence I have reposed in you had not been misplaced, and therefore while anxiously awaiting an answer to my last in fulfillment of your promise of Sunday evening, gave you a gentle chiding for what apparently seemed your negligence, as I was not then aware you had written one which I did not receive. Read it in the spirit in which it was written. But, Emily, why did you not send the first one too. Surely it would have not been stale to me, for if you knew how gladly I welcome, and how fondly I treasure every thought which they contain, you would certainly not deprive me of that pleasure. If in the hours of sadness the perusal of mine, cheer you, how much more so will the perusal of yours add to my happiness. Truly, Emily, you have in George one who honestly endeavors to promote your happiness; one whose chief pleasure is in sharing your joys and sorrows; one in whom you can and I hope will place implicit confidence. The past must be the criterion by which to judge of my sincerity. If that does not sufficiently prove it, what will? Anything in my power to accomplish shall not be left undone to convince you.

Emily, speak not so harshly of Sue. We all have our faults. What you have said in regard to her is too true, but before believing anything which emanates from such a source, first ascertain whether it is really correct. Gossip is the favorite pastime of many nowadays—therefore be cautious. Everything should be carefully considered before entitled to belief, and let us also cautiously guard one's own actions, "charity begins at home."

Have no fears of my mentioning anything which transpires whilst I am at your home. I have learnt long ere this to heed not his remarks. He seems determined to frustrate my hopes, but shall not. You are the one to whom I look.

. . . Now Emily, I have not counted the words but have tried to write you a long letter. I was at a party last night at Kate Felix's until 12 o'clock and it is now only 6 o'clock, so you will see I did not rest much last night. Awoke this morning at 5 o'clock. It was a long party and very pleasant. Would have been more pleasant had you have been there, at least to me. I shall see <u>somebody</u> early tonight, unless we are rudely by prevented, until then <u>forget me not</u>. No more. I remain

Truly yours
George

———————•◆•———————

March 26, 1859
Saturday

Emilie,

May the day end as pleasantly as it began, for <u>early</u> this morning, instead of <u>one</u> as anticipated, I was the fortunate recipient of <u>two</u> precious little "billet doux" which you may rest assured were carefully read and then <u>contents</u> stored where they cannot be burnt. The latter one, written after we parted last night, shows that after I leave, you do not entirely forget me, Amo te.

Oh, what pleasure it would have given me to have been by your side in that "cozy little room" when you were suffering so, for I do think I might have slightly cheered your loneliness, or at least sympathized with you, if my sympathy were worth anything <u>to</u> you.

You are a good prophet, but I hope you will in future prophecy <u>clear</u> weather, when we cannot be debarred from our engagements. Perhaps it rained just because you said it would.

You shall not be <u>disappointed</u> in hearing from me today, and if my notes give you any pleasure in their perusal, most cheerfully will I at any time, write and as frequently as you wish. If their contents are as gratifying to you as yours are to me, most gladly will I make them as long as I can, so that in "hours of sadness" you can spend a few moments in reading them, and know that George was truly and sincerely interested in endeavoring to do anything which would give you pleasure. But Emily I sometimes get sad too, and yet I am not permitted to save those I receive from you. Hereafter, with your permission, I shall do so, and you I hope have confidence enough in me to know that they will be well taken care of. Trust me, confide in me and you shall never regret it.

But Emily, perhaps you have not time to read more. In hoping you have time to return a long answer which I can keep. I remain as ever

Truly Your
George

"Oh, kindly, often think of me
And I will fondly think of thee"
Pleasant be thy dreams, and may thy heart prompt now and
then a prayer for George . . .

March 29
Noon

Emily,

Well, I suppose my last note did not deserve an answer, and I
again write hoping this one may meet with a better fate. You
might have written, as you promised on Sunday evening, for this
has been a very dreary morning, and only a line or two would
have been very cheering. I presume some reasonable excuse prevented you and shall therefore patiently await an answer to this
one, if you deem it worthy, have time, and can trust me without
a request to burn it. When will you learn to confide in me?

. . . What a forgetful mortal I am, never thought of your album
until we had nearly reached the Depot on Monday morning. "To
err is human, to forgive divine." Will you forgive George?

What is the use of my writing such long letters when you won't
answer. You must not forget this time, if you do I will pull somebody's ears, and shall not have the "favorite" on Wednesday
evening. Won't you write?

Very truly
Yours
George

April
Friday Morning

Dearest Emilie,

Was hardly fairly seated in my "old armchair" yesterday evening, after parting from you, when in drops the "little vixen" who
made himself comfortable until 10½ o'clock when he started for
home wondering why I did not accompany him, and what I wanted here at that time of night.[18] The truth was, I remained for the
purpose of writing to my own dear Emily, but after reading your
long letter several times, for it was such a good one, I concluded
to go home, and write early this morning, so here I am before the

---

18. Sadly, the "little vixen's" identity is unknown.

clock has sounded the hour of six, engaged in endeavoring to fulfill my promise. Don't I always try to make good all the promises I make to you, and will I not <u>always</u> endeavor to do so. Only give me an opportunity, if I fail then chide me harshly if you will.

Had a long and very pleasant walk again this morning, and would gladly have had my own dear Em by my side, never mind, we will soon have rambles together. Won't you go to the Cemetery some pretty afternoon? I had a pleasant saunter through it myself this morning. Oh, how I love to muse o'er the graves of those who were once as gay and happy as your own George, but who now alas "sleep the sleep that knows no waking" in the "silent city of the dead," Mount Kalma, where the weeping willow gently kisses the tomb of the slumbered who rests beneath, and flowers—those bright emblems of mortality on which the kind hand of affection has planted o'er the grave of some dearly loved one, fill the air with fragrance. How sorrowful, to read the tributes of love, engraven upon the marble tablets, but how much more sorrowful would it be could we read the thoughts and feelings which are engraven upon the tablets of the heart of those who have lost some near and dear friend. From the dead the living should learn a lesson, for we know not how soon we may rest among them.

"Leaves have their time to fall,
And flowers to wither at the north winds breath,
And stars to set—but all,
Thou hast all seasons for thine own, O Death."

How true it is, then, that we should be ready to meet him, that we should be prepared to "walk through the dark valley of the shadow of death, and fear no evil" but having on His staff, placed our trust on a merciful God—enjoy a glorious immortality in that world of bliss where "the wicked cease from troubles and the weary are at rest." For your sake dear Emily I shall pray, that my faith may be strengthened, and will you continue to pray for me, will you offer a supplication to the Throne of Grace for your own dear George, for "the prayer of the righteous availeth much." How glad I am that you will love me, that you have that deep abiding confidence in me, that my feelings have met with a ready response in your own heart. I did not think you were tired writing to me, and am glad it gives you so much pleasure, which let me assure you is mutual, but oh, you tease me so, and sometimes do not seem like the same Em that writes me such beautiful, kind, affectionate letters. Of course I forgive you but do lay aside your reserve, are we not <u>one</u> in feeling? How sad it was to separate from you after spending such a pleasant evening. The walk there and home, though was pleasanter to me than the visit, and I am so glad we postponed it. I am never happier than when my own dear Em is by my side. How soon will we always be so, will you share my sorrows and joy.

Friday evening, 7 o'clock

Dear Emily,

I had written this far when I was compelled to close, and just this minute got time to finish. I am very tired, working hard all day.

. . . Dear Emily I did not take offense at what you said last night, because I do not think you desire to offend me, but oh you do tease me and sometimes by your indifference worry me a little, a second sober thought makes it all right. I know you like fun and I like you for it, and what a consolation it is to have you ask forgiveness as you do. Indeed were it not for your letter I would hardly know what to think of you. In them I think "from the fullness of the heart the mouth speaketh." Do I not judge right? Your mother's daughter was served right for being so disobedient, but I am sorry your throat got so very sore. Truly those who won't hear must feel.

. . . Do not say your letter was uninteresting. It was the most so I ever received, and oh, how I wish this would be so to you. Indeed, Emily, I feel as though there is a sad deficiency in this one, which was caused by the hasty manner in which I have had to write it. I shall promise and try to do better in the future. Any mistakes or errors you will excuse.

I have several times made up my mind to ask your father's consent to our proposed union but when it comes to the point, I fail for want of courage.[19] I will talk to you about it on Wednesday evening. I am so afraid, I know not why, that he will refuse. But I <u>will</u> ask him. More anon on this matter.

Well dear Emily I will stop. I would like to have written much more for it is really a great pleasure to write to one in whom we have all confidence, whom I devotedly love. Emily, answer all my questions and write me a good long letter. Please excuse the haste in which this is written, I have been in such a hurry. Lew

---

19. This is the first instance where Brooks mentions plans of marriage.

has just come in and is playing the flute while I finish. No more dear Emily. Hoping to see you this evening I remain

Very truly
Yours only
George

April, 1859
Monday Evening

Dearest Emily,

Having to work busily tomorrow, and fearing were I to postpone writing until then you might be disappointed in receiving an answer as soon as anticipated, I have stayed from Harmonic [Group] to enjoy myself that more pleasantly in holding secret communion with my own dear Emily, in confiding to her care and keeping those sacred thoughts which come gushing up from the deep fountains of the soul, and fill my heart with a deep, abiding love, which has I hope dearest Emily, met with a ready response in thine own heart. Has it not Emily?

Like yourself I was an unusually attentive listener of [Reverend] Fry, and was forcibly imbued the great truths which he so beautifully expressed. Never have I listened to a sermon which gave me so much pleasure; never have I heard a discourse which so thoroughly filled my soul with a sense of its own sinfulness and of the joy and delight which they who live continually in the fear of the Lord will experience when they walk the golden streets of the Beautiful City, singing praises to the Most High God. I am glad you were happy and prayed for George at the communion table, Emily. I feel as though you did not love me because of my failure to embrace the religion of Jesus. May I hope that ere another season passes we may be <u>one</u>, and shall stand at the table of the Lord, and seal anonymously a mutual pledge of love for Christ.

Dear Emily, nobly have you done your duty in asking the forgiveness of your father—happy am I to hear that you are again friends. Willingly, cheerfully, will your George unite with you in forgetting the past, in forgiving <u>all</u>, and in looking forward to a bright and glorious future. I shall ask his consent to our union at the very first opportunity, though it is a delicate matter, and will require the sacrifice of many previously cherished ideas of independence. Were it not for the confidence you express I would entertain many fears of success.

I know dearest Emily, we shall be very happy, that you will earnestly endeavor to make George so, and he will faithfully perform his duties. An attractive, happy home with contentment, it matters not how humble it may be, brings a two-fold delight. Oh, Emily, would we were already bound by those sacred ties which bring true happiness. Tell me <u>your</u> thoughts on Wednesday evening—let no timidity prevent you—<u>we are one in heart</u>, therefore let the expressions of our hearts be candid, frank, and sincere.

Any arrangements you may make will be cheerfully complied with, only drop me a line stating at what hour, where etc. I must come. If her reception is on Wednesday evening, we will take the next for <u>our evening</u> as you propose. Do not deprive me of that or I do not know what I should do. My earnest wish is that it may not long be so, that we may soon spend all our evenings together.

But Emily, I have written several other letters and it is now getting late. I think this is a little longer than yours, though I did not make any calculation. At any rate, I shall try to do better in future, and hope you may receive some pleasure in perusing this one, never mind. I shall at no very distant day eat some of <u>your</u> dinner, of which I think I shall be remarkably fond, especially on account of the cook.

I have a rich joke to tell you about Harry catching me last night. What a sly codger he is. Hope Sue and him will go off— even if we "Em, and George" must set them an example. Well Good night, dear Emily—think of and pray for George, and he will remember thee.

I am so anxious to hear what your father said and patiently await for Wednesday.

I remain
Yours only
George

April, 1859

. . . Never mind your father, he will relent some day, and then your happiness will be much greater. What do we care what answer he gave. He has opposed us all the time, and as you are satisfied to love without his consent it makes but little difference. If your mother is on our side we want nothing more. I know Emily you will be true to me, will endeavor to make my life happy, and you know George will also endeavor. Would we were one now, how anxiously I shall wait for time I can call you mine, from whom no one can separate you. We will keep it a secret as long as you wish, or until the time, consequently it will not be kept very long. Oh, Emily I love you dearly, am so sad and lonesome without you. It is a wonder no one intruded yesterday evening. I wish it would always be so.

Emily, dear, forgive this short uninteresting note. I am "very, very tired and sleepy" and do not think you can half read this. In fact I can scarcely keep them open, but I could not fail to write to you.

Hoping to see you tomorrow evening, and that you will often think of George

I remain

As ever

Your George

Write soon a long very long letter, do not let this short one deter you.

Good night, locked in balmy slumbers safe repose, you may be perhaps dreaming of your George. It is 15 minutes of 12 o'clock.

------◆------

April 11, 1859

Monday noon

Dear Emilie,

As I told you yesterday evening your long, long letter was not received until Sunday morning, but oh how welcome it was; how cheering to my heart were the hopes and sympathies which it contained. Though I have highly prized and fondly cherished those which I have heretofore received, yet how much more do I value how much more dearly I will and do cherish the last one. With what pleasure did I dwell on the frank avowals you have made, and read the candid confessions of an honest heart, and let me assure you my own dear Emilie that they found a ready response in my own heart. It was a very agreeable surprise, as I had no hope of hearing from you until this morning, and such a bright beginning on a sabbath morning, made the day although a dreary one, very pleasant and beautiful to George. My heart was happy, happy to know that you thought George worthy of your trust and confidence, worthy to share your joys and sorrows; trials and pleasures. Emily, you shall not be disappointed, your confidence shall not be betrayed, you have reposed trust in one who will make every effort to render your future life a happy one. But I shall write and speak more on this anon.

. . . Do not forget your present but my dear Emily you shall not always be unhappy or I will be because George cannot make you happy. You shall not always be doomed to spend your days under your father's roof or it will be because you will not forsake it for George. Our pleasure shall be no longer married so much to [concern] for others, our feelings shall no longer be hid. Your candor in professing is viewed as the promptness of a generous heart, and if there be life below or hope above, our hearts which have as yet near confessed the tender secret, but let it silently and strongly swell responsively to the bidding of <u>love</u>, and our souls hold sweet and sacred communings of pure happiness and delight. Oh, Emily, how impatiently I wait for our meetings. How fondly I long to behold the dark eyes flashing out joy to mine, as you kindly welcome me. With you I sincerely trust we may not be stopped by intruders on next Wednesday evening.

. . . In return for your good long letter I return you this one, though it is not by half so interesting and satisfactory as yours was to me. I did not count the words and have written in a great hurry. I am very busy but can, as Mr. Hay said yesterday about a certain young man whom he called on—I wonder who it could be—"Take time" to write to my own dear Emily. You can, at full liberty, to make your letters as much longer as you wish, as you may rest assured they will be read every word. Write so that I can get the answer by Wednesday morning. I will stop by the store for it and will get it then safely.

You will excuse this long letter but as we can only write once a week I must make this as long as possible and endeavor to make them interesting, though I fear I have sadly failed in this case.

I will bring yours along on Wednesday if you will read it to me as you promised, though I had no difficulty in reading every word and imagining much more. Now don't fail to write a long, long one. Adieu then dear Emily, until we again meet

Truly Yours
George

P.S. I hope this may safely reach you. If it should fall into the hands of the enemy, you know who he is, I would not there be few, and how sadly you would have to suffer. My earnest prayer shall be offered for its safety

Yours Only
George

----•◦•----

April 15, 1859

My Dear Emily,

Perhaps you did not expect to hear from me this morning. If so I sincerely trust this may prove an agreeable disappointment, if it does not unfortunately, like yours of yesterday, fall into the hand of the Philistines.

I did not rest last night. Sat up until after 12 o'clock talking with my father, and he wishing to take the morning train of cars for the west at 3 o'clock, gave him my room and went into ladies parlor, where I lay on the sofa until it was time to awaken him to start. I did not sleep but could you have known how many plans were laid for our future happiness, how many air castles were built, you would surely have thought your George really foolish. But my dear Emily they were not all mere vagaries; there were some which may and can be realized and that quite speedily, which I shall explain on next Wednesday evening. How long it will seem until then.

Father, whom I had not seen for over a year, left this morning for home, and though it would have at any other time have made me feel sad, yet the recollection of yesterday evening drove away all sadness, and rendered me truly happy. With what pleasure did I dwell on the cheerful assent you fondly gave, and oh, Emily if George does not make you happy it will not be because he will not make an honest endeavor to do so. I have now so many things to tell you. Henceforth you only shall be my confident; you only will I trust, unworthy as I am, and Emily will you not place more confidence in me, will you not make your George some return for the fondness and affection which he will lavish on you. Truly dear Emily, I shall endeavor to merit it. Oh, could I but have you by my side this afternoon, how much I could tell you that prudence dictates should not commit to writing when so much danger of detection exists. I will look for a long, very long answer to this before Sunday sometime. I would ask it sooner but I know your opportunities for writing will not allow you to. Perhaps I may go to Columbia on Friday noon and return on Saturday evening. If not I will let you know in time so that I shall not miss seeing you at choir. If I do not go on Friday I will go on Tuesday and return on Wednesday, perhaps may go on Monday. Could you not go along at that time?

. . . Knowing that I should be remembered in your prayers to the throne of grace, and hoping you will often kindly and fondly think of me, while we are separated. I remain until next we meet, and ever after

Truly your faithful
George

If your father knew all what would he say. He must at no very distant day. May I not communicate what matters my judgment warrant to Lew?

———————•◦•◉•◦•———————

April 23, 1859
Saturday

Dear Emily,

Oh, were my tongue as rich in language as is the coloring in Fancy's loom, it were all too poor to express the least part of the joy and pleasure which the perusal of your long and interesting letter gave to George. How glad was I to know that you were truly happy; that the same feelings which had prompted me in writing also actuated you. Truly, my dear Emily, our souls' deep dreams shall yet be realized; our warm affections have not gushed in vain; and soon, I sincerely trust <u>very</u> soon, will they blend in one un-severed stream of pure and sacred love, on which no ripple of sorrow or discontent may ever come. Let us then be frank, honest, trustworthy and true, and with a firm reliance on God, "He who looketh down with great mercy," look forward to many years of happiness and peace, earnestly hoping that he who has so ceaselessly endeavored to separate us may yet have cause to regret his course. [Your father's] efforts have only resulted in binding us closer, if such can be. I have always endeavored to conduct myself as consistently as possible, and the only excuse he can have is my poverty, not wishing his only daughter to make such a sacrifice. Previous to my visiting you he was apparently the best friend I had but alas, what a change, he now treats me more like a dog, in a manner that I heed only for your sake. I am somewhat of a philosopher, looking very coolly on provocation, and am more inclined to laugh than become angry, but had he not been your father I would have reminded him of it ere this. But as you very correctly observed on yesterday, "What can't be cured, must be endured," and we will therefore have to get along without any encouragement from him which though very unpleasant can very easily be done, when hearts beat in unison, and hope lends her cheering rays to dispel all gloomy thoughts and forebodings. He will find out something very shortly which will surprise him more than ever.[20]

It would have been gratifying to me indeed could you have seen my dear old father. He is a real jolly old soul, I know you would like him, though he is gone and it is now too late to show the original.

I shall endeavor if I don't forget to bring along his picture on Wednesday evening.

You passed on the opposite side of the street on Tuesday, when I showed him, and told him who you were and whom I <u>expected</u> you to <u>be</u>, and also showed him your picture at Keet's but did not give him the last idea of <u>when</u>, and he did not mention the subject after I left.[21] On Wednesday before I saw you, he told me Gus Burnet spoke of you and also of me, but said he had never seen me, but heard I made <u>occasional</u> visits to your house. I may go home shortly and will then inform him or write. Tell your mother [of our engagement] as soon as you like and also your father. When he hears won't there be <u>fear</u> and won't George keep out of his way to save my precious neck. But he must know it <u>before long</u>, the sooner the <u>storm</u> is over the better. Tell <u>no one else</u> if you wish it kept a secret. I will confide it to "Lew" for him I can trust. It will be as safe, perhaps safer than with ourselves. I have particular reasons for telling him which I will explain on Sunday eve. Harry shall <u>not</u> know it for awhile. Suppose Sue and he had gotten the window awhile before I left. Would not they have found <u>something</u> out. They might have <u>known all</u>, which they do not now.

With you I hope Sue and Harry will yet become "twins of one flesh," but he is such a fickle mortal. I remember when Sue said I

20. Brooks and Emily are already engaged.
21. Asahel G. Keet's Photographic Studio was active in Harrisburg starting in the mid 1850s. He and Brooks were friends.

was fickle, and only intended to sport with young ladies feelings. Indeed many others said so, and I must confess there was some truth in it, though I did it unintentionally and I may say innocently. Experience taught me better, I am now so no more, but am satisfied, and none but my own dear Emily shall share my lust, and every effort of mine shall be to increase her happiness, to render her path through life bright and beautiful.

Like yourself I could talk much easier and with more freedom than I can write, and would have been very happy could I have been with you in your loneliness. Indeed, Emily, it does appear very long until Wednesday evening, and for a while, only a little while, we will have to bear it. Yet I am glad you find so much pleasure in writing to me. I can fully appreciate your feelings and sincerely hope you may find as much in my company.

"Liz and Jeffy" must enjoy themselves greatly, and when they return we, Emily and George, will take some fine afternoon and visit them. A person with his means might have got "his pet" something better to live in than the "old warehouse," but that is better than none at all. In truth she is very lucky to get into it, and if she really does love him, can do so there as well as in a "three story brick hut." Remember fortune is very changeable, those who are rich today may be poor tomorrow and we should therefore be ready for the worst. In times of prosperity we should prepare our hearts for adversity, for we know not when the evil hour may come.

Dear Emily, I am indeed very sorry that I cannot join myself to our church on the coming Easter Sunday, but I do not yet feel that I have yet reached that standard of Christian excellence which would warrant such a step. I do wish I were a good Christian, continually walking in the fear of the Lord, but do not feel free from the many sins which cling around me, and my heart repels the idea of making an open profession, when I am not at heart changed, have not received mercy from he "who tempers the wind to the shorn lamb." I am sorry, very sorry, dear Emily, that my failure in this respect distracts from your happiness and love for me, but I must and will stick to principle and right, even though I should lose all else in the world beside. You will go, and when engaged in the solemn services, oh Emily do breathe a prayer for George, yet he may yet find grace, and become a true and faithful member, earnestly endeavoring to promote the glory of God, "The prayer of the righteous availeth much" pray then for me. Let no sinful thoughts enter your mind, drive them far away from you. If it was my influence which prevented you from leaving our church I am glad of doing what I conceive to be some good. I keenly feel the deep interest Reverend Hay has taken in my welfare, he is a good man, comes nearer my ideal of an honest consistent preacher, than any I have hereto met. Would I were like him. Think I shall try to become so as nearly as I can.

I am not tired reading your letter. It is a good long one but not too long. I am very anxious to hear the conversation Sue and you had about the fair, and shall look for you to tell me very soon. How thankful I should be to Annie Stephenson. Had it not have been for her, we should never have met, and then George would not have known Emily. But everything is for the best. It seems the fates ordained it thus, and how happy I am that it is so. We are now engaged and let us banish all fear and candidly peer into the future, openly confess all, and endeavor to do such things as will promote our happiness. Hoping to soon see you and enjoy one of our long social chats, more social than any heretofore. I remain until then,

Very Truly Yours
George

Write soon and very long. Monday morning I believe you promised

———•:•◆:•◆•———

May
Sunday Night

Dearest Emilie,

'Tis night, the time for mind's free breathings in a purer clime; the time when after daily cares, when the busy hum of industry is hushed we enjoy rest and calmly review the past, consider the present, and make high and earnest resolves for the future. But, oh, what delight does it give to read and remind the precious tokens of the confidence and esteem of those we love; hope appropriate, after leaving the sanctuary of God, after parting from my own dear Emilie, to spend the remainder of the evening in answering these tokens.

Dear Emilie, I love you. I love to answer your frank affectionate letters. They are the golden links that bind me the more closely to thee, for in them many of your most sacred thoughts have found expression, which had else remained unknown to George. To them I owe much of my happiness, for I am <u>so</u> happy in the thought that <u>my own dear Emilie loves me</u>. Make me thine only, and the gentle whisperings of thy voice within shall be enough to strengthen me. I do not know how to thank you for stealing from the hours of slumber, an hour or two and devoting them to George. Truly you <u>are</u> a good kind soul. How my heart leaped with joy when you gave me the letter this evening, and if mine was really interesting to you, how much more so was yours to me.

Yes, dearest Emilie, I should have loved to have had you with me this morning, and shall as soon as I can avail myself of your consent to take a ramble in the "silent city of the dead." But how sinful it was if you wish yourself beneath the sod. You may have had troubles, you may have suffered much, but are we not born to trouble. It is God who "doeth all things well" and not for us to refuse to trust in him but turn to Him in the hour of trouble. He is able to save unto the uttermost. I know you are not unhappy now, you certainly should not be so. You have everything your heart wishes for, a more comfortable home than George is able to give you, kind parents, and if you act the part of a dutiful daughter, I know they will love you, they do love you. It is only George who has caused your unhappiness, your estrangement from your dear father, merely because you received the attentions of <u>one</u> whom he liked very well until he feared I might become <u>his son</u>. I sincerely trust if he is wrong he will see his error, and treat me differently in future, for the past I care not. He is freely forgiven, too well you know, that all that has transpired will be forever kept a profound secret. He is to blame some, and perhaps I am much more. I should have been less taunting, and not have laughed when he was angry. I am glad to hear from you that he now thinks well of me, that he is not angry but will freely and cheerfully give his consent to our union, when I know we shall be happy, very happy. I will endeavor to be kind to him, and know I shall please him, and our home, humble though it may be, shall always be a pleasant one for him to visit, and see how his dear Emilie can assume the duties and responsibilities of a dear wife. But Emilie it is growing late, I must to bed and will finish unless prevented, tomorrow noon. Excuse the writing, it is very bad, for I have written hurriedly. Pleasant dreams to you then, and may thought of George not mar thy slumber. Adieu Emilie, I shall pray for you.

———◆•●•◆———

May, 1859

Dearest Emilie—

I am an early bird. Have had a walk, and am now writing to you before it has struck 5 o'clock. I have just read what written last night. I will wait anxiously for what you have to tell me on Wednesday evening. I would ask your father's consent but cannot get a chance, to have him alone, and will talk to you about it on Wednesday evening. Never mind, it won't be long, for the reason that I won't wait. I will make a chance, if I can't get one.

I'm glad you love flowers. I am and always have been so very fond of them, and in fact can't do without them. How I should love to have a little yard, in which I could cultivate some choice ones, but a few crocks at a window will have to suffice until I can get a better place.

Emilie, I have often felt unhappy and sad at the many indifferent remarks you have made, but now know you better and freely forgive. I love to see you lively, love to see you free of fear, and my father will too for he is such a jolly old soul. We will some day soon take a trip to see them in the mountains. They live very humble, they have robbed themselves so that their only son could obtain a little to start in the world, but live very happily, and I really think I am very undutiful in not visiting them. But I am kept so busy, my mother is a good Christian, and daily prays for me. She has been very good to me, so much so that I scarcely feel the loss of my own dear mother.

Indeed you must have a pleasant place among your flowers in your cozy room with a little bird chirping its merry ways so sweetly, and am glad it gives you so much additional pleasure to acquire and answer the letters of your own dear George.

If you are going to send me a more interesting letter next time I should like to see it. I am afraid you can't though don't be discouraged "if at first you don't succeed, try, try again."

For your sake dear Emily I shall go to the Tuesday evening meeting and endeavor to find peace. Do, dear Emily, pray for me. I will go.

Don't be surprised to see me around for you some fine afternoon, when we will take a long walk. Have a raging party to ourselves, and George will crown you "Queen of May." The first one I am not very busy I will come.

Now dear Emily I shall close. Remember these [paper] sheets are very large, and my letter is therefore a very long one. Hoping you will answer soon, a long, long one. I remain

As ever
Your own
George

May 5, 1859
Thursday night, 10¾ o'clock

Dear Emily,

Have worked hard all day ruling for your father. Regretted my conduct of Tuesday and for your sake endeavored to do all I could to please him today, even foregoing the pleasure of writing to my own dear Em. After supper went to lecture, at which there was a very large attendance. Came from thence to [the] bindery, and had been here but a few minutes when "Lew" came with whom I have had quite an interesting conversation for nearly two hours past, on my soul welfare. I was glad he came, it did me good to see him take such an interest in me, to know that his professions were fully exemplified in his conduct. Like your own self he talked with me long and earnestly and endeavored to clear away the many doubts which cling around me. Oh, Emily, he is an honest, true friend, and his departure left me sad and lonely. Would I were like him, in spirit, Emily pray for George, cease not in your efforts.

We shall not long be separated, soon I hope very soon I will be with you always, and then you can aid and assist me in securing the "pearl of great price." Oh, Emily, how happy we should be, with a home, in which, though humble it may be, we could spend all our evenings together. I now miss you so very much, and it is so long to wait from Wednesday to Wednesday. Well, if matters go as I would wish them I shall endeavor to tell you something by next Wednesday.

Indeed, my own dear Emily, the time did seem long until I heard from [you]. I do really think this has been the longest week I have ever spent. But Wednesday evening came at last, and with it the happy heart and cheering smiles of my own dear Emily. Oh, tis sweet to know there is an eye that waits our coming and grows brighter when we come, that the warm affections of your heart beat for George alone. Truly Emily you have made me happy, truly you must love or have confidence in me. Do you remember how beautifully Mr. Hay spoke of the marriage two some Sundays ago, of the confidence which it required in a young girl to leave father and mother and cleave onto <u>one</u>, for better or worse.

Be not surprised if you hear of our marriage. The fact of my making inquiry about several houses, will set the tongues of all the gossips in motion. Well let them go. We don't care, and on next Wednesday evening, I may have more plans to disclose.

[remainder missing]

May 6, 1859
Friday morn

Dearest Emily,

Please give me a definite answer, so that I can inform "Lew" how to act. I would prefer adhering to the time originally set—Thursday evening—and if Mr. Hay will not stay to secure the services of Mr. Bishop or anyone else whom you may designate. Please give me an immediate answer.

Try and be at choir this evening, if your duties will permit you, if not I shall be round at 8, tomorrow. Everybody knows it. I am teased by nearly every person I meet.

Excuse haste etc. I have been lifting and cleaning up, and am very nervous

Truly Yours
George

May 9, 1859
Monday morning

Dearest Emily,

Frank has just given me your note, and I hasten to answer for it does seem very long since you have written to me.

I am a forgetful mortal, think of nothing now but you. Have your father print cards for our wedding. We will send a few to some of my friends who reside at a distance merely as a compliment, they cannot attend. I may also send a few to some of my relations in town perhaps. We will talk over this on Monday evening. I wrote to Mary Hynicka this morning, extending her a cordial invitation to come. When the cards are printed will send her a more formal one. Should she accept, with your consent I will invite one or two more.

Your plan for reception on Friday and Saturday evenings I admire. It is decidedly the best and will not cause any ill feeling. All who wish are perfectly welcome to come. In regard to sending invitations I think the sooner the better. Only a few days remain. Do as you think best in all things. We will talk the matter over this evening.

Soon my dear Emily, will we mutually promise to "love, honor and cherish" for "rich or poor" "better or worse," until death do part us. Our responsibilities are heavy, we are entering upon an important era in our life. We must now throw off the giddy frivolous amusements of youth and seek enjoyment and purer happiness in those of more usefulness. We are but on the first rung of the ladder of life, let us climb up together, each helping the other. May God in his grace render our life a happy one. May no sorrow occur to mar it.

I am in haste dear Emily. Have much to do. Hoping soon to see you

I remain
Yours only
George

***

Having for a time made a truce with Theodore Scheffer, George and Emily started their life together on May 19th, 1859. Surrounded by friends and family, they were married at their church, First Evangelical Lutheran, now known as Zion Lutheran, in Harrisburg.[22]

---

22. Historical Society of Pennsylvania; Historic Pennsylvania Church and Town Records; Reel: 691.

*George Brooks and Emily Scheffer on their
wedding day. (Source: Brooks Family Collection.)*

CHAPTER TWO

The Fates are Against Me

June 1859–March 1861

⊷⊷⊷•⊙•⊷⊷⊷

G EORGE AND EMILY spent the summer of 1859 settling into married life in the home of Emily's father, Theodore Scheffer. Though they hoped to afford their own home, George's sole source of income, his book bindery, was struggling. Harrisburg, surrounded by farms and relying on a heavily agricultural economy, was feeling the brunt of an economic downturn that had started a few years prior.

Although the beginning of the 1850s had seen rapid economic expansion in the United States, the economy had slowed by the latter half. In part, the downturn was due to a decline of the international economy along with the failure of a large bank, the Ohio Life Insurance and Trust Company. The economy was further stymied by the Supreme Court's Dred Scott ruling, which made slavery in the western territories permissible and discouraged northern investors from pursuing westward expansion. The entire country was affected by the downturn, but primarily agricultural trades in the north felt its brunt. Northerners placed blame on the south's aggressive pro-slavery agenda, and although the initial financial panic ended shortly, a real recovery was slow. Unemployment soared and businesses went under.[1] George wrote to his father that July, lamenting the problems his own business was facing:

---

1. McPherson, James M. *Battle Cry of Freedom: The Civil War era.* Oxford University Press, 2003. 189-191. Ross, Michael A. *Justice of Shattered Dreams: Samuel Freeman Miller and the Supreme Court during the Civil War Era.* LSU Press, 2003. 41.

Letter from George Brooks to his father
July 16, 1859
Harrisburg

Dear Father

Your favor came safely to hand, and I had partly answered it nearly two weeks ago when I was interrupted, and today again commence anew.

. . . I am glad to hear you have had so favorable season for the growth of your crops, and presume should I visit you, I would meet with superb entertainment. In green corn season I may come up if I am not too poor. You must bear in mind that times are hard and I find it hard work creeping along. By the time I am out of debt, if I shouldn't fail before I got so, I expect to be somewhat of a financier. My business is now passing through a dull season and money is very scarce until after harvest. Can barely be got at all.

I am glad to hear you have been employed as Superintendent of the new road to Broad Top, and wish you abundant pecuniary success.

. . . My better half returns her kindest thanks for your wishes for her future welfare, and would like greatly to see her new mother. That, however, cannot be until next year unless you come down for I cannot bear the expense of coming up.

I have not heard from any of our friends or relations for some time and presume most if not nearly all of them have forgotten me. Very well, let them. Though poor now the day may come when I can as easily cut their acquaintance as they now can mine.

Mr. Evans' Bible has been done for a week or two. How shall I send it?

Write soon. Wife and self sends love to mother, Annie and Mattie.[2] When in a humor I will [write] more at length in a week or two. I do not feel like it now. Accept <u>our</u> best wishes for your future as well as present health etc etc and we remain

Very truly
Your affectionate S & D
George and Emily

---

2. George's half sisters.

❊ ❊ ❊

Unfortunately work didn't materialize, and by 1860, George was forced to close his bindery and look elsewhere for work. He set his sights first on Pittsburgh, where he applied to Duff's Mercantile College and hoped to find more work than in Harrisburg.[3]

As George headed west, the upcoming presidential election was dominating news across the country. Vast political changes were underway, including the collapse of the Democratic Party, which had dominated politics since the turn of the century. Southern Democrats, strongly pro-slavery, took their place, and forced Northern Democrats to consider compromises over slavery. After a failed Presidential convention and unable to agree on policy or a candidate, the party split and chose two different candidates, John C. Breckinridge, a Southern Democrat, and Stephen A. Douglas, a Northern Democrat.

Meanwhile, the Republican Party nominated Abraham Lincoln, a westerner and a moderate, who was firmly against the expansion of slavery in new territories. Unlike the more liberal contenders for the nomination who proposed the abolition of all slavery, the party hoped Lincoln's moderate platform would attract more conservative voters in states like Illinois and Indiana.

With the candidates chosen, decades of discussion and unrest had reached their paramount. It was clear that electing a president meant voting for or against slavery, and therefore, to the south, for or against war.[4]

———◆•●•◆———

Recommendation letter for George A. Brooks
from Reverend Charles A. Hay
Harrisburg Feb 13 1860

Mr. DeHaven,

Dear Sir,

Tho' personally unknown to you, I take the liberty of giving my friend, Geo. A. Brooks, Esq. a line of recommendation, to be presented in case he sees fit to offer you his services in your publishing establishment. He has been for some time a teacher in my Sunday school, and has carried on his "State Capitol

---

3. Various correspondence between George Brooks and his wife. Brooks Family Collection.
4. Wagner, Margaret E, Gary W Gallagher, and James M McPherson. The Library of Congress Civil War Desk Reference. Simon and Schuster, 2009. 124-127.

Bindery" from which he has sent forth much work that is highly creditable. He has disposed of that establishment and is on a tour of observation—seeing a new location for business. Should he for a while be engaged in your house I have no doubt he would give complete satisfaction.

Very respectfully,
Charles A. Hay

George Brooks' Mercantile College Recommendation
Pittsburgh 16 March 1860

This Certifies that the bearer Geo A. Brooks is a graduate of this College having attended a full course of lectures and gone through a full of exercises in Double Entry Bookkeeping and having passed a highly satisfactory examination upon the same, he was awarded the Diploma of the institution.

It is also due to Mr. Brooks to state that his habits of industry and persevering application to business. This taste for neatness, precision and accuracy (exhibited during his attendance at College) indicate rare qualifications for any department of business, and which, with a little experience will certainly speedily place him in the first class of practical accountants and businessmen.

Respectfully submitted
P. Duff
Principal, Mercantile College

Letter from George Brooks to Emily Brooks
March
Pittsburgh, Pennsylvania

[Emily,]

You no doubt wonder at the strange heading of my letter. Just as I sat down to write Will Duff came to my desk, and got me to do a little favor. Whilst doing it he said he would address my letter, and I accordingly began where he had finished. If it had taken me longer I suppose he would have went on writing to you. On Monday or Tuesday my Diploma will be made out.

. . . If I could get a good situation here I would not mind staying here awhile, for to make money.[5] I could endure the dirt and

---

5. A "situation" refers to work.

smoke for a season, but there is but little hope, and if I cannot get one west I shall have to fall back to my good old, staunch friend, Mr. J. G. L. Brown, who has ever taken a lively interest in my behalf.

But more on this anon. I must now close after writing you so long a letter and thus returning good for evil. Give my kind regards to all my friends, and remember me particularly to Mary Hummel, Lew, in fact all, and also my [Sunday school] classes.

Love to mother and pap, and all the boys. Don't fail to write every day and thereby greatly relieve the monotony of my life and the loneliness which I experience without you.

But think of me often, pray for me daily, and you can rest secure in the love of

Yours only
George

Accept a thousand kisses and kind and loving. Don't fail to write.

✳ ✳ ✳

George returned home to Harrisburg for the summer of 1860 after news arrived that Emily was expecting their first child. Still struggling to find work and without the finances to move the small family out of Emily's parents' home, George and Emily's father again found themselves at odds. On September 7th, 1860, George and Emily welcomed their first child, William Denning Brooks—affectionately called "Willie."

George spent little time with his newborn son before he was forced to look elsewhere for work. This time, he headed to Philadelphia, hoping to find a stable job. He arrived by early October and looked for printing work, but had little luck. His once optimistic and cheery nature disappeared from his letters home, as homesickness and stress took their toll.

——————◆•◆•◆——————

Letter from George Brooks to Emily Brooks
Oct 13, 1860
Philadelphia, Pennsylvania

Dearest Emily,

Nothing of any importance has transpired since writing yesterday and my chances of securing a situation are if anything worse. I came very near yesterday securing a situation but was disappointed. A few days ago the "Press" who have heretofore had their paper worked at other offices, purchased a new improved double cylinder press and Mr. Brown said if I can arrange it so as to learn to run it by November 1st when they intend to commence needing it, I might have the situation. It is to be put up in the pressroom of the North American, and the pressman on that paper agreed with Mr. Brown to learn me. Mr. Knife, a clerk in the office, overheard the conversation, and having some friend of his own, he . . . caused a disagreement between Mr. Brown and him and he accordingly refused to have anything to do with it. I went yesterday and saw him myself, but he was very angry and it was of no use. They have accordingly made arrangement to employ another man who is now running a similar press on the "Post" and who thoroughly understands it. I was very sorry because although it would have been very hard work, and would have required me to have been up all night— every night—still it would have for the present paid me $17 per week and with a prospect of an increase. We would, of course, have had to board as I could not have left you alone in a house all night, and besides rents are so high. Jones's, where I am now writing, lives about 2½ miles from his work and yet pays $180 a year. Jennis lives in West Philadelphia on Darby road above thirty-second street and pays $250, and neither of them have room to turn round for a yard. Mr. Marris' house would rent for $750, so you can form an idea of how much it takes to live in the city. I get so very lonely every day, and wish I was in old Harrisburg along with Emily and Willie.

. . . I have a notion to go to Baltimore and from there on South until I get something to do, or my few dollars run out. It will be almost impossible to get anything to do here. There are hundreds of printers idle, and in offices I have been in they have applicants every day for work and as to getting a clerkship it is almost out of the question. Mr. Brown says whenever an advertisement appears in the "Press" for a bookkeeper or clerk, there would be from fifty to a hundred applicants before noon. He says if I would wait here a month or six weeks he might work me into a place in the Press, by degrees, but I would have to work all night and sleep in daytime. But this I could not afford to do as I would not have money enough to pay my board. I therefore can see no other way than to go South, where I am informed work is plenty, but oh, how hard it will be to leave you and dear little

Willie. I think and pray for you every night and only wish I could see you for I am so lonely, but every cloud has silver lining and I trust better days will soon come. What shall I do, give me your advice. Excuse my writing, it is in a cold room and my hands are stiff. Don't forget to write immediately, direct 1128 Oxford Street, Phila. Write the direction very plainly. Love to all my friends, don't fail to write and believe me as ever

Yours only
George

Take care of Willie and kiss him for me

————◆•◆•◆•◆▬▬▬▬

Letter from George Brooks to Emily Brooks
Oct 22, 1860
Philadelphia, Pennsylvania

Dear Emily,

I did intend writing to you on yesterday but having gone to church and when in the house becoming deeply interested a book which I was reading I postponed it until this morning. But I have been running around all day and have not had time. It is now nearly just getting dark.

Today I went to Johnson's for work but they have barely any, though they think they may have in a few weeks. I was sadly disappointed, as I did expect to have gone to work, but alas I was born in an unlucky stay, and the fates are against me. I do not know what to do. What little money I have is fast dwindling away. I have no means of getting it without work and you need and should have some. Bear, dear Emily, as long as you can. As you say better days are in store for us, and when I once again get work, we shall again make some headway, but how I hardly know unless I get a good situation, for today I have inquired at over some dozen boarding houses as to price of board and the cheapest I could find was a meanly furnished room in a fourth story without gas, or water, which could be had with board at $8 per week and I judged from appearances the board would not have been very good. In order to live even at such a rate I would have to make at least $12 per week, while I have no hope of a job at which I can make more than $8 or $9. Now is not our prospects gloomy, I do not write this to frighten you but merely to show you how matters really stand and again to ask you whether I had not better leave the city and seek something elsewhere, in the meantime having you remain in your unpleasant position. Now what do you say? Give me a fair and candid opinion and as a true wife, nerve yourself to bear up under the trials which seem to surround us. I have not heard from you since Friday, though as I have not been to Oxford Street since morning there may be one there for me now. Hereafter direct everything you send me until further orders to care of J. G. L. Brown, 417 Chestnut Street, where I will be sure to get them. I intend removing my boarding place down to the city nearer business tomorrow morning.

. . . Dear Emily, I am very lonesome without you. Willie I should dearly love to see and have something to pass my evenings with. It will soon be too cold to pass them without fire and remember that costs a dollar a week extra, which would make my board $5—ours $9—Now what chance have I, or rather we. How I wish we were in some little far off village, where undisturbed I might secure some occupation, and we could pass our lives pleasantly. But I must stop, it is getting near dark, this paper is not ruled, and it is hard to write in an office among a dozen hands and the noise of presses etc etc

So goodbye, dear, until you hear from me again when I trust to have better news. Say nothing to anyone. There are many idle printers here, and many working on half pay, but good night dearest. Kiss our dear Willie for me, take care of him be good and kind and you will always have

Yours only
George

Letter from George Brooks to Emily Brooks
Thursday evening, Nov 8. [1860]

Dear Emily,

Your kind favor of Tuesday morning was safely received by your very humble servant on Wednesday noon, but so busy was I that I did not give it a reading until after one o'clock on Thursday morning to which time I had to work; I commenced yesterday morning at 7 o'clock, and worked steadily until 1 o'clock but work has run out now and today several of the hands in our office are out of work. It may commence in a day or so again. I did not go to bed until I read your letter and consequently slept very soundly more so than I had not read it. Today I again read your letter, and with what feelings of pleasure, how sincerely your

George A. Brooks around 1860. (Source: Brooks Family Collection.)

description of the visit which Willie and yourself made to Mary Barritz's seemed to me, and how I envied you and sorrowed that I was unable to participate with you. Sincerely you must have felt happy and proud of "our Willie." Indeed, dear, I am truly glad you were in such a glorious mood and so heartily enjoyed yourself. Do by all means go and spend an afternoon with Mrs. Denning, she will be glad to see you, will treat you kindly. I am glad she is so much pleased with Willie, I only wish I could see him. Lida Gray is a queer fish, Mr. Sertzer is very kind. Go to Mary Boyer's if you can, I am glad you have at last got to singing, and trust when we get together we shall enjoy ourselves more than we formerly did at that amusement.

I got a letter from Keet today in which he said he had an excellent photograph of you, and says the group and mine are nicely colored and he will have yours done as soon as he can. He was been a good friend to me and says he misses me very much. I will try in a day or so send you a few dollars again, enough if I can to pay Sally Bryan, and then perhaps you can get another one for which you can pay at some future time. I am very poor now, and gave you my situation in my last letter.

Keet wants me to come up on Thanksgiving. Maybe I may, and go from there to Washington if I get work.

This afternoon Brenizer and I dressed up a little and took a walk around the city. We walked all afternoon, though I wanted to come home and write a long letter to you, but he would not let me, said he wanted company, and I could write this evening. Well evening is here and they are now hurrying me to get ready to play. It is almost impossible to write, amid such a scraping of violins, etc. I am almost out of my senses. They are truly trying to see how much discord they can make to annoy me.

As this is all my paper I must close. Give my love to mother and all my friends. I will write more at length tomorrow if I do not work. Give Willie a kiss for me.

Love to all friends and I will ever remain

Yours only
George

I have written this in less than ½ an hour

✳ ✳ ✳

Busy trying to find a stable job and somewhere affordable to live, George was many miles from his home on November 6th when Americans voted for president of the United States. Sixty percent of Dauphin County residents, in which Harrisburg is located, cast their ballots for Abraham Lincoln and the Republican party. As expected, the south had voted for the pro-slavery Southern Democratic party and carried eleven southern states. Northern Democrat Stephen Douglas took 29 percent of the popular vote in the north, but Lincoln won in all of the free states except New Jersey. He carried 40 percent of the popular vote which secured enough electoral votes for his victory. The country had made its choice.[6]

George's letters cease after early November, suggesting that he headed home to Harrisburg for the holidays. On December 20th, South Carolina voted to secede from the Union, and started the New Year by deploying troops to Fort Pulaski in Georgia on

---

6. Wagner, *Desk Reference*, 127.

January 3rd. Six days later, Mississippi seceded too, followed by Florida, Alabama, Georgia, Louisiana, and Texas. Still, many thought that war could be avoided.[7]

Life's duties continued for George. Emily was increasingly frustrated with their financial situation, and her father continued to stir up problems and accused George of being lazy. By late January, George headed south as he had proposed and found work in Washington, D.C.

———————

Letter from George Brooks to Emily Brooks
Jan 27, 1861
Washington, D.C.

Dear Emily,

Yours written on the 20th instant enclosing one for mother was safely received on Friday noon, and although I have since made inquiries concerning the one you wrote on Inauguration Day, it has not come to light, and I presume never will. You may possibly have wrongly directed it, or it may, indeed have never been mailed unless you done it yourself. However, let it go though I am sorry it did not reach me. Remember, "write often and direct carefully" and if I do not write often then once for Emily it is almost impossible as we have to be on duty about sixteen hours out of twenty-four. Don't you neglect, when I come home you shall see my diary from which you can put together [what] little time I have. I will write as often as I can and endeavor to relieve your sadness as far as possible for you know that I desire to. But you have our Willy to cheer your hours of sadness—I have nothing.

I was so very glad to receive a letter from Mother [Scheffer], I suppose you read it. Does it not breathe the spirit of a true Christian? She who is most cause to complain calmly hopes I may be more fortunate in the future—is sorry matters have occurred as they are, but does not, like some who have up if any cause, strike me down willingly and denounce my motives, does not charge me with being a <u>curse</u> to our family and blazen my apparent inconsistencies to the public as crimes.[8] Indeed, Emily, I have had to bear what would almost have aroused the ire of a saint. But enough of this. It is useless to speak of it now. It is past, but

---

7. Wagner, 66-67.
8. Brooks is referring to the negative accusations of Emily's father, Theodore.

cannot be erased from my memory. I will write to Mother, to-day likely—yield all I can to her, but not one inch to Father [Scheffer]—at least not until I am free, permanently, from imputations.

Last night I got to bed at 2 o'clock but arose at 8 this morning in order to go to the post office, where fortunately I received your letter of Wednesday afternoon. I was so glad, and shall answer that length. Have I not always been returning good for evil? Did I not write long letters to you from Philadelphia, Pittsburgh and from wherever I have been? Tis true, on last Sunday I wrote you a short length one, but I was tired of writing. As I had written four, I think, before I commenced yours.

I am glad Sue Pugh was so fortunate in getting the "best man living." Indeed she has been very fortunate for if the worst ones, for instance as am I, should be so highly prized as you sometimes say I am—how perfect must Sue be? I am glad we can thus far boast of one thing more than they can. Willie—to whom she was so kind, and with whom she was so very much pleased with. Give my kindest regards to Emma, and through her to all of them.

I have not the least objection to you going home in May or any other you may desire—and if you should prefer company take Callie along and go when Mrs D. wants you.[9] May is about the prettiest season you could visit that region, as then, everything is dressed in the verdant, gorgeous appearance of spring—and if you love rustic scenery—if you admire the beauties of nature as much as I do—I know you would be pleased.

I am glad to hear you have been paying general visits to all of your friends. I like to see you evince a sociable, lively disposition. Remember me kindly to all whom you visit.

My picture must be a horrible caricature—judging from the opinions which I have received concerning it. Lew first wrote to me in regards to it saying I was awful—and now you say it is no picture at all. But never the less it didn't cost much for I wouldn't have ever received the money, and maybe I may like it.

I am sorry to hear Willy is so fretful and has such a severe cold. You should be very careful of him—especially if he is cutting his teeth, and also be very careful of his eyes. For they are such a beautiful blue eye—the prettiest thing about him. Be very kind and careful and deal very tenderly with him for he is our only fortune thus far.

---

9. Brooks' parents' home.

How my heart leaped with joy when I read that you had again renewed your vows at the Communion Table of the Lord—again partaking of the emblem of your faith in Christ—in his astonishing blood—nothing you could have done would have given me more sincere pleasure than that—for you know—indeed, you sacredly know—the sorrow that your indifference in that respect before my leaving had given me. Though not a Christian myself—not feeling that I was prepared to make any open declaration of my faith for—(you know the difficulties which surround me)—still none outside of the arc of safety loved more truly to attend Church than myself, none took more interest in Sunday school classes, and in all the affairs of the Church. I have always taken a lively interest indeed. I may say my conduct in everything has been consistent save in pining, at least my intentions have been good—none regret more than I do my situation—and none feel sadder than I when I see all my old companions gathered around the table of the Lord. I shall try—and you must pray as becomes a good Christian for my success. Do not be discouraged, persevere and you will be successful.

You did right in paying my friend Fred at once, but you did not tell me what he said. I will send you money in this tomorrow—if I can. Everybody in this city use gold and silver nearly. We got paid off in it—and I can scarcely send it in a letter—so I must get paper money—which to get good—for your use I can hardly do. A Pennsylvania bill can hardly be found in this city and Virginia money will not—in these troublesome times—pass in Harrisburg or anywhere else for its full value, north of the Mason Dixon line.[10] I also want to send Mr. Keet some but do not see how I can do it unless I see someone from Harrisburg, who is going up or wait a week or two and send a draft for $20 out of which you can pay Keet. Since I have been here, I have made about $40—of which I have paid Brown & you $10—paid board etc & have $14 on hand in cash. Out of which however must come two weeks board which will not be due for two weeks more however as we pay by the month. The only thing which I have purchased for myself was pair of boots which I really needed at $6 50/100. You can see in my diary in which I keep a regular account, how economical I have been, more so than I have ever been before.

---

10. At this time, states and regions issued their own paper bills, and sometimes didn't accept or offered a lower exchange rate for bills from different areas.

. . . And so Mrs Miller has been over to see you. She is very sociable indeed, and you should improve her acquaintance. Her boy may be very fine but nothing like our blue eyed pet—but judging from your letter the mother is becoming better looking than the Babe, as you say everyone is telling you, you look so well. I guess they were only flattering you endeavoring to make you a little vain. You know—in comparison with me—you are of no account—as especially now—I have not shaven since the third of January and have a formidable mustache—as Jerry—my roommate says—"three hairs and two dirts."

But here I have spun out two pages and besides have joined in discussion on politics, several times, which is going on between Jerry and another border, in our room, and I will now bring my letter to a close—by criticizing yours somewhat. It always makes a letter look better to commence a paragraph with every different subject, where one does not glide into another, look how I do. Also, always when you begin a sentence prefix it with a capital letter after every period or stop always begin anew with a capital letter. In fact, Emily, take my letters—say this one—for a pattern in the two respects I have mentioned and also in punctuation etc., and see how nice a letter you can write me next time. Try and improve. You will not find a kinder teacher than me—nor one from whom you would sooner learn.

And now I will bring my letter to a close by saying that I will write as often as I can. I know my letters do, or at least should dispel all gloom and sadness from your mind. Besides you have Willy to cheer you, and therefore, if I do not write so often, you should excuse me. But I want you to write say about three times a week. It would be so cheering. I have nothing to relieve the tensions of a life here, which let me assure you Emily is a very hard one and yet don't pay well. We have to always be at the office night and day—ready to go to work—and yet in consequence of public affairs we do not get very much work—and besides among these printers I am, though considered good—a slow hand.

Several have been discharged and thrown up their stations already. But here I close. Give love to your Mother and all. Regards to Val Hummel, May, Bell, in fact all of them. Mary Boyer, Gussie, Kate, Annie, and Emma Van Horn, in fact all my friends and a thousand kisses for yourself and Willy and believe me as ever.

Yours only,
George

———◆•◆•◆———

Letter from George Brooks to Emily Brooks
February 10, 1861
Washington, D.C.

My Dear Emily,

Again do I, after having already written four letters, commence my accustomed one to you. I received your short one of Saturday and your long one of the 5th on Friday noon, and how cheering they were to one none can tell.

I was sorry to know you were sick on Sunday and have been so unwell since but trust you will be fully recovered when you receive this. I am also sorry to hear of Willie being so sick and think you should consult Dr. Roberts, both in regard to him and yourself. Don't neglect to have him vaccinated in May or as soon as you can. I really laughed at your foolishness or surreptitiousness in regard to his cutting his upper teeth first. What in the world that can have to do with his living I can't imagine. Don't for a minute think of such nonsense anymore.

I am sorry the little rascal's legs are bowed so badly as you say and you should keep him off his feet as much as possible. In some things, after all, he takes after his momma. Be careful of him.

In going up the Avenue yesterday who should I meet but Emma Hummel, who you say is in Washington. I was so glad. It did me so much good and cheered me so to meet a familiar face and grasp a friendly hand in a strange city. She looks very well. Intends staying here til after March 4, but does not like the city. By her special invitation I will call and see her, perhaps, next Sunday afternoon.

I thought I told you once where I boarded and gave you a full description of my room, family, etc. However here goes again, and should anything occur by which I might be necessary to write to me or send a dispatch, I board with Misses Stone, corner of 3rd and E Streets.

You need not pay Mr. Keet the $1 you owe him. That I will settle when I come home. If I could get the money for that Piano stock I would dispose of it, and your father could wait until I pay him, as the money would now be so useful to me in starting business, but these times I do not see that I can sell it.[11] I sometimes have

---

11. This is the first instance where Brooks references his plan to return to Harrisburg and start a business, which, from other correspondence, sounds like it would have likely been a mercantile.

a notion to send it to your father. Emily, you had better be making inquiries in regard to a few rooms we can occupy. You need not engage any but just enquire and inform me or some cheap little house because if I come home I want some place to stop at and you must have it ready for me, for you know I cannot and would not if I could go to your father's. But I must stop and go to church this evening, will finish after.

Well, Emily, I have just returned from the Lutheran church corner of 11th and Massachusetts Avenue. Rev. Mr. Butler is pastor and preached from verb [sic] "be ye not weary of well doing." He is not a very good preacher, and has but a small congregation. Besides he is so far from where I board I shall not soon go again.

Today I got a letter from Mr. Keet—a good long one—in which he gives me much news. He says he sent you the $10. He also told me if you wanted money and I did not wish to send it by mail I should just send him an order and he would give it to you. He is very kind and I shall thank but do not expect to avail myself of it. He said before you need not pay for your picture.

Emily, today I told Sen in writing to him to engage Bigler's room next [to the] P.O. for our business. Now, I do not want you to say anything about it yet. I however desire your assistance, in fact you can assist me greatly now. Without commenting, me or yourself in any way feel cautiously, that is ascertain what people think of such a business etc. But Emily when I hear from Sen again, I can write more fully in regard to it and for the present let it rest.

It seems to me I can hardly write a readable letter today so I will close and will try and make amends by writing during the week. Time is slipping by quickly. In one more month I shall, if everything goes well, be home with you and making arrangements for a permanent business. Won't it be pleasant to be again reunited. Now make some inquiries about a cheap house or a few rooms.

Give my love to your mother and all friends and believe me

Ever your George
I can scarcely write today

Letter from George Brooks to Emily Brooks
Feb 24 1861
Washington, D.C.

My Dear Emily,

I have just returned to my room from dinner, and snugly ensconced besides a good warm stove. I shall endeavor to answer in detail your four letters, received from you during the past week. I am sorry that so many have accumulated and remain unanswered, but I have worked so very hard this week, that I have scarcely time to read them, let alone answer. For the past week I have worked every day eighteen out of twenty-four hours. Once or twice I only had three or four hours sleep. Many of the hands went to sleep while at work, so completely were they done out, but I was considered the best "pluck" in the office, always so cheerful. Last night however I asked Mr. Mattingly if I might go off, and notwithstanding many others he would not let any go but me, I quit work half past nine, while those remained had to work until nine this morning. Never will I work again so hard as I have done this winter. I can stand it very well. I have not felt like giving out yet—in fact Mr. Mattingly said he let me off because I have been so faithful which was a compliment, but I know I will feel it hereafter, it will injure my health, which is of more account than anything else. But it will prove, to you at least, that I am not lazy as has been charged. I can work when I have it, and <u>never</u> failed to please anyone for whom I worked. But I must begin on your letters and may not get through.

On last Tuesday on my way to dinner I went to the P.O. and how gladly was I surprised to find two letters from you. The first one I opened was dated the 17th but before answering it I will glance over the one I only partly answered on last Sunday. I have written to Mr. Small and received an answer from him in reference to the dues owed to the Benevolent Society—and that is paid out of a draft which I send Mr. Keet. You blame with being close with my money—why you say so I can't imagine. How much do you suppose I can save out $15 & $16 a week? Besides look at the debt I have paid for I had to borrow the money to come on with. Since working here saved $50 which I think is doing very well and of that—including what I send you today—you will have received $30 or over. I think I am doing very well and you should not blame me.

Don't ask me to bring you anything from Washington. Why Emily, everything is so high here, we can get them much less in Harrisburg. I will, however, have to get our Willy a carriage if we stay in Harrisburg.

Emily, I was so surprised when opened your letter of the 17th. It was so well and neatly written, I even thought some lady friend had written to me—married as I am. But on reading "my dear George" I knew it could be from none other than "my dear Emily."

I am sorry you deferred to your "Paps" determination that I should never write his house again—of course I never intend to but I was in fact had made up my mind almost to write to him—returning "our correspondence" and giving him the (Pecan) Stock when you informed he had retracted his formality—all the agony I have suffered—all the insult, detraction and vilification which has indulged in and against me, came rushing back to my memory, and I could not—though I felt like forgiving him. Oh, Emily, for your sake and for your sake only, I have borne much. I was advised to prosecute him and vindicate my character, which he had so fondly maligned—in a court of justice, and so deep did a sense of [fury] weigh upon my spirits, and so far was I influenced by their chat, had it not been for your sake and your mother's I would have done so.[12] I am glad I did not. It would have been better for me but I can live down my enemies—and let them see who George is—but your father's business would have so suffered. It would have been a blow from which he never would have recovered.

I am speaking frankly—there are one or two in Harrisburg who know all the facts. But I will leave this subject never to mention it again and I trust you will never refer to it.

. . . By the by here is [the letter] you wrote on the 15th which has missed its turn—and the first thing which strikes me in it is our new chair which you bought for Willy. How I should like to see the little rouge in it. Give him a thousand kisses for me.

Lew has sent me a "Telegraph" containing an account of the parade and I received the "Union" and from reading them there must have been a gay day in Harrisburg. Oh how I would have enjoyed it. Lew wrote to me about it. I received his letters yesterday and your description was very interesting. It must have been the proudest day Harrisburg ever witnessed. But of course I miss all such treats. We had a very fine display of United States

---

12. Brooks doesn't often reference Scheffer slandering him, but it appears from this reference that it may have played a part in the failure of Brooks' bindery the prior year.

troops here but I did not even see them. We had worked from eight the morning previous until 7 and one half, that morning, night straight ahead. I then went to bed and slept til one—and went to work right away—and worked until 7 the next morning.

You had better not come to Washington on the 4th of March [Inauguration Day], you might get shot. There may be bloodshed in the City on that day. A riot is anticipated and the city is fairly full of US Troops. Sentinels pace the beats before their quarters—day and night—and everything here presents a martial appearance. Mr. Sinclair stopped here quietly on Saturday morning. There was no excitement—no enthusiasm—in fact he scarcely elicits any notice and none but office hunters make any effort to see him. I am afraid, very much afraid, of war.

In regard to those rooms of Mrs. Davis I can give you a definite answer next week, for I will then know whether I will go out of business or not. In Lew's letter today he says everybody advises us to go into it—we must get along well—but he says he can't get the money and consequently will have to back out. I have written to Keet to have the room secured one more week. I intend making an effort to do it myself. If I can raise $300 or so I will start and it will be pleasanter than if we had a partner. To be sure I would have liked to have had Lew in but if I can raise it will now take you as a partner. How much money can you raise and put in? Of course I will give you half of the profits. But if I can only start we shall have a nice little room back of it for you and Willy and when I want to go out you can be shopkeeper. Oh if we can only commence, I know we can get along so well and live so happily. But more of this next week when I trust I can give you better news. If I can't get into business—why I can't tell—when I will come home—I will not come unless I can get something to do. As much as I love you and Willy I must defer seeing you if I can't get anything to do by coming home. So I have, as you see, a very strong incentive to endeavor to raise the means. The one more week will determine, pray for my success the prayer of the righteous meaneth much.

. . . Well Emily I at least send you a little "bunch" of money. Today I wrote to Mr. Keet sending him a draft for $20 from which he will deduct the amount he paid to the Benevolent Society. You can call for the rest. Now Emily be sparing, for you may need some of it to get a house ready, or rather rooms for me before I come. You need not pay your account bills, or anything of that kind. You know there will be some expense incurred in moving and fixing up and you must here keep as I may not be able to send you any more.

In answer, Emily, to your accusation that I do not love you anymore, I simply reply in the expressive language of an old and beautiful song:

"think not beloved, time can break
enter the spell around us cast
Or absence from my bosom take
The memory of the past
My love is not that silver mist
From summer blooms by sunbeams kissed
To a fugitive to last
A fadeless flower it still retains
The brightness of the earlier stains"

A thousand kisses for Willy and yourself. Love to friends

Yours Only, *George*

-------◆·◆·◆-------

Letter from George Brooks to Emily Brooks
[Monday, March 4 1861, Inauguration Day]
Washington, D.C.

[Beginning of letter is missing]

. . . when I sent you that it was all I had and my board was not paid. Last week and this week will be required to pay my board and passage. I don't mean to say you are extravagant, but merely to show you no more will come. It is all we have, and moving and something for me to eat when I come will require a little, and my chance of earning any more here will be done on Thursday.

On Sunday morning I went to Episcopalian Church. It was such a beautiful day, the church was very full, preaching very good. In afternoon I went to Catholic Church, finest I have ever seen, crucifix of solid gold, finely frescoed. In evening city was greatly crowded. Trains arriving all afternoon, it being an extraordinary occasion the senate held an extra or rather a Sunday session. So crowded I could not get in. Went from there to Capitol Hill, and made my first call on Emma Hummel. She was so glad to see me and wondered why I hadn't called before. Spent my time pleasantly. At 9 left and come to Senate, where I stayed until 11, and came home. Of course, you won't like it, but she promised to take me to Congressional Cemetery today, near where they live, and after the inauguration I went out there and she went with me. We found it such a beautiful place. Came back before dusk and I came home.

Today has been a <u>great day</u>, although cloudy in morning, the sun rose bright and clear by 10, and everything betokened a fine parade. The city was crowded to suffocation almost. Sentinels were placed upon the housetops on the lookout for danger, and army troops, infantry and artillery were stationed in different positions of the city apprehending an attack. At 1 the procession with the President elect left Willard's, and escorted by more companies than I could number marched up the Avenue. It was a glorious sight. Mr. Lincoln and Buchanan were in the same carriage with Hamlin. After the procession arrived in the Capitol, I secured a good position near the stand and heard every word of his Inaugural address. It was a grand sight. On the platform with him appeared all the Senators, Members, and Judges and all the foreign ambassadors in full Court dress. Mr. Lincoln spoke about 20 minutes. He is a fine looking man, not by any means like any picture I have seen of him. His address had a good effect, no disturbance occurred. All passed off finely and I first saw an Inauguration of the President, which I will long remember and more fully describe when I come home.

Inauguration of President Lincoln, March 4, 1861.
(Source: Library of Congress.)

Tonight the ball takes place. It will be a magnificent affair. But I am very tired. Write to me at once, and I will write on Thursday.

A thousand kisses to our Willie and Emily. Remember me to your mother and all friends

Truly Yours
George

❋ ❋ ❋

George's fear of war was well founded. By the day of Lincoln's inauguration, the seceded states had already formed their own government. Lincoln's speech was direct and to the point, outlining that he had no intention of abolishing slavery in states where it already existed, but that "the Union of these States is perpetual." Though the new president did not want to go to war, he plainly stated that he would defend and preserve the Union. "We are not enemies, but friends," he said to the audience gathered before the unfinished Capitol building. "We must not be enemies. Though passion may have strained it must not break our bonds of affection. The mystic chords of memory, stretching from every battlefield and patriot grave to every living heart and hearthstone all over this broad land, will yet swell the chorus of the Union, when again touched, as surely they will be, by the better angels of our nature."

Three Months Will Soon Be Over

April–July 1861

TO SOUTHERN CITIZENS, President Lincoln's inaugural message was interpreted more as a threat than a plea for peace. Friendship was out of the question. Two days later, the Confederate Congress authorized the recruitment of 100,000 volunteers for twelve months' service. On March 11th, the seceded states adopted the Constitution of the Confederate States of America. While some sections were almost identical to that of the United States' Constitution, other sections, including the one that protected the institution of slavery, were very different. Some Southerners, including Confederate President Jefferson Davis, argued that the rebellion was over the issue of states' rights, while others, including Vice President Alexander H. Stephens, insisted that slavery was at the cornerstone of the Confederacy. Northern abolitionists took Stephens' position as proof that slavery was the cause of the national crisis.[13]

Diplomacy was proving futile. Since before its secession, South Carolina had been calling for the Federal military to abandon their outposts guarding the Charleston Harbor, a tactile reminder of the North's unwillingness to allow the southern states to remove themselves from the Union. Only one of the outposts, the antiquated and indefensible Fort Moultrie, was occupied by a significant body of Federal troops. At the end of December, with tensions unbearable after South Carolina's vote to secede, post commander Major Robert Anderson moved his men to the more easily defensible, but uncompleted, Fort Sumter.[14]

---

13. Wagner, *Desk Reference*, 6, 68.
14. Catton, Bruce. *The centennial history of the Civil War: The Coming Fury.* Doubleday, 1963. 144, 153.

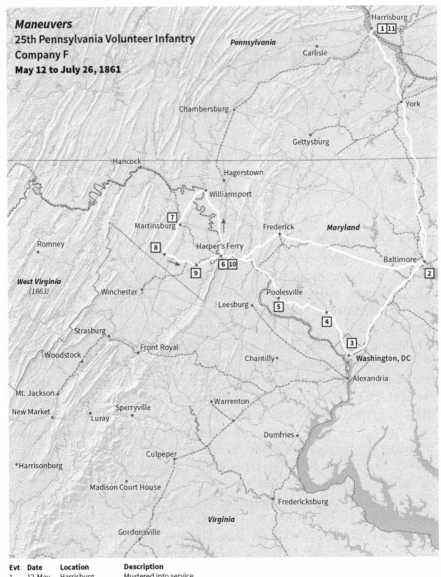

Maneuvers
25th Pennsylvania Volunteer Infantry
Company F
May 12 to July 26, 1861

Evt	Date	Location	Description
1	12-May	Harrisburg	Mustered into service
	15-May	Harrisburg	Departed for Baltimore
2	16-May	Baltimore	Parade through city
3	17-May	Washington, D.C.	Quartered at arsenal
4	30-Jun	Rockville	Bivouacked
5	1-Jul	Poolesville	Bivouacked
6	2-Jul	Harpers Ferry	Encamped on Maryland Heights; engaged in light skirmishing
7	8-Jul	Martinsburg	Encamped
8	15-Jul	Bunker Hill	Encamped
9	17-Jul	Charlestown	Bivouacked
10	18-Jul	Harpers Ferry	Returned to Maryland Heights and encamped
	23-Jul	Harpers Ferry	Departed for Harrisburg
11	26-Jul	Harrisburg	Arrived; mustered out of service

South Carolina troops seized Fort Moultrie and the other unguarded Federal posts in the harbor. Confederate forces monitored Fort Sumter from their new outpost at Fort Moultrie, and prevented any supply ships from reaching the Federal garrison in the middle of the harbor. Essentially under siege, the Federal troops were running out of supplies, and in early April President Lincoln was forced to send a fleet of ships, capable of using force if necessary, to the isolated fort. By the time the first of the supply ships reached Charleston Harbor, Confederate Brigadier General P. G. T. Beauregard had demanded that the fort be surrendered and prevented supplies from reaching the fort. After Union forces declined to surrender, Confederate guns around Charleston Harbor opened fire at 4:30 A.M. on April 12th. With the big naval guns yet to be placed in the new fort, the Union garrison at Fort Sumter had little with which to mount a resistance. The next day, the fort was surrendered and President Lincoln called for 75,000 volunteers to serve for ninety days. The North and South were at war.

In April of 1861, the Federal army consisted of only 16,000 men, and was far smaller than the combined militias of the seven states composing the Confederacy (they would eventually be joined by four more). The Union would have to recruit, equip, and train volunteers and local militias to be soldiers.[15]

After the firing on Fort Sumter, a patriotic fever ignited in both the North and South and led many men to enlist for a variety of reasons. Some wanted adventure, or to see combat. Others felt an obligation to their country, state, or their ideals. Men on both sides had been raised in a nation that had declared and fought for its independence less than a century before. Stubborn, determined, and with a staunch belief in freedom, the sentiment of men north and south was much the same.

While some carefully considered the decision of going to war, others were quick to sign up for a fight. The majority of Northerners thought that the war would be over within the span of three months' time and that the Confederacy would crumble at the first show of northern aggression. Young men's ideas of war consisted of parades, dashing uniforms, cheers from ladies, and hopes to "see the elephant" (experience combat) and then go home before

---

15. Wagner, *Desk Reference*, 4, 6, 243.

the weather turned cold. In those early months of patriotism and courage, no one knew what the war would become.[16]

After over a year away from home, George Brooks returned home to Harrisburg after Lincoln's inauguration. Having raised sufficient funds to open a store, he rented out a storefront and started preparations with Emily. But the war put George's long anticipated plans on hold. In late April, he volunteered for a group that adopted the name "The Lochiel Greys." The Greys, also referred to as the "Guards," were commanded by prominent Harrisburger Henry McCormick, and were comprised of many of Harrisburg's wealthier and more prominent citizens. George enlisted as a Private but was soon promoted to Fourth Sergeant.

Rarely touching on politics in his personal correspondence, his motivations for joining aren't completely clear. In time, he would grow to be one of the best recruiters for the regiments in which he served, but he always appealed to patriotism and liberty and avoided purely political issues. In a recruitment letter to the local newspaper, the Pennsylvania Daily Telegraph, in July of 1862, he wrote that "the great principles of liberty must be perpetuated; our government, in all its original purity, must be preserved." Like many Northern men, George probably didn't believe in the institution of slavery, but didn't particularly want to go to war over it. Once the war had started, though, the threat of the dissolution of the country was motive enough to take up arms.

A call of 42,000 more volunteers was put out on May 3rd, by which time the Lochiel Greys had already reported for training.

———◆•●•◆———

Pennsylvania Daily Telegraph
April 25, 1861

THE "INDEPENDENT RANGERS" – Capt. C.M. Donovan, the "Ross Rifles," Capt. Wm. H. Miller, the "Verbeke Rifles," and the "Lochiel Guards," are the names of the four military companies recently organized in this city. We believe that each have the full complement of men, and are anxiously awaiting an acceptation of their services by the Governor.

---

16. Wagner, *Desk Reference*, 461-462.

Pennsylvania Daily Telegraph
May 3, 1861

JOINED CAMP CURTIN – The "Lochiel Greys," Capt. Henry M'Cormick, of this city, joined Camp Curtin this morning, to which place they were escorted from their "headquarters" in the Exchange to the camp ground by the Repass Cornet Band of Williamsport. The company is mostly composed of the sons of our wealthiest and most respectable citizens, and a finer looking set of young men never tread *militaire*. We expect to hear great tidings of the "Greys."

✳ ✳ ✳

In the early months of the war, recruiting and rendezvous stations both north and south were overwhelmed with volunteers. Camp Curtin, the largest Northern rendezvous camp of the war, was quickly established in Harrisburg, and over the course of four years would organize and send off over 300,000 volunteers, including the Lochiel Greys.

Harrisburg, located at the intersection of many rail lines and turnpikes, was an ideal location for moving supplies and organizing recruits from not just Pennsylvania but many northern states and the regular army. Uniforms, weapons, ammunition, boots, canteens, knapsacks, and blankets were only some of the items necessary to ready new soldiers for the field.

A sketch of soldiers drilling at Camp Curtin. (Source: Harper's Weekly, May 11, 1861.)

When it came to learning how to be soldiers, however, there was no formalized training. If regiments remained at their rendezvous point for long enough, they might perform rudimentary drill to pass time, but how long they remained could range from hours to weeks. It wasn't until after they departed that some thought was given to readying regiments for combat, and in fact some would find themselves under fire having barely learned how to march.[17]

If a regiment did have time for some instruction, its quality could vary. Especially in the first months of the war, training was often left at the discretion of the volunteer officers, who were oftentimes inexperienced themselves and had varying motivations for how much they were willing to learn and how long their men should be drilled.[18]

Upon mustering into service, the Greys were assigned as Company F of the 25th Pennsylvania Infantry. Half of the 25th was comprised of the "First Defenders"—the first five Pennsylvania companies to report to Washington earlier that year. With the addition of five new companies, including the Lochiel Greys, the regiment was placed under the command of Colonel Henry L. Cake of Pottsville.[19]

The regiment was issued gray shell jackets, trousers, and forage caps furnished by the state government.[20] Wealthy friends and politicians donated other equipment like "havelocks," a hat cover intended to ward off summer sun and heat, and waterproof gum blankets for the soldiers to sleep on. The gum blankets saw much use, but the havelocks soon proved to work more as a miserably hot head bag, and most soldiers eventually tossed them to the wayside.

17. Miller, William J. *The Training of an Army: Camp Curtin and the North's Civil War*. White Mane Publishing Company, Inc. 1990. V.
18. Wagner, *Desk Reference*, 465-466.
19. Bates, Samuel Penniman. *History of Pennsylvania Volunteers: 1861-1865*. Harrisburg, PA, 1871. 225—230.
20. Field, Ron, and Robin Smith. *Uniforms of the Civil War: An Illustrated Guide for Historians, Collectors, and Reenactors*. Globe Pequot, 2005. 121.

———————•◦•———————

Pennsylvania Daily Telegraph
May 9, 1861

VOTE OF THANKS.
Head Quarters Lochiel Greys,
Camp Curtin, May 8th, 1861.

At a meeting of the Lochiel Greys the following preamble and resolutions were unanimously adopted:

WHEREAS, Mr. John Rice of the city of Philadelphia has kindly presented to each member of our company a most excellent and serviceable silk oiled cloth covering for head and shoulders, well known to our gallant "Tars" as a "Sou'-Wester."

Therefore be it resolved, That we, the Lochiel Grays of Harrisburg, do hereby tender our warm thanks to Mr. Rice for the marked and un-looked for favor which he has so generously bestowed upon us.

Be it further resolved, That the above resolutions be published in our daily papers, and a copy of the same be forwarded to Mr. Rice.

HENRY MCCORMICK, *Captain.*
WM. W JENNINGS, *1st Lieut.*
GEORGE FISHER, *2nd Lieut.*
A.J. FOSTER, *President*

❋ ❋ ❋

After a short period of organization, the regiment left to defend the nation's capital, where an attack was feared. With the Confederate capital of Richmond only about one hundred miles south, Washington, D.C.'s civilians had spent the prior weeks sandbagging and fortifying important public buildings while anxiously awaiting soldiers and firepower.

The 25th marched south to Baltimore, where southern sympathies were strong. A month earlier, on April 19th, angry Baltimore citizens had attacked Federal troops passing through the city, leaving four soldiers and twelve civilians dead. Marshal of Police George Kane received much of the blame due to his pro-Southern stance. As the 25th Pennsylvania made their way through town, many expected they would also be attacked, and tensions ran high. Nonetheless, they passed through without incident, and prided themselves on being the first regiment to carry the Stars and Stripes through the city after the riots. Upon arrival in Washington, D.C., a flurry of correspondence commenced as the Greys explored the city and began drilling and training.[21]

———•◦•———

Pennsylvania Daily Telegraph
From the Federal Capital
Washington May 17, 1861

Will you please publish the annexed card in acknowledgment of many favors received at the hands of our Harrisburg friends. We arrived here about half past ten last night, having marched through Baltimore with our flag at the head of our company. We were the first military to bear our national banner through the city. Our friends will be gratified to learn that the marching of our boys elicited considerable remarks, and we were taken for regulars. We brought up the rear—the post of danger—and were cheered several times.

Yours, &c., *HENRY M'CORMICK.*

CARD:
The Lochiel Greys would hereby acknowledge a strong sense and appreciation of the generosity of the citizens of Harrisburg during our encampment at Camp Curtin. The remembrance of our kind treatment and the trust that the feelings which prompted it still exist will go far to smooth the rough pathway of the soldier's fortune.

We must acknowledge our indebtedness to Col. Geo. A.C. Seiler and other officers on duty about the camp, for their uniform attention and gentlemanly bearing toward us.

To the ladies who so many and so often cheered our hearts by their presence and kind words we would avow a determination to deserve on our return still more attention on their part, and to those especially who so actively plied their needles for several days in our service, we are ever grateful. We also publicly express our gratitude to the estimable lady who by her generous donation supplied our company with comforts we should otherwise have lacked.

---

21. McPherson, *Battle Cry of Freedom*, 285-6.

We also thank Mr. H.W. Hoffman, the generous dairyman who would insist upon supplying us with cream all the time we were in Camp Curtin. Mr. Platt, in presenting us with white head covers, has entailed upon us a debt to be appreciated under the coming summer sun. Another set of kind friends presented us with gum blankets; but to enumerate all the kindness we received would be a task beyond your room for patience.

Col Coverly of the Jones House must accept the warmest thanks for his bounteous and elegant collation given on Wednesday afternoon, and we proudly trust we may be able to reciprocate. Among the brightest spots in our memories will be that of the overwhelming kindness we received from the citizens of Harrisburg for the past few weeks. Pledging ourselves not to prove unworthy of their favor on behalf of the LOCHIEL GREYS.

Pennsylvania Daily Telegraph
Washington, May 17, 1861
Author Unknown

My heart leaped with joy on last evening when I witnessed the entrance of the "Lochiel Greys" into the Federal Metropolis. To see so many intimate friends ready and willing to sacrifice the dear ones at home, all future prospects, and their lives, in defense of the glorious "stars and stripes," filled the heart with rapturous emotion. My sincere prayer is, that amidst the carnage of battle, in the hour of success, in the times of adversity and tribulation, He "who doeth all things well," will shield them from traitors, and return them home safely to the bosoms of those who are now shedding bitter tears for their safe delivery, and praying for a victory of right over the rebellion. The company is quartered in the Union building, corner of Sixth street and Pennsylvania Avenue, but will, this afternoon, be removed to the Arsenal, about one and a half miles below the city, along the banks of the Potomac, until Monday, at which time they will march to Arlington Heights, on the Virginia side of the river, where they will be permanently stationed.

Mr. M'Cormick, the gentlemanly captain of the Greys, by his decorous bearing, indefatigable exertions, and kindly attentions, has attached those under his command to him with indissoluble bonds. Lieutenants Jennings and Fisher have also gained the good will and confidence of their compatriots, and I venture the assertion that there is no corps in the service in which a more brotherly feeling is exhibited than the "Lochiel Greys."

The young men connected with the company have been busily engaged for several hours this (Friday) morning writing letters to the anxious at home, and I supposed many have reached them ere this hurriedly-written epistle has arrived at its destination.

There are now in this city from 30 to 35,000 troops, all eager for a brush, and it is generally conceded by all that Gen. Scott is so perfecting his arrangements as to be able to advance forces into Virginia within a few days. I think in the course of a few days you may look for exciting news. May "Darkness and the gloomy shade of death" environ the rebels 'till mischief and despair drive them to break their necks or hang themselves. Such is the wish of thousands of patriots in the land. Yours, Respectfully,

HARRISBURGER.

Pennsylvania Daily Telegraph
From the Federal capital
Head Quarters of the Lochiel Greys,
Fort of West 4½ street,
Washington, May 19, 1861
Written by Corporal Eugene Snyder

Before leaving home we promised to pencil you a line whenever an opportunity presented itself. You will not, of course, look for any items on such little things which from time to time occur among the Greys. On Thursday morning we left our loved ones at home to march to Washington in defense of our country.

Our route to Mason's and Dixon's line was very monotonous, but from the line to Baltimore it was one continued ovation. The American flag could be seen floating from the houses, barns and tree tops in every direction—at nearly every house the ladies and children saluted us with waving handkerchiefs and cheerful smiles, but singular to say we saw few men and less approval from them. At Cockeysville we met our gallant friend Capt. J.M. Eyster, Lieut. J. Wesley Awl and many other of the Cameron Guard. On our march through Baltimore we brought up the rear, and were generally taken for regulars guarding the Carbondale City Guards, who were un-uniformed. We [line illegible] found one living soul patriotic enough to salute our flag, which was carried by Mr. Parker, and the only colors displayed by the troops.

After we passed Ross street many ladies saluted and praised us as we marched by. From Ross street on to Washington depot the crowd cheered us; at one place nine rousing cheers were given for the "Lochiel Greys," the only company that dared carry the United States flag through the Monumental city. While at the depot the crowd gathered around us and talked freely with us. They, almost to a man, deprecated the ruthless attack of the 19th ult., blaming Marshal Kane in no unmeasured terms. They say all the police are secessionists, but they treated us kindly nevertheless, for which they have our thanks.

Our guard, under control of Sergeant [George] Brooks, were not so well secured as we. They tell us that even the women shook their fists at them. These tokens of little ill feeling towards our self-sacrificing and patriotic soldiers. I verily believe that had not the Michigan regiment been in front of us, and the Government forces closely at hand, we should have had a hot reception. Our muskets were loaded with conical balls, and each man had his supply of caps and cartridges, ready for any emergency. We had made up our minds fully what to do in case of an attack, and that was to do anything but run away. We arrived in Washington at eleven P.M., and quartered in Union Hall, corner of Sixth street and Pennsylvania avenue, until about four P.M., yesterday, when we were marched to our present pleasant and agreeable quarters, on the bank of the Potomac, close to the U.S. Arsenal. While in Union Hall our boys had but one meal supplied them—there is a restaurant under the Hall, where some of us had ordered a supper the night we arrived. Tired and hungry as we were, and with the smoking beef before my eyes, I had to leave it. It went "mighty" hard, but the duty of a soldier is to obey; I did obey, and slept soundly upon my blanket on the floor until morning. No dinner was furnished the Greys; but by invitation from our respected citizen, A.J. Jones, Esq., whom we met on the avenue, E.H. and myself dined with him at the National, just across the way. While at the National, we had the pleasure of meeting His Excellency Gov. Ramsey, well known to Harrisburgers. While at Union Hall, Mrs. Gen. Cameron, Mrs. J.D. Cameron and Mrs. Burnsides called to see us. We also had the pleasure of a visit from John L. Speel, pleasant Harry Thomas, and several Washington residents, formerly of Harrisburg. Our first supper at our new quarters, after having no dinner, was a cup of coffee. After supper General Cameron called to see us, and was received with roaring cheers and many warm welcomings. Major Brua. Cameron, J.D. Cameron, Esq., also visited us. How delighted the Greys were to see all those familiar faces. It seemed so much like home. Up to this time every man was well and in good spirits, but the extraordinary drill of *two hours and twenty minutes* before breakfast, with empty, craving stomach, created much dissatisfaction and some sickness. I am sorry for this, as it was the first, and I do sincerely hope it will be the last cause for any complaint, because we love our gallant Captain and Lieutenants. We have been living so much like a band of patriotic brothers that it would be a pity to mar those pleasant feelings. We are greatly indebted to our Captain and his friends for our quarters, so beautiful and cheery. At first we were told that we were to be quartered on Arlington Heights, a prominent summer resort for Washingtonians. We should liked to have gone there, but we are perfectly delighted with our situation. It will take some time to get in working order and have our *cuisine* suited to our wants or actual necessities, all things considered. The U.S. Arsenal is in front of us. It is from here we obtain our provision, and I believe we shall be well supplied, because, as I understand, our townsman, Francis R. Shunk, is the Assistant Commissary. When our boys were told of it, all the boys said "bully for that." As I am "weary and war worn," and will be called for duty in a few minutes, dear TELEGRAPH I will bid you adieu, hoping to let you hear again from me in the course of our stay here.

YOURS, *Cpl. Eugene Snyder*

P.S. – A copy of the TELEGRAPH would be thankfully received at any time by the Greys. For the information of those who may wish to send anything to any members of our company, I would say the proper direction is "Lochiel Greys, Capt. Henry M'Cormick, Advanced Cameron Regiment, Washington, D.C."

✳ ✳ ✳

The Greys were fortunate in that their billet at the Arsenal provided them access to training from regular army soldiers, and as a result they received far better schooling than most early war

Artillery pieces line the lawn at the Washington Arsenal. (Source: Library of Congress.)

units. Despite the bad food and long hours of drill, soldiering proved to be a gallant adventure for the men of the 25th. Their optimistic and spirited tone shines through their letters home, as does their naive eagerness to go "see the elephant." Their enthusiasm only grew after May 24th, when Union Colonel Elmer Ellsworth was shot dead while removing a Confederate flag from a rooftop in nearby Alexandria, Virginia. As the first prominent Union officer to die, his name and actions stoked patriotic fires of the north.[22]

George Brooks himself went to see the spot where Ellsworth had fallen and wrote home to tell his family. Although appearing to enjoy his new life as a soldier, he was homesick and relations with his wife, Emily, and her parents had worsened. His send-off to war had been an unhappy one, and Emily rarely wrote to him. When she did, she complained of money and accused her husband of not loving her anymore. Still, he tried to soothe her concerns and remind her that "three months will soon be over"—a sentiment that many men in uniform were sending to loved ones at home.

---

22. Wagner, *Desk Reference*, 8.

———◆•◆•◆———

Letter from George Brooks to Emily Brooks
Washington, D.C. May 23, 1861

Dear Emily,

I am very much disappointed in not hearing from thus far, and cannot imagine why you have not written to me. Nearly everyone in the company has received a letter or paper, whilst I have not. Consequently you may suppose I feel very much neglected. Yesterday evening I borrowed a "Telegraph" from one of our boys which is the first news I have had from the capital of the old Keystone, except a letter which Will Hyers had from Gussie Parkhill.

We are now located, as I said in my last, in a beautiful spot on the bank of the Potomac, a short distance from the Navy Yard and Arsenal and U.S. Garrison, and within view of Alexandria opposite where we can see the flag of the Confederate States (a very large one) unfurling its serpentine folds to a Southern breeze.[23] About 800 or 1000 troops are stationed there—southern ones—and there being some fears of an attack, heavy pieces of artillery are stationed every evening. Today one regiment from New York, about 1000, were sent over to Alexandria, and we do not know how soon lively times may be upon us which will be gladly hailed as we are now tired of our monotonous life. We have, however, delightful opportunities for bathing, and enjoying ourselves in many ways—but I sadly miss you and Willie. But three months will soon be over. Our living is very poor, and our uniform, save our overcoat, much poorer. Sometimes we get fresh tough beef but generally we have only boiled mess pork which is nearly all fat and was put up several years ago. This and a tin full of water or coffee constitutes our supper and breakfast. Sometimes we get one tin full of bean soup for dinner.

Did you see the notice which [I] received in the "Telegraph"? What does dad and mom now think of my departure? How are all my friends, and what kind of business has the store done? Have you made any arrangement with Blessing in regard to store. Please write at once and give me particulars in regard to everything.

---

23. The next day, Colonel Elmer Ellsworth and his regiment would remove the flag with disastrous effect.

A batch of letters just now came, nearly everyone got something save myself. Do write. Take good care of Willie. Give my love to all, and believe me as ever

Yours only,
George

--------◆--------

Pennsylvania Daily Telegraph
From the Federal capital
Head Quarters of the Lochiel Greys,
West 4½ street, at
Washington, May 28, 1861
Written by Sergeant George A. Brooks

MESSRS. EDITORS: – The "Greys" are still quartered near the extreme end of 4½ street, in a commodious building fronting the United States Arsenal, and pleasantly located on the eastern bank of the Potomac; and the mechanical skill of many of our members have served to render it very comfortable by the addition of many convenient improvements. We are as happy, cheerful, and contented as soldiers could be expected under the circumstances; and between swimming, ball-playing, letter-writing, and last, but not least, drilling, we manage easily to pass the time. Our inactivity is, however, becoming very irksome and monotonous, and we are anxiously awaiting orders to march, preferring glory to safety. How soon our wishes may be gratified we cannot tell—a soldier's future is very mysterious—though on Saturday last we had every reason to believe our company would soon be wending its way to 'glory or the grave.' On that morning, through the kindness of Captain M'Cormick, the company were permitted to visit the city, under the charge of Sergeant Kemble, for the purpose of witnessing the funeral of the lamented Colonel Ellsworth, but before the procession had started, a general alarm was sounded from the commandant's headquarters, bells were rung, messengers were seen flying in hot haste in every direction, and an order arrived, commanding our immediate return and preparation for marching. Everyone in our noble company leaped with joy at the welcome news, and we obeyed with alacrity, only, however, to be ready—clothing and blankets packed—to hear our orders countermanded, the alarm having been caused by a skirmish between picket guards. With melancholy feeling we settled down to our usual routine and again await and order to charge.

To-day, in company with our gallant Lieutenant Jennings, I made a tour through that portion of Virginia lying between the chain bridge, three miles above Georgetown and Alexandria city, about eight miles below Washington. Having been provided with passes from General Mansfield, and well armed with knives and revolvers, we visited the Arlington House, formerly the residence of the venerable G.W.P. Custis, and more latterly occupied by Colonel Lee, of the Confederate army, and now in charge of the Eighth New York regiment, and found much to interest us. When seized by the United States troops, Colonel Lee's servant occupied and still takes care of the ample gardens and lawns which surround it; much of the furniture and many of the paintings of Mr. Custis still remain, and nothing has been disturbed, save a few rooms which are occupied as officer's quarters. Wandering from thence down the river and among the hills, we visited a number of camps, and were frequently challenged by picket guards; but having the necessary papers, we experienced no difficulty. Arriving at Alexandria, we were, through the kindness of the officer of the day, shown through the Marshall House, made memorable as the place in which the heroic Ellsworth was so brutally assassinated. The house is under a strict guard; but many passes are granted to visitors and the oil cloth sprinkled with this blood has been carried away in small pieces, to preserve as mementos of his untimely death. Retiring from the sorrowful sight we took passage on a steamboat, passing a New York steamship having a prize in store, and arrived safely in the city by evening, having spent a pleasant day.

Guard mounting is one of the institutions of camp life, and a splendid one it is, too, especially when the days are wet and raw and the nights cold and gloomy. Each guard is composed of three reliefs—each relief being two hours on duty, and four off— and commences every morning when the old ones are relieved. The ceremony is an imposing one—a certain number of men are detailed from each company in the regiment and marched under the care of the First Sergeants to the parade grounds, where they are carefully inspected by the Adjutant and furnished with a sufficient supply of cartridges for any emergency—the Regimental band, ours being the Ringgold Band of Reading, one of the finest in the city, playing the meanwhile, after which they are regularly received and presented to the officers of the day. They are then marched to the guard house. During the day and early part of the night time passes pleasantly enough, but from midnight till morning it is decidedly gloomy. Sleep will endeavor to exert its sway, and it is a hard enemy to contend with when frames are fatigued and stomachs but poorly satisfied with cold unpalatable bites—snatched during the intervals of duty—from which the gluttonous Greenlanders, notwithstanding their predilections for greasy food, would turn from with loathing and disgust. It has, however, its pleasures too, as gathered around the cheerful evening camp fire, we rehearse the familiar incidents of boyhood, and though our lot is sometimes hard we enjoy it. The reveille sounds at 9½ o'clock at night, and tattoo at 5 o'clock in the morning, between which hours no one is allowed to pass without the countersign. Our friends in Harrisburg are not forgetful of us. Within the past week Messrs. Boyer, Simons, Hickok, Haynes and many others have paid us friendly visits, and such an evidence of interest in our welfare is quite cheering and not soon forgotten. G.A.B.

P.S. I just have seen an article in the TELEGRAPH, stating that Lieut. Awl, of the Cameron Guards was the first to carry the American flag through Baltimore. This is not the case. Mr. Parker, of the Lochiel Greys, first unfurled it in the streets of that city, Thursday, May 16, 1861. G.A.B.

Letter from George Brooks to Emily Brooks
25 Regt. Penna. Volunteers
Washington, D.C. June 2nd, 1861

My Dear Emily,

Your long and welcome letter of May 31 was safely received this morning and you cannot imagine how gladly it was received. But you chide me with having forgotten you, when I have really written oftener than you, notwithstanding you have every facility for writing while I have every inconvenience to overcome.

In regard to provisions, I have only to say if you cannot afford it do not send them. Nearly everyone in our company has however received something, and I of course feel somewhat behindhand. Our accommodations are not very good—sleeping on hard floor every night, and having only pork and bread—sometimes beef and a little dried beef, bologna, cheese, butter etc etc would come very good for a change. I think the Express Company forward provisions free. Frank could easily ascertain and being a good customer of the Company might have it done. I am surprised however at your being so very economical as to deny yourself sufficient food merely because the rent is not made up yet. Do not despair. God keeps those who humbly pray and have faith.

So George Blessing has refreshed the store. Very well. You must now do the best you can, and tell Daniel to watch everything closely, and be as saving as possible asking your advice in everything. Business is no doubt very dull, but try and do the best you can. If we could only get our money from the Government. I could send you $15 or so which would lay in a good supply of fine candies, but we will not receive any until our time is nearly up—which will be very inconvenient. Give all the time and attention to your business you can. Don't only spend your evening but spend more time in the day if you can. Again, don't say I "do not care how you can get along only so I am safe myself." If all my actions whenever I have been employed have not been for you and Willie, I can only say I cannot do more. At the expiration of my three months I will have about $50 from the government which will be something [to] begin on again if you can only get along so long. Now be energetic and do your best. If after sending Harper Witman and Co. $10 for fine candies, you can spare me $2 I will be much obliged. You ask me to get a furlough and come home a day or so saying "Gus Ball does so every Sunday and thinks something of his wife." You must remember I am much further away from home than he is. Would have to travel through an enemy's country—that soldiers cannot get away so easily as musicians—and that I have no money to pay my way home and back. You cannot imagine what pleasure it would give me to see my dear little Willie and yourself but I must forget that pleasure two months more and then I will come home, in fact all of us will, as the soldiers are very badly treated. Some of the Company in our regiment not getting more than two meals a day. Emily, what did your pap say when I shook hands with him to go—that he hoped I would go for three years. Really it seemed as though he was glad to get me off. But I can't think of leaving you and Willie unless I could get something better than what I now have and was able to have you with me. But I don't expect anything better. I am glad Willie pleases everybody so. Indeed we have been blessed with a lively babe.

. . . I am very well, in fact my health could not be better, but eating hard pork, salty, and sleeping on a floor is a high price for health. If your pap comes to Washington I suppose of course you would have him come and see me. Tell him I would be glad to see him, would get off a day and show him the sights around the city, and give him the best accommodations our quarters would afford. His visit would pay him well. Tell him to bring Willie along. I will not kill him, unless love would do so, and will send him home safely again. I hardly know what I would do were he and you to drop suddenly on me someday. Nothing could please me better. It would be such a surprise.

If you send me a small box don't forget to have Frank send you some letter paper like this and some envelopes. I am nearly out and have not a penny to get any. Don't forget.

But I will close. Remember me to Val Hummel, Dr. Hay, Mary Hummel, in fact all my friends. Miss Rawn. Give my love to Aunty Ann, pap, mother and boys.

Write soon to me so that I may know what is going on. Will Sieg sends me the Telegraph regularly. Give my kindest regards to Mr. Keet, Sen. Kinard etc etc.

Kiss Willie and be good, kind and careful to him, pray for him and me and believe me as ever

Yours only
George

I send you some geranium, sweet Williams etc, plucked from the gardens of the Arlington House Virginia, by myself, and also a piece of the oil cloth on which Ellsworth fell at Alexandria, which I cut off on the spot myself.

Letter of Recommendation for Promotion
The Prep Office
Philadelphia, June 20, 1861

Hon. Simon Cameron,
Secretary of War:

Dear Sir—Learning that three Lieutenants are to be appointed from the Lochiel Greys, 25th Reg. P.V., I would most earnestly commend to your consideration Mr. Geo. A. Brooks, now a member of the Company, for one of said appointments. Mr. Brooks

Officers of the 8th New York State Militia pose on the steps of Arlington House. (Source: Library of Congress.)

learned his trade with me, and I always found him to be intelligent, industrious and faithful. A young married man, unfortunate in business, I feel confident that if you confer upon him one of the appointments it would be worthily bestowed, and it will be regarded as a favor to

Yours very respectfully
J.G.L. Brown

<hr />

Pennsylvania Daily Telegraph
Twenty-fifth Penna. Regiment.
Washington, June 24.

The Twenty-fifth, or advance regiment of Pennsylvania volunteers, Colonel H.L. Cake commanding, have just received marching orders, but do not know their destination. They will break camp this afternoon. The officers and men are in high spirits at the prospect of active service. They have been provided with tents, ambulances, transportation wagons, and, indeed, all the necessary equipage of camp life.

------◆◆◆------

Pennsylvania Daily Telegraph
From the Lochiel Greys
Rockville, Montgomery Co., M.D.
Sunday, June 30, 1861.
Written by Corporal Eugene Snyder

After a suspense of a week's duration, we at last got orders to "march forthwith" from our lovely quarters on the Arsenal grounds in Washington, D.C. To-day one week ago we were ordered to be in readiness to march, as the telegraph notified you of at the time. Wagons, tents, provisions, and all the necessary articles for a moving army, were furnished us. All rejoiced over the news to march. The "Greys," so anxious to signalize themselves before returning home, manifested their job by cheers, cap tossing, &c. But soon the orders were countermanded, and thus we lay until Tuesday, when we resolved to pitch our tents upon the green sward before our house, where we encamped until yesterday afternoon, after we had given up all hope of seeing active service.

When our orders to march were received, such a yell of enthusiasm I ever witnessed. Immediately our tents were leveled with the ground, and all hands were at work packing such things as they deemed needful into their knapsacks, and such as good be dispensed with were carefully placed in boxes "until our return," as the hopeful ones would say. All things ready, the companies of our regiment were in line, headed by the Ringgold band, in marching order. It may be well to add that but half of the 25th were ordered off. The two Ringgold companies remain at the U.S. Arsenal and three companies at Fort Washington. The regiment on march was made up in the following order, under the command of Lieut. Col. Selheimer and Major Campbell, the popular M.C. from the Schuylkill district: First, the "Lochiel Greys;" then the Carbondale City Guards, under Captain Darte; third, the Doylestown Guards, (bearing the regimental colors,) Capt. Deans; fourth, the Allen Rifles, Capt. Yeager; and fifth, the National Light Infantry, Captain McDonald, of Pottsville.

We took up our line of march at 3 o'clock, P.M. From the United States Arsenal grounds, up Four and one-half street, up Pennsylvania avenue to the Treasury Department (where we were *not* paid off,) and then halted for a few minutes. The weather was intensely hot and the men stood it like veterans, not a man giving way to the scorching heat. From the Treasury we marched to the reservoir on Georgetown, all the time in blissful ignorance as to the exact place where we were to encamp. After refilling our canteens we again moved on a few miles on the road to Rockville until we came to a Rev. Mr. Nourse's, well known to some of the members of the Greys, where we again halted, filled canteens and took up our march until sun down, at which we had then marched some ten miles from our quarters. This our officers considered good enough for an evening's march, and hence ordered us to bivouac on a new mown hay-field for the night. After spaces had been assigned to each company, arms stacked, knapsacks unslung and accouterments, &c. off, we foraged for wood, built camp fires, made coffee, supped and laid down upon the ground to sleep. This was the first bivouac, long to be remembered by us all, and a social bivouac it was. The evening sky was clear—the air was balmy, and every breeze came laden with the scent of the new mown hay. At about 9 P.M. the sentinels were stationed, tattoo was beat, and soon we were en wrapped in soothing slumbers. There we lay for the first time in an enemy's country with the weary sentinels around and God above us watching and protecting us while nature's sweet restorer strengthened us for the morning's march. So far nothing has happened to the regiment. The march and the camp were admirably arranged which gave us more confidence in the skill and ability of our superiors. Our surgeon-in-chief, Dr. Owens, and his assistant Dr. Renald, are constantly administering to the wants of those who had intimations of sickness. The parents and relations of the Greys may rest assured that the sanitary condition of the company is in safe hands. Our line of march from our first bivouac to this place will be described to you at another time. The day is quite hot, and we shall in all probability spend the rest of it and the coming night in our present camp, which is on the Fairgrounds—a beautiful grove with excellent water and large and comfortable buildings in which our men are now seen "snoozing," others singing and some wondering what the folks at home are thinking of them, whether so and so is at church and who's with them, &c., &c.

Our destination is Poolesville to join Col. Stone's command. This place is on the front line just where the most important move of the Federal forces is to take place. It is to be hoped that the Twenty-fifth, and particularly the Lochiel Greys, will give a good account of themselves.

Letters to the Greys should be directed as usual to Washington, from whence they will be promptly forwarded to us wherever we may be.

YOURS, &c., *E.S.* [Cpl. Eugene Snyder]

———————

Pennsylvania Daily Telegraph
July 2, 1861
Author Unknown

THE TWENTY-FIFTH REGIMENT, Pennsylvania volunteers, Col. Cake—to which the "Lochiel Greys" are attached—left this city yesterday afternoon, but where to I am unable to say. It is my impression that they went to Seneca Falls to join Col. Stone's command. When I last visited their quarters all were well except two or three, who had a slight attack of Gen. Price's disease, though not super induced by the appearance of the enemy. The Lochiel boys bow submissively to all hardships, and I did not hear any complaints uttered by any of them as to the rigid drilling requisite to make a hardy and enduring soldier. They seem in excellent spirits, and do not desire to return to their homes without having a brush. As one of them remarked to me a few days ago, in a spirit of animation and patriotism:

When I left my mother's house, and in fact when the glorious stars and stripes were assailed by a ruthless and fratricidal horde at Fort Sumter, I resolved to go forth with a determination to die under that banner, and if God willed it so, I would "shuffle off this mortal coil" breathing the sentiments of the satirist: *Dulee et decorum est pro pratria mori-* "it is sweet and glorious to die for one's country," or to quote the words of Hale, of Revolutionary fame: "I regret that I have but one life to lose for my country."

Nobel sentiment, indeed, and well spoken!

✳ ✳ ✳

Soldiers and citizens alike were eager for a fight and fear ran high in Washington of an impending attack by Southern forces, but the Federal volunteers were ill equipped and poorly trained. Union General in Chief Winfield Scott, a hero of the War of 1812 and the

Mexican American War, was doing his best to train his army of volunteers. He had served with many of the Confederate generals he now would have to fight against, and knew an invasion of the south would be difficult and costly. He cautioned that an invasion "might be done in two or three years . . . with 300,000 disciplined men. The destruction of life and property on the other side would be frightful, however perfect the moral discipline of the invaders."

That army of 300,000 had yet to be mustered and trained. Instead, Scott proposed combining naval blockades with military maneuvers to secure the Mississippi river, in effect "envelop[ing] the insurgent states and bring[ing] them to terms with less bloodshed than by any other plan." It was dubbed the Anaconda Plan due to its proposed surrounding and constriction of the south, and it was immediately rejected by the public and press as being "too slow." Many thought an immediate display of the superior force of the Federal army would be sufficient to end the rebellion. With the initial volunteers' three month enlistment expiring by the end of summer, and harvest season and winter on the horizon, most wanted a quick end so they could return to their lives and families.

While strategy was formed, some of the soldiers around Washington, after receiving a couple months of training, were sent to Union-sympathizing western Virginia to separate the area from the rest of the state. Under the command of Major General George B. McClellan, they aimed to secure a buffer between the Confederate-sympathizing portions of Virginia and the east and west running rail lines in Maryland and Pennsylvania. The Union separated and occupied portion of Virginia would become part of the Union as the state of West Virginia in 1863.

In early June, McClellan's forces had won a skirmish at Philippi, Virginia (modern day West Virginia) after surprising their Confederate adversaries. The Rebels fired one volley and then turned and retreated through the town. The quick victory delighted the northern press, who dubbed the incident "the Philippi Races." It also encouraged Northerners that an easy end to the war could be at hand, and immediate action should be taken.

Giving in to public and political demand (including that of President Lincoln), General Scott ordered Brigadier General Irvin McDowell and his poorly trained army to advance into Virginia. The plan was to push Confederate forces further away from the nation's capital and reduce fears of a Confederate attack. Meanwhile, out in Western Virginia, General Robert Patterson's 18,000 man Division would harass Confederate General Joseph E. Johnston's 12,000 men, keeping them away from McDowell's advance and preventing their participation in the upcoming battle.[24]

With orders to support western Virginia operations, five companies of the 25th Pennsylvania– D, F, G, I and K, reported to Colonel Stone's Brigade, of Patterson's Division, at Poolesville, Maryland on July 1st. From Poolesville, they moved via Point of Rocks to Sandy Hook, and then on to Harpers Ferry where they encamped opposite the town on Maryland Heights. Harpers Ferry and the Federal arsenal there were held by Confederates at the time, and an attack to take the town was planned for July 6th. Before that date, orders were received to march north to Williamsport and then across the Potomac to Martinsburg, Virginia, where the rest of Patterson's men were concentrated.

On July 3rd, while moving southward into the resource-rich and Confederate-held Shenandoah Valley, Patterson's advanced forces had squared off against the soon to be famous Colonel Thomas J. "Stonewall" Jackson near Hoke's Run. Despite outnumbering the Confederates two to one, Patterson's men were outmaneuvered and forced to retreat. Jackson's orders were only to delay Patterson's advance, so after doing so he moved southward.[25] The following day, Patterson's full command moved unabated to Martinsburg and encamped slightly outside of town.

The 25th Pennsylvania arrived at Martinsburg on the 8th and joined the 7th Brigade, 3rd Division of Patterson's command along with the 17th Pennsylvania, 1st New Hampshire, and 9th New York. Bored, exposed to the hot summer climate, and nearing the end of their enlistments, most of the men were growing more eager to return home than fight. They named their new billet "Camp Misery," reflecting their sentiments.

―――――――◆•◆•◆―――――――

Letter from George Brooks to Emily Brooks
Three Months Vols.
On the Virginia Shore, opposite
Williamsport Md. July 7, 1861.

Dear Emily,

After writing to you this morning, we started from our quarters near Sharpsburg and marched to Williamsport, Md, arriving just

―――――――――――――

24. Wagner, *Desk Reference*, 245-246, 333-334.
25. "Battle Summary: Hoke's Run, WV." 2016. 10 Jul. 2016 <https://www.nps.gov/abpp/battles/wv002.htm>.

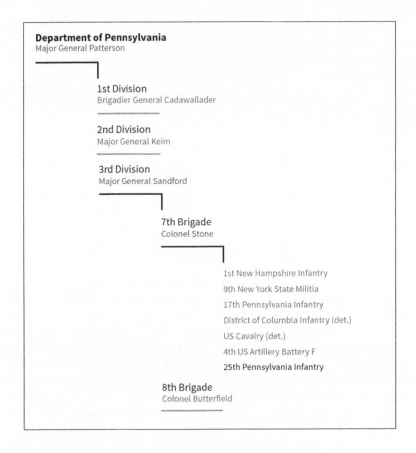

Department of Pennsylvania
Major General Patterson

1st Division
Brigadier General Cadawallader

2nd Division
Major General Keim

3rd Division
Major General Sandford

7th Brigade
Colonel Stone

1st New Hampshire Infantry

9th New York State Militia

17th Pennsylvania Infantry

District of Columbia Infantry (det.)

US Cavalry (det.)

4th US Artillery Battery F

25th Pennsylvania Infantry

8th Brigade
Colonel Butterfield

about Church time, though we were debarred the privilege of going. Whilst resting in the town, however, I received a copy of the "Morning Telegraph" of Saturday, which is the only news I have had. After remaining in Williamsport an hour, we marched to a woods back of the town to get a shady place for a camp or rather bivouac, as we have no tents with us. We had barely got our equipment off when the 1st Penna Regiment appeared in sight and I nearly broke my neck in my hurry to get to see them knowing the Cameron Guards were among them. Among the first whom I saw was Theo—looking fat and hearty, and you may believe I gave him a hearty shake of the hand. I saw many whom I know, in fact all of them. It was a joyous reunion and we all enjoyed it. This afternoon we again started on our march and had to wade over the Potomac, which is about ½ a mile wide, though not very deep. When the regiment approached the shore we had all to take our pants, shoes, drawers, stockings off and hold our clothing up while we crossed.

I have just been detailed for "officer of the Guard" tonight. I must therefore close though it is hard to march all day and stay up all night. But so soldiering goes.

We are now bivouacked on the ground where a battle took place a few days ago. Tomorrow morning we go to Martinsburg, Virginia where over [18,000][26] troops are now encamped. I will write to you from there and may in the morning see Theo. I had no time to talk to him today.

Kiss Willie and believe me

Yours only
George

————◆•◆•◆•————

Letter from George Brooks to Emily Brooks

[Beginning missing]

. . . I am pleased to hear Mr Lambert called. He told me he would. He was very pleasant and we were all so glad to see him. We drilled in the hot sun especially for him and his wife who is such a lovely woman, appears so good natured and kind that no one could help loving her. But in speaking of him you take occasion to again, as you have time after time before, doubt my love for you. You say my letters prove it, they are not warm enough. Deeds, not words, is a better criterion by which to judge, and in the mere matter of writing who evince the most affection. You, surrounded by comfort, with scarcely anything to do, and every convenience and faculty for writing can only pen me one short letter in three weeks, whilst I subject to the rough treatment of camp life, marching day after day, sometimes rising at 2 in the morning and marching until sunset and then going to bed, having no tent and no light save the brilliant twinkle of the stars in the deep blue firmament who seem like silent sentinels guarding the portals of heaven, can and have written to you at least 12 times in the same period. Surely Emily, you are very unjust, and a moments reflection would satisfy you. Besides, if any one would have cause to complain I would, for you close not by sending me a kiss or anything at all from you or Willie, but by saying Theo

---

26. Brooks said there were 28,000 troops which was a vast overestimate.

will be home in a week or so and you and <u>Willie</u> will be glad to see <u>him</u>. Perhaps it is right, but it is not so cheery or pleasant to me.

Supposing it <u>barely possible</u> my last four or five letters may not have reached you. I sent one direct by Fred Blessing, and yet sufficient [time] has elapsed, others have received letters but still none from you. Verily I am patient.

On Monday morning at 2 o'clock having been off on picket duty all night until then, we started from Martinsburg for Winchester, Va, where the enemy are encamped. The whole body except the first regiment all moved. Gen Patterson's main column about 23,000 men taking the main road and one column, about 6 or 7000 taking the backroad. There was a train of over 1100 four horse wagons from which you can form an idea how immense our army is. I was placed in command of the rear guard, and we heard firing and rumors of an attack in front, but none occurred, the enemy fled before us at a small place called Bunker Hill. They had over 800 cavalry encamped but a few shots from our artillery sent them off in haste, leaving their camp fires burning, a load of corn, etc. We encamped there during the night. Continued firing all night between pickets and next day our artillery were sent out to batter down a barricade which they had erected in the road, but finding they had them for miles this side of Winchester and had labored for weeks upon them to make them effective, they returned and on Wednesday morning at 2 o'clock we started on our march, the whole body moving on the same road. Just think about 30,000 men and a string of 1100 wagons. It took them until after 12 midnight to arrive at our camp. We marched on slowly, our Company being on the left of the 7th brigade until we reached a small place called Middlesway, where we were informed the enemy were strongly entrenched and had masked batteries erected in a woods covering the road opposite the brow of a hill beyond the town. Almost a line of battle was formed. Every regiment available were assigned a position, <u>and out of the whole army our company was one of two selected to occupy the most dangerous and important position</u>, that of <u>skirmishers in advance</u>, right and <u>left of the main body of the army</u>.[27] We went forward at a double quick, not a man in our company wavered, not a <u>cheek blanched</u>, every one appeared

27. This may have been a reflection of Company F's ability to effectively drill and maneuver thanks to their training at the Washington Arsenal. Other units who had received a more lacking education wouldn't have possessed the skill and discipline to skirmish.

anxious, ready and willing, gayly laughing over our chances, as though we were going to select partners for a dance. Arriving at our position in front we were halted, deployed as skirmishers, and then the Colonel rode up and said he wanted two men to volunteer for a dangerous duty, in which the chances of being shot was 99 in 100 and asked those who would go to step out. When the whole company stepped to the front, this was more than the most sanguine captain could anticipate, and he had to select two men. After they had gone a short time we started forward rapidly and after us the main column following, and after we had gone two miles the report was found to be a false one, it having originated from a small body of cavalry who fled on our approach. We reached Charlestown about 4. It is a small but lively little place, the country town having a Courthouse, some fine churches, splendid residences and very pretty girls. The people are nearly all Secessionists and many fled on our approach. We took a cannon, a quantity of powder, and two secession flags, parts of which I send you. It is the place where John Brown and his four companions were hung. We are encamped near the place.

The Cameron Guard came from Martinsburg after us. Last night I was over to see them and saw Theo. He is well and will soon be home.

P.S. The flitch we now have to eat is full of maggots, but we must go it or starve.

Mr. B.L. Etter, Pallock and Rawn all came over to see us the day we got here. They could not get done shaking our hands they were so glad to see us.

But here is my last scratch. Good bye dear, give Willie a kiss, remember me to all and believe me as ever

Yours only
George

P.S. Will Hyers has not been very well for several days. He does not stand it so very well but complains considerable all the rest are well. Yesterday we had a letter from Robert Muench announcing the death of Joshua. We are all very sorry and I was appointed to draft resolutions expressing our feelings. He was in my mess.

———•◆•◦•———

Pennsylvania Daily Telegraph
July 19, 1861
Author Unknown

OUR VOLUNTEERS. – All companies from this city are now with Gen. Patterson's column, in pursuit of the retreating rebels. An engagement is daily expected, so that it is not probable "our boys," whose term of enrollment expires this week, will return home for several days yet. May they go safely through the approaching struggle, do credit themselves and the city they represent, and come back with "brows bound with victorious wreaths." When they do return we can promise them a heart-warm welcome, and a reception worthy of heroes. Thus far they have borne themselves like American citizens, like law-abiding men, like heroes, without fear and without reproach. No country in the State or Union has sent forth worthier sons, and no people have more reason to be proud of their defenders. Then, too, most of them do not come home to rest in ease after their three months of life in camp, but the great majority of them propose to re-enlist for the war, and aid in planting the stars and stripes on every foot of rebel soil. In letters from the State Capital and Cameron Guards, Verbeke Rifles and Lochiel Greys, which we have seen, the brave boys tell us that though a soldier's life is hard, and his fare rude, yet they do not feel like yielding up their standard for other hand to defend and for other arms to bear onward through rebel regions to victory. All honor to our valiant volunteers. Let us at once make arrangements to give them a fitting public reception on their return. Every man of them cannot have an individuality of wide renown attached to his name, but we can at least testify our admiration to each company in mass, and then welcome with open arms each son, brother, friend, in whose personal fame we have near and sacred interest, and whose return to hearth and home under circumstances so glorious, brings from the overflowing heart "Thoughts that do often lie too deep for tears."

✳ ✳ ✳

The Federal advance into Virginia started slowly and quickly exposed just how unprepared the Union army was to wage war.

With the understanding that General McDowell would attack the Confederates outside Washington near the town of Manassas on July 17th, General Patterson took his men—most of whom were still far closer to civilians than soldiers—across the Potomac on the 15th. The orders Patterson had received from Washington were muddled, and the best he could determine was that he was to demonstrate against General Johnston to keep the Confederates occupied near Winchester, but he was not to take undue risks and wage a battle that could possibly be lost.

After the brief skirmish on July 16th, Patterson stopped his men at Charlestown on the 17th and, well aware that the enlistments of some of his three-months regiments were coming due, and with orders seeming to dictate caution, he took no further action. The following day, he continued further north to Harpers Ferry, thinking that he had done his duty in keeping Johnston in the Shenandoah Valley while McDowell attacked outside Manassas on the 17th.[28]

However, the battle hadn't taken place. McDowell's army didn't leave Washington until July 16th, and the Confederates learned of their departure quickly via telegraph. Over the next four days, both sides maneuvered their forces toward battle. Johnston's army, unabated by Patterson, continued south and boarded trains toward Washington. Patterson's reputation was ruined by the arrival of Johnston's men outside Manassas, increasing Confederate strengths to slightly greater that of McDowell's 28,000 men.

After initially taking the advantage, McDowell's green and poorly commanded soldiers lost the upper hand and were forced to retreat. Becoming entangled in civilians who had traveled from Washington to watch the Union victory of which they had been assured, a chaotic mess soon ensued as soldiers and civilians alike skedaddled back to the capital.

The Union's defeat at First Manassas was a shock and embarrassment to the North. With nearly 3,000 Union and 2,000 Confederate casualties, it was the first indication that the war would not be as easily won as had been anticipated. The Confederacy also found the battle unsettling due to the human cost and the missed opportunity of pursuing Union forces and perhaps even taking Washington.

---

28. Catton, *The Coming Fury*, 442-5.

Both sides would spend the next few months abandoning their ideas of a short war and training and reorganizing their armies. Blamed for their parts in the defeat at First Manassas, General McDowell and General Patterson were both relieved of their commands. McDowell was replaced by Major General George B. McClellan, who had gained fame via several victories in western Virginia earlier in the year.[29]

With its enlistment at an end, the 25th Pennsylvania left Harpers Ferry on July 23rd and returned to Harrisburg via Baltimore. They were mustered out on July 26th.[30]

———————

Pennsylvania Daily Telegraph
July 25, 1861
Author Ulrich & Bowman's Dry Goods

SOLDIERS RETURNED. – The clever company of Lochiel Greys arrived home this morning all in good condition and with hearts buoyant and strong. Should our country call them they will again make their watch word *"Lochiel Greys."* For the present many a family has been made glad, and the social circle advantaged, and as they will want some little rubbing up, we will just say at Ulrich & Bowman's they can get any little dry goods fixens they may want.

Return of the Lochiel Greys.
Author Unknown

The Lochiel Greys, of this city, Capt. Henry McCormick, reached home this morning at five o'clock, and were received by the First City Zouaves at the west end of the bridge. Notwithstanding the early hour at which the boys arrived, a large crowd of friends and acquaintances turned out to welcome them. The members of the company are literally bronzed by exposure, but in good heart and splendid health. Some of them have so much improved in physique that their wives and sweethearts at first failed to recognize them. There are men in the ranks who barely passed official muster, now returning with appetites like saw mills, and muscles as firm now as they were previously flaccid. The Greys

---

29. Wagner, *Desk Reference*, 246-247.
30. Bates, *History of Pennsylvania Volunteers*, 225–226.

have *unanimously* voted to re-enlist for the war, and will no doubt return to the tented field in a short time. Had the Greys reached home last evening, as expected, our citizens would have turned out *en masse* to welcome their gallant defenders.

The Greys made a parade this forenoon, and were greatly admired for their fine soldierly appearance, splendid marching and accurate drill. It is generally conceded that no regiment from this state contained a finer body of men than the Lochiel Greys. The company is a credit to our city.

❋ ❋ ❋

By the time the Lochiel Greys arrived home, President Lincoln had signed two bills authorizing the enlistment of a total of one million volunteers for three years service.[31] Most of the Lochiel Greys wouldn't remain in Harrisburg for very long as they joined and helped form new three years' regiments. For many, the three months' war that should have already ended was just beginning.

---

31. Bates, *History of Pennsylvania Volunteers*, 10.

CHAPTER FOUR

The Seat of War

August 1–December 31, 1861

———•◦•◦•———

T HE DEFEAT AT First Manassas and call for three years'
troops kicked off the war effort in earnest. In August of 1861,
the Federal army recruited and reorganized, and Congress got to
work writing bills to wage war. Legislation was passed to build
three new naval vessels, called ironclads, and to pay for the war,
they levied the first Federal income tax in US history. Meanwhile,
Federal troops lost yet another battle at Wilson's Creek in Missouri. At the end of the month, the navy proved more successful by capturing two Confederate ports guarding an important
Confederate access point to the Atlantic—Hatteras Inlet in North
Carolina. Out west, border-state Kentucky seemed dangerously
close to leaving the Union. Across cities and towns in the north,
hundreds of thousands of men who had not enlisted with a three-
months' regiment flooded into muster locations. Even though
most signed up for three years of service, many still thought the
war would be over in time for Christmas.[1]

Upon returning home, the majority of the 25th Pennsylvania's
men reenlisted in various new organizations. Colonel Cake returned to Pottsville and formed the 96th Pennsylvania Infantry,
which was composed of many 25th veterans.[2] George Brooks remained in Harrisburg and started recruiting his own company of
one hundred men.

Most of the men Brooks signed on were from Harrisburg. He
also found willing soldiers in a militia unit from Dauphin County
called The Manada Furnace Company. The Manada boys were
composed primarily of residents of East Hanover Township,

---

1. Wagner, *Desk Reference*, 10–11.
2. Bates, *History of Pennsylvania Volunteers*, 382–410.

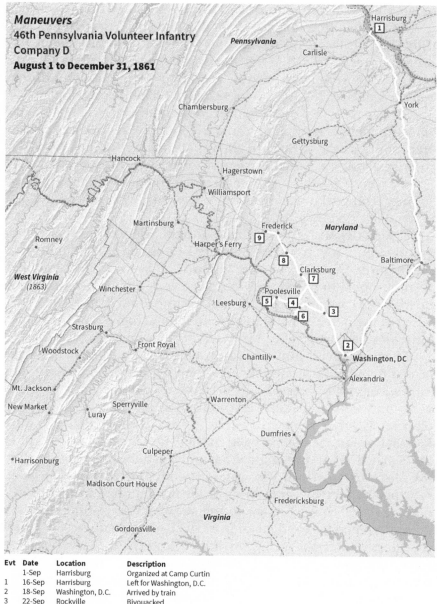

Maneuvers
46th Pennsylvania Volunteer Infantry
Company D
August 1 to December 31, 1861

Evt	Date	Location	Description
	1-Sep	Harrisburg	Organized at Camp Curtin
1	16-Sep	Harrisburg	Left for Washington, D.C.
2	18-Sep	Washington, D.C.	Arrived by train
3	22-Sep	Rockville	Bivouacked
4	23-Sep	Darnestown	Encamped
	21-Oct	Darnestown	Moved in support of action at Ball's Bluff
5	22-Oct	Edwards Ferry	Bivouacked
6	24-Oct	Outside Muddy Branch	Moved a few miles from Edwards Ferry towards Muddy Branch and named the new camp "Williams"
	26-Oct	Muddy Branch	Camped along the C&O Canal near the Muddy Branch Creek, "Camp Knipe"
7	4-Dec	Little Seneca creek outside Clarksburg	Quartered in buildings on the way to Frederick
8	5-Dec	Urbana	Bivouacked
9	6-Dec	Frederick	Entered winter quarters, "Camp Matthews," slightly outside of Frederick

located a few miles east of Harrisburg. Many of them were employed at a pig iron furnace located in the small town of Manada. They had drilled throughout the summer and participated in small parades dressed in red shirts and black trousers with a red stripe. They were instructed by a woman, Miss Houtz, until they reported to Camp Curtin to join George Brooks' company.[3]

Brooks took just over fifty men to Camp Curtin. There, he met up with a fellow veteran of Company F of the 25th Pennsylvania, Harrisburg druggist Edward "Ned" L. Witman, who had also tried to raise a full company but had located slightly fewer men than Brooks. Both groups were eagerly accepted by Colonel Joseph Farmer Knipe who was rushing to raise a regiment and get into action.

Before departing from Camp Curtin, Brooks and Witman's groups would join to form Company D of Knipe's 46th Pennsylvania Infantry. Both Brooks and Witman had been elected Captain of their groups, but based on Brooks' success finding more recruits, he took the captaincy and Witman became First Lieutenant. They adopted the name of Witman's group, The Verbeke Rifles, so called for their main benefactor, Mr. William Verbeke of Harrisburg.[4]

Electing officers and placing prominent politicians in positions of command was a common practice early in the war. Brooks and Witman had received good training with the 25th Pennsylvania and were more experienced than many other newly minted officers. Colonel Knipe, however, was a true soldier. A native Pennsylvanian, he had enlisted in the Regular Army in 1842 after his learned trade of shoemaking proved too dull. He served in the Mexican-American War before leaving the army in 1847 and returned to Pennsylvania to work for the railroad. In the 1850s, he rose to the rank of major in the state militia, putting him in a prominent position and location at the beginning of the Civil War.

Shortly after the firing on Fort Sumter, Pennsylvania Governor Andrew G. Curtin instructed General Edward Williams, commanding the state militia, and the then Major Knipe to select a spot for Pennsylvania's military training ground in Harrisburg. Williams and Knipe knew Harrisburg and selected the fair grounds—a well situated piece of land that was close to water and transportation by turnpike, rail, and canal. On the day of its

---

3. Moyer, Nevin W. *Military Milestones of Old Paxton Township 1714–1946.* The Triangle Press, Penbrook, PA. 29.
4. Bradley, *Surviving Stonewall: A story of volunteers who became veterans fighting against Thomas J. "Stonewall" Jackson.* CreateSpace, 2016. 26.

Colonel Edward "Ned" L. Witman, 1861. (Source: George C. Bradley Collection.)

opening, Knipe climbed to the top of the fair hall with a large flag and shouted down to the gathered townspeople "What shall we name the camp? I propose the name of Governor Curtin!" and so Camp Curtin was born.

After helping organize and train many three-months regiments, Major Knipe was given permission from the governor to raise his own regiment. With the rank of colonel, Knipe recruited up his 46th Pennsylvania Infantry with alacrity.[5]

At the time, ten other regiments were being formed at Camp Curtin, and as volunteers arrived from all over the state they

5. *The Bugle*: Quarterly Journal of the Camp Curtin Historical Society and Civil War Round Table, Inc. Summer 2007, Volume 17 No. 2.

Brigadier General Joseph Farmer Knipe. (Source: Library of Congress.)

were selected by colonels to join their regiments. Knipe's patriotic nature got the best of him, and he was eager to be the first to compose his regiment. To do so, he took some volunteers who would later prove to be less than ideal soldiers—51 out of 965 recruits were forty years of age or older. Some were younger than the minimum age, including four youngsters in Company D who fibbed about their age to enlist. Others would later prove to be rowdy and cause disciplinary problems, and the companies of Irish and Germans would develop a deep dislike of one another in the months to come.[6]

While volunteers of mixed quality filled out the ranks, James Levan Selfridge was named Lieutenant Colonel of the 46th. At thirty-six years old, he had been a captain in the three-months service with the 1st Pennsylvania Volunteer Infantry. Before the

---

6. Bradley, *Surviving Stonewall*, 27-8.

war, he had worked in the mercantile business in Philadelphia and his hometown of Bethlehem, Pennsylvania.[7]

Pennsylvania Daily Telegraph
September 5, 1861

DAUPHIN COUNTY SHARP SHOOTERS. – Mr. Geo. A. Brooks, of this city, a member of the Lochiel Greys, is now in command of a company of volunteers, recruited from among the young farmers and hunters at Manada Furnace, in this county. The members of this company have the reputation of being excellent marksmen, having used the rifle almost from their infancy. They showed their good judgment in selecting Capt. Brooks as their commander, as he will bring into the service an experience which will go far to increase their efficiency. The company is attached to Col. Joseph F. Knipe's Regiment.

✳ ✳ ✳

The new regiment started training as companies joined from the surrounding counties, and they were soon issued equipment. In a letter dated October 7th, James A. Peifer, an avid writer in Company C who penned many letters home over the course of the war, recalled the issuing of equipment:

We then proceeded to the commissaries and received shoes, two pair woolen stockings, underclothes, canteen, knapsack, and the most useful article—a blanket. They are a great deal heavier than those others we received in the three-months service, and a blouse. But overcoats we did not receive, and have none today yet. We were now once more rigged in Uncle Sam's clothes and looked like fighting. We had no arms and therefore no duty but guard duty.[8]

As an officer, George Brooks was required to purchase his own uniform. So, still outfitted in his civilian clothes, he set to work

---

7. Coffin, Selden J. *Record of the men of Lafayette : brief biographical sketches of the alumni of Lafayette College from its organization to the present time.* 1879. 178.
8. Peifer, James A. and Carolyn W. Abel and Patricia N. McAndrew. *Bethlehem Boy: The Civil War Letters & Diary of James A. Peifer, Company C of the 46th Pennsylvania Volunteer Infantry.* Moon Trail Books, 2007. 18–49.

training his freshly-equipped company to be soldiers on the same ground on which he had learned only five months prior. With hundreds of thousands of soldiers reporting for training across the North, weapons were in short supply, and many regiments, including the 46th Pennsylvania, began their training unarmed.

After about two weeks of drill, on September 16th, the regiment received marching orders to report to Washington, D.C. to be assigned to a brigade. They took down their tents, packed their knapsacks, were armed with outdated and inaccurate muskets, and were presented with their regimental flag.

————————

Pennsylvania Daily Telegraph
September 17, 1861

INTERESTING CEREMONY.
Presentation of a Stand of Colors to the 46th Penna. (Knipe's,)
Regiment.

The ceremony of presenting a stand of colors to the Forty-Sixth regiment of Pennsylvania volunteers, Col. Joseph F. Knipe commanding, took place in the rear of the State Capitol about 6½ o'clock last evening, and was witnessed by an immense concourse of ladies and gentlemen of our city.

The regiment left Camp Curtin about 4 o'clock P.M., and marched to the State Arsenal to receive their arms, cartridge boxes, &c., and as fast as each of the companies were supplied they filed off into positions in rear of the public buildings.

These proceedings did not terminate until near six o'clock, when the regiment was formed into three columns facing the rear of the capitol, after which the color-guard were marched to their position in the front and centre to receive the colors.

Shortly after these arrangements, his Excellency Gov. Curtin presented himself on the steps of the Capitol, in company with Quartermaster General Hale, and several of his aids in full uniform, when the band struck up the "Star Spangled Banner," and the regiment was brought to a present arms.

Gov. Curtin then made the presentation speech in his usual eloquent manner, during the delivery of which he was frequently interrupted by outbursts of applause from the soldiers and citizens. The colors were received on behalf of the regiment by Lieut. Colonel Selfridge, whose speech on the occasion was brief, but replete with patriotic allusions, which were also loudly applauded by the multitude. After the presentation ceremonies, the Governor returned to the Executive chamber, and the regiment proceeded to the railroad en route for Washington.

The flag presented to the regiment is one of a number ordered at the extra session of the last Legislature to be furnished to all regiments from this State in the service of the general government. It is made of silk, fringed with yellow, and differs from the ordinary flag in the blue field, which contains beside the thirty-four stars, the coat of arms of the State, and the name of the regiment, painted on one of the white stripes. There is nothing new in its general design, it being precisely similar to the old regimental flags beneath whose glorious folds the gallant Pennsylvania line marched in the revolutionary struggle and in the war of 1812.

As the regiment who was made the recipient of the flag last evening, has marched to the seat of war, we have taken the trouble to compile a list of its organization, which will be the more acceptable to our readers from the fact that its chief officer and others are natives of this city:

FORTY-SIXTH REGIMENT.
Colonel—Joseph F. Knipe
Lieut. Colonel—James L. Selfridge
Major—Arnold C. Lewis
Adjutant—Geo. W. Boyd

Co.	Name	Hometown	Captain
A	Logan Guards	Lewistown	Joseph A. Matthews
B	Frisbie Infantry	Pittsburgh	William L. Foulk
C	Lehigh Valley Guards	Lehigh County	Owen A. Luckenbaugh
D	Verbeke Rifles	Dauphin County	George A. Brooks
E	Reading Rifles	Reading County	Cornelius Wise
F		Pittsburgh	Benjamin W. Morgan
G		Potter County	James H. Graves
H		Potter County	William D. Widger
I		Scranton	Richard Fitzgerald
K	National Guard	Shamokin	Cyrus Strouse

These companies in point of *personale*, drill and general good appearance, will bear a favorable comparison with any others in the service. That commanded by Capt. Foulk, the Frisbie Infantry, is an exceedingly fine looking body of men, and have achieved a proficiency in drill which speaks volumes for the energy and industry of their commanding officer.

Altogether the regiment is composed of the right material, and under the lead of its experienced and gallant commander, Col. Knipe, it will be found always ready when duty calls.

❄ ❄ ❄

After their send-off, the regiment marched to the railroad station and boarded trains. James Peifer's letter of October 7th outlines the journey from Harrisburg to the nation's capital. For many of the men who had not served in a three-months regiment, it was their first time away from home.

We started about ten that night and arrived at Baltimore next day, the 17th. About noon here we halted till about 4 P.M., when we boarded another train. We soon moved on, reached the Relay House, 15 miles from Baltimore, where we took in water and wood. We were branched off on the Washington road.

We reached Annapolis Junction about dusk. The road here is guarded by the Massachusetts 1st Reg't. Here we stopped about an hour to let several trains pass.

We soon moved on again through a beautiful country, but very thinly populated. We reached Washington about nine in the

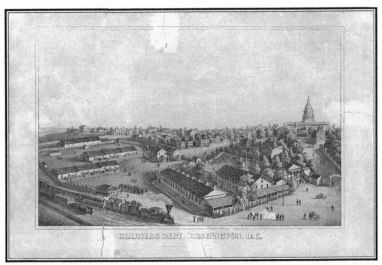

Early in the war, the Soldier's Rest in Washington, D.C. was the first stop for many newly arrived regiments. (Source: Library of Congress.)

evening, marched to some street, forgetting the name, behind the new capitol building in course of erection, where we stacked arms; and proceeded to a large building erected for the purpose called the Soldier's Retreat.

Here we received coffee and bread and beef tongue, very good. After all, being fully refreshed a little. By the way our colonel (Knipe) waited on us like a father, did not eat until the men were all finished. We then marched out Pennsylvania Avenue about one mile, where our Colonel secured quarters in a large four story building. Were soon all snugly ensconced on the floor and prepared for a good night's rest, as we were very tired, as it was now two o'clock. We slept very sound.[9]

------◆◆◆------

Pennsylvania Daily Telegraph
Correspondence of the Telegraph
Author Unknown
Washington, Sept. 18, 1861.

I had the pleasure today of taking by the hand my young friend Col. Joseph Knipe; also Capt. George A. Brooks and Lieut E. Witman. The regiment landed in the capital about three o'clock this morning and marched up the Avenue as far as Woodward's building, where it stayed until about twelve o'clock, at which time the boys packed up and moved east of the Capitol. They will likely be quartered there until they become proficient in drill. For healthy and stalwart looking men few regiments can cope with the Forty-sixth; and I feel satisfied that when the time for action comes no corps will render better service.

ERATO

❋ ❋ ❋

The next morning, September 18th, the regiment was awakened about seven and given time to wash and explore the city. With guards, check points, and thousands of soldiers occupying the area, they were unable to enjoy much sightseeing. Two hours later, they formed up and marched back to the Soldier's Retreat where they had breakfast. Afterward, they marched through the city with the band playing past the White House and Treasury building.

---

9. Peifer, *Bethlehem Boy*, 18.

Continuing out of the city, they halted around four o'clock at Kalorama Heights, overlooking Georgetown and Alexandria. Here they pitched their tents and officially formed their "messes"—pairing off into groups of six to fifteen men who would march, cook, and tent together.[10]

Remaining at Kalorama only a few days, their marching orders were received September 21st. The regiment was to relocate to near Darnestown, Maryland, and join the regiments of their new brigade. James Peifer recalled the march:

> We marched out of the field, when it commenced to rain hard. We marched through Georgetown, raining in torrents. About 10 o'clock we reached Tennallytown (Tenleytown), wet to the skin, where we halted and expected to take quarters. But soon the command, "forward, march" was given, and we moved on again, feeling the worst of it and not knowing where our journey would end. It was still raining and I was so tired I could hardly move anymore, as it was very muddy. About 2 o'clock Sunday morning, 22nd, we halted at a large woods, containing several buildings used to hold agricultural exhibitions, near Rockville, Md. Having marched 17 miles here, we took up quarters much to our relief. We were soon all retired. John Fetter and myself laid on a table. But I could not sleep, as all my bones hurt me, and I was wet to the skin and felt so chilly.

The next morning, the cold and sore soldiers awoke and had breakfast. By ten, they were back on the road, the rain having ceased.[11] They traveled six miles from Rockville when a disgruntled private suddenly shot and killed the regiment's Major, Arnold Lewis. The *Telegraph* told the tale in Harrisburg:

Pennsylvania Daily Telegraph
Particulars of the Shooting of Major Lewis.
Darnestown, Sept. 26.

A tragic occurrence was witnessed near this village yesterday in the Pennsylvania Forty-sixth, Col. Knipe, on their way to join

---

10. Messes were an informal division of the company, and as such, their size was left up to the regiment. Many documented messes were around 6 men in size, however mess lists drawn up after the Battle of First Winchester and discovered in Captain Brooks' correspondence numbered around 15 men each. Myers, Ben. "Model Company." Retrieved February 20, 2017 from benjmyers.com/model-company.

11. Peifer, *Bethlehem Boy*, 19.

Gen'l Banks' column. In the regiment is a company composed principally of Irishmen, who have given the commander much trouble. When near Muddy Run, two of the men got engaged in a fight, and one of them, named Lanahan, of company I, a very bad character, was, by order of Major Arnold C. Lewis, tied to the rear of a baggage wagon. After proceeding about a mile, it was reported to Major Lewis that Lanahan was at large with a loaded gun in his hand. The Major, accompanied by Assistant Surgeon W. Charles Rogers, rode towards Lanahan and ordered him to give up the gun. Lanahan refused, and while the Major was in the act of getting off his horse to enforce his order, Lanahan retreated a few steps, took deliberate aim, and shot the Major in the back with a ball and three buckshot.

The latter fell and expired in three minutes, without uttering a word. Lanahan was secured, and the body of the unfortunate officer was placed in a wagon and guarded to the camp. Lanahan is now in the hands of the Provost Marshal, and will be tried by a drum-head court probably today. The murderer is a resident of Scranton, Pennsylvania.

Major Lewis was thirty-two years of age, was married about a year ago, and leaves a widow but no children. He served in the Mexican war, and on the breaking out of the present rebellion, was editing the Catasaqua (Lehigh county) *Herald*, which occupation he resigned to enter the army. He was dearly beloved by the whole regiment, and his death hangs like a pall upon the spirits of his associates.

❋ ❋ ❋

Shocked, the regiment continued on to Darnestown after Lanahan was arrested, arriving around four in the afternoon. Marching through town and passing hundreds of camps, they found their new brigade around seven in the evening and made camp. Their tents soon arrived and they pitched them quickly. By nine, after some coffee, most of the men were sound asleep from sheer exhaustion.

The next morning they awoke and pitched their tents properly in rows, naming their new camp "Camp Lewis" in honor of their fallen Major. Around them were camped about 4,000 other soldiers of their new brigade, the 1st Brigade, Major General Nathaniel Banks' Division. As was common early in the war, the

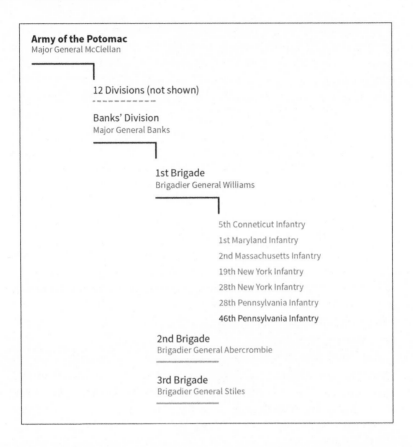

Army of the Potomac
Major General McClellan

12 Divisions (not shown)

Banks' Division
Major General Banks

1st Brigade
Brigadier General Williams

5th Conneticut Infantry
1st Maryland Infantry
2nd Massachusetts Infantry
19th New York Infantry
28th New York Infantry
28th Pennsylvania Infantry
46th Pennsylvania Infantry

2nd Brigade
Brigadier General Abercrombie

3rd Brigade
Brigadier General Stiles

brigade consisted of a mix of unit functions, including infantry and artillery. With the addition of the 46th Pennsylvania, it was almost 5,000 strong.

Nathaniel P. Banks had a successful political career before the war, serving as Speaker of the House and Governor of Massachusetts. He sought the Republican nomination in the 1860 election, but was unsuccessful against Abraham Lincoln. After his defeat, he accepted a job as director of the Illinois Central Railroad and occupied that post for a short time until volunteering for military service in 1861. As one of the first politicians to be handed a generalship, his commissioning as a Major General immediately inspired resentment amongst West Point educated and career generals.[12]

---

12. "Nathaniel P. Banks." National Archives and Records Administration. Accessed September 08, 2017. https://www.archives.gov/boston/exhibits/banks.

*Major General Nathaniel Prentiss Banks.
(Source: Library of Congress.)*

Pennsylvania Daily Telegraph
October 15, 1861

SWORD PRESENTATION. – *A Patriotic Letter.* – The morning previous to the[ir] departure for the seat of war . . . Capt. George A. Brooks was presented with a handsome sword by the officers and his fellow teachers of the second department First English Lutheran Sabbath School. The following letter, acknowledging its receipt, breathes forth the true spirit of patriotism, and shows the kind of material our regiments are composed of :

Camp Lewis, Oct 1, 1861.
From Capt. George A. Brooks

Gentlemen: – The confusion incident to a new encampment, and the repose necessary to a long and arduous march, has prevented me until now from tendering my sincere and heartfelt thanks for your present of an elegant *sword, sash* and *belt*, just previous to my leaving home with my company for the "seat of war."

Such manifestations of the feelings and sympathy of those with whom we are closely associated are at all times cheering and encouraging; but coming, as this does, from my most intimate friends, as well as those to whom it has been my privilege to look for counsel and advice—and with all of whom I have been for years past engaged as a humble co-worker in a glorious cause—I cannot too highly prize it, or too dearly cherish the friendship of the givers. While I fully appreciate your motives, I feel that I have not merited such an evidence of your favor. I may have been faithful as a teacher, in one sense-indeed, I loved to teach; but I lacked many of the most essential qualifications for so responsible a position, and while I humbly endeavored to do my duty, and am conscious of having secured the love and esteem of many of those to whom I ministered as a teacher, yet I keenly felt my incompetency, and was more fitted to have fallen at the feet of Gamaliel and receive instruction, than to have endeavored to impart it.

In my new sphere, I need not assure you that it will still be my aim to endeavor to be *faithful,* and believing, as I now do, that no sword was ever drawn in a worthier cause, I trust the blade, which through your unexpected kindness I now wield, may never prove recreant to its trust. "The Union must and shall be preserved." By all the great memories that cluster round our history as a nation—by all the hopes of the freest government upon earth, and the great principles of liberty which have been achieved for us, and which we *must* maintain, we will meet those traitorous rebels and convince them that the hearts of our citizens are loyal—that whilst our "swords are thousands our bosoms are one," when our cause is just, as it now is. As for myself, I have now an additional incentive to do my duty, and should I, through the kindness of an over-seeing Providence, be spared my life and breath until the end of this unnatural war, and return home in safety, I trust I may not have disappointed your hopes, and will crave no higher boon than the plaudit of "well done, good and faithful servant."

Again thanking you, gentlemen, for your generosity and kindness, I remain

Very truly, your friend,
GEO. A. BROOKS.

✳ ✳ ✳

Knipe's mixed bag of recruits started to become more apparent after Major Lewis' death at the hand of Private Lanahan. Tensions

Brevet Major General Alpheus Starkey Williams. (Source: Library of Congress.)

flared between the Irish, Germans, and Dutch-Americans. The problems among the men were nothing new—for decades, religious, economic, and social differences had put the Germans and Irish at odds with one another. Further complicating the situation, Germans whose families had immigrated the century or two prior looked down on both groups. As October arrived, the regiment continued to drill, but disagreements and bad conduct slowed their progress. German-descended James Peifer wrote home and spoke bluntly of his concerns for the regiment:

> We cannot agree very well with the Irish. We are drilling about five times a day, but that does no good to some of our men, as they are too stupid to learn. We do not expect to see fight in a hurry yet, as our Reg't. is not drilled well enough yet.[13]

The regiment needed discipline, and on October 12th, the arrival of their brigade commander would in time provide the

13. Peifer, *Bethlehem Boy*, 20.

guidance they needed. Brigadier General Alpheus S. Williams was a resident of Detroit, Michigan, a graduate of Yale, well traveled, and had worked in a variety of professions before the war, including lawyer, judge, bank president, newspaper editor, and the Postmaster of Detroit. He was also a veteran of various Michigan military organizations throughout the 1840s and 50s. Williams had hoped to command Michigan troops and was disappointed to find that none of his regiments were from his home state, but quickly took a liking to his brigade and set to work continuing their training. His pre-war professions suited him well for the massive amount of administrative work needed to maintain a 5,000 man organization, and he quickly set to work streamlining daily tasks. He also soon proved that he cared deeply about the well-being of his soldiers, and the men took a liking to him too, nicknaming him "Old Pap" Williams.[14]

The 46th Pennsylvania was the newest organization in Williams' command, with the other regiments having formed in May. Their efforts to improve continued, intermixed with the boredom of camp life and the uncertainty of their future.

Still overshadowed by the death of Major Lewis, scandal seemed to follow them. In mid-October the shortest soldier in Company D, Private Charles D. Fuller, was found out to be a female in disguise. Fuller, given name Hattie Martin, had hoped to accompany her male companions in the adventurous life of a soldier. Unfortunately, her plan was foiled. The *Pennsylvania Telegraph* was flooded with inaccurate articles about the event, even reporting the death of Colonel Knipe at her hands. In truth, the only casualty was Private Fuller's disguise.

———◆•◆•◆———

Pennsylvania Daily Telegraph
October 16, 1861

More About the "Female Soldier" Who Reported the Murderous Attempt on Colonel Knipe.

At Camp Caloramo [Kalorama], Washington city, a hospital nurse was wanted. A choice was soon made from this company, furnishing recruits from Georgetown—one of the enlisted was the lucky one for the position. The choice was made with much

---

14. Williams, Alpheus Starkey. *From the Cannon's Mouth: The Civil War Letters of General Alpheus S. Williams.* U of Nebraska Press, 1995. 18-20.

regard for the mild, youthful and amiable disposition and the winning manners of the one appointed. The nurse, from kind and pleasing manners, soon made hosts of friends, and had a large acquaintance in the regiment; was known by the name of Charlie, but was always addressed Doctor. He was very active, very communicative, knew how to extract teeth, prescribe, &c. In fact with all pertaining to the department of nurse, and even surgery, he was perfectly conversant. Charlie was graceful, good address, and rather under the medium height, and made a neat and tidy looking soldier, chewed and smoked the best tobacco in the camp, and occasionally had no objection to a "smile" of first rate liquor.

✳ ✳ ✳

The "smiles" of alcohol Fuller enjoyed were the downfall of her life as a soldier. After getting into the hospital's liquor supply, an inebriated Fuller disclosed she was a woman. She fled, creating a story about Colonel Knipe's demise to get to the Rockville train station and then continuing to Baltimore. There, she was arrested at a hotel bar while still in uniform. According to her account, her stint with the 46th Pennsylvania wasn't her first in the military. She also claimed that all of the officers of the regiment were aware of her gender since her enlistment, which, if true, means Captain Brooks was in on the secret. However, her story and the newspaper accounts telling it are full of misinformation, and the full truth is probably lost to time.[15]

Fuller was briefly a celebrity in Harrisburg, the newspaper remarking ". . . when she arrives at home [she] will don and wear the crinoline with as much grace as she did the breeches." When she passed through town a few days later, however, she appeared in trousers, a wool shirt, and "a military cap setting jauntily on her head," which, according to the paper, allowed her to "play the 'boy' to perfection."[16]

With a reputation now marred by scandal, the 46th Pennsylvania settled into a routine of picket duty, a task that involved long, boring hours standing guard. Despite the unpleasant duty, many enjoyed camp life during the mild weather of October, 1861. James Peifer commented, "I am well and hearty, and growing fat, as we have plenty to eat—and what does a man want

---

15. Bradley, *Surviving Stonewall*, 33-4.
16. *Pennsylvania Daily Telegraph*, October 10th and 19th, 1861.

more than enjoyment of good health, a good appetite, and plenty of exercise."[17] General Williams was similarly pleased with their situation:

> We have had very fine weather for some days, with splendid moonlight nights. Within the hearing of my camp are probably eight or ten regiments, all with excellent bands, besides several camps of artillery, cavalry, and independent zouave companies with bugles and trumpets. In consequence, we have a profusion of music at all hours, but especially during the moonlight evenings. The hillsides and projecting knobs which lie around our circular-formed valley are covered with tents, and at night when the lights are lit and the camp fires blazing and the bands playing the scene is very striking and beautiful.[18]

The beauty and romanticism of camp life wasn't lost on Captain Brooks, but his personal letters seldom reflected it as he remained at odds with Emily and her father at home. More than a year of financial troubles had only contributed to their resentments, and pay could be slow to reach the troops. Brooks hadn't been paid since leaving Harrisburg in September. As an officer, he also had the expense of buying his own uniform, and by mid-October it had yet to arrive.

———————————

Letter from George Brooks to Emily Brooks
Camp Lewis Oct 17, 1861

Dear Emily,

Your long and very welcome favor of Oct 11 reached me on Sunday afternoon when Col. Knipe arrived, and I was so pleased that you had thought so far to minister to my happiness as to send me our dear Willie's picture. It was such a treat and I will treasure it safely, in fact I open my trunk nearly every day to look at you and him. Col. Knipe gave it to me, and said if he had have had time he would have called and paid you a visit. On Sunday he sent for me to come to his tent and I was greatly surprised to meet my R. S. Muench who had come along with him. It is a great pleasure to meet a Harrisburger. He spent the day with us and left on Monday afternoon.

---

17. Peifer, *Bethlehem Boy*, 21-23.
18. Williams, *From the Cannon's Mouth*, 22.

Col. Knipe also brought from Governor Curtin my commission as Captain and had it dated back to September 2, from which time I will likely receive pay, which will be half a month more than I am entitled to. Do not, however, mention this to anyone, for I was not mustered in then, although I was really in the service, engaged in raising a company.

I am sorry to say I have not yet received my uniform. On Sunday our Quartermaster went to Washington with his teams, and I sent by him for it. He went to the Express office and ransacked the whole office, when they informed him they had forwarded it to Annapolis, Maryland, supposing our regiment had gone there. I today wrote to Washington, Annapolis, and to Mr. Sayford concerning it. I trust it may yet come though my prospects look gloomy.

I wish it would come as all the other officers in our regiment being uniformed I feel very flat. In your letter you take occasion to give me a scolding in regard to purchasing a new pair of boots when I already have so many. You are mistaken. The boots are for Lieut. Witman and not myself, though I must soon get a good heavy pair of field boots for winter as I shall need them badly, staying out all night on picket and all kind of dangerous duty, and I must have dry feet, they are essential to health.

So Maggie Etter is soon to be married, well, I wish her joy and only wish I could be present at her wedding. Please tell me when it will come off, as I today got the Colonels' consent to make a visit home in a month or so, if we do not get too far into Virginia.

Still, I would like you to go to father's and spend your time whilst I am away, where you would not constantly be reminded of your dependence and the obligations you are under to your kind and loving father. However, do as you think best and I will submit.

. . . I am sorry I have no money to leave with you or to send you now as I would cheerfully do so, but I must wait until our paymaster comes round when you shall hear from me at once, and I shall remit to you at once and you can buy what you want—silk drapes or anything you need, and when I return I will bring you a nice present. So don't fret, it will come by and by, but as to sending you a present from this neighborhood, why it would be almost impossible. We can scarcely get the common necessities of life, let [alone] anything fit to send you for a present.

Remember me to all friends. When you write to father, give him my love and Annie and all. Try and go up awhile as he is very lonesome now.

We are still lying at Camp Lewis and our men are being well drilled. Today we heard heavy firing off to the Southwest and presume a battle was going on. We are all anxious for a brush with the enemy ourselves and our regiment is now under marching orders. I wish we would stay here just two weeks more, and I would then feel our companies would be better fitted to meet the enemy. But we are ready at any time.

It is getting late and I must close so good night. Give my kind regards to all friends, love to pop and mom, and believe me as ever

Yours only

George

A thousand kisses for yourself and Willie

Write soon and direct as usual

❈ ❈ ❈

September and early October were mostly quiet strategically as both sides continued to recruit and drill. Operations in the 46th's vicinity along the Potomac river consisted of Union pickets on the Maryland shore peering at Confederate pickets on the Virginia shore. Sometimes shots were exchanged, but rarely caused any harm. General Williams wrote that "There is a strange excitement in the prospect of shooting at one another across the river. We have had, however, very little picket firing and do not encourage it. The Rebels appear on the opposite bank, but so long as they remain quiet we do not trouble them."[19]

Their peaceful camp life continued until October 21st when a raiding party crossed the Potomac and encountered some Mississippi infantry. A skirmish began and Colonel Edward Baker, a former Republican congressman and senator who was eager for a fight, decided to offer reinforcements. His men struggled to cross the Potomac in only four boats and arrived slowly. In the meantime, the Confederates organized more men. In the skirmishing, Colonel Baker badly positioned his men and was then killed, after which his men started to fold and retreat toward a steep bluff overlooking the Potomac. With no means of escape, more than

---

19. Williams, *From the Cannon's Mouth*, 29.

half of the brigade became casualties.[20] Though it was already too late to help, regiments, including the 46th, were rushed in the direction of the firing in case a larger Confederate attack followed. Despite a hurried, forced march, they arrived too late to be of assistance, but did arrive in time to see the wounded and get a taste of the truth of war. James Peifer wrote home that, "It was the most pitiful and awful sight I ever saw! It chilled my blood when I heard the groans of the poor fellows as they lay there in pain. I then got the idea of the horrors of war . . ."[21]

Not only was the defeat at Ball's Bluff another blow for Union morale, it also raised questions about the capabilities of politically appointed officers. In response, congress formed the Joint Committee on the Conduct of the War in early December. Intended to help determine the causes for battle losses, the committee extended its interests until it had direct impact on the selection of officers and military strategy. Despite its 'oversight', the committee proved to have little positive effect on the war and was at times blamed for negative outcomes and poor officer morale.[22]

Having seen the horrible aftermath of battle, the 46th and its brigade had still avoided it. They made a new camp at Muddy Branch, Maryland, and assumed they were settling in for the winter. The weather was turning, and the cool fall nights they had recently enjoyed were now cold and rainy. They built winter huts, complete with log sides with the cracks daubed with mud and moss. They made the roofs out of tents and affixed a door on one end and a stove on the other. Crates and barrels were used to top off the chimneys, and sometimes would catch fire "causing alarm to the owners and much excitement in the adjoining tents."[23] Nonetheless, the men were happy with their tidy camp, and their drill and discipline was improving. General Williams wrote that he had "a very busy brigade and am much pleased with it. I fancy it is far the best in the division in all respects, in drilling, policing, good order, and cheerful discharge of duty." Even on cold picket duties where the men weren't allowed to make fires and some lacked winter coats, they still went "with wonderful cheerfulness."[24]

---

20. Wagner, *Desk Reference*, 248.
21. Peifer, *Bethlehem Boy*, 25-28.
22. Wagner, *Desk Reference*, 371.
23. Boyce, Charles. W. *A brief history of the Twenty-eighth Regiment New York State Volunteers.* Buffalo, NY, 1896. 21.
24. Williams, *From the Cannon's Mouth*, 29-30.

———•◦•—

Pennsylvania Daily Telegraph
November 5, 1861

VERBEKE RIFLES. – This fine company, under the command of
Capt. Geo. A. Brooks, of this city, are now in Gen. Banks' division
of the army at Darnestown, Md. The company number ninety-
one men, nearly all of whom are residents of Dauphin county.
By reference to an advertisement in to-day's TELEGRAPH it will
be seen that then more men are wanted to fill the company up to
the maximum standard of 101. Patriotic young men desirous of
serving their country cannot find a better opportunity of doing so
than enrolling themselves with the Verbeke Rifles. Capt. Brooks
is a good officer, and having himself served as a private in the
three months' campaign, intimately knows and fully appreciates
the wants of the soldiers, and supplies them to the best of his
ability. Those desiring to enter the service with the Rifles can
obtain all the necessary information by calling on W.K. Verbeke,
Walnut street.

———•◦•—

Pennsylvania Daily Telegraph
The Verbeke Rifles.
Camp Knipe, Near Muddy Branch, M.D.,
November 11, 1861.
Written by George A. Brooks

MR EDITOR: – Since writing to you from Edwards Ferry, General Banks' Division, instead of advancing on Leesburg, as was
then anticipated, has fallen back near its former position, a
short distance from the Muddy Branch, about twenty miles from
Washington, and the glorious Forty-Sixth are now encamped in
the midst of a dense pine forest—quite a romantic and pleasant location—affording us great protection from the keen winds
which already prevail in this climate.

We have rendered our canvas houses as comfortable as inge-
nuity can make them, and I can assure you *necessity* invents
many comforts; but the opinion is prevalent that winter quarters
will be taken nearer Washington, where provisions, forage, &c.,
can be more easily and readily secured, as the roads to this point

are in an extremely bad condition. There were rumors however, afloat to-day that we would winter in or near Frederick City, and others that our division would soon be sent on some naval expedition Southward. We sincerely and earnestly hope that the latter may prove the case.

We are now progressing rapidly in regimental drill, and bid fair to become one of the most efficient regiments in the service. During our sojourn at Camp Lewis, schools for the instruction of officers were instituted and successfully prosecuted, and while there our regimental drills and the soldier-like appearance of our men were highly commended. Colonel Knipe takes a pride in his men, has proved himself a competent and careful instructor, a thorough disciplinarian, and one well worthy to command—and is ably assisted by our good natured and clever friends, Lieutenant Colonel Selfridge and Major Matthews, both of whom are intelligent and experienced officers; whilst your townsman, Adjutant Boyd, being an old "Lochiel," is, of course, well qualified for his position. Indeed, we have every advantage which "The power of through-the magic of the mind, linked with success—assumed and kept with skill," can give, and our only regret is the quality of the arms with which we have been furnished. These, it is expected, will soon be exchanged for those of more modern construction—a more effective weapon—and then should the cool, determined "Old Keystone" boys ever become engaged in a conflict, Pennsylvania will have cause to be proud of the gallant Forty-Sixth. Death upon the battlefield has no terror for her sons if with them die their foes.

Our Brigade, composed of the New York Twenty-eighth and Connecticut Fifth regiment, beside our own, under the command of General Williams, of Michigan, a graduate of [Yale] and an old regular army officer, sends out strong detachments daily on picket or grand guard duty on the Potomac, distant about two miles from our camp; and though during the summer and fall months the duty was a pleasant one, yet as the chilly blasts of winter sweep along its banks, few now consider it a desirable position. From four to ten men are placed upon each post, and are not allowed any fire during the twenty-four hours they are on duty. The rebel pickets thickly line the Virginia shore, but the distance being too great an interchange of shots has not yet taken place.

To-day Anthony Helmerich, Company D, Verbeke Rifles, received a letter containing information of the death of his uncle in Germany, and the interesting fact of his falling heir thereby to the snug little sum of $18,000. Fortune favor thus the brave.

Little sickness prevails in our camp, and none at all of a serious nature in the Rifles. The boys are all in the best of spirits. More anon.

SOLDIER.

✳✳✳

Most companies were down a few men since they had left Harrisburg, and George Brooks received his anticipated trip home to recruit in Harrisburg, hoping to fill his Company from 91 men to a full 101.

———————

Pennsylvania Daily Telegraph
November 15, 1861

Good For the Forty-Sixth Regiment and the Verbeke Rifles Particularly. – Capt. Geo. A. Brooks of the Verbeke Rifles of this city and neighborhood, arrived here last night on special military service. The captain is looking remarkably well, and represents the "Rifles" as being in an excellent condition—both as regards to health and fighting trim. The captain brought with him the sum of *seventeen hundred dollars*, being the amount forwarded by the soldiers of his company from their pay to their wives and families in this city and vicinity. The money has been deposited with the County Commissioners, and will be duly handed over to those entitled to receive it. Capt. Brooks informs us that since the last "pay day" the men of the regiment to which he is attached—Knipe's gallant Forty-Sixth—have sent home to their families the sum of *eighteen thousand seven hundred dollars*. Such action as this speaks volumes for the honor and nobleness of heart of our gallant volunteers.

✳✳✳

Finally having received their pay, some soldiers used their money responsibly but others did not. Discipline problems related to alcohol ran rampant in many units. The 5th Connecticut, also in Williams' Brigade, recorded a murderer in their ranks after one man attacked another "in a drunken fury."[25] James Peifer, dubious of his own comrades' actions, told his family, "I am sorry to say that some of the men do not know how to spend their money properly. They go out and buy liquor and come to camp intoxicated . . ."[26]

The army was restless, and 1861 seemed to be coming to a close without any significant developments. After the defeat at Manassas, President Lincoln grew increasingly frustrated with General-in-Chief Winfield Scott's handling of the war. Old and in poor health, Scott resigned on November 1st, leaving Major General George B. McClellan in command of the Union armies.

McClellan was a graduate of West Point, had served in the Mexican War, and was an official U.S. observer of the Crimean War (1853-1856). As a skilled administrator, he was successful in helping to organize and train three-months recruits into soldiers. He instilled discipline and pride in his men, and his dedication and care earned him a devotion that few other generals would ever enjoy.

Unfortunately, he was too timid to use the soldiers he had so well prepared. Although his army was better trained and supplied, General McClellan insisted Confederate forces in Northern Virginia outnumbered his 120,000 man army (in truth the Confederates had about 45,000 men). McClellan continued to train and equip despite pressures from Washington and the public to do something.[27] For the 46th Pennsylvania, Williams' Brigade, and the thousands of soldiers along the Potomac, that meant more picket, drill, and waiting.

———◆◆◆———

Correspondence of General A. S. Williams
November 24, 1861

BRIGADE DRILL

The past has been a tolerably pleasant week and I have improved it by a review of my brigade and brigade drills, in which all my regiments are maneuvered together. We make a great show in these "evolutions deluxe," especially as they are mainly done in double-quick, and the regiments being very well drilled the movements are made with wonderful precision and accuracy.

---

25. Marvin, Edward E. *The Fifth Regiment Connecticut Volunteers.* Hartford, CT, 1889. 41.
26. Peifer, *Bethlehem Boy,* 31.
27. McPherson, *Battle Cry of Freedom,* 360-65.

Would you not like to see four or five regiments rapidly to the front in "echelons" forming squares all in one grand oblong parallelogram, then separating into squares of single regiments, oblique and direct; in short, taking all manner of offensive and defensive positions and all moved without confusion or disorder and controlled as by a single thought to the same end?

Mine is the only brigade in this division which has these drills, and consequently we have a large crowd of spectators from the three brigades and from the host of civilian employees of the army. It was quite an imposing affair, *we* all think. I found a large field of many hundred acres where I could form my regiments in one line. After marching in quick time, each regiment marched past in double-quick to the music of its own band. It was very handsomely done, for all my regiments but one have been nearly five months in service and move on the double-quick with the regularity of veterans. They trot off with knapsack packed, canteen and haversack and cartridge box, with forty rounds of ball cartridges, as if nothing was on their backs. On the whole, you see, I am well pleased with my brigade, and what is perhaps more important, I think the brigade is well pleased with me, but this may be fancy.[28]

———————◆•◆•◆———————

Pennsylvania Daily Telegraph
November 27, 1861

RECEIVED NEW CLOTHING. – The Forty-Sixth Pennsylvania regiment, (Col. Knipe,) in Gen. Banks' column, at Darnestown, Md., have received new suits of clothing, excepting overcoats, which they expect in a few days. Their old overcoats are serviceable but much worn—The Verbeke Rifles, Capt. Brooks, of this city, are attached to this regiment.

❋ ❋ ❋

November 28th was Thanksgiving, and the Brigade attended services and some arranged for turkeys to be delivered to camp.[29] Rumors had been circulating about a move to establish real winter quarters, and on December 4th suspicions were confirmed.

---

28. Williams, *From the Cannon's Mouth*, 34-33.
29. Boyce, *Twenty-eighth New York*, 22.

They left their huts behind and begrudgingly departed camp with a destination of Frederick, Maryland. They moved over rough, muddy roads through Darnestown, and paused about two miles distant for a dinner of crackers and pork. After covering thirteen miles, the men halted in a field and pitched their tents, but the ground was frozen and they had trouble pounding in the stakes. Wet to the skin with perspiration, they made fires in front of their tents and soon began to feel better. A call for "hot coffee" went around and everyone came limping—their ill-fitting shoes having made their feet sore and blistered—over to get their cup filled.

The morning of December 5th they were awakened, had roll call and coffee, and then struck tents and were back on the move. They marched through Clarksburg, Maryland, the first town with brick buildings they had seen since leaving Washington in late September. They admired the ladies—who were rumored to be Secessionists—as they passed through town.

By noon they arrived in Hyattstown and paused for dinner. Rations were getting low and some men bought cakes in town. Then it was on to Urbana where the regiment took shelter in various buildings. They removed their damp clothing and headed out to the local farm houses to pay for a meal.

The next day they arrived at Frederick and halted, tightened up their ranks, and marched through the city led by General Williams on horseback with colors flying and music playing.[30] Outside of town, they camped in a maple grove at the foot of the mountains overlooking the city.

———•◆•———

Pennsylvania Daily Telegraph
From Col. Knipe's Regiment.
Correspondence of the Telegraph.
Camp Matthews, near Frederick, M.D.
Wednesday, Dec. 18, 1861.
Written by George A. Brooks

MR. EDITOR: – Though the "melancholy days" have passed, and the hoar frosts of winter should be upon us, yet the weather continues delightful, and the atmosphere is mild and balmy. It is now as warm and clear as a May day in our clime, and the bright moon sheds as mellow a light as ever illuminated the beautiful

30. Williams, *From the Cannon's Mouth*, 38-9. Peifer, *Bethlehem Boy*, 36-9.

night of that land of romance and love, fair Italy. Indeed, this favorable freak of nature is exceedingly beneficial not only to the personal comfort but to the health of the brave boys now in the field, and it is a pleasant reflection that the hand of Him who rules the destinies of nations is manifest in all. We sincerely trust the weather may continue, and that the "Christmas dinner" may be eaten in the open air beneath the clear blue sky, should our friends, living in peace and plenty at *home*, surrounded by every comfort, give a substantial evidence of their sympathy and encouragement, by sending us one. Having gone forth in response to the call of our country, with our lives in our hands to battle for the liberties of all, we have sacrificed the *comforts* of home, but not the *ties* and *rights*, and therefore claim at least an equal share of the "Christmas gifts." Don't forget.

This morning the reveille sounded at an early hour, orders to march were landed, three day's rations were hurriedly cooked, the camp long before daylight was a scene of bustle and systematic confusion, and rumors of a chance for a skirmish with the rebels being circulated, our boys were in a glorious mood. Though surprised at the order, as all had anticipated spending a portion of our winter here, yet they greatly preferred the toil of a march and the hardship of a bivouac, with the prospect of a "brush," to leading the monotonous life of camp duty so far from any apparent danger. The genial, invigorating rays of the morning sun served to brighten the general joy and hilarity which prevailed, and every preparation being made, we awaited with eagerness the order to "strike tents." But, alas for the mutability of early hopes, the orders were countermanded, and we have again settled down to the usual routine, and will in all probability in a few days begin erecting our winter quarters.

Our proximity to Frederick renders our wintering here very pleasant in every respect, save the inducements for the clandestine introduction of liquor into camp by a set of unprincipled harpies, who hang like carrion around our camp. Col. Knipe has, however, instituted rigorous measures to suppress it, and a colored man and German shoemaker living close to camp being caught in the act, received a severe castigation. Lanahan, the murder of Major Lewis, is still awaiting his sentence. There is no doubt of his execution, and he seems fully prepared and anxious to die. In an interview which I had with him just before leaving our camp near Darnestown, he seemed deeply penitent and was affected greatly on my conversing with him upon the subject. The way of the transgressor is hard.

Col. Ruger, of the Third Wisconsin, is Provost Marshall, and a portion of his regiment are detailed as Provost Guard. He succeeded Capt. James Wenrich, of the 29th Pennsylvania, formerly of Harrisburg, who discharged the responsible duties of the position with great credit. The headquarters of the Third Wisconsin is in the old barracks, which was erected in 1812. The building now presents quite an antiquated appearance.

Senator Wilson, of Massachusetts, has introduced a bill into Congress abolishing sutlers in the army, which I am confident will meet the condemnation of nine-tenths of the volunteers in the field. Army fare is poor living at best, especially when—as often the case—the crackers are musty and the pork half spoiled, and to deprive them of an opportunity of spending a portion of their hard-earned means in such luxuries as they may desire, is unjust and uncalled for. It is mistaken philanthropy.

Lieut. Edward L. Witman, of the "Verbeke Rifles," has been seriously ill for several weeks past, but is now rapidly recovering, and will—after a few weeks spent in recruiting his health—be ready again to take the field. He has the well-wishes of every member of the "Rifles." More anon

SOLDIER.

※ ※ ※

For the murder of Major Lewis, Private Lanahan was sentenced to death by hanging. His upcoming execution cast a shadow on many men of Williams' Brigade, including Williams himself, who was said to have had tears in his eyes upon being notified of the young man's conviction. He remembered the cold day of Lanahan's death in a letter home:

———•◆•———

Correspondence of General A. S. Williams
December 23, 1861

THE EXECUTION OF LANAHAN
We had an execution by hanging a private of my brigade on the parade ground today at 2 P.M. The culprit was named Dennis Lanahan. While on a march just three months ago, he deliberately loaded a musket and shot the major of his regiment, the 46th

Pennsylvania, simply because the major had compelled him to follow a wagon, and on his refusing had tied a rope to him for a short time. He was partly intoxicated at the time, but when sober was a very bad man. He has been in the hands of the provost guard of the division ever since, and after one or two trials set aside for irregularity in the order organizing the court, he was finally condemned a few weeks since.

I received an intimation for the first time yesterday that he was to be executed today, and this morning a party from Frederick began putting up the scaffold on a knoll in the center of the field we use for drills. At twelve o'clock I received the notification of the execution. The unpleasant office was performed by the Provost Marshal, and my brigade was present only as spectators. The day, as I have mentioned, was half-sleety, half-snowy, and with a high, cold wind. The ceremonies were very short. The rope was adjusted, a Catholic priest whispered something to the prisoner, a black fellow pulled the cord and let fall the drop. The man fell about two feet and literally died without a struggle. There was but an almost imperceptible drawing up of his legs and not a movement besides. The troops marched off leaving a small guard, and the affair was all over in ten or fifteen minutes.[31]

❋ ❋ ❋

While his army stagnated in camp, General Banks petitioned General McClellan to allow him to cross into northern Virginia and advance into the northern Shenandoah Valley to take the strategically important Confederate town of Winchester. Scouts reported that Confederate forces in that area were around 4,000 strong with generous estimates never topping 7,000 troops, and there was little chance for reinforcement. The isolated Confederates were a fair match for Banks' 5,000 man division. Hoping to take the initiative, Banks wrote McClellan: "Nothing would delight this division more than to make the expedition to Winchester which . . . I believe to be entirely feasible."

McClellan didn't agree and refused Banks' proposal. He also refrained from taking any action to reopen the Baltimore and Ohio Railroad which had been severed below Harpers Ferry and damaged in several locations. While the press fumed over McClellan's inaction, Banks sulked. His men would be staying put.[32]

---

31. Williams, *From the Cannon's Mouth*, 43-44, 46.
32. Cozzens, Peter. *Shenandoah 1862: Stonewall Jackson's Valley Campaign.* The University of North Carolina Press, 2013. 50.

By December, all knew the war would not be over by Christmas. Spirits sank further as the men fought homesickness approaching their first Christmas away from loved ones. Private James Peifer wrote home lamenting the lack of festivities and the homesickness felt by he and his comrades: "I can tell you our hearts ached and we wished as we never wished before."[33]

As an officer, George Brooks had a few more of the comforts of civilian life for Christmas at the house where he boarded in Frederick. Having been away from home for the majority of the time since the beginning of 1860, perhaps Brooks' homesickness had become familiar to him. After an uneventful Christmas, he wrote home to his wife on his 28th birthday on December 31st, but, perhaps preoccupied with the persisting tensions at home, made no reference to it or the new year.

———————◆●◆———————

Letter from Capt. George A. Brooks to Emily Brooks
Camp Matthews 46th PV
December 31, 1861

Dear Emily,

I am very glad you sent me your picture, it is quite a fine one <u>and</u> were you as good looking as your <u>dearly beloved</u>, it would fascinate almost any poor mortal but nature ordained it otherwise. I have the advantage and our boy is flattered every day about his beauty simply because he looks so much like his "daddy." But your picture is an exact likeness. It looks very much like my "Dorathea" and it will be treasured accordingly. I wish you would at once have Master Willie's taken in his Zouave uniform and send it at once.

Col. Knipe met father Scheffer on St. John's night at Buchlers and said he could not get done talking about our Will. The Col. said he spoke of bringing Willie and you over to see me and appeared to be very proud of his son in law. Perhaps from what I hear he has reason to be. But what has made him take such a sudden fancy to me, I am now no better than ever before and simply endeavor as I have always heretofore done, to do my duty, I am glad and proud his opinion is beginning to change and shall try to merit it.

The day I received your note I wrote to you answering it. You must not be so impatient.

---

33. Peifer, *Bethlehem Boy*, 46.

In regard to the uniforms, Mr. Sayford will receive pay from the Company for the first ones, but I am afraid our other things such as Lieut. Witman's boots and the portfolio to which I so much needed are forever gone, lost. They may turn up sometime.

I am glad to hear father was down to see you, and that he looks so well and hardy. I wonder what put it into his head about me having money in bank. My pay is $130 per month, we were paid on the 1st of November and left Harrisburg Sept. 16. There was not two months pay due me. I gave you $100 and had to pay for all my outfit, etc, etc, which is very expensive. Besides having to find myself during two months just past—I do not think I have done so bad, and on next payday I will send you home a good sum. But there are many little expenses of which you have no idea, which eat up money very fast. I shall be as economical as I can but among other officers, I cannot be mean, it is not my nature.

Col. Knipe told me that as soon as Lieut. Witman would return I might visit home, but I judge by that time we will have marched from our present location and be nearer the enemy. I will be able in a day or so, or at least a week to say something more about it. I am waiting to hear from Lieut. Witman. If he does not soon expect to return I want you, Willie and pap to come over and spend a few days in Camp with us. We will treat you to our best in fact initiate you into camp life.

Remember me to all my friends, girls and boys. Tell Valle Hummel I received his kind letter and will answer soon. Write to me often. Write to me soon. Letters to me are like flowers in June. Love to pap and mom, Theo, Frank and all the other boys.

I remain your affectionate husband,

George

❋ ❋ ❋

Writing from his cold tent, Private James Peifer again put pen to paper on December 31st, and unlike Captain Brooks, was feeling rather nostalgic. "I wonder what the new year will bring upon us," he mused. "I hope and wish that the coming year may bring this rebellion to a close, and return all who are spared to their dear firesides."[34] Peifer's sentiments were shared by many as 1861 gave way to 1862, but none could have imagined the horrors the new year would bring.

---

34. Peifer, *Bethlehem Boy*, 45-49.

CHAPTER FIVE

Masterly Inactivity
January 1–February 28, 1862

———◆●◆———

T HROUGHOUT NOVEMBER AND December of 1861, Confederate General "Stonewall" Jackson's men had harassed the Baltimore and Ohio (B&O) Railroad and the Chesapeake & Ohio (C&O) Canal in an effort to disrupt northern commerce. The B&O had been severed at Harpers Ferry earlier in the year, but Jackson continued to prod at the remaining eastern stretch and also made several attempts to disrupt the 200 mile C&O which ran between Cumberland, Maryland and Washington, D.C. Both were critical to the northern economy and war effort. In December, Jackson had sent men north to destroy Dam No. 5, the oldest dam along the canal, but the entire expedition proved a folly. Little damage was done to the aging dam and the Federals had it patched and running shortly after Jackson headed back to Winchester.

Many of his men, especially those from the Deep South that found the cold Virginia winter almost unbearable, hoped to enter winter quarters and resume campaigning in the spring. Jackson had other plans. He knew he had the advantage and was eager to act on it before the Union forces were able to train and reinforce their ranks. He was also afraid that keeping his men in one place would be more detrimental to their health than staying active and on the move. In a letter to his commander, General Joseph E. Johnston, Jackson said that "if this place is to be held by us, our true policy, in my opinion, is to attack the enemy in his present position before he receives additional reinforcements, and especially never to permit a junction of their forces at or near Martinsburg." Johnston agreed and approved a plan to attack Union forces under General Kelley at Romney, Virginia. Jackson's men, now 7,500 strong after the arrival of General Loring's Division,

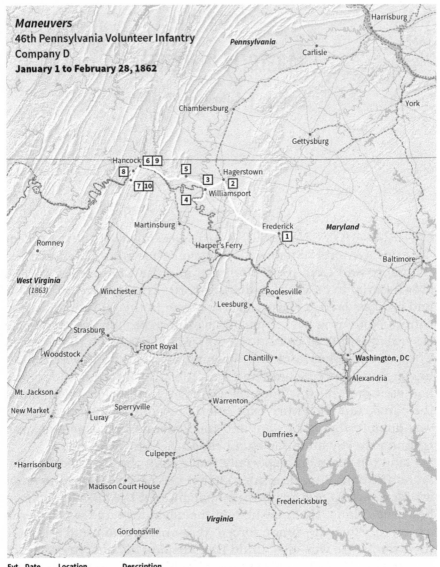

Maneuvers
46th Pennsylvania Volunteer Infantry
Company D
January 1 to February 28, 1862

Evt	Date	Location	Description
1		Frederick	In winter quarters since December 6th
2	6-Jan	Hagerstown	Marched from Frederick (twenty-six miles in 10.5 hours)
3	7-Jan	Williamsport	Quartered in warehouses
4	9-Jan	Falling Waters	Picket duty
5	10-Jan	Clear Spring	Quartered in Lutheran Church
6	11-Jan	Hancock	Arrived at 3:00 p.m.
	24-Jan	Hancock	Rebel shelling of town
7	25-Jan	Hancock	Expedition to within two miles of Bath (Berkeley Springs); returned to Hancock
8	28-Jan	Dam No 6	Guard duty at Dam No. 6 along the C&O Canal
9	8-Feb	Hancock	Returned to town
10	23-Feb	Hancock	Expedition to Sir John's Run, Bath, and back to Hancock

spent New Year's Eve packing five days rations and drawing ammunition.[1]

While the The Verbeke Rifles welcomed 1862 in winter quarters outside of Frederick, Maryland, Jackson's men were on the march in the early morning hours. Captain Brooks started his journal that day. The war seemed to be progressing slowly in Frederick, but Brooks kept busy with drilling his men and travelling into town. There, he would periodically take up accommodations at the "Central House" and spend nights socializing.

From the Journal of Capt. George A. Brooks
Journal Commencing January 1, 1862

NEW YEAR'S MORN, JANUARY 1 1862. Fine day. In morning went to city of Frederick to pay respects to General N. P. Banks, in compliance with Northern custom, after which sauntered around city with Captain Morgan.[2] Met an old Harrisburg friend Geo. W. E. Blessing, with whom I spent portion of an afternoon, and went with him to see Charley Platt who is lying ill with Typhoid fever. He is slowly recovering, but greatly prostrated. The beauty and fashion of the city were on the pare, and the city presented a fine appearance. In the evening visited some lady friends in company with Captain Morgan. After which went to Central House and retired.

THURSDAY, JANUARY 2. Arose early and walked to camp. Nothing new or stirring today. Tomorrow the anniversary of St. John in Masonic language. Will be properly observed by the order, having been postponed.

FRIDAY, JANUARY 3. Clear morning, but very cold. Started off to city with company of five others. "True and loyal men" to join in celebrating the anniversary of the patron Saint of our glorious order. Lodge opened at 11½ o'clock where after some preparatory business we were formed in twos and marched, proceeded by the band of the Massachusetts 3rd, to the Lutheran Church, where we were eloquently accepted by the chaplain of the same regiment. Many new incidents in Masonic history were presented and it proved very instructive. Private, non-commissioned, and many

1. Cozzens, *Shenandoah 1862*, 56-66.
2. Captain Benjamin W. Morgan, Company F.

Brevet Brigadier General James Levan Selfridge.
(Source: Library of Congress.)

of the most distinguished commissioned officers of the army, high and low, rich and poor, mingled together in perfect harmony and equality, thus showing the beauty and grandeur of the order. After lecture returned to lodge and were towards evening, "called off from labor to refreshment." The banquet was well gotten up and everything passed off well. In evening took a lunch with Cols Knipe and Selfridge, after which visited some lady friends. Too stormy to go home. Consequently stayed at the Central House all night.

SATURDAY, JANUARY 4. Arose early and started for camp. Quite a sprinkle of snow fell during the night. Officer of the day—Sun came out and warm, making it very muddy. Towards evening blew up very cold.

SUNDAY, JANUARY 5. Cloudy and cold morning. In afternoon seven of our companies, accompanied by band went to church in Frederick to the good old tune of "Come ye disconsolate." Being senior Captain present took command of the battalion. Heard fine sermon from Rev. J McCord. Everything passed off well. Retired to camp and found we had been ordered to cook two days rations. Some probability of a march. Began snowing briskly about 4 o'clock. Read until late.

❋ *❋* *❋*

The rumored march was due to General Jackson pressing General Kelley near Romney. Jackson's advance and attack were stymied by the inexperience of his troops paired with frigid weather, forced marches, and hunger. Small skirmishes broke out on the 3rd and 4th with minimal effect, and Kelley's outnumbered men managed to retreat across the Potomac river, the C&O running along it, mostly unscathed. Jackson was furious, and ordered his artillery moved up to shell the town of Hancock, Maryland, which rested along the C&O. Mostly occupied with civilians, Jackson's men had inhibitions about lobbing shells across the river as they carried out their orders. Owing to darkness having fallen, minimal damage occurred and no one was injured.[3]

On January 5th, Jackson placed his infantry along the heights opposite Hancock and sent Colonel Turner Ashby across the river under a flag of truce with a message: Surrender Hancock or in two hours the town would be shelled and taken. Brigadier General Frederick W. Lander, in command of Union forces in Hancock, respectfully rejected the offer and sent Colonel Ashby on his way. Lander evacuated the town and posted what little infantry he had (mostly green Pennsylvania troops) around the town with water buckets to quell any fires.

Jackson's motives were unclear—there were stores of Federal equipment warehoused there, but the river was swollen and ice choked the fords, so getting any captured goods back across would've been difficult even without Lander following. Perhaps Jackson hoped to bluff the Federals into abandoning Hancock. Whatever his true plan, the artillery barrage began at two P.M., several hours after it was promised. Federal artillery responded, and the exchange continued until about dusk with no ill effects.

Under the cover of artillery, Jackson sent one group of men to the illusive Dam No. 5 to actually destroy it, and another to the Grand Cacapon River railroad bridge. The first party failed, but the second succeeded.

As night fell a heavy snow arrived, and the Federals in Hancock headed inside and wrought far more damage on the town than

---

3. Cozzens, *Shenandoah 1862*, 67-79.

Scenes from Hancock, Maryland, as sketched for Harper's Weekly. (Source: Harper's Weekly, *November 8, 1862.)*

Jackson's bombardment. Looting and stealing food, they burned firewood and furniture indiscriminately to keep warm. Meanwhile, the Confederates huddled on the opposite bank, most lacking blankets and food because their wagon train was miles behind.

That evening, General Lander sent a message to General Banks requesting that Banks' men either cross the Potomac and take Jackson from behind or send five regiments to reinforce Lander and he would attack himself. Banks, though wanting for action, had to first seek approval from General McClellan. In the meantime, he dispatched General Williams' Brigade, including the 46th, on a forced march to Hancock.

———◆◆◆———

From the Journal of Capt. George A. Brooks

MONDAY, JANUARY 6. At 12 o'clock was awakened by orders "to march" but upon inquiry did not feel warranted in arousing the men. Has snowed since 9 o'clock about four inches deep and still snowing. Laid down again, but had not fallen to sleep ere I was again awakened, ordered men to pack up and prepare for a march at once. Whilst they were getting ready and the wind blowing a perfect hurricane, wrote letter to "Telegraph." After

Major Cyrus Strouse. (Source: Author's collection.)

the usual delay incident to departure we left camp at 6 o'clock precisely. Thus we bid adieu to a pleasant location, around which many pleasant memories will ever linger and cherish as one of the bright spots in life. On reaching the pike we were formed by the Nineteenth and Twenty-Eighth New York and the Fifth Connecticut, and our regiment taking the advance were soon trudging on our weary way towards Hagerstown through the snow, the roads being quite slippery. Everyone seemed to be in fine glee. On the way we passed through the fine and patriotic towns of Boonsboro and Funkstown about 4 and ½ o'clock reached Hagerstown, a distance of 26 miles through the snow, a march unparalleled in the history of the present rebellion. But nine stragglers remained behind, and when the band struck up in Hagerstown all marched as if they were just starting on a holiday excursion. We were quartered in the court house, church, and the citizens almost overwhelmed us with kindness. Coffee and sandwiches were served in abundance and our regiment will ever remember the hospitable and generous people of

Hagerstown. Company quartered in Junior Hall. Took supper myself at Washington House. Met George B. Ayres and Mr. McCormick, Esq. After which in company with Adjutant, Captain Strouse, and Horace Jones.[4] Started out to see the elephant—met Mr. Gauntz the sheriff of the county and accompanied him to his residence where we were hospitably entertained. Got to bed by 11 o'clock, the party meeting Lot Allen of Middletown and the Adjutant seeing the "elephant" to his satisfaction.

Pennsylvania Daily Telegraph
January 6, 1862
From the 46th Penna. Regiment.
Written by Captain George A. Brooks
Camp Matthews, 1 o'clock A.M.,
January 6, 1861.

We have just received orders to march, and whilst the men are preparing to "fall in," I hastily drop you a few lines. On Christmas day the weather which had previously been mild and pleasant, suddenly changed, and since that the cold has been very severe. No drills have taken place, and our holidays have generally been spent in erecting winter quarters, by building, with logs and mortar, about four feet high, and securely placing the tent upon the top, making a roomy house. Some have purchased small stoves, while others have built fire-places in them, rendering them very comfortable. Yesterday we completed ours, the company, but alas, are not permitted to enjoy them. Half an hour ago we received order to march, and will soon be on our way.

This evening information of a very important nature was brought in, and our whole division are now under marching orders. I think we will go to Williamsport, about twenty-five miles from our present location.

Though the weather is very inclement and cold—it having snowed an inch or two on Saturday, beginning again this evening, is now four or five inches deep and still coming down very fast, yet the men seem anxious to see more active service, even though coupled with hardships, and a commendable feeling of patriotism preface the whole regiment. We are, however, ill(y)

---

4. At this time, George W. Boyd was Adjutant. Captain Cyrus Strouse was in Company K. Horace C. Jones was a Private in Company C.

prepared for a forced march at this time. Every body is completely "broke." On Tuesday the paymaster should have made his
appearance, and our requisition for shoes and clothing would
have been filled in a few days. Many of the men are now nearly
barefooted, very few have stockings worth wearing, and some
none at all. We will be unable to take our tents, and how we will
stand a march in the snow, and tomorrow night will be spent,
should the tents not reach us, I will explain in my next.

We will likely get into an engagement, and if should be so
fortunate, rest assured the 46th will come out with flying colors. Promising to write again in a few days, I remain, as ever a
SOLDIER.

P.S. Send all letters, &c., to "Frederick," as before.

———————◆•◆•◆———————

From the Journal of Capt. George A. Brooks

TUESDAY, JANUARY 7. Cold morning but clear. Slept well,
arose early and saw men have breakfast. At 9 o'clock received
orders to march and by 10 were on our way. Many were almost
barefooted but stood it bravely and marched like men. About
1 o'clock reached Williamsport and quartered in several large
warehouses at the lower end of the town. Very muddy and cold,
after the boys were comfortably fixed went up town. Took tea at
the house of a strong Union woman named Mrs. Long. Had the
pleasure of meeting two fine young ladies, Fanny Carson and
Estelle Hughes. Spent portion of the evening with them. Stayed
in quarters but too cold to sleep.

❋ ❋ ❋

Williams' forced march through the snow proved useless. Banks,
in submitting Lander's request to McClellan, had shown a more
cautious side due to the winter weather. He told his commander
that he was concerned that crossing the Potomac could lead to
another Ball's Bluff scenario and it might be best to wait until
Spring. McClellan, always careful, agreed. Williams' men were
told to remain in Williamsport for the time being. General Jackson had already turned his troops south on the seventh, knowing
that the element of surprise had been lost.

General Lander urged Banks to join him at Hancock and begin a pursuit into Virginia. He simultaneously asked McClellan to cross into Virginia with or without Banks. Banks and McClellan both declined, and instead McClellan forwarded orders that Lander should go to Romney where General Kelley's men, who had just helped repel Jackson, were positioned. Lander was instructed to direct a withdrawal of Kelley's men across the Potomac to Cumberland, almost forty miles west of Hancock, where they could go into camp for the winter.

General Lander arrived at Romney and set Kelley's men in motion on a cold, muddy, and miserable march that felt more like a retreat. The weather worked against him, and with the men already in poor shape after spending several months in the field, illness spread and morale dropped.[5] Meanwhile, George Brooks and the 46th were still in Williamsport with little to do but try to keep warm.

———————◆•◆•◆———————

From the Journal of Capt. George A. Brooks

WEDNESDAY, JANUARY 8. Very cold morning, could not sleep during night. Sketched nearly all night. In morning, sun came out warm making it very muddy. Towards evening blew up cold and at night sleeted again. Spent night writing home and to paper after which went to hotel, Mrs. Anderson's. Hailing and sleeting very fast. Just before going to bed was sent for and arrested three of our men, belonging to companies K and J for forcing an entrance into a private family's residence. In company with Col. Selfridge and Major Matthews.[6] Took them to guard house—raining very fast. Got to bed by 12 o'clock with adjutant.

THURSDAY, JANUARY 9. Early at camp, after which returned and took breakfast at "Globe." Cold, unpleasant, and very slippery. Tired staying in this locality, having no quarters with Company and feeling lost. How rapidly absence of a controlling power saps and undermines the discipline of a company. In afternoon ordered to go on picket by my own request at Falling Waters—a dangerous locality and the scene of an engagement during the three month's service. Dined at Mrs. Long's. In evening received

---

5. Cozzens, *Shenandoah 1862*, 80-91.
6. Major Joseph A. Matthews. Promoted to Colonel 128th Regiment P. V., November 1, 1862.

orders to join our Brigade and start for Hancock in the morning. Took tea at Mrs. Long's and spent evening in company with Estelle and Fanny. Found them all very kind and pleasant. Took quite a fancy to Estelle, a very sensible, patriotic, warm hearted girl, and will ever remember with pleasure the brief though fleeting moment spent in her society. Went to Mrs. Anderson's where a large party of merry lads and lassies of the town were assembled. Tripped the light fantastic toe till 10 o'clock. Made the acquaintance of many pretty girls and greatly enjoyed myself. Good bye to my evenings in Williamsport, they have been few but pleasant.

FRIDAY, JANUARY 10. Slept soundly and arose early. Everybody in great glee at the thought of marching as we are heartily sick of our present location, in all things save the kindness and generosity of the people. Started at 11 o'clock, sun shining warmly—very muddy. Marched steadily and reached Clear Spring, a pleasant little town, about 4 o'clock. Quartered in Lutheran Church.[7] Took tea at "Union Hotel" after which spent evening and night in family of Lutheran minister, Reverend M. Curtis, a very fine, sociable man.

SATURDAY, JANUARY 11. Started by 8 o'clock, morning clear and cold. Marching very good on the pike. On the road, crossed the summit of the Blue Ridge Mountains at a summer resort called "Fairview." The finest and most extensive view I have ever seen. Reached Hancock about 3 o'clock, just as it began hailing, but which soon turned into a very severe rain. Waited in the street an hour, waiting on quarters, by which time we were completely drenched to the skin. Finally secured very comfortable quarters in a "Secesh" house. Carpet still on the floor, and everything scattered around the house, evincing the haste in which the affrighted residents had gathered together a few valuables and left on the day of the bombardment of the town by the Rebels on Sunday last. Was greatly amused on going into the kitchen shortly after our arrival to find the boys indulging in tomatoes and other canned fruits found in the cupboards. Some were reading valuable works. The family who left were evidently of refinement and intelligence. Took supper at the house of a family formerly resident of Juniata. Slept in quarters.

---

7. St. Peter's Lutheran Church still stands at 30 S Martin Street, Clear Spring, MD.

✳ ✳ ✳

After their brief stay in Williamsport, Williams' Brigade had been ordered to Hancock where Williams was instructed to take over command of the town from General Lander. Williams found the town in a state of havoc:

> I found here five regiments of infantry of the newest and most mobbish species. During the shelling of the town on Sunday previous [January 5], the people had left their houses, food, furniture and all, which our troops . . . had occupied and literally appropriated to themselves. Food, furniture, forage, fuel and all had been used and destroyed without thought or decency. Three of the regiments were new and had been armed with Belgian [rifles] the day of the attack. They knew nothing of camp, garrison, or other military duty, and were literally a mob firing their loaded muskets right and left and playing the very devil generally.

He immediately set to work "beginning a reform," and with the help of his reliable brigade appointed a provost marshal, placed guard outposts around town, closed down the bars, and arrested a number of especially rowdy soldiers. Finding a place to house all of the soldiers was also problematic, and they filled up every building, barn, and even some canal boats. Others were forced to bivouac outside in the cold.

Williams was anxious to prepare Hancock because reports indicated that Jackson was located only six miles away near the town of Bath, and after the weather improved, he would renew his attack. While sending out scouts to gather more information about Jackson's position, Williams cautiously sent his wagons two miles out of town. If they were attacked, he feared they would have "a scene of confusion that I am not anxious to witness."

Telegraph communication was established between Williams and Kelley's men in Romney, and Williams was instructed to keep his men ready to march at any time in case Kelley was attacked. Lander, out at Romney with Kelley, was "in a constant stew—at times full of fight" and asked Williams to join him. Williams was hesitant, fearing the expedition would result with "frozen feet to hundreds, if nothing more disastrous."

Lander would later curse Williams' hesitance, but it wasn't without reason. While Williams' men were anxious to cross into Dixie, they were poorly prepared. Many were without socks, and hundreds were almost shoeless. Requests for thousands of shoes went mostly unanswered, with only 500 pairs received for a two-month period. "Just fancy in this age soldiers left without shoes in this war for the Union," Williams wrote home. To his relief, higher command rejected Lander's proposition for an advance.

On their third day in Hancock, intelligence indicated that Jackson was instead moving further south toward Unger's Store, and seemed to have given up on Hancock.[8] In truth, Jackson's men were suffering greatly, having been exposed to the elements and poorly fed for days, and were barely in good enough shape to reach Unger's Store, let alone attack Hancock.

Many of the worn out Confederates hoped for a break, but fate would prove otherwise. While they sloshed through muddy roads, scouts reported that the Yankees had left Romney. Jackson was elated, and considered his good fortune a miracle from God. After only a few days rest, he had his men on the road to Romney on January 13th.[9]

From the Journal of Capt. George A. Brooks

SUNDAY, JANUARY 12. Fine Morning. Cleaned out our quarters and put on as good a Sunday look as we could. Very muddy. The recent bombardment did but little damage. About noon met Lieut McDonnell of the 110th PV and Lieut Ricketts of Matthews' battery. About noon received orders to keep men together, as an attack was anticipated, and by 2 o'clock were ordered to pack up and march out of town as the Confederates had threatened to shell the town. Started off with our baggage and encamped in a large field back of town. No bombarding, however, occurred, but a general anxiety prevailed. Got our tent fixed by dark.

MONDAY, JANUARY 13. Fine morning though very cold. Officer of the day. Raised markee [sic]. Received letter from home. One from Emily. Wrote to landlord at Clear Spring. Am in sole command of camp no field officers being present. Sat up late reading and began a flirtation with Estelle or rather wrote a letter of thanks for kindnesses received. After 12 o'clock visited guard house but did not make "grand rounds." Very stormy and snowing very fast.

---

8. Williams, *From the Cannon's Mouth*, 54-7.
9. Cozzens, *Shenandoah 1862*, 93.

————◆•●•◆————

Pennsylvania Daily Telegraph
January 13, 1862
Author Unknown

THE VERBEKE RIFLES. – This gallant body of volunteers, representing Harrisburg in the Forty-Sixth Pennsylvania regiment, Col Joseph F. Knipe, at present located with the army on the upper Potomac, is suffering for want of necessary clothing, including shoes and stockings. Our attentive correspondent attached to the 46th regiment, in his last letter, alluding to some contemplated military movement, said: "We are, however, ill(y) prepared for a forced march at this time. Everybody is completely "broke." On Tuesday the paymaster should have made his appearance, and our requisition for shoes and clothing would have been filled in a few days. Many of the men are now nearly barefooted; very few have stockings worth wearing, and some none at all." The patriotic Treasurer of the York Aid Society, Mrs. Dr. Roland, after reading the letter stating the above facts, in the Morning Telegraph, a few days ago, at once sent us a letter offering to furnish the suffering men of this Company with *one hundred pairs of stockings*, if we would give her the necessary directions to insure their prompt and safe delivery. We have, in reply to this truly generous offer, sent that lady the name and address of Capt. Brooks, and we presume it will not be long until the gallant boys of the "Rifles" are well provided for in the way of stockings, which they will owe to the noble-hearted generosity of one of York's most patriotic daughters.

————◆•●•◆————

From the Journal of Capt. George A. Brooks

TUESDAY, JANUARY 14. Cold morning. At an early hour the Paymaster Clerk arrived with Pay Rolls. After rolls were signed marched to town and received money. Co "D" being second company paid. Received as my share $262.50. Received heavy mail, none for me save papers. In evening went to town and visited military Masonic lodge, in company with Colonel. Work very poor, conducted loosely. Got in camp by 9 o'clock. Snowing very fast.

❄ ❄ ❄

Jackson arrived in Romney on the 14th, and he set to work forming plans to disrupt Lander's communications and threaten his flank. Orders were given to begin the operation on the 18th, but only Jackson himself was confident in his plans. Dissent ran through what was left of his ranks, with a third of the men ill or on furlough. Desertions were becoming more common, and even the most loyal of men were disgusted after the rough campaigning they had recently endured. Jackson finally realized his plans were unrealistic with the current state and morale of his officers and enlisted men, and cancelled his orders. Instead, he started preparing them for winter quarters.

Still, Jackson was pleased with the outcome of his campaign. A colonel under him wrote that "in two weeks, and with trifling loss, [Jackson] had placed the troops opposed to him, while preparing for an aggressive movement, upon the defensive; had expelled them virtually from his whole district; had liberated three counties from their rule, and secured the supplies in them for the subsidence of his own troops."

Realistically, and despite his optimism, Jackson's maneuvering that January had little ill effect on the Union strategy in the area and did more harm than good by demoralizing his men and introducing distrust into his command. Winter ice had done a better job of blocking up canal traffic than Jackson had. Even the Union withdrawal from Romney had been planned by McClellan all along in an effort to mass his troops for the winter and prepare them for a spring offensive. If anything, the campaign had just highlighted the weaknesses of Jackson's men—the Yankees had shown themselves equals at forced winter marching and had proved the uselessness of the Virginia militia under Jackson's command. If only McClellan had allowed Generals Lander and Kelley to attack as they wished, Jackson's army might have been defeated on the mud and snow covered road to Romney.

Months of occupation by both sides had left Romney in disrepair and filthy: illness ran rampant and the troops detested the location. By the third week of January, Jackson started moving his men back to Winchester to keep an eye on Banks. He left General Loring's men, along with some local militia and what was left of Ashby's cavalry, behind to hold the area.

Loring's command was understandably unhappy to be left behind, and Loring knew that due to the terrain the area was highly indefensible if the Yankees did decide to attack. Jackson laid telegraph wire from Winchester to Romney, but even with direct communication, Loring was fifteen miles closer to the Yankees than he was to support from Jackson. Worse yet, intelligence accurately indicated that Union troops outnumbered him almost three to one. Fearing the outcome of remaining in his current position, Loring and some officers who shared his concerns drafted a petition outlining their peril. After forwarding it to Jackson as protocol demanded, he also broke protocol and sent a General to hand deliver the petition to President Davis. Davis agreed that Jackson was wrong to leave Loring exposed, and had the Secretary of War order Jackson to move Loring back to Winchester. Jackson followed his orders and then promptly resigned, citing interference with his command as the primary reason and stating that he was "no longer useful here when what I do in the field is undone by the secretary of war." But after an appeal from the Governor of Virginia, Jackson remained.

During the near disintegration of Jackson's command, General Lander was at work planning the exact scenario General Loring feared. After a denied request to attack Winchester with Banks, Lander submitted a new plan to march on Romney with Banks making a demonstration at Martinsburg to distract Jackson. McClellan agreed to the plan, but heavy rains made the Potomac too difficult to cross. While waiting for the waters to recede, Lander modified his plan based on a new map that showed roads of which the Federals hadn't been aware. He now planned to circle around Romney and attack Loring from the east—a weak spot that Loring himself had pointed out to Jackson. McClellan approved the revised plan, too, and Lander selected February 3rd to begin his advance.[10]

From the Journal of Capt. George A. Brooks

WEDNESDAY, JANUARY 15. Cold morning, and snow being wet made walking very bad. Rumors of moving into town, and efforts are being made to quarter our regiment in town. Nothing

---

10. Cozzens, *Shenandoah 1862*, 96-103.

important occurred today. Went to town in evening to procure Lieutenant Witman's pay roll.

THURSDAY, JANUARY 16. Cold disagreeable morning. Stayed in town all night at the residence of Mrs. Bridges who has a fine son of the firm of Bridges and Henderson and two very pretty and intelligent daughters. Have some notion of boarding with them, in morning did not go out, first sent for company having procured quarters in a fine large warehouse. Got very damp and uncomfortable. By noon the boys came in, carrying knapsacks, baggage, stores etc. Towards evening got pretty well fixed, having made bunks and put up general conveniences. Had some trouble with men, money being plenty and whiskey too easily procured. Sent several to guard house. Placed guard on quarters. Sent home $250 by Adjutant, who has leave of absence to visit Harrisburg.

FRIDAY, JANUARY 17. Fine morning, but very disagreeable walking. Considerable trouble with men. Received letters from Emily and from Wm. H. H. Sieg, enclosing one from Mrs. Roland of York, PA, offering to supply the company with *one hundred pairs of socks*. Quite a timely present, and will write concerning it. Nothing very important occurring. Have taken boarding at the house of Mrs. Bridges. The girls are very pretty, intelligent and pleasant, but strong sympathizers with the Confederates—we have very lively and spirited arguments.

SATURDAY, JANUARY 18. Raining or rather sleeting. Rumors of a forward movement. Received information of the probability of our receiving Minnie Muskets and Sibley tents. Gratifying news, as our arms especially are very poor, and a regiment drilled as we are should receive a better weapon. My old Lieut Colonel of the three months service, John Selheimer, arrived today on a visit. Wrote letter to "Telegraph" after which took a bath and went to boarding house. Wrote to Dr. Witman.

SUNDAY, JANUARY 19. Raining but air moderate. Wrote to Emily a long letter and also one to Wm H. H. Sieg concerning his kindness etc. Sent him specimen of Virginia money. Wrote to Sayford, read Goldsmith and spent portion of afternoon in conversation. Spent evening in writing.

MONDAY, JANUARY 20. Raining hard and very muddy. In fact this is decidedly the muddiest place I have ever been in, worse, far worse than our old haunts at "Muddy Branch." Received letter from "Ned" [Lieut. Witman] who appears to be recovering slowly but expect soon to be able to join us. Anxiously await his arrival, as my duties will then not be so laborious. Wrote him a long letter. Put up and sent off over $700 for the men which in connection with what was previously sent off, amounts to over $1000.

TUESDAY, JANUARY 21. Raining, turned to snow. Officer of the day. Bought sash and belt costing $15 as my old ones are too worn for holiday movement. About 9 o'clock began snowing. Glorious news from our army in Kentucky. Zollicoffer the rebel General killed, also Bailie Peyton. The engagement took place on Sunday morning and resulted in a complete route of the enemy. Boys all overjoyed at the news, but sorry that we are compelled to be here in a state of "masterly inactivity." A well drilled regiment, while many others just entering the field are thrown at once into active service. Heard from home through Captain Luckenbach.[11]

WEDNESDAY, JANUARY 22. Very murky morning. No trouble whilst on duty. Confederate pickets seen on other side. Received a long and very pleasant and affectionate letter from my new friend, Estelle. Must reply as an answer is requested. In evening William Bell arrived, bringing me a letter from Emily. A very long one. Saw Adjutant in morning who had just arrived from home. Many messages from friends.

THURSDAY, JANUARY 23. Bleak, dreary morning. Have not seen the sun for over ten days and from present indications may not see it for some time to come. Exceedingly muddy. Ordered out on battalion drill, which occasioned much dissatisfaction. Marched below town, or rather waded through the mud, and after resting on a hillside came back and held dress parade in front of Gen. Williams' quarters in order to let him see how ridiculous it was to order men out in such weather. Received letter from home. Yesterday Mrs. Bridges, the wife of Robert Bridges, a fine agreeable young woman came from St. James College, a pleasant addition to our family. Received a pressing invitation from Mrs. Ann Louisa Boles, daughter of Judge Boles to call and see her, which I will of course do.

---

11. Owen A Luckenbach, Company C. Promoted from 1st Lt. to Captain, September 4, 1861; discharged on Surgeon's Certificate, October 20, 1862.

```
┌─────────────────────────────────────────────┐
│  State of {  issued under the Act  { Virginia.│
│             of the Corporation.               │
│                                               │
│              {  Vignette:    }                │
│  Winchester, {  Agricultural } Oct. 3, 1861.  │
│              {  Implements.  }                │
│                                          H    │
│  No. 8128.                       Done by the  │
│           Corporation of Winchester.          │
│                 FIVE CENTS.                    │
│  Payable in Virginia Bank notes by the        │
│  Treasurer to Bearer on presentation of       │
│  these due bills, in sums of FIVE DOLLARS.     │
│  W. A. B. Coffroth,     J. R. Bowen,          │
│           C. C.                    Prest.      │
└─────────────────────────────────────────────┘
```

(Source: Pennsylvania Daily Telegraph, January 21, 1862.)

Pennsylvania Daily Telegraph
January 21, 1862

CONFEDERATE "SHINPLASTERS." – Captain Brooks, of the Verbeke Rifles, now stationed with the army at Hancock, Md., has sent to a gentleman connected with this office, a sample of "Shinplasters" issued by the various town, borough and city corporations in "Dixie," for the purpose of keeping the "machinery in motion." The sample before us represents the value of "five cents," and was issued by the corporation of Winchester. The picture on the left corner of the note was evidently intended to represent a juvenile god "Mercury," but looks more like the battered impression of a worn-out wood-cut of a turkey buzzard. Directly below this is a large-sized figure "5," enclosed in checkwork. The right end of the note contains a similar figure "5," flanked above and below with a continuous "border." The main body of the note reads as follows:

The note is printed on miserable, flimsy brown paper, with a texture, soft and greasy as a cast off finger rag, and is altogether a curiosity.

From the Journal of Capt. George A. Brooks

FRIDAY, JANUARY 24. The same morning we have had for some time past. No variation. About noon company of the NY

Twenty-eighth crossed the river on a scouting excursion, under cover of the artillery, who were posted on an adjacent height. The company returned by noon. About 4 o'clock six videttes were seen upon the hill, opposite Hancock, and shortly after one of our wood boats was fired upon by the Rebels from the water station about a mile above town. In evening, Col. Selfridge being officer of the day, detached my company to go over the river, and returning. But upon visiting General Williams he objected.

————◦•◦————

Pennsylvania Daily Telegraph
January 22, 1862
From the Forty-Sixth Penn'a. Regiment.
Hancock, Jan. 19.
Written by Captain George A. Brooks

MR. EDITOR: – We have been so busily engaged in changing quarters and receiving the kind and ever welcome attentions of paymaster Sherman, that I have been unable to write earlier concerning our march from Frederick to Williamsport via Hagerstown, and our subsequent arrival at the "deserted village" of Hancock. But "better late than never."

Leaving our camp, near Frederick on Monday morning, January sixth. Just before daylight we were joined by the Nineteenth and Twenty-eighth New York, and Fifth Connecticut regiment—all belonging to the brigade of General Williams—our regiment taking the advance. The snow was about four inches deep, and the weather very cold. The men were in excellent spirits, and although we "trod on slippery places," yet all marched well and cheerfully. Along the route, and especially in the pretty little villages of Boonsboro and Funkstown, we were cheered with every demonstration of loyalty to the Union. The stars and stripes floated gracefully from the windows of many dwellings, and many a fervent wish and hearty God-speed were given us. At half-past four o'clock in the afternoon we reached Hagerstown, having marched a distance of twenty-six miles through the snow, the toes of many being entirely exposed, and leaving but nine stragglers behind—a feat unparalleled in the history of the present rebellion. As we entered the streets of Hagerstown the band struck up a lively tune, and the men marched as though they were just starting on a holiday excursion. We halted in the public square, and were soon snugly ensconced in comfortable quarters. The citizens almost overwhelmed us with kindness, and coffee and sandwiches were abundantly supplied, after which the men were given the freedom of the city. It is a pleasant and neat town, quite a brisk business place, and ever will the Forty-sixth Pennsylvania remember the hospitable reception given them by her generous and benevolent people.

On Tuesday morning at ten o'clock we were again formed, *every man being in his place*, and started for Williamsport, having been detached from our brigade and ordered to report to Col. Leonard of the Thirteenth Massachusetts, acting Brigadier-General, where we arrived at noon, distance seven miles. We quartered in large open warehouses below town, on the river bank, remaining there until Friday morning. The men suffered greatly, it being very cold, and having no stoves. The feet of several were frozen badly. Many of the citizens were very kind.

On Friday morning we received the very cheering news that we were again to join our brigade, and by eight o'clock were under way. Marched steadily and reached a small place called Clear Spring, and starting from there on Saturday morning at an early hour, arrived in Hancock about 3 o'clock, just as it began raining severely. It was nearly an hour before quarters for the whole regiment could be procured, by which time all were pretty wet. Our company, the "Rifles," was finally placed in a very comfortable "secesh" house, and everything evinced the haste in which the affrightened [sic] occupants had left during the bombardment of this place on the Sunday previous to our arrival. The carpet still remained on the floors, papers, letters &c., were scattered through the rooms, and a fine collection of books evinced the taste and refinement of those who had resided therein. Visiting the kitchen shortly after we were located, I found the boys regaling themselves with canned fruits and other edibles, having made fire in a large cook stove, and all the culinary appliances necessary being convenient, they were generally "at home."

On Sunday morning rumors were current that the Confederates would probably make an attack upon us, companies were ordered to stay in quarters, and every premonition of "lively times" was apparent. About noon we were ordered to leave, as the enemy had threatened to bombard the town, and retiring in good order, halted on a hill back of the batteries of Captains Matthews and Knapp, who occupied a commanding position. All anxiously awaited the appearance of the rebels but they came not, and after remaining three days in camp we again removed to town and are now quartered in a large warehouse, in the principal street.

Considered the hardships and exposure which we have encountered during the past few weeks the regiment is enjoying excellent health; very few are seriously ill, and not *one* of the "Verbeke Rifles," is unable to be about—though some have frozen feet and severe colds.

Since our arrival here we have been short of provisions, but this was owing to bad roads and the sudden transportation of a large body of troops here. Today, however, a full supply arrived, and we only await orders to advance.

Promising to write again in a few days,

I remain as ever,
SOLDIER.

P.S. – Letters should be directed, "Co. D., 46th P.V., Gen. Williams' Brigade, Hancock, Md."

———————

From the Journal of Capt. George A. Brooks

SATURDAY, JANUARY 25. Snowed during the night, but this morning the sun rose bright and clear, the first time we have seen it for over three weeks. Still some chance of Cos. K and D going over the river and am only awaiting orders. Should be pleased to plant the colors upon the "sacred soil" and have an opportunity of try the mettle of our "boys." About 11 o'clock received orders to be ready to march at a moment's notice. Were delayed over half an hour by a deserter coming across the river. Crossed the river in a large flat. A company from the Fifth Connecticut having first crossed. Had many applications for permission to accompany me. Marched up the hill cautiously, my company acting as reserve, and the Fifth Conn. being thrown out as skirmishers. After advancing about two miles toward Bath, discovered three pickets who we drove in, after rolling the timber which they had prepared for a bridge into the river. We returned all safe from our first expedition to the "sacred soil." The girls were all glad to see me as they had many fears for my safety. It is strange—surrounded by every comfort home can give, by kind warm-hearted friends who take so deep an interest in my welfare, it but gives a striking instance of how unnatural a warfare we are engaged in. Warm sympathizers, ever secessionists, praying for the successes of the South, yet they regret to see those in the great Federal Army put on the armor and go forth to fight the unholy rebellion. Strange.

SUNDAY, JANUARY 26. Fine morning, though cold. Officer of the day. Spent much of the day at my "new home," where I do indeed enjoy all the comforts. Our family all rigid "blue stockings" have family worship morning and evening, and they are so very kind. Verily our lives have fallen in goodly places. In evening trotted "pony" out to supply train to visit pickets, after which spent the remainder in religious controversies with the girls and Robert. Spent our time profitably—had dress parade.

MONDAY, JANUARY 27. Cold morning and cloudy. Had a good company drill—first one for many weeks. In afternoon had battalion drill in a large field adjacent to the town. In evening raised thirty four dollars for the band in addition to sixty already contributed. Making in all ninety-four. Received orders to march and take charge of Dam No. 6 on the Potomac 8 miles above Hancock. To start at early hour.

THURSDAY, JANUARY 28. Raining or sleeting. Very ugly morning to march. Started at 10 o'clock. Snowing very fast. Just before leaving received our new gum blankets which came quite

The rugged country around Dam No. 6 (guard wall visible in lower left corner), captured in the early 1900s. (Source: Western Maryland Regional Library.)

opportunely. The girls all felt sorry at seeing me go. It broke up our small social circle, and I felt very sad at leaving a place in which I had enjoyed so many home comforts. But thus, it is life. The best friends must part, and I bow in submission to my fate, trusting my absence may be short. We took the tow path for our march, being informed that the road was better. Passed some of the most rugged scenery I have ever seen. Saw a few Confederate pickets but they gave us no trouble, no doubt considering discretion the best part of valor. Arriving at Dam No. 6 found no quarters. Halted Company, stacked arms, and borrowing horse from Cavalryman, went in search of shelter, which I found at a lock 2 miles above. Returned and took company up. Pretty comfortable house. Wagon containing rations did not arrive. Met unpleasant evening. Bought straw enough for beds.

WEDNESDAY, JANUARY 29. Slept comfortably. An ugly, disagreeable night. Had no guard on duty save at quarters. About 9 o'clock wagon containing provisions arrived. Borrowed horse from Cavalryman and rode up to lock 3 miles above on a scouting expedition. Cautioned everybody being adjacent in reference to selling liquor. Made some inquiries concerning country, people, etc. In afternoon rode down to pickets at the Dam. No 6. Changed the position of sentinels and rode below dam a few miles on a prospecting town. Gave orders securing all boats and preventing all crossing either river or canal. Rather unpalatable news to some who had been crossing daily. In evening wrote a few lines to Colonel after which read til very late "Elsie Venner" by Oliver Wendell Holmes.

THURSDAY, JANUARY 30. Snowed and rained all night and snowed very fast this morning. Sent letters off by Cavalryman— slept soundly on a board wrapped in my blanket. At 9 borrowed horse from Mr. Clay and started for Hancock. Took the county road which runs through one of the most dreary regions I have ever seen for a distance of 8 miles. Snowing very fast. Reached Hancock at 12 A.M. found everybody at headquarters in good spirits. Asked and answered innumerable questions. Saw Dr. and my sick who were left in old quarters, all getting along finely. After seeing Quartermaster and attending to necessary business—went to "home" where friends enjoying the comforts and joys of society, friendship and home, after taking a hearty dinner and bid adieu and started for company at 4. Rode along quite briskly, awhile I left the pike when the road wound round among the ravines through the mountains. One of the most lonesome and picturesque roads I have ever traveled. The road being very bad. I could not go along over a walk and loving solitude at times, began reflecting upon the vicissitudes and adventures in the life of a soldier. Before I had gone far the lengthening shadows of evening stole on apace, and of all the dark dreary regions, this was one. Arrived safe at the house of Mr. Clay whose horse I had been riding, and walked from there to quarters. Distributed mail and papers among the boys. Received letters from Wm. H. H. Sieg, Mrs. Dr. Roland, A. J. Keck, and Dr. H. O. Witman. Glad to know he is recovering.

FRIDAY, JANUARY 31. Did not go to bed last night until near midnight, first finishing a wild weird tale "Elsie Venner" by O.W. Holmes, the only one I have read for many years. Many original vivid imagism [sic], but on the whole quite skeptical. Beautiful clear morning. Whilst breakfasting, boys brought information that a man from other side wished to cross, averring he was an escaped prisoner. Buckled on my pistol and taking a trusty man, crossed in boat, got him in, and returned. On examining him he stated he had just escaped from the rebels who had taken him prisoner. Did not know much concerning the movements of the Confederates. In morning wrote to Capt. A. D. Collin, an old friend in the "Reserve Corps" after which rode to Orleans, a small place five miles above occupied by Captain Douglas and has company from Gen. Landers' command. Stayed but a short time making the acquaintance of Captain Douglas, a fine Scotch gentleman. Rode leisurely home. In evening rode to Dam 6, visited pickets, shared some general information, and returned just at dark. Spent portion of evening with a young girl at a neighboring farm house. Returned to quarters and had just began examining some letters which were to be sent over the river, when the mournful intelligence was brought that one of my men on picket at Dam 6 had been drowned in the lock. Hastily saddling and bridling the horse and procuring a lantern, I rode in great haste to the lock and found alas, it was too true. Amos M. Wenrich was no more—he fell in the "line of duty" and though not gloriously upon the battlefield yet a patriot offering up his life upon the altar of his country. Always a mild, quiet inoffensive boy. Ever ready and willing to perform any duty which devolved upon him, intelligent and of a pious mind, he was a model soldier, and ever

*Amos M. Wenrich, a farmer from Dauphin
County, Pennsylvania, just outside of
Harrisburg, was 19 years old when he drowned
on duty. The locks near Dam No. 6 still exist and
can be visited. In person, imagining a deadly
fall on an icy night while laden in heavy winter
army gear isn't difficult. Amos' older brother,
John, was killed a little over a year later at
Gettysburg. (Source: Moyer, Nevin W., Military
Milestones of Old Paxton Township, 1946.)*

will his memory be cherished green in the heart of his companions in arms. Thus life flit away.

"The good die first
Whilst they whose hearts are dry as summer's dust
Burn to the socket"[12]

What food for reflection? What a theme for the practical reason
to dwell upon?

❇ ❇ ❇

Amos Wenrich was the first man to die under George Brooks'
command, and his untimely death took a toll on the Company. As
the cold, wet weather of January came to a close, they remained

---

12. From William Wadsworth's "The Excursion"

on guard duty along a desolate stretch of the Potomac, keeping at eye on the imposing Dam No. 6. Twenty-seven miles upstream from Dam No. 5, Dam No. 6 stretched 475 feet across the Potomac. Large guard walls were necessary to protect the canal and its lock, culverts, and inlet channels from floods. The dam raised the upstream level of the river by about sixteen feet in normal conditions, meaning a fall into a lock or inlet would be at least that far. Patrolling the slippery rock walls at night in worn out boots was treacherous, and Amos would have been weighed down with a heavy winter coat.[13] He wouldn't be the only soldier to lose his life guarding the C&O.[14]

From the Journal of Capt. George A. Brooks

SATURDAY, FEBRUARY 1. Cloudy morning. Drizzling rain. Arose early and made arrangements for sending Amos to Hancock, having no way in which to inter him here, and not being able, on account of Sunday intervening, to send him home. Sent him down to Hancock on small flat boat. His melancholy death has thrown a gloom over the whole company and checked the general hilarity of the boys. Wrote long letter to Emily, giving a description of our life during the past week, having delayed writing takes longer than usual. In evening rode down to Dam with countersign, but did not stay away. Have been so antsy since we have been up here, and have lost so much sleep feel somewhat worn out. Did not go to bed until late, reading in Byron.

SUNDAY, FEBRUARY 2. Bright clear morning, though pretty cold. Meat having run out, boys had to take "cracker breakfast." Wrote to "Estelle" and Lieut Witman, long letters—invited to dine with Mr. Clay and just after dinner, Captain Luckenbach, Snally, Dr. Wilson and Mr. Lamer rode up from Hancock on a visit to me. Had them take dinner. Afternoon flat came up with seven days rations, besides bringing a large mail containing letters from Lieut Witman and Col Selfridge. Amos M. Wenrich's remains were taken charge of by Company "A" and would be buried with all the honors of war.[15] In afternoon my friends went

---

13. Gray, Karen. "Dam 6 and Its Associated Structures." *Along The Towpath* XLVI.3 (2014). C&O Canal Association. Web. 20 Dec. 2015.
14. A week later, Company I also lost a man, Private James Barrett, by drowning.
15. Wenrich was buried in Hancock, MD, but the author was unable to confirm the current location of his grave.

home. Am sorry orders came making me stay another week as I did want to return and again enjoy the comforts of home and the society of brother officers. But this is soldering. In evening read Byron until a late hour.

MONDAY, FEBRUARY 3. Arose early. Snowing very fine but fast. Indications of a regular snow storm. Never saw or heard of weather equal to what we have seen for several weeks past or in fact since Christmas. Sent four of my men over to Virginia today on a deer hunt. About 2 o'clock they returned bringing a fine fawn and had a fine mess of venison for supper. In afternoon wrote to Mrs. Dr. Roland of York, and David Wenrich concerning the death of his son Amos. Poor hand at consoling. In evening flat came up bringing no provisions, the supply train from Hagerstown not having arrived. Borrowed enough from Captain Morgan, Co. F. In evening went to Mr. Clay's and from there elsewhere, returning at 10. Where ignorance is bliss tis folly to be wise.

TUESDAY, FEBRUARY 4. Snowed nearly all night. Got ready to take a hunt and started with six men for the "sacred soil." Ran around all day but did not see any deer, though there were indications of large quantities about. Returned by 3 o'clock very wet but feel well and am glad I went. Have most excellent appetite. Forgot to mention receiving a letter yesterday from Col Selfridge and some papers, also letter and paper from "Snally." In evening wrote to A.G. Keet, Wm H.H. Sieg, and Emily, after which sat up reading Byron's Sara.

WEDNESDAY, FEBRUARY 5. Very cold but clear morning. Attending to matters in general and securing a horse from Mr. Clay started for Hancock. Rode down the towpath, rather a wild, fractious beast, but reached Headquarters by 12 P.M. Glad to see everybody. Went to quarters, saw boys, all in good spirits—sick, all well or nearly so. After going to quartermaster and attending to some general business went "home." Surprised and glad to see me, indeed one of the girls had remarked in my absence that she "was afraid they thought too much of Captain Brooks." Feel proud that I have made such warm friends and trust I may be able to reciprocate the many kindnesses I have received at their hands. Colonel away at Frederick, consequently did not return.

THURSDAY, FEBRUARY 6. Spent one of our familiar home evenings—so pleasant. So sociable. So cozy. Before bedtime had our usual lunch and after family worship retired. This morning when I awoke it was sleeting or hailing, and continued so much of morning. At 10 went to officers school for instructions in light infantry drill although pretty familiar with the manual and tactics in general, yet found the school very beneficial and am sorry my absence prevents attendance, always being anxious to learn. After school saw Colonel and was assured we would be recalled from our station at Dam No. 6 on Saturday. Learned all particulars concerning arms, etc. Took dinner at "home," after which visited the grave of my unfortunate man Wenrich who was drowned. At 3 o'clock started for Dam No. 6 reaching quarters at dark. Boys all glad to see me. Had a large mail for them. Blowing up very cold. Read until late.

❆ ❆ ❆

After several victories in January had secured Union control of eastern Kentucky, President Lincoln issued General War Order No. 1, which instructed land and naval forces to make a general movement by February 22nd. Lincoln had reached the end of his patience and issued the order to force McClellan into an offensive.[16]

A few days later on February 3rd, General Lander started an advance on Romney, but just a quarter mile out of camp the men were told to cancel their movement. The General had collapsed with intense pain and chills brought on by the onset of sepsis from a bad leg wound he had received at Ball's Bluff. Bacteria had entered through the wound and infected the soft tissue of his bones, and forty year old Lander knew he was dying.

The knowledge of his impending doom seemed to inspire him to do something of meaning, and so he ordered his men out again and continued to monitor his campaign from his sick bed. On February 6th, when his men arrived in Romney, they found that Loring's men had already left and returned to Winchester. With the Confederates clear of the area and the railroad able to be reopened, Lander considered his campaign a success and instructed his men into camp on comfortable, high ground near the Paw Paw Tunnel.

On February 9th, the Confederate war department promoted General Loring and transferred him to Georgia in an attempt to separate him from General Jackson. Jackson, still bitter from the petition incident, wasn't sorry to see him go.

---

16. Wagner, *Desk Reference*, 13, 251.

Jackson's men were faring poorly in Winchester. Many fell sick and there weren't enough supplies for the quantity of soldiers camped there. So many were sick that the army had to appeal to townspeople to donate food, but there was little to give. An outbreak of scarlet fever and typhoid only made matters worse, and Jackson's ranks were dwindling—a roll call in February showed 6,404 men were present and 7,355 were absent. Intelligence indicated that Union forces were massing along the Potomac and an advance by Lander, recovered for the time being, and Banks, seemed imminent. Jackson told his commanders that he would need 9,000 men to hold the valley, but no one knew where they would come from.[17]

From the Journal of Capt. George A. Brooks

FRIDAY, FEBRUARY 7. Cloudy morning and pretty cold—wrote to Lieut "Ned." Looked over Army regulations. Sent guard over river with Mr. Dawson. At noon received visit from Capt Waller of New York Twenty-Eighth, commanding at Sir John's Run and through him information that our whole brigade were under marching orders. Immediately after his departure I took horse and went to Hancock post haste. Brigade had not moved but had been ordered to. Had every arrangement made. Got ambulance to bring my sick back. Found a wagon with four days rations and our new rifles and ammunition had been sent up to me and in case our regiment moved I was to cut across the county independent and join them. After procuring some medicine started back. Rode fast and arrived at Dam before 6. In making a fast trip ambulance and wagon containing goods had arrived safely. Boys in great glee—examined new guns—a beautiful arm. In evening went girling for an hour or two after which returned and took a complete bath and put on clean clothing. Will march tomorrow to join the regiment. Being relieved by Company "I."

SATURDAY, FEBRUARY 8. Very cold morning, arose early and unpacked guns. Beautiful arm. Distributed them with ammunition and repacked old guns etc. Loaded wagons and by 11 sent company off under command of Lieut Geiger.[18] Kept one man on each post and stayed at old quarters myself until arrival of

---

17. Cozzens, *Shenandoah 1862*, 103-7.
18. John W. Geiger. Dismissed July 6, 1863.

Company I which was not til 3 o'clock. Left and taking my men along walked to Hancock a distance of 12 miles in less than three hours. Very warm. Found our company all safely ensconced and all very glad to leave the dreary desolate despair in which our lot fell during the past [End of entry]

SUNDAY, FEBRUARY 9. Beautiful morning at reveille call. Have very sore throat and severe cold brought on by fast walking. In morning had inspection of quarters only. Spent remainder of morning in reading. Spent afternoon in quarters and in evening, after writing home, recited the Presbyterian Catechism which I have not done for fourteen years. Remember them pretty well, first impressions last longest. Information came to headquarters that Company I who relieved me at Dam No. 6 drowned one man in the same place my unfortunate Wenrich lost his life.

MONDAY, FEBRUARY 10. Very fine morning. Feel very unwell and have a very sore throat. Unfit for duty, but Lieut being officer of the guard had to remain at quarters. In morning went to officer's school. Considerable difference of opinion in regard to new drill to be adopted. Mail brought no letters from home. Very strange and cannot account for not hearing, long ere this received one. Judge everybody is well. Very fine dress parade. Afterwards drew fifty pairs of pants. Nothing new or stirring. Some indications of moving into our new Sibley tents about a mile from town. Received every kindness and attention from my friends in my new home.

TUESDAY, FEBRUARY 11. Glorious morning. Felt somewhat better though throat is very sore. Towards noon began snowing and was quite stormy. Spent day until noon at home. After dinner went to quarters. Dropped into Capt Matthews. Saw him, Ricketts and Godbald.[19] Received several members of "Telegraph" but still no letter. Spent evening reading Byron and political discussions.

<hr>

Pennsylvania Daily Telegraph
February 11, 1862

THE VERBEKE RIFLES.
Capt. Geo. A. Brooks, of this city, attached to the 46th Pennsylvania regiment, in Gen. Banks' column, on the Potomac, from

19. All were members of Matthews' battery.

all accounts, are winning golden opinions from the military authorities for their effectiveness and through military discipline. Recently the Rifles received the high compliment of being one of two companies selected from an entire brigade to make a reconnaissance in the direction of Bath, Va. This small force was afterwards augmented by the addition of one more company. The expedition after marching, or rather skirmishing, for over two miles, saw none of the enemy save a few pickets, who were driven in. Towards evening the companies returned to camp, first throwing in the river some timber which the rebels had prepared for erecting a bridge over the Potomac to bring Jackson's army over. The letter from which we derive the above particulars adds, "had we met any of the secession rascals there would have been "fun." The "Rifles," generally, are in the enjoyment of good health, and anxious for a passage at arms with the enemy.

———•◦•———

From the Journal of Capt. George A. Brooks

WEDNESDAY, FEBRUARY 12. Beautiful morning—air mild and balmy and sun shining gloriously. Streets very muddy. When mail came in received a long letter from Emily, in which she expresses sufferance at not hearing from me. Immediately sat down and answered it. Rumors of our moving to camp tomorrow. No news of any importance.

THURSDAY, FEBRUARY 13. Fine morning. At 9 went with Company as a fatigue party to our new camp location, very pleasant. Meadow land, gently sloping hill and water plenty. Terraced our tents and generally fined them up. Returned to town by 1 o'clock and found Lieut Witman who has been absent for some time sick. He looks finely, far better than for many years past. Very glad he has come as it will relieve me from onerous duties. In evening ran about town with Lieut after which went home. Col Selfridge, Quartermaster Cadwalader and Adjutant Boyd spent the evening with me.[20] Very pleasant. After some conversation among the 'children' and family worship we all went to bed.

---

20. George B. Cadwalader. Promoted to Assistant Quartermaster U. S. Volunteers, July 8, 1863.

✳ ✳ ✳

On February 13th, General Lander, having temporarily recovered enough from his illness to return to the field, joined his men and started them toward Bloomery Furnace. The last Confederate forces in that vicinity, four understrength militia companies, occupied the area. Lander hoped to use his aggressive advance to shame Banks and Williams into action. The ensuing operation lasted about thirty hours, during which his men marched forty-five miles, crossed the Great Cacapon River via pontoon boats, scattered the Confederate militia and took over one hundred prisoners. Lander returned to camp exhausted but victorious. He wrote to McClellan telling him that all Confederate forces had been cleared from the district and that "General Williams could move over the river without risk."[21]

While the newspapers made mention of Lander's success and he reported to McClellan that he had reopened the B&O Railroad between Cumberland and Hancock, Williams saw it differently. He had controlled the rail line half way to Cumberland for a month prior, and had established a telegraph line between Hancock and Cumberland twice. Furthermore, his men had already been doing reconnaissance and picket throughout the region where Lander claimed his success for days before he had even arrived in the vicinity. General Williams wrote home, annoyed with the situation:

> In truth, until last Sunday Gen. Lander knew nothing of the railroad or the other side of the Potomac for twenty miles above. The whole of that region has been held by my pickets, who have had possession of the railroad bridge over the Big Cacapon and below for five to ten miles. I confess my astonishment, therefore, to see in the Baltimore papers today a long account of Gen. Lander clearing the line of the railroad and opening the route for Gen. Williams' brigade to cross, and a complimentary order of the Secretary of War to Gen. Lander for his valuable services.[22]

In the grand scheme of things, Lander's actions and the accolades that followed, warranted or not, were of little meaning. The Bloomery Furnace affair was mostly overlooked by Confederate leadership. The Western theater was on the verge of collapse after Fort Henry on the Tennessee River was captured on February

---

21. Cozzens, *Shenandoah 1862*, 108-13.
22. Williams, *From the Cannon's Mouth*, 59-60.

6th, opening the river for Union traffic into the deep south. Bowling Green, Kentucky was evacuated on the 15th, and the same day Fort Donelson on the Cumberland River was surrendered.[23] Paired with other victories, in three weeks, Union troops had gained control of Kentucky, Missouri, and much of Tennessee. The blockade was squeezing the south's economy, and McClellan's 155,000 man army stood opposite the Confederacy's 40,000 near Manassas Junction. Perhaps the largest blow was the absence of any European country backing the rebellion—a financial and political bolster that the Confederacy knew was required if they stood any chance of succeeding. With defeat seeming imminent, the Confederate Congress enacted a conscription act to keep the armies in the field past spring.

Back in Washington, General McClellan faced his February 22nd deadline to start the campaign he had planned in October when he accepted command of the Army of the Potomac. Still insisting that the Confederates had 150,000 well equipped and trained soldiers at Manassas instead of the 40,000 poorly prepared men that were actually there, McClellan devised another option. He presented President Lincoln with a plan that he said would bring "the most brilliant result." By landing his entire army at Urbana, a port near the mouth of the Rappahannock River, and marching up it toward Richmond, McClellan would leverage the railroad and his capture of the James and York rivers to protect his flanks and supply his advance. Lincoln accepted the plan.

In the Shenandoah Valley, Banks indicated his readiness to begin operations by February 11th. He had created a large and reliable network of civilian spies, including white Unionists, free blacks, and runaways. Jackson's weakness in numbers and morale were communicated back to Banks, who in turn told McClellan that "the enemy was never in a feebler condition than at this time." He was certain that he and Lander could occupy Winchester and Leesburg by March 1st. Feeling the pressure of Lincoln's impatience for action and the logistics of planning his Peninsula campaign, McClellan consented to Banks' request to cross the Potomac at Harpers Ferry by the end of the month. Banks started his brigades still in Frederick toward Harpers Ferry, leaving Williams at Hancock for the time being.[24]

---

23. Wagner, *Desk Reference*, 14.
24. Cozzens, *Shenandoah 1862*, 114-5, 117-9.

—•◆•—

From the Journal of Capt. George A. Brooks

FRIDAY, FEBRUARY 14. Rain, misty morning. The streets very muddy. Went to Oyster Saloon with Lieut Witman and got my first "steer" since arriving in Hancock. Got holster for pistol. Making preparations for moving. Lieut Witman brought a letter from Emily and also a fine Colt pistol. Everybody at and around home well and lively. Wrote long and spacy [sic] letter to Emily in regard to matters in general and Willie's picture in particular. Spent evening at home.

SATURDAY, FEBRUARY 15. Pleasant morning. Lieut Witman detached as "Inspecting Officer" at Ferry across Potomac. Sorry so soon to lose him, after his return from so long an absence. But such is the fate of war. Done nothing out of usual routine, save having a dress parade, at which the news of our recent victory at Roanoke were read. For evening after parade went over with Lieut Witman and several friends to "Dixie." Returned after dusk, Lieut Geiger being officer of the guard, could not go home until after "tattoo." Snowed some in the morning.

SUNDAY, FEBRUARY 16. Pleasant morning. Sun shining beautifully. Had regular inspection. Coming out in white gloves. At 10 received orders to march to camp at 1. Started for camp at 1½ o'clock. Road somewhat muddy. Camp pleasantly located on pike a mile from Hancock called "Camp Wilson." After seeing boys comfortably fixed went into town and spent evening and night at home in the pleasant society of my new friends, Helen Mar, Fuller, Persilla, Robert, Morgan and "mother" reading Spurgeon's sermons etc. Drank cup warm tea for a very severe cold.

MONDAY, FEBRUARY 17. Rain, cloudy morning. Sleeted somewhat during night. Did not get up until 8 o'clock. Cold some better. Got a team from quartermaster and sent out enough of lumber to cover our tent floor. Went out to camp and by 3 had our "old quarters" comfortably fixed. Received orders to march into town. Had a grand review of the whole command. Information of the recent capture of Fort Donelson. Generals Johnson and Buckner and 15,000 men by our forces read Glorious news as it was considered one of the strongholds. Three times three hearty cheers were given by the whole brigade which made the very welkin ring and amid the music of bands and the booming of cannon we had four grand dress parades. It was magnificent, glorious, inspiring and our only regret was that we were debarred from participating in it. In the evening called at my old home and after spending an hour or so started for camp. Large and beautiful campfires all along the principal streets of Hancock and the headquarters of every regiment and the homes of a number of citizens illuminated. Reached camp at 9.

TUESDAY, FEBRUARY 18. Clear morning. Sun out finely. Officer of the day. Went with regiment into town to escort the Nineteenth New York out, they leaving our brigade for Washington to be placed in the artillery service. Marched finely and everything went off pleasantly. Returned to camp, marching very muddy. Received letters from Frank and Emily also one from Estelle, quite too devoted for a friendly correspondence. Have my tent fined up pleasantly and now live very comfortably. Spent evening in writing to father of Amos M Wenrich and also to Frank. Having a very bad cold did not make "grand rounds" but after reading awhile went to bed. How pleasant must home be.

WEDNESDAY, FEBRUARY 19. Cloudy raw morning. Began sleeting early. Adjutant not being present and everybody waiting, mounted guard myself. After superintending firing of old guard went to quarters. Spent morning in reading, Horace took dinner with us. In afternoon wrote long letter to Emily. Received package from home containing paper envelopes etc. Has rained very hard all day. After dress parade went to town and spent very pleasant evening at "home." Dropped in at Headquarters to see Colonel and Major etc. Came out to camp at 10. Very dark and raining briskly.

THURSDAY, FEBRUARY 20. Cloudy raw morning. Very muddy. About noon went to town and dined at "home." Spending portion of afternoon. Had ambrotype taken and paid boarding $10.50. Spent part of evening at Headquarters. Highly complimented on the appearance of my Company, etc. Spent remainder of evening in company with Lieut Witman and Morgan at "home" after which adjourned to saloon and had a fine mess of oysters. From thence went home, quite cold and freezing—walking very rough. Reached camp at 10½.

FRIDAY, FEBRUARY 21. Clear morning, very cold. Too cold to sleep and awoke with a very severe cough. Received letters from

Mrs. Roland or Miss Darker and also from Theo K Scheffer. Also a fine box of stockings—fifty—a donation from the aid society of York. Came very importantly and quite an acceptable present. Ever will we remember the gracious, warm hearted benevolence. Wrote to Theo.

SATURDAY, FEBRUARY 22. Cloudy morning. At 10 regiment formed and marched to town where the whole brigade was formed in line and after review by Gen Williams were marched to a large field adjacent to the town where the brigade was formed into a square facing inwards. The farewell address of Gen Washington was then read after which the "Star Spangled Banner" was sung. The regiment then formed into a line, prepared for review and had the finest the brigade has ever had. After the review marched to quarters. Spent evening in town at "home" very pleasantly and started for camp at late hour, having first spent some time at Headquarters to hear particulars in reference to Jackson's rumored approach. At 10 were ordered to cook two days rations and march at midnight.

SUNDAY MORNING, FEBRUARY 23. Companies ABC+D started at 1 o'clock for Sir Johns Run, distance of six miles. Raining and very muddy. Many sunk in mud up to their knees and none but few had dry feet. Reached Sir Johns at 4 o'clock and laying on the bare ground slept til morning. At 11 crossed the Potomac and moved on cautiously toward Bath. On reaching there found no enemy but all along the road was evidence of the devastation they had made. Bath or Berkeley Springs is a pleasant little place, beautifully located and one of the finest and most famous watering places in the country, but is now almost desolate. Leaving Bath we pushed on to Hancock and crossing the ferry were soon again in camp. Spent evening at Colonel's. Took supper at Dr Wilson's and taking some medicine and had whiskey purely for a very severe cold. Went to bed.

————◄•◆•►————

Pennsylvania Daily Telegraph
Author unknown

FROM THE FORTY-SIXTH PENNSYLVANIA REGIMENT – The Forty-Sixth Pennsylvania Regiment, Col. Knipe, of this city, is now encamped about one mile from Hancock, and the other regiments comprising Gen. Williams' (Third) brigade in or near the town. The brigade has been under marching orders for the past four days. They were ordered, on the 24th, to cook three days' rations, to be carried in haversacks, and four more to be taken with them in wagons, to be ready to march next morning after daybreak—to leave all camp equipage behind—the baggage of the officers and camp materials to be taken, after they marched, to Hagerstown, and there to be stored.

On Sunday morning [the 23rd], near midnight, Companies A, B, C and D, (the Verbeke Rifles, Capt. Brooks, of this City,) of the Forty-sixth regiment, were ordered out and marched on short notice, with two days' cooked provisions in haversacks. The night was very dark, and rain began to fall before they left the camp. After marching through mud shoe-mouth deep, and in many places to their knees, they arrived, about an hour before daylight, on the Potomac, at a point called "Sir Johns Run," six miles from their present camp. The men, after they halted, suffered severely from the cold, as no fires were permitted to be made until the day had dawned. After several hours' rest, they crossed in a flat to the Virginia side. Here they found two companies of the Sixty-second Ohio regiment encamped, guarding a bridge, which had been lately erected in place of one burned by the rebels on the 3d of January last. Information had been received that several companies were on their march, via Bath, to destroy the present structure so lately built, and to prevent their approach the detachment was so suddenly called out. They arrived in Bath, about two and a half miles back of the river, and there learned that several companies, which had been encamped beyond there on the Winchester road, pulled up stakes and made a hasty retreat on their approach. They returned to camp that night, taking a different road home, and crossed the river opposite Hancock, seven or eight miles from Bath.

———◆•◉•◆———

From the Journal of Capt. George A. Brooks

MONDAY, FEBRUARY 24. Clear morning but very windy. After purchasing a few necessary articles went to camp. Many of the tents blown down. Could not do anything for the wind. Cleaned out trunk, packing up to send home. In evening got orders to prepare for a march, after which went to town. Spent evening or portion of which at home. Transacted some necessary business and came to camp. Very cold.

TUESDAY, FEBRUARY 25. Very cold night and morning but clear. Anxiously awaiting order to march. Wrote letter and began pay rolls at 10 o'clock. Finished them by 12.25 the quickest work yet done. After dinner shot mark [sic] and was detailed as officer of the day to report at headquarters at once. Mounted Grand Guard and borrowing Major Matthews' horse, made grand rounds or visited the guard and pickets. Stopped in town and slept all night at home. Spent very pleasant evening.

WEDNESDAY, FEBRUARY 26. Fine morning. Roads drying up finely. Spent morning in attendance of duties. Received long letter from Emily, the best, most happy one that she has ever written. Put me in a glorious mood. Took dinner at home and went to Headquarters. After Grand Guard mounting went home. Met Kate Byers, the most beautiful girl I have ever beheld—a perfect little fairy—and as pleasant and amiable as she is pretty. Returned to camp after dress parade. In evening wrote to John Hook, Miss. Louise Durker and Mrs. Roland. William Sayford and Emily.

Letter from Capt. George A. Brooks to Emily Brooks
Camp near Hancock
February 26, 1862

My Dear Emily,

I was today exceedingly surprised at the receipt of a letter from you so unlike your usual style—so happy and good-natured, that I at once answer it, trusting by my promptness to secure a continuance of your favor. It was long too, and bore every evidence of an endeavor to please me, and well have you succeeded for I must confess I was astonished. Do please, my dear Emily, write always so, won't you. It so pleasantly recalled old times, making me so happy, until several complemented me on <u>my</u> unusual <u>happy</u> appearance.

You must have had quite a grand parade and although it was a glorious sight to see over 2,000 men in uniform, marching etc, yet you should see one of our reviews when as high as 30,000 have been out, Infantry, Cavalry, and Artillery. I would however, gladly have been with you and looked on. Besides, I would have loved to have seen <u>our dear little wife</u> dressed up so neatly, waving her handkerchief, and giving our Country's defenders a hearty God speed. And our Willie too enjoyed it. I only wish I had him in camp a week or two. I would make a regular young soldier out of him—and teach him all kinds of antics.

By a letter from Theodore I was aware that he was a first Lieutenant in Capt Dorsheimer's Company and was glad to hear of his success. I have no doubt he will get along finely. When you write inform me to what Company, or rather regiment he is attached and what is the position of the Company. Dr Jones must be working wonders in your city and I trust he may successfully cure your mother and Kassie.

So you have had a letter from Maggie and she appears to be very happy. I am glad to hear it. She has some faults but is a good girl and will try to do her duty. I trust he is a good man and will make a kind husband. Are they at housekeeping? If so we might after the war make them a pop visit and also take a look at some Pittsburgh friends.

Is Sen Kennard with Harry Davis or is he in town altogether. I want to write to him but not knowing his whereabouts have postponed it. I saw the local in regard to his visit to Mr Buchaman and thought it quite a good joke. Give him my kind regards.

So you often think of me, and how happy we will be on my return. Our Willie is so lively, affectionate and lovely, and our family. Small as it is will be a pleasant one. You, Emily, can make it so, all rests with you. If home is made a pleasant happy one, if all the little comforts which a wife can only invent are brought into requisition and everything done with an eye to make it attractive there I will always be found in leisure moments. Then without harsh words or looks, Willie can be trained up in a "kind loving way" in the "fear and abomination of the Lord" and we will sing together as our days gone by spending our time so happily. None can love you better than your own dear George and place implicit confidence in my actions, words and judgment, for in everything I never forget you myself the interest of our family. By prayer, by becoming a firm, sincere Christian, you can only hope to live happily and enjoy the fellowship, and society of good friends, drawing around you a circle of those who will sincerely and tenderly love you. To be good is to be happy. You must teach Willie he has a father and show him my pictures. It will aid him to recognize me when I come home—and rest assured, I will do so as soon as I can.

We are now under marching orders and expect to move on tomorrow morning—perhaps very early so I must go to bed. I have been writing all evening and it is now after 11.

Give my kind regards to Val Hummel and family. Mary, Sue, Bella, etc, Keet and family, in fact everybody. Love to pap, mom and boys. Give Willie a good kiss and tell him to hurrah for Co. D and the Union and saving a thousand kisses for yourself, believe me as ever

Your affectionate husband

George

———————•◦•◦•————————

From the Journal of Capt. George A. Brooks

THURSDAY, FEBRUARY 27. Cold, clear morning. Little snow. Ordered again last night to cook rations, but no orders to march. Cold unpleasant day. Prepared for review and muster tomorrow. Spent evening in town at home. Rumors of a general move received credence. Went to camp at 9.

FRIDAY, FEBRUARY 28. Very windy, cold morning. On account of being so stormy mustered in Company streets for payment after which began preparing for a march. Spent greater portion of afternoon and evening in town and my good friends at home were very sorry to see me depart. Had very interesting, warm and spirited arguments with Mrs. Mary Broderick, a bitter secessionist whom I met. It is strange, very strange, how confident Southern sympathizers are of the ultimate supremacy of Southern rule: How they grasp at every straw which will give the faintest hope of salvation. Poor, deluded mortals mistake patriotism, worthy of a noble cause and time. Started for camp and packed trunk, an order being received to form and officers baggage be boarded. Wrote to Emily and acknowledged one from Estelle.

✳ ✳ ✳

On February 25th, Union forces captured Nashville, Tennessee, the first Confederate state capital and industrial center to fall. It seemed like the Union was winning the war.[25] In the Shenandoah Valley, Banks and Lander were ready to make their advance.

---

25. Wagner, *Desk Reference*, 15.

Anxious to see a successful operation, General McClellan himself was opposite Harpers Ferry to direct the crossing of Banks' troops across the Potomac and into Virginia. There was immediately a problem when it was discovered that the pontoon boats made specially to span the river wouldn't arrive. They were built in Washington with the intention of moving them up the C&O Canal, but the engineers had failed to check their width, and soon found that they were too wide to fit through the canal locks. McClellan fell mercy to the press over the snafu, despite Banks' men creating a makeshift bridge and entering Harpers Ferry on February 26th. Hoping to make a good show for a thus far blundered advance, McClellan decided that instead of advancing Banks on Winchester, which could possibly lead to defeat, he would instead focus on rebuilding the severed B&O railroad. To that end, he ordered Lander and Banks back to Williamsport where they would cross the Potomac, join forces, and occupy Martinsburg.[26]

---

26. Cozzens, *Shenandoah 1862*, 119-21.

CHAPTER SIX

Sacred Soil
March 1–April 30, 1862

WHEN NEWS ARRIVED that General Banks had crossed the Potomac, General Jackson knew he was outnumbered six to one and that there was no hope of holding the northern Shenandoah Valley. "Now we may look for war in earnest," he wrote in personal correspondence, ". . . if this valley is lost, Virginia is lost."

He ordered his command back to Winchester on February 27th, leaving Martinsburg to the Yankees without a fight. The movement sent Winchester residents into a terror, wondering if their town was next to be abandoned. Some waited for evacuation while others took matters into their own hands and fled. Not everyone was terrified, though, and pro-Union residents took the Union forces' closeness as an opportunity to cross into Union-held territory.

On the 28th, McClellan, his staff, two infantry regiments, some artillery, and cavalry entered Charlestown, which was devoid of defenders save some Confederate cavalry that left town without a fight. A third of the enslaved black residents left their masters to head north. The Yankees found the most resistant group to be Charlestown's women, who hurled insults and accusations at soldiers and Northern press alike.

The next day, General Williams marched twenty-three miles from Hancock to Williamsport and immediately started moving his six regiments across the Potomac toward Martinsburg. With only one boat available, they crossed one company at a time.[1]

---

1. Cozzens, *Shenandoah 1862*, 121-5.

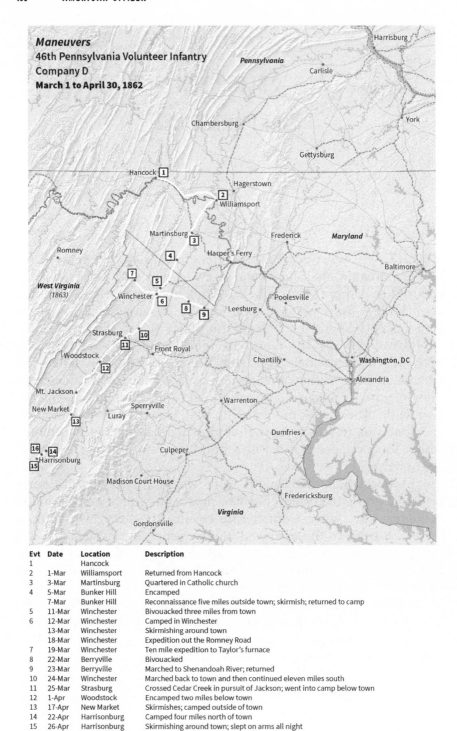

Maneuvers
46th Pennsylvania Volunteer Infantry
Company D
March 1 to April 30, 1862

Evt	Date	Location	Description
1		Hancock	
2	1-Mar	Williamsport	Returned from Hancock
3	3-Mar	Martinsburg	Quartered in Catholic church
4	5-Mar	Bunker Hill	Encamped
	7-Mar	Bunker Hill	Reconnaissance five miles outside town; skirmish; returned to camp
5	11-Mar	Winchester	Bivouacked three miles from town
6	12-Mar	Winchester	Camped in Winchester
	13-Mar	Winchester	Skirmishing around town
	18-Mar	Winchester	Expedition out the Romney Road
7	19-Mar	Winchester	Ten mile expedition to Taylor's furnace
8	22-Mar	Berryville	Bivouacked
9	23-Mar	Berryville	Marched to Shenandoah River; returned
10	24-Mar	Winchester	Marched back to town and then continued eleven miles south
11	25-Mar	Strasburg	Crossed Cedar Creek in pursuit of Jackson; went into camp below town
12	1-Apr	Woodstock	Encamped two miles below town
13	17-Apr	New Market	Skirmishes; camped outside of town
14	22-Apr	Harrisonburg	Camped four miles north of town
15	26-Apr	Harrisonburg	Skirmishing around town; slept on arms all night
16	26-Apr	Harrisonburg	Moved camp two miles north of town

Union troops ford the Potomac at Williamsport, Maryland. (Source: Harper's Weekly, July 6, 1861.)

From the Journal of Capt. George A. Brooks

SATURDAY, MARCH 1. Arose at 2 o'clock having slept with Morgan. Built a fire and awakened men. Camp a glorious sight everything hustle and confusion, and large fires lifting their fiery tongues heavenward lighted up the sky. Moved out of camp before day carrying knapsacks and halted in Hancock to bid them a farewell and load our knapsacks on a wagon. Started for Williamsport at 7½ o'clock. Lieut Witman again joining the company. Day cool but sun shining brightly. Passed Fairview at noon, the Fifth Connecticut in the lead having started before us. At Clear Spring took a short road to Williamsport, reaching there two miles ahead of the Conn[ecticut] Fifth and took up our quarters in the old warehouse. Men very tired having marched twenty-six miles, a hard march. Took tea at Mrs. Long's where I first met "Estelle." Went to bed early—everybody being tired.

SUNDAY, MARCH 2. Raining and very disagreeable. Troops were crossing at ferry all day but we being on the left of our brigade will probably not cross before tomorrow. Spent day with

Company. Many of men under influence of liquor, the bane and curse of the army from the fountain—from the highest officers to the lowest. Took tea and in fact stayed at Mrs. Long's. Met Capt Betts in the evening also Lieut Marble who slept with Lieut Gorman and self. No news of any importance. Must leave all our baggage behind and take no clothing save what we have on our back. Rather hard.

MONDAY, MARCH 3. Cloudy morning. At an early hour prepared to cross river. Were all safely landed in "Dixie" and started for Martinsburg over the same road I had marched in July last, under very different auspices.

When we reached Falling Waters, the losers of the contest during the three months service, it began raining and rained very hard until we reached Martinsburg. Ordered to quarters in new Catholic church, the priest protesting greatly against such a "sacrilegious preceding." Promised him to take every care of the church and prevent all from entering the altar. Very fine church, warmed by heaters and very comfortable, especially to men drenched to the skin. One of the finest alters I have ever seen, being of pure Italian, inter-laid with Cyrane [sic] marble, ornamented with golden and silver crucifixes etc. Made request of men to keep outside of the railing. Called on Miss. Campbell and were invited to tea at 8. Rained very hard consequently did not go but instead at Mrs. Basts' a few doors off. Slept soundly in church.

❋❋❋

General Lander's 12,000 man division, also instructed to join Banks at Martinsburg, was supposed to have arrived before Williams. McClellan had feared Lander would engage with Jackson on the road to Bunker Hill, and so he had ordered Banks to send Williams post haste to Martinsburg in support. But when the 28th New York of Williams' Brigade was the first to enter Martinsburg on March 2nd no one—Williams, Banks, or McClellan—knew where Lander was. Later that day they would receive word that Lander's command had been delayed after the General had fainted on the 1st. They waited for twenty hours in the hopes he would recover, but soon realized he would not. He died at 5 P.M. on the 2nd while his men, now temporarily under the command of Colonel Nathan Kimball, started southward.

Williams' advance men found the town of Martinsburg, a town with a reputation for pro-Union sentiment, "in a state of utmost confusion," with property plundered by Virginia militia and most of the shops boarded up as both Northern and Southern sympathizers had fled in their respective directions.

As the rest of Williams' men trickled across the Potomac company by company, they made their way to Martinsburg. All 5,000 men arrived by March 3rd and encamped anywhere they could find space. Barns, businesses, and private homes were descended upon by soldiers hoping to escape the winter elements.

Meanwhile, in Winchester, Jackson was unsure of his next move. General Johnston was planning to withdraw from Centreville to behind the Rappahannock River, which would expose the Manassas Gap Railroad and Jackson's back if he were to remain north of Front Royal or Strasburg. Further complicating matters, Jackson struggled to get reliable intelligence about Union strength, and enlistments were expiring, further reducing his own troops. He hadn't yet decided to leave Winchester without a fight, but it increasingly appeared to be the only option.[2]

From the Journal of Capt. George A. Brooks

TUESDAY, MARCH 4. Clear morning. Very cold. Spent all day in town awaiting orders to march being in suspense as to our destination. In afternoon put up tents preparatory to marching into camp tomorrow. In evening rode out to our camp, took dinner and tea at Mrs. Basts' in company with Lieut Witman. Slept with Witman at a house adjoining church. One year since Inauguration of Lincoln. How horrible is war.

WEDNESDAY, MARCH 5. Rainy and very muddy. Ordered to march to camp, but just before going received orders to march to Bunker Hill. Started at 12½ reaching Bunker by evening, camping in an orchard belonging to Mr. Boyd, brother in law of C J Faulkner and a very warm secessionist. Place very familiar having laid here during the three months service under Gen Patterson over two days and then beat an inglorious retreat. Got tents up before dark. Ground rather marshy.

THURSDAY, MARCH 6. Rested all day, momentarily expecting orders to move forward. Wrote to Emily. Visited Conn. camp in search of tobacco, finding none. Information of the Rebels threatening Winchester.

---

2. Cozzens, *Shenandoah 1862*, 128-30.

FRIDAY, MARCH 7. Awoke with "long roll" at 4 o'clock, all out and line formed in five minutes. Moved about 1½ miles in direction of Winchester, but seeing none of the enemy returned at noon. Started with the Fifth Conn., two companies of Cavalry and one section of battery to make a reconnaissance, our regiment taking the left. After proceeding about five miles met about 100 [of Ashby's] cavalry in a woods, who gave us a brisk skirmish, but pushing us too rapidly they gave way and retreated towards Winchester. After firing a few shots after them as a parting benediction from our battery, we retraced our steps. Had it not been for the impetuosity of "whiskey"—the evil of the war, we could have surrounded and captured the entire body. As it was satisfied, having for the first time witnessed firing and "smelled powder." Three of our cavalry were wounded and two horses shot. Captain Cole of the cavalry being killed instantly.[3] Reached camp by evening, all in the best of spirits.

❊ ❊ ❊

General Williams was in good spirits too, writing home, "I don't know what is ahead, but I think we shall drive them forward without much trouble."[4] Banks, more cautious than Williams, also found himself optimistic by the 7th. Lander's former division was expected to arrive on the 9th, which would provide overwhelming numbers. Banks also had an efficient network of spies feeding him accurate estimates of Jackson's troop numbers. Deserters provided even more information—one disgruntled private telling Banks the strength and position of every regiment of the Stonewall Brigade (trained by the famed Jackson himself) and corroborating rumors that Jackson would abandon Winchester as soon as within twenty-four hours. On March 8th, General Banks submitted a plan to McClellan to advance on Winchester.

McClellan, however, was more concerned about the whereabouts of General Johnston who, reports indicated, had left Centreville and Manassas. McClellan responded to Banks' plan without orders, and instead with a request that Banks determine if a portion of Johnston's men might be heading toward Winchester. With an absence of direction, Banks decided to move forward.[5]

3. Marvin, *Fifth Connecticut*, 62.
4. Williams, *From the Cannon's Mouth*, 62.
5. Cozzens, *Shenandoah 1862*, 131-2.

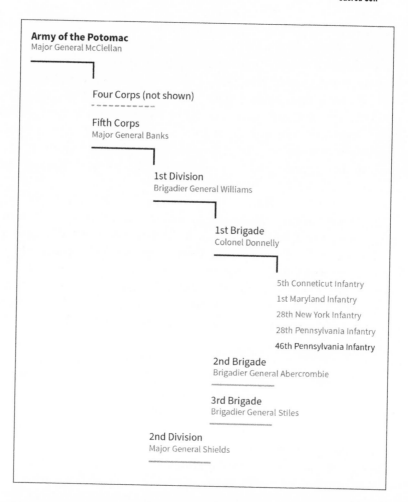

Army of the Potomac
Major General McClellan

Four Corps (not shown)

Fifth Corps
Major General Banks

1st Division
Brigadier General Williams

1st Brigade
Colonel Donnelly

5th Conneticut Infantry
1st Maryland Infantry
28th New York Infantry
28th Pennsylvania Infantry
46th Pennsylvania Infantry

2nd Brigade
Brigadier General Abercrombie

3rd Brigade
Brigadier General Stiles

2nd Division
Major General Shields

Outside the Valley, a Union victory had been earned on March 7th at the Battle of Pea Ridge in Arkansas, which helped retain Missouri as a Union state. But the next day, off the coast of Virginia at Hampton Roads, a naval battle ended in the worst defeat yet experienced by the eighty-six-year-old US Navy.[6]

The same day, thoroughly frustrated with McClellan's lack of action and the pontoon boat debacle, President Lincoln issued War Order No. 2, which outlined the immediate reorganization of the Army of the Potomac into five corps. The order was a clear slight to McClellan who had rejected the idea earlier in the winter, saying he wished the army gain some combat experience first to show which generals would be best to take command.

---

6. Wagner, *Desk Reference*, 15.

Under the new corps system, General Banks was placed in command of the new Fifth Corps, and General Williams moved up to command Banks' old division, which was now designated as the first division of the Fifth Corps. Brigadier General James A. Shields was placed in command of the second division. Williams' Division was composed of three brigades—the first, his old brigade, was now commanded by Colonel Dudley Donnelly who was promoted from the 28th New York. Brigadier General J. J. Abercrombie commanded the second brigade, and Brigadier General George H. Gordon the third.

Matters for McClellan only got worse. On March 10th, he finally advanced across the Potomac against the Confederate works at Manassas, and found that Johnston really had left and the formidable artillery within the forts were actually painted logs. The press, public, and Congress were thrown into an uproar. In response, on the 12th, Lincoln issued War Order No. 3 which relieved McClellan from his duties as General in Chief and left him to concentrate on his command of the Army of the Potomac.[7]

———•◆•———

From the Journal of Capt. George A. Brooks

SATURDAY, MARCH 8. Fine day. Done nothing save drill. In afternoon took supper at home of Mr. Bell, a strong Union man, just inside our picket lines, a <u>mason</u>, and spent evening in pleasant conversation with his daughters, two very intelligent girls. Played euchre and find them generally well accomplished in the refinements of polished life. Must again avail myself of the opportunity.

SUNDAY, MARCH 9. Glorious morning—officer of the day. Regimental inspection but instead of going out with company visited the 13th Mass. and listened to a stirring and patriotic sermon by their chaplain, a man of sound sense, eloquent, and one who fully understands and appreciates the spiritual wants of soldiers. Mutiny in Co "A" on account of their position in the regiment being changed. Company "D" detailed as guard and nearly the whole company put under arms. In afternoon took splendid dinner at Mr. Bell's and spent a very pleasant afternoon. Read the poetic effusions of Carlton Hughes who before troubles

---

7. Cozzens, *Shenandoah 1862*, 146-8.

taught a school in this neighborhood, and was surprised upon seeing his picture to find upon inquiry that he was a brother of Estelle Hughes, with whom I have been corresponding for some time past. Returned to Regiment and came out on dress parade. Spent portion of evening in Company with Col Selfridge, after which went to camp, visited guard, made "grand rounds" and went to bed.

MONDAY, MARCH 10. Awoke before day with orders to march with one days uncooked rations taking only blankets. After forming in line on pike, and standing in rain one hour nearly, were ordered to quarters and began at once preparing three days cooked rations. Laid all day anxiously waiting orders to march, understanding a formal movement was being made on Winchester by all of Banks' Division.

TUESDAY, MARCH 11. Formed early, the day fine and clear. Moved at 7 o'clock our Brigade taking the right and our regiment the right of the Brigade. Companies "K", "I", "A" and "D" my own company were selected as skirmishers and sent in the advance. [End of entry]

WEDNESDAY, MARCH 12. Arose by four o'clock having slept soundly on the leaves with naught save the sky for a covering. Marched out on the main road, stacked arms and awaited the passage of General Hamilton's Brigade who took the advance, we taking up position on the left of our own brigade. The day was a glorious one. During the night all trace of the enemy disappeared, and nothing occurred to mar the grandeur of our entrance into the "paradise of secession" with flying colors. We marched through the principal streets of the town and encamped beyond it. But one "American flag" greeted our arrival and but few smiles, the citizens having been under secession rule so long, that its deformed [sic] had become virtues prejudicing them in its favor—we trust such illusions may soon be dispelled. Encamped on fine ground near the residence of <u>James M Mason</u>. In afternoon visited the city, spent evening in camp.

⁂ ⁂ ⁂

Jackson wanted to make a stand at Winchester, but couldn't risk losing his army or allow Banks to slip away to Richmond. Johnston's withdraw from Manassas and refusal to send reinforcements gave Jackson no option other than to move further south, drawing Banks deeper into the Shenandoah Valley. After eight days of wagons transporting army stores southward, Jackson started withdrawing his troops from Winchester on March 9th. The next day, with a combined 30,000 Union troops approaching from the north, he declared martial law in Winchester and started arresting pro-Union residents out of fear that they would pass information to the Yankees. Those loyal to the Confederate cause hid valuable possessions and anything that might identify them as secessionists.

When Banks halted on the night of March 11th, Jackson was secretly hopefully that he could still launch a night attack against the unaware army as they slept. But poor communication, a problem from which Jackson often suffered, foiled his plans, and he was forced to fully evacuate town that evening.

On March 12th, General Williams and many others had expected an assault on Winchester's defences. Instead, they entered a town almost devoid of militants and the greatest resistance came from the townswomen.[8] During an occupation of the town a month later, John M. Gould of the 10th Maine lamented, "We had already seen Rebel women, but in all our travels we never saw any so *bitter* as those of Winchester."[9]

James Peifer of the 46th Pennsylvania recounted an exchange in which Kate Sperry, a Winchester resident, and several friends were walking down the street on which General Banks' headquarters were located. Seeing the Stars and Stripes hanging above their path, the women stopped before passing under it. "Kate, do you intend to walk under that dirty rag there?" asked one of the girls. "No, never!" replied Sperry, and so the women crossed the street so as to avoid walking under the flag. One of Banks' Zouave guards, overhearing the exchange, called out to them "Misses! I think you have a dirtier rag under the skirts of your dresses." Peifer remarked in his retelling of the event, "They of course blushed and no doubt thought, 'ain't that a monster', but I say bully for the Zouave!"[10] Luckily for the "she-devils" of Winchester, Union policy and standing orders prevented retaliation, both physical and verbal, from the Yankees, and the Zouave could've been shot for his comment.

---

8. Cozzens, *Shenandoah 1862*, 133, 137-42.
9. Gould, John M. *History of the First - Tenth - Twenty-ninth Maine Regiment.* Portland: Stephen Berry, 1871. 108.
10. Peifer, *Bethlehem Boy*, 76.

On March 12th, Jackson's men camped between Cedar Creek and Strasburg, and by the 16th, they had arrived and camped at Red Banks. Jackson's primary goal remained keeping Banks in the Valley so he could not reinforce McClellan's anticipated movement on Richmond. By stopping at Red Banks, Jackson hoped that their position was far enough south to give him the freedom to maneuver but not far enough to make Banks think that he had left.[11]

——————•·•·•——————

From the Journal of Capt. George A. Brooks

THURSDAY, MARCH 13. Fine and clear. Had fine drill and wrote long letter to Emily, sent in town at noon and received good barbering. Missed afternoon drill. On dress parade in evening. Nothing of any importance in a military sense except several small skirmishes with the enemy took place in several directions. Afternoon all quiet.

FRIDAY, MARCH 14. Very foggy morning. At reveille whole regiment including staff marched to Milltown Mills and all took good wash.[12] Nothing stirring today. Drill all day.

SATURDAY, MARCH 15. Fine day. Very pleasant. Nothing save drill. Wrote to Emily and evening in town with Morgan.

——————•·•·•——————

Pennsylvania Daily Telegraph
From the 46th Penna. Regiment.
Winchester, Va., March 15.
Written by George A. Brooks

MR. EDITOR: – While the continued success of the Union cause is borne upon every southern wind, and our brethren in arms in the South and Southwest are flushed with victory, and crowning themselves with imperishable honor, the great mass of the people at home should not, in their admiration of heroic deeds and acts of personal courage and bravery, forget the less bloody, though equally important, conquests which the right flank of

---

11. Cozzens, *Shenandoah 1862*, 144-5.
12. Milltown Mills was located one mile from Winchester on the Valley Pike. Frederick County Photo Album Index. N.p., n.d. Web. 11 Sep 2012. <http://usgwarchives.net/va/photo/frederick/>.

An early 1900s view of Milltown Mills near Winchester. (Source: VAGenWeb.)

the "Grand Army of the Potomac" have within the last week, so gloriously achieved Winchester, the boasted "paradise of rebellion," and key to the great valley of Virginia, is ours; Yankee feet have at last trodden upon one of the most sacred spots of Virginia's "sacred soil;" the home of James M. Mason, the famous Confederate minister has been invaded, and fortifications and defenses which required great skill and much labor to erect, has been quietly taken possession of without even one of the chivalry "dying in the last ditch."

On Tuesday morning, after a week's preparation, we left Bunker Hill, the command of Gen. A. S. Williams taking the advance, the 46th Pennsylvania on the right. After proceeding about four miles, a small detachment of the rebel cavalry were discovered in a small woods, in which we had had a skirmish the Friday previous, and companies "K" and "C" were thrown upon the right, and company "D" upon the left of the main road as skirmishers, advancing cautiously, the rebels hastily withdrew, falling back upon a larger force. When within about five miles of Winchester, they appeared in considerable numbers, when four companies under command of Major Matthews were deployed as skirmishers, company "K" taking the left, and 'D" the extreme right, and for over two miles we had quite lively times; considerable firing took place on both sides, and a general engagement was anticipated. Two companies of Maryland and a detachment of Michigan Cavalry, supported the skirmishers, occasionally making a dash at some exposed point of the enemy, and as the shell and ball of Capt. Matthew's battery, stationed in the rear to cover our advance, whistled over our heads, now and then answered by a shell from our rebel friends, plowing up the ground in front of us, and intermixed with the peculiar whir of Minnie musket balls, &c., all combined render such excitement quite pleasant and exhilarating to those directly engaged, while outsiders might have better appreciated it. We pressed them so hard that they were compelled to slowly retreat, and securing the ground we had gained by a strong picket guard, we bivouacked for the night, sleeping fully equipped. The opposing cavalry were all of Ashby's famous regiment, in pretty strong force, with some artillery. As we afterwards learned, nine were killed and some wounded. Only one of our men was injured—a member of company "C"—being shot in the thigh. All the boys behaved gallantly, and acted like veterans, and only require a broader field to fully show their efficiency.

On Wednesday morning, General Hamilton being senior Brigadier, took the advance, and upon moving forward found that the enemy had retreated during the night; the "stonewall brigade" was *non est;* Winchester was entered, her ramparts scaled and taken without firing a gun, and as we entered the city the same faces which had the evening before *wept* with sorrow at the retreat of the brave Jackson's force, *smiled* upon and greeted our arrival, but corroborating the fact that interest, not principle, is the great lever which controls the actions of the mass of mankind.

We are now snugly encamped on a beautiful hill on the edge of this city. Taking a ride this morning around the fortifications, we find them thorough, evincing some skill in their conception but poorly executed. They had, however, taken advantage of a number of fine natural positions, and planted strong batteries upon them, but these were all removed save a few gun carriages.

I know it will be gratifying to the numerous friends of Sergeant John Care of company "D," to hear of his promotion to the position of First Lieutenant. Care was a member of the "Lochiel Grey's," during the three months service, and since his connection with the 46th, has attracted the attention of all by his soldierly bearing and gentlemanly deportment. The promotion is a worthy one, and reflects credit upon our gallant Colonel.

Promising to write more regularly hereafter, as our movements are now becoming more interesting, I remain as ever,

SOLDIER.

P.S. – Direct letters, Company "D," 46th Regiment, Penna. Vol., Gen. William's Division, Winchester, Va.

————————◦•◦•◦————————

From the Journal of Capt. George A. Brooks

SUNDAY, MARCH 16. Cold raw day. Regular inspection. Muddy. Spent morning at Colonel's quarters. In afternoon stayed in tent and in evening read Byron.

MONDAY, MARCH 17. Fine morning. Took an early walk with Lieut Witman through town—saw a beautiful woman, first one since our arrival at Winchester. Had fine drill.

TUESDAY, MARCH 18. Had drill today. In evening was ordered to proceed out the Romney Road, on a scouting operation with three days uncooked rations. Started at 5 o'clock, was promised a guide but not coming we trudged along alone wading creeks knee deep. When within two miles of our destination found one or two good Union men who were fleeing for a place of safety from the presentations of the Secesh Cavalry who nightly scout the country for the purpose of impressing. They accompanied us and we reached the residence of Robert Brown Esq by 8, who very kindly threw open his house, parlor, and all for our men who were wet and tired, built large fires in old fashioned country fireplaces, and we were very soon comfortable. Put on strong guard and had them kept on the alert all night.

WEDNESDAY, MARCH 19. Pleasant regular April day, cloudy now and then. All started on a scouting expedition towards Taylor's Furnace. Found the people entertain great fear of Northern troops and we being the first ever seen in this region, they hastily fled from their houses on our approach. Found many expressing Union sentiment when they saw us who were at heart rabid "Secesh." On reaching the furnace found the cavalry had been there but one hour before and taken two fine horses but failed to find Mr. Been [the owner] at home. Went on one mile further hoping to "bag" some of them, but received information that the Company of Captain Sheets, about 120 men, had moved from Russell's Mills to Cottonwoods some five or six miles further on, and it being too far concluded not to pursue them further. Took a fine Colt from Mr. Piper, a Captain in the Rebel service, and confiscated him. Returned to quarters at Mr. Brown's some 10 or 11 miles distant. Met Colonel who came up along with Chaplain to inform us that the reg't were under marching orders, and we should return at once. After eating a small bite, again started and reached camp by 9 o'clock. Very tired, the men having marched over 28 miles in 12 hours. Brought "Dixie" down safely, and immediately went to bed.[13]

THURSDAY, MARCH 20. Had no drill this morning men being generally tired. In afternoon had fine battalion drill, lasting until dress parade. It being [first] one for several months everything went off finely. In evening went to bed early. Received papers from home. At noon took ride on "Dixie," who glides along quite nicely. Yesterday Gen Shield's Division moved towards Strasburg. In evening started for Theatre but raining very hard came back after spending a few minutes at Sutlers.

FRIDAY, MARCH 21. Raining, ugly morning and very muddy. Received mess chest today. Perfect godsend. Got it fixed in tent and had things cleared up generally. Put stove up and had good warm fire going making everything comfortable and feeling quite at "home." Straightened up all my books generally, and brought up diary from notes. Wrote to Frank and read and smoked. In evening Colonel sent for me and on going over to Headquarters found he wanted a euchre companion. Myself and Lieut E. S. Witman received appointment of aid de camp from Col Donnelly acting Brigadier. Glad to see "Ned" go up but very sorry to leave him. Trust it may be better for him and secure to his benefit.

SATURDAY, MARCH 22*. On arising found ground covered with snow. Began raining after breakfast making it very muddy. Wrote "Fuller and Helen" at Hancock. Rode out to 84th on my new horse "Dixie." Saw Miles and Mather. Got marching order. Had the blues all day. In evening wrote "Daily Telegraph," Estelle, etc, Witman ordered to report.

*Attention: Correction. Have gotten one day ahead somehow. Today is really Friday [the 21st].[14]

---

13. Dixie or "pony" as he sometimes says, was Brooks' new horse.
14. The exact day Brooks got a day ahead is unclear. His dates are correct when they entered Winchester on March 12th, but somewhere between then and the 21st he seems to have added an extra day. During this period, he doesn't mention any outside events with which to check his dates against. After this point, the dates are correct.

✳ ✳ ✳

Upon his removal as General in Chief, McClellan's first action had been reevaluating his Peninsula plan. He attributed Johnston's withdrawal to a leak of his intention to land at Urbana, and thought his only option was to land further south, and therefore out of Johnston's reach, at Fortress Monroe, which was already in Union hands. Then, he would move up the James River Peninsula, which meant seventy miles stood between his army and Richmond. Lincoln, anxious for any progress, accepted this new plan on the conditions that Washington was kept safe and Johnston would not be allowed to move back to his old position at Manassas. At long last, on March 17th, McClellan set the Army of the Potomac in motion.

Earlier in the month, McClellan and General Banks had decided that Shields' Division was enough to occupy Jackson in the Valley. Shields was to entrench at Strasburg and scout the surrounding country while repairing the railroad between Strasburg and Manassas Junction. Williams' Division was to return to Centreville, outside Washington, to support McClellan's efforts against Richmond. To free up Williams, Banks first had to determine the location of Jackson to be sure an attack wasn't imminent.

To that end, General Shields' Division entered Strasburg unopposed on March 19th. Moving about five miles south, he correctly determined that Jackson's army was below Woodstock, and after considerable meddling by Ashby's cavalry, returned to Strasburg for the night. Considering his mission completed, Shields moved his men back to Winchester the following day. The march back was grueling and made further miserable by rain, and put the men, who felt their efforts were mostly for naught, in a foul mood. Shields and Banks, however, were ecstatic. Based on how far Jackson was from Winchester, Banks wrote McClellan that he could start Williams' Division toward Centreville immediately.

———— ◆ ————

From the Journal of Capt. George A. Brooks

SATURDAY, MARCH 22. Cloudy. Cooking rations having to march at 12. In town and out at 84th PV. Saw Col. Murray and urged Mather's appointment to Lieutenancy. Had "Dixie" shod. On return to camp received box from Sayford containing uniforms. Also a box containing pound cake, oranges, apples, pears, candies, etc, etc from some source unknown. This very pleasant to receive such a surprise from kind friends, to know that some one cherishes your friendship. At 12½ started our regiment being in rear of the whole division. Reached Berryville 11 miles encamping.

SUNDAY, MARCH 23. Pleasant, cloudy. Started at 9 our reg't being in center of brigade, left in front. Upon reaching the Shenandoah about 4 miles from Berryville found the bridge broken and men were sent forward to construct a pontoon bridge. After lying on road side over two hours orders came and the brigade marched back to Berryville, and ordered to be in readiness to march at a moment's notice to Winchester. General Jackson having on [Saturday] evening attacked the place supposing we had left and fighting having been going on already today. No particulars concerning it have yet arrived.

❋ ❋ ❋

While Williams' Division was starting for Centreville, Stonewall Jackson's 4,000 men, now in higher spirits and better health, had also set out and had moved almost thirty miles in one day to arrive in Strasburg. Shields' reconnaissance had appeared to Jackson as an advance and then a retreat, with the only explanation for such behavior being that McClellan was moving Shields back to Washington to support the offense against Richmond. To keep all of Banks' forces in the Valley, Jackson would strike at Winchester.

Ashby's cavalry harassed Shields outside of Winchester on the 22nd, but Shields and Banks weren't alarmed—after all, just two days ago Jackson's army had been many miles away. It took three separate couriers to convince Shields that something was amiss, at which point he called up reinforcements, but still didn't think Jackson was approaching in force. An artillery duel broke out, during which General Shields was seriously wounded and had to be taken from the field. Colonel Nathan Kimball took command, and at twilight pushed Ashby's badly outnumbered troopers south. The Rebel cavalry continued six miles while Kimball continued to the outskirts of Kernstown where he camped for the night.

Colonel Ashby indicated to Jackson that with just a few companies of infantry, he could surely take Winchester the next day. He said that only four Union regiments and a couple batteries of artillery remained in Winchester, and that they were preparing to fall back to Harpers Ferry. Where Ashby got this information is unknown, because it was terribly incorrect. Shield's entire division was in Winchester with no plans of leaving. Jackson accepted Ashby's plan to move the next day.[15]

On the 23rd, while Williams was paused near Berryville, Jackson advanced his small force against Kimball near Kernstown. After taking the offensive in the morning and attacking Kimball, Jackson realized that he was in truth facing a full division of 8,500 men. He changed his tactics immediately, and attempted to hold his ground until nightfall when he could retire under the cover of darkness. But his men started running low on ammunition, and an overwhelming number of Union soldiers were now pushing Jackson's line back. Unable to hold, Jackson retreated, abandoning his hopes of attacking Winchester and leaving 718 Confederate and 590 Union casualties behind.[16]

Though Jackson had suffered a tactical defeat, he had still accomplished his objective, and the fight at Kernstown had rattled Lincoln and Stanton in Washington. Banks was also dubious of his chances of success after getting information out of two Confederate prisoners from Jackson's staff. They had smartly lied, telling their captors that Jackson expected thirty thousand reinforcements at any time and once they arrived, he would attack again. Banks immediately recalled Williams' Division from Berryville.

McClellan, busy launching his Peninsula campaign, telegraphed Banks that he should push Jackson hard. Kimball acted to that effect on the 24th when he surprised Jackson with the strength of his advance. Kimball was about to attack when Banks showed up with the vanguard of Williams' Division and cancelled Kimball's plans. With 20,000 men available, Banks moved slowly forward, placing Kimball five miles south of Strasburg and Williams on the outskirts of town on March 25th.[17]

Here Banks waited, telling McClellan that he feared Jackson would be reinforced. McClellan told Banks he didn't think that would happen and that Banks should continue to push Jackson. But Banks, no more aggressive in nature than McClellan, chose to ignore his commander's unusually wise advice, and let March draw to a quiet close.[18]

15. Cozzens, *Shenandoah 1862*, 147-56.
16. United States. National Park Service. "First Battle of Kernstown." National Parks Service. Accessed July 17, 2016. http://www.nps.gov/cebe/learn/historyculture/first-battle-of-kernstown.htm.
17. Cozzens, *Shenandoah 1862*, 218, Williams, *From the Cannon's Mouth*, 66.
18. Cozzens, *Shenandoah 1862*, 219.

From the Journal of Capt. George A. Brooks

MONDAY, MARCH 24. Awake at 11 last night. Many not yet asleep and orders to strike tents and march at once. At 12 started and reached Winchester by 6 or rather encamped or bivouacked 2 miles this side of it awaiting orders. At 8, again started, marching through Winchester and eleven miles beyond without resting. City full of wounded the slaughter being terrible on both. Our loss was primarily in the 84th and 110 PV and 5 Ohio. Col Murray of the 84th killed. On our way along the road most ambulances were filled with wounded. Over one hundred bodies being dead unburied on the battlefield three miles from Winchester. Road filled with stragglers returning from the battle having been separated from their regt. Rumor of a fight ahead. Threw off knapsacks and hurried on chasing Jackson until evening. Bivouacked and men having no blankets could not sleep though very tired having marched for 48 hours without any rest. Never will I forget the excitement of the chase and the men could not have kept up had it not been for the prospect of a fight. Slept very cold not even having an overcoat. Towards evening our battery had a fight with the rear of Jackson's army and they retreated until evening when night put a stop to slaughter, alas how horrible a thing war is. The sad reality but few reached.

TUESDAY, MARCH 25. Up very early. Did not sleep of any account night being very cold and having no covering not even an overcoat. Started after our friend Jackson again. Considerable firing ahead but we were too far off to be in any danger. Indications were made of a stand by the rebels and we were hurried on but they rapidly retreated—Crossed Cedar Creek the rebels having burnt the bridge at this place. Saw some wounded soldiers and a few feebly made graves by the roadside, the leg and foot of one remaining unburied. Pursued Jackson and reached Strasburg, a small village on the north fork of Shenandoah and on the Orange and Alexandria Railroad, sixty one miles from Manassas. Going into camp a short distance below Strasburg. T'was here such a bold stand by the rebels was anticipated. On our arrival found the town nearly deserted, nearly all the inhabitants having gone with the retreating army of Jackson. Knapsacks did not come up.

WEDNESDAY, MARCH 26. Poor night's sleep. Beautiful morning. Knapsacks arrived. No drill. No news from any direction. In afternoon took ride with Morgan a few miles out the Stanton Pike, visiting Huntington's Battery and several of the Ohio regiments. "Dixie" getting lame from a stone bruise returned earlier than anticipated. Received two last knapsacks. Intended to write in evening but being very tired went to bed early.

THURSDAY, MARCH 27. Glorious morning. Company drill. Had general cleaning up of arms, accoutrements, etc. At noon were ordered out, it being rumored that Jackson was making an attack upon our right. Our whole brigade soon in motion, and after resting on the road over an hour, found it was "no go" and returned to camp. Sutler arrived, bringing mail, none for me. Saw Billy Bell. Spent evening in writing and conversation.

Pennsylvania Daily Telegraph
From the 46th Pennsylvania Regiment.
Strasburg, VA., March 28, 1862.
Written by George A. Brooks

MR. EDITOR: – The recent stirring events in this region have so sadly deranged our minds, that you will pardon me for not writing earlier, though I know some uneasiness may exist among those who have friends in the 46th regiment, P.V., concerning it.

On Saturday morning our brigade received orders to march, and by one o'clock were on their way towards Centreville, being ordered to join the "Army of the Potomac" under General M'Clellan at that point, the other brigade of our division having preceded us, leaving Gen. Shields in command at Winchester, strongly predominates, though a few loyal hearts gave us a cordial welcome. Continued our march on Sunday morning, but on arriving at the Shenandoah river found the bridge broken, and men were at once sent forward to construct a pontoon bridge, the regiment the meanwhile resting upon the roadside. Just as we were in readiness to move forward, the whole brigade was ordered back to Berryville, from whence it started at 11 o'clock P.M., for Winchester, making a forced march, the night being very dark—and arriving within sight of the city just as the sun rose, when a halt was made, and while momentarily awaiting for the order, and as each rumor of the terrible battle of the day before reached us, the excitement became intense, and our boys were eager for the fray, as it was anticipated that Jackson might possibly renew the attack.

From what we could learn relative to the attack, it appears that Jackson was misled concerning the evacuation of Winchester by our troops, supposing our whole force had left, save a small detachment as guard, and consequently expected an easy victory, as on Saturday afternoon, only an hour or two after our departure, Ashby's cavalry were drawn up in line, only a few miles from the city, and two pieces of artillery placed in position. Towards evening an advance was made by the rebels—four companies of our brigade, including one from the 46th Pennsylvania, under command of Major Mathews, holding them in check until General Shields' forces arrived, when a small skirmish ensued, during which the General was wounded by the bursting of a shell.

On Sunday morning, Jackson having been reinforced, the attack was renewed with more vigor, followed by very severe fighting, the rebels slowly giving way, and late in the afternoon a desperate charge was made by several of our regiments, taking five or six pieces of artillery, and ending in the utter rout of the rebels. It was during this charge that the gallant Col. Murray, of the 84th Pennsylvania fell, while leading his brave boys on to victory. Thus has another hero been offered a sacrifice upon the altar of patriotism—another generous, noble-hearted man—one whose loss will be keenly felt—taken from among us—but ever will his memory be cherished. Peace to his ashes.

By seven o'clock we were again ordered forward, and marching through Winchester found all excitement and confusion, people running to and fro, ambulances loaded with wounded, whose groans were truly distressing, waiting to be unloaded at the temporary hospitals which had been prepared, and everything betokening how terrible the contest had been. As we proceeded along the Strasburg pike, the road was nearly filled with ambulances and stragglers from the field of battle, nearly all bearing some trophy of the fight, and all, more or less, begrimed with powder. Shortly after passing the battlefield, in which our two hundred dead bodies still lay unburied, we threw off our knapsacks, so exciting did the pursuit become, and by evening, when within two miles of Cedar Creek, on the other side of which Jackson was encamped, weary and nearly worn out, having marched for nearly forty-eight hours, we bivouacked for the night, building large fires, and lay down upon the ground without any blankets, and many not having overcoats. The night was cold, but all arose in the morning ready to push forward, and with some slight skirmishing by our batteries in front, we reached Strasburg about noon or a little after. Jackson, however, proved too skillful at retreating to allow us to catch him, but we harassed him so much that he was compelled to bury many of his dead, which he had taken with him, along the roadside, in order to lighten his wagons. It was in fact the greatest rout of the war, and while our loss was large, yet his was double that of ours. The pomp and pageantry of soldiering was very fascinating, quite romantic, but when we see the dreadful realities of war as we did on that day, the heart sickens with horror over the bloody slaughter; yet the rebellion must be crushed.

The whole of the Fifth army corps are now lying around Strasburg awaiting orders, Gen. Banks being here in person. I cannot tell you more.

Lieut. Witman, of company "D," has been detached and is now acting Aide de-camp to Col. Donnelly of the 28th New York, who commands our brigade, Gen. Williams having been promoted to the command of the division, formerly under command of Gen. Banks. The promotion of Lieut. Whitman to such a responsible position will gratify his many friends at home. More anon.

SOLDIER.

Direct letters to "Winchester, Va," until further orders.

———•◦•◦•———

From the Journal of Capt. George A. Brooks

FRIDAY, MARCH 28. Fine morning. Sun out beautifully. Day very warm. Had company drill in morning, and in afternoon had battalion drill. Fired by company and wing—firing and drill went good. In evening rode over to Strasburg and visited home of a Mr. Krebb, who I found quite an agreeable old man. Has a son in the secession army, a Colonel, though was greatly disappointed at the gentlemanly conduct and behavior of our troops. Is related to the Spanglers of York, and Kelley of Harrisburg with both of whom I am well acquainted. Returned to camp promising to return and dine with him. Lieut brought me a looking glass and billiard ball from Secessia.

SATURDAY, MARCH 29. Cloudy morning. About 9 began sleeting very fast. Fixed up my books and wrote letter to Emily. In evening Witman came over. Nothing of any importance. Made out requisition for clothing for next three months for men wanting many things which they never thought of. Had meeting of officers at Col tent. Had quite an interesting school. Rained hard all day. Spent evening in reading.

SUNDAY, MARCH 30. Rained very hard last night. Many of the men had to get up being flooded out but did not have much trouble myself until morning when awakened found my tent floor completely covered, swamped, and one of my feet in the water. No inspection. Did not go out of tent except to dig ditch, etc. Fixed up trunk, looked over some old papers, read Byron, newspapers etc. Plenty of company—wrote to Mrs. Long in acknowledgment of letter and box she so kindly sent me. Received long letter from Emily and half a dozen "Telegraphs." Plenty of news. In evening wrote another long letter to Emily and six pages for "Telegraph" after which fixed diary, read awhile and went to bed. Still very stormy and raining occasionally. Lieut Geiger officer of guard. Must sleep alone.

MONDAY, MARCH 31. Glorious morning. Detailed as Field Officer of the day, going on duty at 10 o'clock. Had regimental inspection. Took company out Geiger being sick. Beautiful day. After inspection took "Dixie" and visited pickets, besides making the round of the camps. Nothing of any importance stirring. Spent evening in camp with Capt Griffith.[19] Just before dusk walked down to picket station at bridge to give them the countersign. A clear, pleasant evening.

TUESDAY, APRIL 1. Cloudy but pleasant. Awakened at 10 o'clock with orders to cook three days rations. Routed out cooks and soon had machine in operation. Went to bed again and up at 5. Prepared to march at 7 o'clock A.M. Drew off pickets and as regiment moved off. Reported to Col Donnelly and was relieved. Left Alick[20] and pony at old quarters, also several who were not very well as we may return. Started at 8 o'clock, considerable delay along the road. Day very warm. Reached Woodstock by 4½ o'clock the advance of our column reaching it shortly after 1 o'clock. Ashby's cavalry with two pieces of artillery made a stand, but gave way

---

19. Patrick Griffith of Company I.
20. Alick's identity is unknown, he may have been a servant.

on our artillery appearing and sending a few shells among them. Rebels retreated burning bridge across Shenandoah about five miles from Woodstock. They attempted to burn bridge over strong creek but our advance was so close that the fire was put out before any damage occurred. As we passed through Woodstock but little Union sentiment was apparent only <u>three</u> ladies having the courage to wave their handkerchiefs. Considerable firing ahead— camped about two miles beyond Woodstock or rather bivouacked erecting spruce and French tents.

WEDNESDAY, APRIL 2. Cloudy. Anxiously awaiting orders to move forward but on account of bridge being burned had to make detail of men to construct one. Considerable firing across river they (the enemy) occasionally driving back our bridge builders. In afternoon went out to river and saw the rebels upon whom our batteries fired some twenty shots to which they occasionally replied. Saw a member of Penn 29th have his head completely blown off. Do not [know] how soon we may move but will likely go as soon as our bridge is built. Yesterday evening wrote to Telegraph. In evening Alick and Dixie came up to join us. Wish we had a Sigel, Rosecrans or somebody whose energy was not completely controlled by cautious ignorance, too bad—We might then do something.

❋ ❋ ❋

On April 1st, Banks finally started his men south. His latest pause wasn't completely without reason. For one, his cavalry was lacking in both quality and numbers and was proving mostly ineffective against the skilled and gallant Ashby. Second, and perhaps most importantly, rations were in short supply and had to be reduced and supplemented by foraging off of the local countryside. This was exacerbated by the poor state of supply lines which had been strained by his advance and also the unfavorable weather. Throughout early April, unseasonably cold temperatures had paired with almost constant rain and snow to make the troops, North and South, miserable, and the roads impassable. And finally, most of the men were without suitable shoes.[21] General Williams lamented on conditions in a letter home:

---

21. Cozzens, *Shenandoah 1862*, 227-8, 236-9.

Forage is very scarce, in fact, all stripped off from this section, and what is worse, our long marches over wet roads have destroyed fearfully the poor shoes issued by the government. I have at least 4,000 men in my division who are shoeless completely, or so nearly so that they cannot march. Shoes issued to my men in Winchester are already entirely worn out![22]

The Yankees' slow progress allowed Jackson to make a leisurely withdraw to a few miles south of Mount Jackson where on April 2nd he took up a strong defensive position on Rude's Hill.

Meanwhile, McClellan's advance on the Peninsula had ground to a halt when it was discovered that Confederate forces were protected behind seven miles of earthworks. Another problem arose when President Lincoln and the Secretary of War, who had approved McClellan's Peninsula plan based on the condition that Washington be kept safe, realized it was in truth little protected. Banks' Fifth Corps had been assigned to protect Washington, but the battle at Kernstown had shaken McClellan enough to order Banks to stay put.

Lincoln's solution was to countermand orders for McDowell's Corps to join McClellan on the Peninsula and instead place Mc-Dowell in Fredericksburg in command of the new Department of the Rappahannock. Lincoln also made General Banks independent of McClellan by creating the Department of the Shenandoah which Banks alone would command. With the creation of the Mountain Department from western Virginia to east Tennessee led by Major General John C. Frémont, there were three independent commands between the Alleghenies and the Potomac River. All three reported directly to Washington, with McClellan presiding over only his forces on the Peninsula. The President and Secretary of War were now in direct control, and only time would prove their efficacy.[23]

———— ··•·· ————

From the Journal of Capt. George A. Brooks

THURSDAY, APRIL 3. Glorious morning. Slept well and feel greatly refreshed. Firing at Shenandoah early and all morning. Sad account in Company L. Sergeant Richards and Privates

---

22. Williams, *From the Cannon's Mouth*, 69.
23. Cozzens, *Shenandoah 1862*, 223, 227-30.

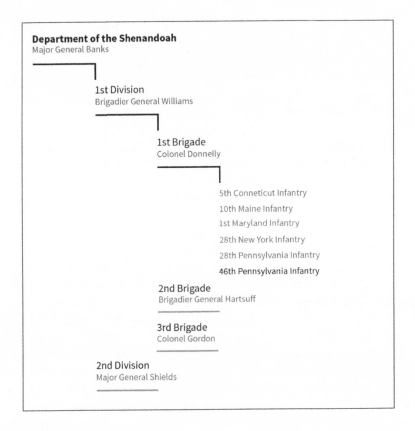

Cannon and Davis whilst crossing the river in a boat were drawn over the dam. Davis escaped, the other two men drowned. Spent day in quarters having no drill and expecting every moment to march. In evening, with Adjutant, went down to Lieut Witman who with the staff occupies the elegantly furnished home on the banks of Stony Creek, of a rebel who has gone South for the benefit of his health, leaving a ward and her sister, pleasant and intelligent young ladies, in charge of it. In evening the campfires on the hills around burned brightly and gleaming from out among the green pines, was indeed beautiful, and the music from bands who were serenading the General, the jocund song and joyous laugh from many a lively soldier, rendered it one of the most beautiful sights I ever beheld reminding me strongly of Moore's description of the beautiful Salla Rookle on her journey toward the Province of Buchoring [sic]. Everybody in the happiest mood. Some very much so.

FRIDAY, APRIL 4. Very fine morning. Officer of the day. After guard mounting drew off the guard. In afternoon took ride with the Adjutant to Woodstock. Saw some very pretty girls but all are very strongly tinctured with secession sentiments in fact the ladies are the most bitter enemies we have. Spent afternoon in reading and in evening again paid Witman a visit returning to camp by 9 o'clock. Men all put up their tents this afternoon there being indications of rain.

SATURDAY, APRIL 5. Raining and very unpleasant day but towards evening cleared up. Was very busy in arranging accounts and everything in readiness for the paymaster on Monday who will probably then be here. Nothing stirring save occasional firing among our pickets.

SUNDAY, APRIL 6. Very fine morning. Had regular inspection. Came out in my new suit which fits me very well. Spent part of day in writing. In evening had a very fine dress parade. Nothing new or stirring. Received long and very interesting letter from Emily.

MONDAY, APRIL 7. Cloudy morning and premonitions of snow. Paymaster arrived yesterday evening and by noon began paying off. Being first ready was first Company paid off but were hardly done as it began raining and soon turned to snow. Whole regiment paid off by evening. Some notion of going home, as I will probably have to go to Hagerstown for instruments for band and can then run down. Got everything ready. Received money from men amounting to $1,553 to be sent home. Money from others rose it up to $2,700. Got a horse intending to start at 1 o'clock and went to bed early. Snowing and blowing furiously indeed will be a dreadful stormy night—but so greatly do I wish to see the beloved ones at home that I would brave almost anything but of life and health.

TUESDAY, APRIL 8. Started on horseback at 1 the wind blowing a perfect gale driving in my face. Having a well filled carpet bag found riding very unhandy—After going a mile found the cold so intense I could not stand it and came back to quarters. Still snowing very fast in morning. Having an opportunity started in Sutlers wagon at 9 o'clock and reached Winchester by evening. Very cold riding. Stayed in h[ouse] at James Mann's boarding house going to bed early it being too troublesome to carry my carpet bag and had no safe place to leave it.

WEDNESDAY, APRIL 9. Still snowing as fast as ever, intended going in the cars but on reaching the depot found that, on account of an accident the day before, they could not run. Visited John S Martin our Quartermaster Sergeant, who has gone crazy imagining himself General McClellan and issuing orders with the most supreme confidence in his authority. Perfectly rational on every other subject. In afternoon [found] an open wagon going to Martinsburg who promised to take me as far as Hagerstown. A Mrs. Harris who had come on to secure the body of her son and Wm H Bell both along. Still snowing fast. Started at 4 and reached Martinsburg by 9. On the way stopped at our friend Bells at Bunker Hill a few moments. Started from Martinsburg at 10½ after seeing a fine specimen of "Constitutionality" on modern Union sentiments. Snowing very fast and very cold.

THURSDAY, APRIL 10. Reached Hagerstown about 4 crossing the ferry at Williamsport about 2. Very stormy so much so the ferryman was afraid to venture over. The coldest ride I ever had but cheered up by the pleasure of meeting the dear ones at home. At 7 started in cars for Harrisburg, arriving there by 12 with what feeling may be imagined not described. All at home and soon Emily and Willie were in my arms. In afternoon after home and friendly greetings distributed and expressed some $2,700 which had been sent by me, meeting many friends and acquaintances. In evening in company with Emily visited Mary Hummel, Mary Ball, and Mary Barnet. Also mother Denning. Met Aunt Betsy whom I have not seen for several years. She is very hale and hearty and I was greatly gratified to meet her. Reached home by 10. How pleasant to be surrounded by the comforts of home, a good affectionate wife and lovely boy. How I wish this terrible war was over and we all, North and South could once more return to our peaceable associations and prosperity would again dawn on our unhappy country. But our flag must be maintained— our honor and government must be sustained at whatever cost. Went to bed feeling tired after three days and nights travel.

FRIDAY, APRIL 11. Up early. Beautiful morning. Intended going at 9 but found I could reach Winchester as soon by returning on the route I came. Went to cars however and saw Aunt Betsy safely off. Came home and spent an hour playing with Willie after which went to Keets' and had photograph taken album size. Had long talk with Lew Mill Hyers. Spent rest of morning

*Captain George A. Brooks stood in full uniform for this
undated photograph. It was likely from the spring of 1862
and was perhaps the image Brooks references in his
April 11th diary entry. (Source: Author's Collection.)*

at home with Willie and Emily. Left $100 with Daddy, $20 with
Emily. Started at 1 bidding a very reluctant adieu to all. Sorry
to leave home but my country calls, tis mine to obey. Got fine
Album photograph of Willie and soon expect one from Emily.
On way to Chambersburg met Aunt Sally in the cars. Arrived in
Hagerstown by 6 stopping at Washington House.

After supper drove toward Williamsport to see our friends
but after going about two miles changed my mind coming back
and spent evening in writing to Emily. In evening before writing

went to Express and saw Band instruments paid for. Went to bed by 10.

SATURDAY, APRIL 12. Up early. Very fine morning. Made arrangements with Etter to carry my carpet bag over having a number of parcels for the men with it. At 7½ started on stage and while it stopped at Williamsport saw my good friend Mrs. Long, Estelle's friend. Potomac very high but crossed ferry safely. Had very pleasant traveling companion the person of Judge Wiesal of Hagerstown. No connection of stage at Martinsburg and after dining at Staub's started with Capt Foulke to foot it. Before starting from Hagerstown were assured by stage proprietor of connection. After walking about four miles overtook sutler's wagon in which we rode to Winchester arriving there about dark. On our way stopped at our friend Bill's and saw the pretty Maggie and her fair and fat sister Rachel. Stood all night at "Jim Mauers."

SUNDAY, APRIL 13. Up very early. Secured seat in hack starting for Woodstock fare $3. Off by 8 reaching Woodstock by 2 and riding from there to camp in ambulance. Glad to get home to camp once more among my boys who were all glad to see me come. Indeed I have contracted a fondness for this nomadic life but yet love home more. In evening went on dress parade.

MONDAY, APRIL 14. Cloudy morning but pleasant. Ground very muddy. Wrote to Sayford. At noon salute of thirty-four guns was fired from Best's battery in honor of our recent victory at Corinth.[24] In afternoon rode to Woodstock and received from Lew $9 overpaid by Lieut Geiger. During the night Howard Etter came bringing my carpet bag. Had a number of letters etc which the boys were glad to receive. This evening the band used our new instruments—German silver—on dress parade which was a decided improvement, and we now possess of the finest and best bands in the service. All the field officers out. Went to see Witman at Headquarters and after return sat around campfire conversing until after 10.

TUESDAY, APRIL 15. Raining and in fact rained all night. Officer of the day. Wrote to "Lew" pasted up company matters in books and made out descriptive list for John J. Wenrich. Spent afternoon in reading the "Profession" by author of "Jane Eyre" etc— an excellent story though not equal to some of her subsequent

---

24. First Battle of Corinth, or the Siege of Corinth, was crucial to Union operations in the Mississippi River Valley.

works. Received letter from Orth dated March 22.[25] At tattoo drew off guards at being too stormy.

WEDNESDAY, APRIL 16. Clear morning and very pleasant day. Wrote all morning. In afternoon took ride on "Dixie" to Woodstock. Saw a company of rebel cavalry fifty-eight in number beside three Lieutenants who were captured by our boys. I believe it was Capt Harper's company. They were really the hardest looking set of fellows I ever saw—no uniforms, in fact regular militia, and had horses which were really a disgrace to the innate creation. All placed securely in links. On returning to camp found an order to cook one day's rations. Made every preparation to march a general forward movement being anticipated.

THURSDAY, APRIL 17. Awakened at 12 with orders to march. Went to bed again and arising at 3 awoke boys. Got breakfast, packed knapsacks, and by 5 were on our way, the Maryland 1st being on the right, our regiment next. On nearing Mount Jackson the great stronghold of the rebels we halted preparatory to a battle expecting a strong resistance would be made but found Jackson had retreated leaving Ashby to cover his rear, burn bridges, etc, and harass our advance. Passed through Mount Jackson, a small village, the rebels burning the bridges across the Shenandoah in the outer edge of the town occasioning us some delay. Mount Jackson is a dilapidated village but every arrangement had been made by Jackson for permanently occupying the place. Three very large fine and ever elegantly constructed hospitals had been erected and large warehouses for the reception of commissary stores etc were built on the railroad. On our approach they burned a large number of cars and a locomotive which they had been using. Their smoking embers were all that <u>welcomed</u> our arrival, and as we marched through the place to the inspiring tune of "Red White and Blue" a sullen look evincing a bitter feeling was all the inhabitants gave us. When within half a mile of the main branch we halted and began reorganizing and thoroughly arranging every detail as Jackson was reported to be making a stand about two miles beyond and a regular battle was anticipated. Field pieces could plainly be seen on an eminence two miles off putting all in the best of spirits. So rapidly had we chased them that the bridge across the Shenandoah proper, a long covered one was saved. Had they succeeded in destroying

---

25. Alexander M Orth of Co D.

it we should have been delayed a week or two. The Vermont Cavalry saved it capturing a Lieutenant who was caught in the act of setting it on fire and killing the horse on which Col Ashby rode—the famous gray stallion who has so long been a prominent mark for our sharp shooters. Everything being arranged we marched over the bridge, threw out skirmishers in heavy forces, our brigade forming by company in mass and advanced steadily through very marshy ground, some places knee deep, expecting every moment a volley from the hill in front. As soon as we moved our batteries in our rear began firing thus covering our approach. The ground was a large level plain extending about a mile and a half between two ranges of hills, well adapted for artillery. It was most an admirable ground for a battle and we earnestly hoped one might take place. We advanced steadily only however to be disappointed as they again retreated throwing a few shells which fell short of us. Our batteries gave them about twenty shells which had some effect. We then followed Ashby's Cavalry before us driving them and reached New Market after dark, bivouacking on a bluff immediately beyond the place. The men very tired having marched from or been up from three in the morning and it being nearly 7. Many of them wet from wading.

FRIDAY, APRIL 18. Fine morning. Sun rose beautifully. Took walk through the town. Quite a brisk place in days gone by. At 9 again started but had to contend with Ashby's Cavalry all the way marched about five miles and encamped on a fine meadow, beautifully watered. In evening went to neighboring farmhouse and had an excellent supper. Alick did not come up this evening. A gust in afternoon.

———◦•◉•◦———

Pennsylvania Daily Telegraph
April 17, 1862

IN ACTION. – By reference to our telegraphic dispatches from Gen. Banks' command, this afternoon, it will be seen that four companies of Col. Knipe's 46th Pennsylvania regiment, in connection with a body of Ringgold's cavalry, yesterday morning succeeded in capturing sixty-one of Ashby's famous rebel cavalry, including three officers.

❋ ❋ ❋

In the evening on April 17th, General Banks telegraphed Secretary of War Stanton to let him know New Market had been captured without Union casualties. Stanton replied with thanks for "the brilliant and successful operations of this day," which left Banks in "high spirits." But others were less enthused by the movement, and correctly guessed that Jackson's retreat was due more to Jackson's own intentions than Banks' actions. Jackson was more than willing to give up Mount Jackson and New Market, and in fact all of the Valley as far south as the North River which lay between Harrisonburg and Staunton. With McClellan threatening Richmond, Jackson needed to keep in contact with General Ewell's Division, which was located near Brandy Station, and Johnston outside of Richmond, while allowing himself the room to maneuver to assist either. Giving up a portion of the Shenandoah Valley was acceptable considering the current circumstances. After marching fifty miles in three days, he moved his men into camp in Elk Run Valley, between Swift Run Gap and Harrisonburg, on the night of the 19th.[26]

Not only was McClellan moving on Richmond, but the war in general seemed to be going in the Union's favor. Earlier in the month, the two day battle in Tennessee near Shiloh Church resulted in a hard-fought and bloody Union victory. Simultaneously, the Confederate stronghold on Island Number 10 in the Mississippi River fell, opening up a significant portion of the river to Union travel. A few days later on April 11th, Fort Pulaski, which guarded the mouth of the Savannah River, fell to Union forces, further strengthening the blockade of the South.[27]

———————◆◆◆———————

From the Journal of Capt. George A. Brooks

SATURDAY, APRIL 19. Cloudy. Indications of rain. Ordered about 2 o'clock to cook rations at 8 received orders to report for picket duty at 9. My Company placed on extreme outposts on main road. Saw a few horses, rebel pickets. In evening extended pickets along woods and remained with them all night. Some difficulty which might have resulted seriously owing to the

26. Cozzens, *Shenandoah 1862*, 243-5.
27. Williams, *From the Cannon's Mouth*, 17.

inefficiency of the officer of the day. No further trouble during night. Rained all day and nearly all night very hard.

SUNDAY, APRIL 20. Rained all night. Spent yesterday evening in Company with girl at tall gate. Rather pretty but ignorant. Men on alert all night but saw nothing. Several citizens coming to our lines sent them back. At 10 were relieved by Company E. On returning to camp found everything terribly muddy and wet but made the best of a bad bargain. Rained all day. Took up my quarters in Adjutant's tent. Cooked company rations expecting to march during night.

MONDAY, APRIL 21. Rained all night and still raining. Adjutant awakened at 1½ with orders to march at 8 in the morning. Before time arrived orders were countermanded. Spent morning in Adjutant's tent. In afternoon read and played cards for amusements. Heavy mail came towards evening bringing letters from "Helen and Tullie," "Estelle," L. R. Witman and last but not least my dear Emily. How pleasant to receive these tiny messengers of friendship and love. Hancock friends as familiar and kind as anyone. Estelle more lively but more cautious and guarded than before, a regular stale-gut like woman. Luther businesslike and frank, Emily confiding like a dear wife should be. What a pleasure to read and reread on a rough dreary day. After dark went over South Creek and took at residence of Mr. Wise about a mile from camp returning by 8, in time to find our shoes which had come nearly distributed by the Lieutenant. Went to bed in Adjutant's tent. Has rained all day and evening as if the very floodgates of heaven had opened upon us. Will likely march by morning, all the boys now having a supply of shoes which they have needed very badly. Our requisition for pants etc is also due but want of transportation prevents the government sending them along. Went to bed in Adjutant's tent.

TUESDAY, APRIL 22. Still raining, but getting colder and some indications of a clear up. At 9 got under way and by 10 the sun came out finely. By noon again became cloudy and was showering all afternoon. Reached a position selected for our camp four miles this side of Harrisonburg. Put up tents. Markee did not come. We are now in the extreme advance our brigade lying fifteen miles beyond or in front of the main body. In evening Lieut Ned came up.

WEDNESDAY, APRIL 23. Fine morning, orders to get ready and accompany Colonel to New Market, on case of Capt Fitzgerald.[28] Saddled "Dixie" and started by 8. Morning a glorious one and had a fine ride, distance of fourteen miles. On reaching New Market found Company "I" of our reg't doing provost guard duty. In afternoon went before Board of Examination testifying on honor as to Capt. F's competency to discipline a company and his general unfitness for a Captaincy. Wandered about town in afternoon. Spent portion of evening in Company with Morgan visiting Mrs Eliza Clinedinst, a very pretty young lady, sweet and amiable disposition, rather Union in her sentiments having visited considerable in the North, but having a brother in the Confederate army—H. MacDowell, Col of 84th PV is her Uncle—older sister an elegant singer, possessing a superb voice favored us with several secession songs. Spent rest of evening in company with several officers playing "muggins."[29] Went to bed with "Caddie" our quartermaster.[30]

AUTHOR'S NOTE: Brooks didn't make an entry on Thursday, April 24th, and consequently made some date errors in his journal. They have been corrected.

FRIDAY, APRIL 25. Still cloudy and unpleasant. Premonitions of rain. No signs of us leaving. Board of examination still slowly moves along. Hearing of our regiment moving today felt very uneasy concerning the company it being the first time I have been absent on a move, and no one being along save Lieut Geiger. Board concluded its labors this evening and tomorrow we will be ready to march for camp. Spent portion of evening in company with Capt Griffith, remainder in rascality. Went to bed at an early hour thinking of home and friends.

SATURDAY, APRIL 26. Fine morning and is clearing up. At 10 o'clock started with General Williams, Col Knipe and Captain Strouse for camp. Stopped several places the Col being almost too unwell to ride. Reached Harrisonburg by 2 o'clock. General very much provoked at Col Donnelly's movement. After waiting nearly an hour General got ready and with Lieut Pitman started for our camp or rather to find it. Past the road but soon found the right one but meeting General Hatch he explained position of Donnelly and the General then returned home. Proceeded to camp

28. Captain Theophilus Fitzgerald of Co E. 28th NY.
29. Domino game.
30. George B Cadwalader

*Friends from Donnelly's Brigade posed together for this image by an
unknown photographer. From left to right: Captain Charles H. Fenn,
Company F, 28th NY; Lt. Darius S. Gilger, Company K, 46th PA; Dr. William
C. Rodgers, Surgeon, 46th PA; Lt. George B. Cadwalader, Quartermaster,
46th PA; Dr. George W. Burke, Assistant Surgeon, 46th PA; Captain George
J. Whitman, Company H, 3rd WI. (Source: Rick Brown Collection.)*

alone—on reaching headquarters found a very brisk skirmish
was going on ahead and our regiment had been ordered out. One
of Company "G" was killed and three wounded. Started out but
found the skirmish over before our regiment reached the place,
the rebels taking to their heels as usual. Returned to camp looking at the body of man killed, Isaac Seely. Saw all the wounded.
In evening about 8 o'clock regiment returned, very tired. Soon
after received a general order to retreat, and wagons were ordered
to move in advance but being short of transportation could not.
Started what wagons we had and laid on our arms all night.

SUNDAY, APRIL 27. Slept on arms all night. At 12 midnight buried man who had been shot. It was a solemn funeral. No useless
coffin confined his breast for in sheet nor shroud we bound him.
But he lay like a warrior taking his rest with his martial cloak
around him. Sad reflection, but we know not how soon our own
turn may come. In morning moved back towards Harrisonburg
and encamped on a hill about two miles outside of the place. Put

up our tents and were quite snugly fined by night. Camp in a fine location but water almost too far off.

--------◦•◦•◦--------

Pennsylvania Daily Telegraph
Harrisonburg, Va., April 27.
Author unknown

Yesterday afternoon the pickets of Col. Donnelly's brigade, stationed eight miles hence on the Gordonville road, were attacked by a large force of Col. Ashby's rear guard, and driven back. One man named Isaac [Seely], of the 46th Pennsylvania Regiment, was killed, and three others were wounded.

The reserve of the 46th Pennsylvania regiment, and a section of Hampton's battery, then advanced and repulsed the rebels. They retreated to a wood, where several of our shells burst in their very midst. A wagon was seen gathering up and carrying off their dead and wounded.

Owing to the horrible state of the road between this town and Col. Donnelly's encampment, and the impossibility of forwarding him supplied, Donnelly has been ordered to take up a new position nearer the town, until the roads are in better condition.

Jackson's main body is encamped near the east bank of the Shenandoah. The bridge over the river was strongly picketed by him, and underlaid with inflammable matter, ready to fire on our approach.

Capt. Brown of the 28th New York is performing provost duty in town. The orderly department of our troops is a convincing proof to the population that our object is but a mission of peace, and that the secession leaders have been guilty of gross misrepresentation and duplicity towards them. All the churches whose pastors are not in the secession army are open today, and the town wears the appearance of a northern country Sabbath.

--------◦•◦•◦--------

From the Journal of Capt. George A. Brooks

MONDAY, APRIL 28. Pleasant morning. Today our new pants came and in afternoon distributed them. They are light blue— those which we have drawn here before being dark blue. Spent day in fixing up my books generally and pasting diary from note

From Gen. Banks' Division

ANOTHER SKIRMISH WITH ASHBY'S CAVALRY.

THE REBELS-REPULSED.

One Man Killed in Col. Knipe's 46th Pennsylvania Regiment.

HARRISONBURG, Va., April 27.

Yesterday afternoon the pickets of Col. Donnelly's brigade, stationed eight miles hence on the Gordonville road, were attacked by a large force of Col. Ashby's rear guard, and driven back. One man named Isaac Kelly, of the 46th Pennsylvania regiment, was killed, and three others were wounded.

The reserve of the 46th Pennsylvania regiment, and a section of Hampton's battery, then advanced and repulsed the rebels. They retreated to a wood, where several of our shells burst in their very midst. A wagon was seen gathering up and carrying off their dead and wounded

(Source: Pennsylvania Daily Telegraph [Harrisburg, PA], April 28, 1862.)

book. In evening did not go out on dress parade but looked on the regiment and it did present the finest appearance I ever saw. All the men were arranged in their new pants and who could not feel proud of the old 46th. In evening received pay rolls and began them.

TUESDAY, APRIL 29. Pleasant but cloudy—worked at pay rolls all morning and at noon went to town. Went to Hospital to see two of my boys. Daniel Dennis and Matthew Taylor—who are both very low of the Typhoid fever. Taylor improving. Dennis very low and are afraid he will never recover. Gala day in Harrisonburg. All the bands of our brigade with the colors of each regiment, escorted by the color guard came to town for the purpose of having a jubilee on the success of Porter's feat at New Orleans, and when they all united in playing the Star Spangled Banner, Yankee Doodle, Dixie etc it made the yard of the old courthouse of Rockingham County ring and the building to echo and re-echo sounds to which it had long been a stranger. The bands afterwards escorted the color through the principal streets, playing in conjunction. Came to camp after seeing Rodgers, Caddie and Adjutant, all of whom are sick at the American House. On arriving at camp found the company had very suddenly been ordered out on picket duty, and after supper started out after them. Found them on the extreme outpost with a company of 28th New York three miles from camp. Visited all parts before going to bed. Clear starry night.

WEDNESDAY, APRIL 30. Cloudy morning. Hurried in to field officer at an early hour and had my company relieved from picket duty. Saw nothing. No causes for alarm during the night. Got to work on muster rolls and got one finished in time for muster and went out with reg't without any breakfast. Intended to have finished them last night. All the companies mustered in. After muster finished the remaining two pay rolls and sent them in all correct. In evening fixed up clothing accounts and wrote long letter to Emily. Just before going to bed an orderly came bringing information of death of Daniel Dennis.

❈ ❈ ❈

Stonewall Jackson spent the end of April planning the best way to keep Banks in the Valley. On April 30th, he started his men on a thirty-five mile march over the Blue Ridge to Mechum's Station. Hoping to complete the march quickly, he made no effort to conceal their movements in attempt to trick Banks into thinking his true destination was Richmond. Instead, after reaching Mechum's Station, Jackson's men would board rail cars and ride west to Staunton where they could form an attack on the Mountain Department, commanded by General Frémont.

Despite having recruited and reinforced his ranks to about 8,000 men, Jackson was still outnumbered two to one by Banks' men alone. Allowing Frémont and Banks to join forces would prove disastrous to Jackson, so before they had a chance to do so he planned to attack them separately. Simultaneously, Brigadier General Richard S. Ewell's 8,000 man division was moving up to Jackson's former position at Elk Run Valley, where he could threaten Banks' flank at Harrisonburg.

At first the ruse worked, and Banks, confident that Jackson was leaving the Valley for good, telegraphed the Secretary of War on April 30th saying "There is nothing more to be done by us in the Valley." The same day, Banks started pulling his scouts and advanced forces back toward Harrisonburg and New Market. The War Department was satisfied to see Banks withdraw because supply lines were still woefully inadequate, and they feared the independent commands of Banks, Frémont, and McDowell were too widely spread. Orders were issued on May 1st for Banks to withdraw to Strasburg and for Shields' Division to join McDowell near Fredericksburg.

Jackson's quick march over the Blue Ridge proved anything but. They were immediately slowed by bad weather, and men and equipment alike took a beating. They didn't arrive in Mechum's Station until May 3rd, by which time Williams and Banks had correctly determined that Jackson was not planning to leave the Valley, and that Ewell had arrived as reinforcements.

Unfortunately, the information was of little use, because Banks had already started his men northward on May 1st. Not only were Jackson's unclear intentions worrying but, to many of Banks' officers and soldiers alike, Banks' withdrawal felt like an unnecessary retreat.[31]

---

31. Cozzens, *Shenandoah 1862*, 254-9.

CHAPTER SEVEN

A Regular Prance

May 1–24, 1862

T HE BEGINNING OF May brought hope to the Union war effort. On May 1st, New Orleans, the largest city in the Confederacy, fell to Union forces, and General McClellan's army was making progress toward Richmond on the Peninsula.[1] In the Shenandoah Valley, soldiers were cheered to hear of the success of their comrades on other fronts, and many thought the war would be over by the Fourth of July. Some even placed wagers on whether they would face real combat before the war ended.

For General Banks, the lull in activity that consumed his army through the end of April and the beginning of May was troublesome. He couldn't be certain exactly where Stonewall Jackson was located. Banks determined that the Rebels had made a move to Port Republic, but beyond that, he couldn't be certain because Colonel Ashby's cavalry had successfully blocked observation anywhere south of Harrisonburg. By May 5th, Jackson had completed a grueling movement of his men from Port Republic to Mechum's Station and then onto Staunton without notice.

Based on Banks' own report to the War Department in April that all was quiet in the Valley, orders were in place for the withdrawal of his men to Strasburg, and also for General Shields' Division to depart the Valley to join General McDowell. In early May, Jackson's unknown intentions increasingly troubled Banks, and on the 9th he wrote Secretary of War Stanton expressing his concerns about Jackson and the division of his command. Unfortunately, Banks' realization was too late: orders had already set the Department of the Shenandoah in motion.[2]

---

1. Wagner, *Desk Reference*, 18.
2. Cozzens, *Shenandoah 1862*, 277, 289.

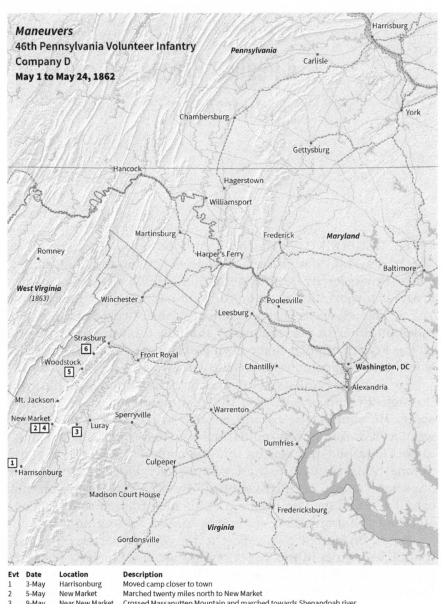

Maneuvers
46th Pennsylvania Volunteer Infantry
Company D
May 1 to May 24, 1862

Evt	Date	Location	Description
1	3-May	Harrisonburg	Moved camp closer to town
2	5-May	New Market	Marched twenty miles north to New Market
3	9-May	Near New Market	Crossed Massanutten Mountain and marched towards Shenandoah river
4	10-May	New Market	Moved back to original camp
5	12-May	Woodstock	Marched to within two miles of town
6	13-May	Strasburg	Moved within six miles of town
	17-May	Strasburg	Moved 1.5 miles to a new camp

From the Journal of Capt. George A. Brooks

THURSDAY, MAY 1. Cloudy morning, misty and drizzling. Got requisition for coffin before breakfast. After breakfast rode into town with squad to dress the corpse and dig grave. Selected spot in the cemetery on my own responsibility and by 10½ Daniel Dennis was buried with the honors of war, having lost his life in the service of his country. Thus have I lost two men out of my little band, one by drowning the other by the lingering torture of disease. Both good soldiers, faithful men. Verily in the midst of life we are in death. In afternoon arranged some business matters and in evening wrote to Keet in answer to a letter from him containing photographs of Emily and myself very welcome visitors; and also to Adjutant General Russel on business.

FRIDAY, MAY 2. Fine day regular spring weather. In fact the finest day we have had this season. Consumed all day in fixing up clothing accounts and arranging business matters generally. Signal corps went to Peaked Mountain escorted by company "F" of 46th and "L" of 5th Conn. Saw Jackson's whole force. Returned by dark. Received letter from Lew but not fancying some allusions burned it. How strange some men become importunate inconsistent suspicions. Really, I am beginning, in fact am, almost already convinced that friendship is but interest that interest is the great lever which controls all our actions. What a theme for reflection.

SATURDAY, MAY 3. Glorious day. Officer of the day. Done guard duty up in regular Camp "Lewis" order. Spring weather will bring soldierly duties stricter. This afternoon had orders to march or rather remove our camp to a better locality nearer Harrisonburg. Removed by 4 o'clock and got comfortably fixed by dark. Our new camp commands one of the finest positions and the most magnificent in which we could have located. Rich fertile fields spread before us in every direction and the valley around Harrisonburg is rich and attractive.

SUNDAY, MAY 4. Another fine morning. After guard mounting and regular Sunday inspection went to town in company of Capt Morgan. Saw Caddie and afterwards meeting some brother officers took walk around town, wandering accidentally into the

Presbyterian church just as services were beginning. Heard a good sermon, but the prayer was decidedly secession in its proclivities. After church came to camp. Just before dress parade had orders to cook two days rations. A movement on a large scale on foot and we are, I believe, ordered to join Gen McDowell at Fredericksburg. Gen Jackson is also moving towards us rapidly with a heavy force and before morning will attack us in which case there will be a desperate battle. Though not possessing one half the force reported to be with him yet our boys are eager and would fight like modern devils.

MONDAY, MAY 5. Awakened at 2½. Slept very little. Morning as dark as blazes. Marched through Harrisonburg and halted on the other side of the town awaiting other regiments to arrive from where we did not move until after daybreak. Marched very slow in morning and by noon were not more five miles from Harrisonburg. In afternoon got along very fast and reached our camping ground about 6 o'clock having marched a distance of twenty miles. Day very warm and road very dusty. Got a good supper in town and met a very fine and pretty young widow.

TUESDAY, MAY 6. Fine morning and will be a very warm day. Yesterday evening Luther R. Witman arrived after we had long and anxiously awaited his arrival.[3] Day very warm. Nothing of any kind going on. In evening took a ride into town and rode over a mile beyond in company with Morgan, Adjutant and Ned Witman. Beautiful evening. Friday Captain Wise returned.[4] Very fine dress parade.

WEDNESDAY, MAY 7. Another very fine morning. In afternoon fixed up my clothing book. Nothing of any account transpired today. Geiger was officer of guard, towards evening evidence of rain.

Letter from Capt. George A. Brooks to Emily Brooks
Camp near New Market
May 7, 1862

My Dear Emily,

    It is so long since I have heard from you that I fear you have become so much enamored with your "mountain home" as to

---

3. Luther R. Witman. Brother of Lt. Edward Witman. Died of wounds received in the Battle of Peach Tree Creek.
4. Cornelius Wise of Company E. Resigned on September 24, 1862.

Adjutant Luther R. Witman, 1861. (Source: George C. Bradley Collection.)

have forgotten your "dear George," and perhaps you have even been transformed into some mountain fairy with Willie as an accompanying angel. Do however, write to me once more, if only to let me know how you are pleased with your visit thus far, how father, Annie and Mattie are and how yourself and Willie are generally.

Since seeing you, and immediately after joining the Regiment, we began moving and ever since we have been on the go—and have twice driven the enemy back. We have been marching steadily for over two weeks, and most of the time have had no tents, so I have had no opportunity of writing, in fact I have none now, and merely drop you a few hasty lines stating that I am well, as I daily await a letter from you, and will reply to it at length!

We are now lying near New Market Virginia but have been further down the valley in fact we lay at Harrisonburg eighteen miles below this for two days and made a reconnaissance out the Gordonsville road, about eight miles, having quite a brisk skirmish one of our men being killed and four wounded. My men and their worthy Captain all came out safe.

We are daily expect[ing] orders to move on towards Gordonsville down the valley of the Rappahannock, and may have some brisk work, but as McClellan has defeated them at Williamsburg, the war will no doubt speedily close and I will once again join you and Willie. But I must close, will write a long one in a few days

Your affectionate husband
George

From the Journal of Capt. George A. Brooks

THURSDAY, MAY 8. Glorious morning. Last night wrote to Emily today received letter from Dr. H. O. Witman.[5] Orders to cook three days rations in the afternoon, news from McClellan of the most joyous and exciting nature and the boys in the best of spirits. Nothing of any special account transpiring in our division and we seem doomed to lead a life of inactivity—those who offered their service long after us have crowned their day with glory. But we will hope on.

✳ ✳ ✳

While the 46th Pennsylvania remained largely inactive, McClellan was, for a change, anything but. On May 3rd, Yorktown had finally fallen after a month-long siege, forcing the Confederates up the Peninsula toward Richmond. They retreated again on May 5th when a battle at Williamsburg resulted in a Union victory.[6]

In the Valley on May 8th, Stonewall Jackson's men, with the addition of Brigadier General Edward "Allegheny" Johnson's Brigade, clashed with two brigades of Frémont's Mountain Division at McDowell, West Virginia. The battle was severe and lasted four

---

5. Henry Orth Witman, brother of Luther and Edward. A Physician in Halifax, PA.
6. Wagner, *Desk Reference*, 256.

hours before the Union brigades were forced to retreat. Jackson gave chase until the 13th, sufficiently pushing the Yankees from the area, and then started his men back toward McDowell. Banks, now without hope of reinforcement from Frémont, was firmly in Jackson's sights.[7]

From the Journal of Capt. George A. Brooks

FRIDAY, MAY 9. Another fine day. Very warm. Before noon started across the Massanutten mountain, one of the range of Blue Ridge, to relieve a brigade of Shields' Division at Columbia bridge over the Shenandoah River. Climbing the mountain was very tiresome, it being four miles to the top. The road very crooked. Halting near the top had one of the finest views I have ever beheld—magnificent beyond description. Wound down the other side five miles, one of the most remarkable roads I have ever seen, admirably graded. Encamped for the night or rather bivouacked near the Shenandoah—glorious night.

SATURDAY, MAY 10. Another fine morning. Owing to some misunderstanding we did not relieve the brigade we had intended but remained in camp. Spent portion of morning in reading. In afternoon in company with Lieut Wm. Caldwell took a walk and bath in the Shenandoah and shortly after our arrival in camp received orders to march at once in great haste were under way by 3½.[8] The woods on fire through which we had to pass, in fact

The Massanutten Mountain in the Shenandoah Valley is a prominent landmark to modern travelers on Interstate 81. (Source: Library of Congress.)

7. Cozzens, *Shenandoah 1862*, 274-5.
8. 1st Lieut. William P. Caldwell of Co. K. Killed in action at the battle of Cedar Mountain, VA August 9, 1862.

nine of the ten miles we marched was in dense forest. Had to pass within ten feet of the fire which was fast sweeping everything perishable before it. Really a horrible and awfully grand exhibition. Passed the mountain by moonlight and in fact the whole march was grand and picturesque not easily to be forgotten. Arrived in our old camp by 10½. Tents all up save my own.

SUNDAY, MAY 11. Another fine pleasant morning. Had regular inspection. Spent remainder of morn in reading. In afternoon wrote to Estelle and in evening visited town in company with Capt. Corliss of the Fifth and Ben.[9] After promenading up and down the principal streets and seeing the flower of Virginia's daughters (but oh, horror, they all nearly rub snuff and chew tobacco) called on Mrs. Clinedist and from there dropped in to see another young lady whose name we did not know. The latter a spirited secessionist. Returned to camp by 9 o'clock but did not get in bed before we received orders to pack up and prepare for a march.

MONDAY, MAY 12. After packing up everything and even putting our knapsacks in the wagon the teams were ordered to move on and we remained shivering by the fire until morning or rather 3 o'clock when we started on our march. Day very warm and the roads exceedingly dusty. Reached camping ground within two miles of Woodstock and bivouacked for the night. Still no letter from home and it seems so strange. Only one within a month none for over three weeks. Took a bath in river.

TUESDAY, MAY 13. Up at 3 but did not get off until daylight. Marched very slow, there being considerable deterioration on the road, and about noon, being within six miles of Strasburg, halted and our wagons which had gone beyond Strasburg were ordered back reaching us by 3. Laid out regular camp and put up tents. Sun very hot and roads so dusty. Jim Brumbaugh arrived today after an absence of four months at Hospital.[10] John J. Wenrich also arrived a day or so ago. Our movements, very mysterious truly, and we all look forward anxiously for future developments.

WEDNESDAY, MAY 14. Rained last night. Glad we were in such comfortable quarters having our tents all up last night. Wrote

9. Captain George W. Corliss, Co. C 5th Conn. Inft. Awarded the Congressional Medal of Honor for bravery during the Battle of Cedar Mountain August 9, 1862. Ben is Captain Benjamin Morgan of Company F.
10. James A. Brumbaugh of Harrisburg, PA. Discharged July 3 1862 by Surgeon's certificate of disability.

to B. F. S. and Wm Sayford.[11] Sent all letters off by mail and we now expect daily mail being much nearer our quarters, or rather railroad communication with the cities and receiving the daily papers one day after their publication. Nothing stirring today.

THURSDAY, MAY 15. Still raining. Detailed as officer of the day but changed with Capt Mills.[12] In afternoon went to hospital at Strasburg. Saw M. Taylor and John Shelly.[13] Taylor nearly well. Shelly looks bad. Gave them $5. Over 1,200 men sick here, a small community, and it is fearful to contemplate. So many thrown together in one place—800 of them belongs to Gen Shields' Division. Only 80 belongs to our brigade. Rode up to fortifications which are being erected on a hill back of Strasburg. Not very formidable. Began raining rapidly. Met "Caddie" and rode with him to camp. Spent evening and some more at Randle's. Went to bed later.

FRIDAY, MAY 16. Still raining. Spent morning at Camp and Randle's part of the time in an interesting conversation with a crass widow whose husband was in the Southern Army. At noon General Banks and staff paid our camp a visit. Also General Williams. Received letter from "Estelle" and a few lines from Dr Harry Witman. "Estelle" very impatient and anxious to hear from me. How full of resorts and expedients is woman. Purchased very fine field or marine glass for $25. Rather high but got good glass and may as well have it as a poor one. Spent portion of evening with a very interesting young widow. Got to bed late.

✳ ✳ ✳

After the departure of Shields' Division on May 12th, Banks' forces were further reduced on the 16th when Colonel Kenly's 1st Maryland, almost 1,000 men strong, was ordered by the Secretary of War to the Union garrison at Front Royal. With only 4,476 infantry, 1,600 cavalry, and 16 artillery pieces remaining in Strasburg, Banks knew his forces were dwindling. Moreover, the town had been filled with months worth of government supplies and sick soldiers. Despite the high spirits of his men, and hastily and shoddily constructed breastworks placed on the south side of

11. "B.F.S." is Benjamin Franklin Scheffer, Brooks' brother in law.
12. Capt. Nathaniel J Mills, Co H. Discharged June 24, 1862.
13. Corporal Matthew Taylor and Private John Shelly. Taylor was discharged when his enlistment expired in September, 1864. Shelly was wounded in the leg at the Battle of Peach Tree Creek, GA. His leg was later amputated, ending his military service.

town, Banks knew he couldn't hold if Jackson were to attack. His concern was warranted, because Jackson, reinforced to 16,000 strong with the addition of General Ewell's men, was well aware of his opponent's vulnerability.[14]

———•◦•———

From the Journal of Capt. George A. Brooks

SATURDAY, MAY 17. Another beautiful morning. Some probability of our moving today. At noon struck tents, packed up generally preparatory to a move and marching one and a half miles across the country, locating in a fine field near water and a commanding position. There being some probability of our staying here sometime fixed our tents up snugly. In the evening the Colonel gave orders for a dress parade but we did not go out. Nothing stirring.

SUNDAY, MAY 18. Glorious morning. Officer of the day. Had fine guard mounting. Stayed in tent nearly all day. Fine dress parade in the evening with prayer by the chaplain, after which we had service and a regular sermon which was attentively listened to by a respectable audience. Camp filled with country people. No unusual movements on foot.

MONDAY, MAY 19. Another fine morning. Company ordered out on picket and, on being relieved as officer of the day, followed them. Stationed on the extreme right with the reserve at the house of a good Union man named Fauber where I had very comfortable quarters. On visiting the pickets in the morning found a very interesting and pretty girl and also a rich young widow with whom I spent a very pleasant hour. Took dinner at Station of Reserve. Visited the pickets in afternoon and spent remainder in reading, etc. In evening took a young lady home, after which went rounds of the pickets and went to bed. The anniversary of my wedding, 3 years.

TUESDAY, MAY 20. Fine morning. Arose at 3 o'clock and visited pickets. Nothing stirring during the night. At 10 o'clock were relieved by Company E and started for camp. Sorry to leave so pleasant a station. Received letter from J. Wesley Awl but none from Emily.[15] Can't imagine why she won't write. Now over a

---

14. Cozzens, *Shenandoah 1862*, 287-9.
15. John Wesley Awl, a Harrisburg friend.

month. Took walk in evening down to pike with Lieut Care and Captain Morgan and calling on a young widow returned by 9. Spent rest of evening at sutler and in my own tent talking etc. Went to bed late.

WEDNESDAY, MAY 21. Another fine morning. A slight sprinkle of rain during the night rendering the morning air pleasant and balmy. Wrote to Wm. Sayford ordering several coats etc. Last night received from him box. In afternoon wrote to J. Wesley Awl concerning Daniel Dennis' death, also sent off box containing Dennis' clothing etc. In evening again wrote to Emily wondering why I do not receive an answer to the many letters I have written. Nothing of any account transpiring. All perfectly quiet.

THURSDAY, MAY 22. Another fine morning. Received clothing etc from quartermaster and distributed it. Kept busy charging all morning. Had company drill. Boys do very well after nearly three months exemption from it. Very warm day. Had short drill in afternoon and a very fine dress parade in the evening. Gen Williams, Gen Hatch, Col Donnelly and portions of the staff of each were present. A number of country girls were present. After parade took walk with Morgan, meeting rather an interesting mountain maid with whom I had nearly an hours' pleasant chat. Returned to camp. Nothing stirring.

FRIDAY, MAY 23. Very heavy dew. Reveille at 5 o'clock. Regiment turned out under arms and had a roll call. Yesterday evening boxed up boys' overcoats, preparatory to sending them home, thus relieving them of a very heavy encumbrance during the coming summer, if we are still in service. Very warm day. Reports, Lieut. Muhlenberg of Best's Battery whilst swimming in the North fork with one of his men and a servant was shot at by a squad of sixteen men who had got inside our pickets. The private was killed and Lieut wounded.

✻ ✻ ✻

The evening of May 22nd found Jackson and Ewell's combined forces bivouacking within twelve miles of the Union garrison at Front Royal. On May 23rd, they started at daybreak to cover the difference. The plan was to strike the isolated and badly outnumbered Union outpost, turn Banks' flank in the process, and place Jackson's force firmly between Banks and any possible assistance from McDowell in the east. Banks would have no choice but to withdraw toward the Potomac to preserve lines of communication, and it would do so without requiring Jackson to make a potentially disastrous frontal attack on Strasburg.

About a mile outside of Front Royal, the majority of Colonel Kenly's men were lazing about camp attempting to stay cool despite the heat of the day. At 2:00 P.M., when Jackson's advance forces arrived and swept through town, they met little resistance and easily pushed startled pickets and the provost marshal guard in their wake. The first indication something was amiss occurred when an incredibly frightened black man rode into the Union camp around 2:30, shouting to the Union troopers that the Rebels were about to "surround you and cut you off." Thinking the man was overreacting to a skirmish between pickets and guerrillas known to be in the area, the Yankees were dubious, but sent two troopers to investigate. Minutes later they returned, as terrified as the civilian. Dozens had been captured in town, and several had been killed by gunshots fired from the windows of homes.

Colonel Kenly ordered his regiments formed, and set fire to stores of equipment in camp. He placed his regiment on a small hill outside of town, and knowing he was badly outnumbered, maneuvered his men in such a way to trick the Confederates into thinking he had more men than he actually did. Two companies of the 29th Pennsylvania and two companies of the 5th New York cavalry arrived and gave aid. Kenly knew he was surrounded by overwhelming Confederate force, and his best hope was to delay them as long as possible to give Banks the best opportunity for escape.

Two troopers rode for Strasburg to alert Banks of the approaching danger. For two hours, Kenly moved his men back and forth and was able to hold his position, but by 4:30 P.M. Rebel cavalry threatened to flank him from the rear. He ordered his small command to retreat across the Shenandoah River. They did so well ahead of the Confederates, who had paused to loot the abandoned Union camps. Kenly ordered the burning of both bridges spanning the river, but the wood was green and the detail of men were terrified by the overwhelming numbers of advancing Confederates. One bridge remained completely intact while the other only sustained damage to one span. Kenly formed a new defensive line on another rise in the terrain and held for

another hour until Confederate cavalry and infantry located fording points along the river and started approaching on his left and
right flank. He had no choice but to order his men northward.

After retreating two miles, Kenly made a final stand, but
was quickly overwhelmed by a superior number of Confederate
cavalry. The majority of the Yankees were captured, including
Kenly himself. With minimal loss, Jackson's men had captured
almost 700 soldiers, wounded and killed another 36, captured
stores and provisions at Front Royal, and captured two artillery
pieces. But most importantly, Jackson was now on Banks' left
flank and in position to cut off Banks' only line of retreat through
Winchester.[16]

❋ ❋ ❋

The afternoon of May 23rd was "intensely hot," and General
Banks had spent it and the evening sorting through incomplete
and at times contradictory reports as he tried to determine what
was happening at Front Royal. The first news had reached him
around 4:00 P.M. when a 5th New York trooper arrived in camp
after riding seventeen miles in fifty-five minutes. He knew little,
though, and Banks gave him a new horse and sent him back for
more information. After another messenger arrived with similarly
scant information, Banks sent him back as well. The two messengers did confirm that something was happening, and so Banks
felt it prudent to dispatch the 3rd Wisconsin Infantry to Front
Royal. Without more information, he was hesitant to do more.

News continued to arrive from various sources. None were
concise and few were accurate, some claiming that up to 20,000
rebels were on Banks' flank and Kenly had been killed. Without
a clear idea of what was actually happening, and knowing how
exposed he was at Strasburg, Banks ordered a retreat. At 10 P.M.,
he started his large wagon train north toward Winchester and
ordered all of his regiments camped south of town to pack wagons
and fall back.

At midnight, the most reliable report yet arrived, stating that up
to 6,000 Rebels were at Front Royal and had decimated the Union
command there. It still wasn't clear who Banks faced—Ewell,
Jackson, or both. Banks considered three courses of action—attack the Confederate flank on the Front Royal road, abandon the

---

16. Cozzens, *Shenandoah 1862*, 287, 294, 298-9, 301-7.

wagon train and retreat over the Little North Mountain to the Potomac River, or make a direct retreat for Winchester. He knew the
first two options would be futile, and that the latter, falling back
on Winchester, would allow him to seize the town before the Confederates had the chance. He could also maintain his lines of communication and draw on reinforcements from Harpers Ferry. The
decision was made, and Banks sent word to the War Department
that he would head for Winchester and to send reinforcements if
possible. Colonel Donnelly's Brigade started out shortly after 1:00
A.M., ordered to retreat to Middletown and remain there until they
received new orders.

The morning of May 24th most men were up before dawn,
if they had slept at all. It was chilly and raining, and for a brief
while it hailed. Banks had been busy overnight, ordering all
but the most critically wounded evacuated from the hospitals
in Strasburg. Commissary and quartermaster stores had been
loaded into wagons. Donnelly's Brigade's trains were already in
position on the Valley Pike, and Donnelly's men were waiting for
Gordon's Brigade's trains to pass so they could fall in on their
rear. Gordon's men were packed, fed, and waiting to fall in behind
Donnelly. Signal stations were set up on high ground to allow
communication between the front and rear of the column. He
was far from a perfect commander, but General Banks had kept
his head through a dire situation the night of May 23rd and the
morning of the 24th. His men were ready to move.

Throwing out a forward and rear guard, Banks attempted
to understand what lay ahead and behind him. The frightened
soldiers generally did a poor job—a detachment of the 29th Pennsylvania advancing only three miles before a few carbine shots
sent them fleeing for the main column. Banks dispatched more
men, but could not wait any longer. Without a clear idea of what
lay around of him, the column moved forward around 9:00 A.M. A
Lieutenant of the 5th Connecticut of Donnelly's Brigade took note
of the spectacle, remembering: "There were half as many Negros
as soldiers, some drivers and some refugees, wagons loaded with
Negro women, waiting on some officers, mess kettles, pans, and
chickens. Then there were droves of beef cattle belonging to the
commissary department, ambulances with sick, all hurrying in
one direction."[17]

George Brooks also recalled the retreat in his diary:

---

17. Cozzens, *Shenandoah 1862*, 310-16.

SATURDAY, MAY 24. Awakened at 3 o'clock this morning with orders to march at once without cooking any rations and not yet having sent off our overcoats had to unpack them. It was raining and we were soon on our way towards the pike being about a mile from it. Passing the cavalry camp found them burning all the forage and reaching the pike found one section of Hampton's battery in positions from which we judged an immediate attack was anticipated. On inquiry ascertained that Jackson was advancing upon us down the valley of the Shenandoah and Ewell was endeavoring to cut off our retreat at Winchester, having the day previous destroyed and captured our small force with a large amount of government store at Front Royal. We moved on rapidly towards Strasburg where we joined the 3rd Brigade, cavalry, artillery, etc, under Banks, making our whole effective force of fighting not over 4,000—with 1,000 sick and unfit for service, beside attached to trains drivers etc and 500 wagons.[18]

On the night of the 23rd, the Confederate captors of Front Royal had celebrated their victory with the local civilians. The tired and hungry soldiers ate lavishly, since Front Royal hadn't yet been hard pressed by the war, and resupplied with equipment, including rifles, left by the Yankees. The festive air didn't extend to Jackson and Ewell, who weren't sure if Banks would move north toward Winchester and the safety of the Potomac, or perhaps try to escape toward Washington. Jackson knew his opponent, and guessed the cautious politician-turned-general would most likely retreat to Winchester. Hoping to get an idea of Banks' early movements, Jackson dispatched cavalry and infantry to monitor his movements.

At 6 A.M. the next morning, Ewell's men set out toward Cedarville. Jackson's men followed at 8, with the rear of his column, which started the day four miles south of Front Royal, not crossing the Shenandoah until 10. Having marched twenty-five miles the previous day, and having endured long marches for many days prior, the men were exhausted.

Jackson paused for three hours to close up his stretched army near Cedarville and filled the time trying to deduce the location of Banks. Finally, a courier arrived around 1:00 A.M. with news that Brigadier General George Steuart's cavalry had found

18. *Brooks Diary.* May 24th, 1862.

the Union wagon train near Middletown, and had attacked in an uncoordinated and undisciplined manner. They captured some trains with sick soldiers and took them prisoner, and succeeded in frightening some wagon drivers, many of whom were former slaves. Steuart successfully sent the wagon drivers scurrying, but neglected to inflict further damage. General Banks and the master teamster quickly got the frightened wagon drivers under control, and Colonel Donnelly deployed the 46th Pennsylvania as skirmishers on the right of the Valley Turnpike, along with a battery of artillery. The 28th New York and 5th Connecticut were placed behind them in column.[19] Captain Brooks recounted the operation in his diary:

> We moved on towards Winchester as rapidly as permissible and everything progressed fairly until within about half a mile of Middletown, our wagon train was attacked in front and a general stampede of teamsters ensued many coming without their wagons, in fact we anticipated a regular prance, or rather it was one. Our regiment being in front was immediately ordered to unsling knapsacks, and everything which would encumber them, load at will and charge down the pike at a double quick a distance of four miles to the village of Newtown driving the cavalry [Steuart's] before us and pursuing them to the sight of the woods about a mile from the pike brought up the battery shelling them several miles. During our pursuit we killed two, wounded one, and taking one prisoner. We then returned to the pike and pushed ahead without any further annoyance of any account . . .[20]

Donnelly's effective pursuit was praised by Banks, who later commented that, "This episode . . . occupied nearly an hour, but it saved our column. Had the enemy vigorously attacked our train while at the head of the column it would have been thrown into such dire confusion as to have made the successful continuation of our march impossible." After Donnelly's men returned to the Federal column, the wagons and soldiers continued toward Winchester.

Steuart had indeed had the option to inflict far more damage on the wagon train, and could have thrown Banks' column into

19. Cozzens, *Shenandoah 1862*, 316-22.
20. *Brooks Diary*. May 24th, 1862.

Colonel Dudley Donnelly, 28th New York Volunteer Infantry. (Source: Boyce, C.W. A brief history of the Twenty-eighth regiment New York state volunteers.)

disarray. With the opportunity missed or unrealized, he returned to Jackson with a useful piece of information: the location and direction of Banks' movement, from which Jackson was confident Banks' target was Winchester. Jackson didn't know how many Yankees remained in Strasburg, if any, and spent four hours feeling out the area to determine if Banks was still located there in force. The pause gave Banks' wagon train precious time to move north.

For the remainder of the afternoon, Banks' rear guard attempted to fend off Ashby's cavalry while Jackson tried to determine the exact location of Banks' infantry. Just before 4:00 P.M., Ashby severed the rear guard of Banks' line at Middletown, but it was still unclear to the Confederates exactly what part of Banks' column they were hitting. A pocket of Federal resistance south of Middletown delayed Jackson another two hours, and it wasn't until 5:45 that he turned his men north in pursuit of Banks' retreating column. Jackson was moving slowly, and General Ewell was growing impatient. Communication problems had slowed his independent advance toward Winchester. Finally, he moved forward without orders from Jackson.

At sundown, General Banks and Williams were within six miles of Winchester and sent cavalry forward to determine if the town was still in Union hands. To their relief, it was, and the Tenth Maine Infantry and five companies of the 8th New York Cavalry had just arrived as reinforcements. Banks continued his train forward and concentrated on the rear of his column which was fending off attacks from Confederate cavalry. For the most part, the gallant maneuvering of regiments protected the Union wagons on their journey north.

Federal infantry started entering Winchester after dark, with the last regiment, the 2nd Massachusetts, not arriving until 2:00 A.M. The soldiers were exhausted, having been on the move since 5:00 A.M. the previous day, with many having fought in skirmishes in addition to the distance they had marched. It was a cold, damp night, and many men did not have overcoats or blankets.[21] Captain Brooks recalled the 46th Pennsylvania's arrival in town:

> . . . reaching Winchester about nine o'clock at night without any further annoyance, and bivouacked on the Front Royal pike, nearly a mile from town, having marched twenty-seven miles, without anything to eat, and having no blankets nor overcoats, we built large fires and passed a sleepless night.[22]

The suffering of Banks' men was easily trumped by the Confederates. Ewell had arrived outside of town at 10:00 P.M., and tangled with pickets until midnight. At that point, his men were kept in or near their ranks until morning, shivering cold and only permitted to nap. Meanwhile, Jackson's soldiers were toiling their way through the darkness, hoping to close the twelve miles of turnpike between them and Winchester before morning. Like Banks, they had been moving, marching and fighting since 5 A.M. the morning prior, yet Jackson continued to push them

---

21. Cozzens, Shenandoah 1862, 322-33, 340-1.
22. Pennsylvania Daily Telegraph. May 27th, 1862.

relentlessly. They stopped and started, skirmishing as they went, and losing men to exhaustion at every stop. Finally, at 3:00 A.M., Jackson halted them north of Kernstown while more skirmishers were sent forward to push Federal pickets back to Winchester. This continued until another officer finally convinced Jackson to let the men rest for two hours, at which point those who hadn't already done so collapsed to the ground, instantly asleep despite the cold.[23] Two hours of sleep would prove far too little for the day ahead.

---

23. Cozzens, *Shenandoah 1862*, 336-9.

CHAPTER EIGHT

Make a Stand

May 25–26, 1862

ALTHOUGH GENERAL BANKS' retreat to Winchester had been successful, over one hundred wagons filled with supplies were lost and his regiments were spread across the countryside. His effective force was around 4,400. The men were aware they were outnumbered at least three to one—in truth it was four to one. They were also aware of the enormous task before them. "This remembrance of this day constitutes one of the most important events in our lifetime," George Brooks wrote in his journal to open his entry for May 25th, 1862.

During the night of May 24th and the early morning of May 25th, Banks and his officers exchanged telegrams with the War Department in Washington. Outnumbered as he was, Banks' only hope was the safety of Maryland, but his slow moving supply wagons would need a head start. The only option that would give him enough time to safely reach Maryland was to start the wagon train north and have his infantry stand and face Jackson outside of Winchester.[1] Expectations were low. "That we should all be prisoners of war I had little doubt," wrote General Williams afterward, "but we could not get away without a show of resistance, both to know the enemy's position and to give our trains a chance to get to the rear."[2]

President Lincoln had spent May 24th at Falmouth, Virginia in council with Generals McDowell and Shields, the latter's command having just arrived after a long march from the Shenandoah Valley. Their meeting resulted in a plan for both generals, with 40,000 men between them, to move in support of McClellan

---

1. Cozzens, *Shenandoah 1862*, 342-3.
2. Williams, *Cannon's Mouth*, 79.

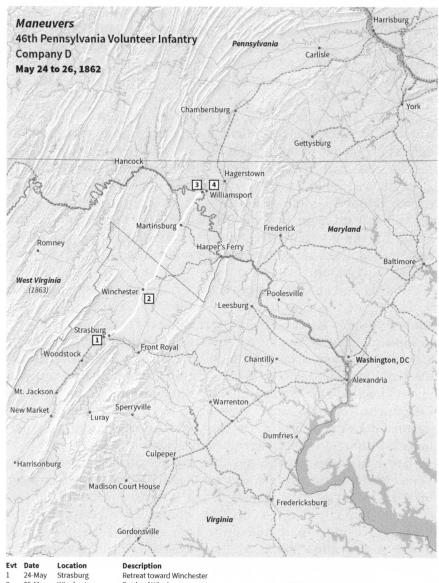

Maneuvers
46th Pennsylvania Volunteer Infantry
Company D
May 24 to 26, 1862

Evt	Date	Location	Description
1	24-May	Strasburg	Retreat toward Winchester
2	25-May	Winchester	Battle of Winchester
3	25-May	Williamsport	Retreated to Williamsport; river was too high to cross into Maryland
4	26-May	Williamsport	Crossed Potomac; quartered in Williamsport

on May 26th. Brushing away smaller Confederate forces in their wake, they would join McClellan and face Richmond with a combined 160,000 troops. Even the cautious McClellan, who still overestimated Joe Johnston's numbers, could hardly manage to fail with so many men at his disposal. Prospects for success had never looked better.

That was, until news of Front Royal arrived just after the plan was put in place. Banks' plight wasn't imaginary. If he were to fail in his defense of the northern Valley, Harpers Ferry and communications with the West would be threatened. Jackson's true strength and objectives weren't known, which meant an attack on Washington couldn't be ruled out. By evening, Lincoln made the difficult decision to send Shields and McDowell back to the Valley to trap Jackson. That meant their 40,000 troops couldn't reinforce McClellan, and would seriously alter his plans for attacking Richmond.

Shields and McDowell were less than happy with the plan, and both reminded Lincoln that they couldn't arrive in the Valley fast enough to help Banks. Lincoln telegraphed Frémont in the West Virginia mountains, asking for him to send help to Banks immediately, but Frémont asked not to be sent. His men were low on supplies and food, and enemy activity in the area made him cautious about dividing his command. Lincoln himself replied, ordering Frémont to "move against Jackson at Harrisonburg and operate against the enemy in such a way as to relieve Banks." Despite Lincoln's efforts, it was clear that Banks' little army was on its own.

The early morning of May 25th was no warmer nor more dry. Those who had managed to get some sleep woke up before dawn to a damp, foggy day, and were well aware of what lay ahead. Colonel Donnelly had his brigade, consisting of the 28th New York, 5th Connecticut and 46th Pennsylvania, up well before dawn, and arranged them on a small elevation called Camp Hill, overlooking and on the east side of the Front Royal Road. The brigade was supported by six artillery pieces and a squadron of cavalry. Gordon's Brigade was located west of the Valley Turnpike on Bower's Hill, along with the support of eight artillery pieces and cavalry. The infantry regiments arranged themselves as best they could, since all of their Generals were still in Winchester and the field was obscured by a heavy fog.[3] George Brooks later remembered their deployment that morning:

---

3. Cozzens, *Shenandoah 1862*, 344-50.

Reveille sounded before day, the regiment fell into line under arms, roll was called and we left our arms in stack awaiting orders. Gen Banks had determined to make a stand; Gen Gordon's brigade forming the right wing of the defense and our brigade, the left, having our center unprotected.[4]

During the night, General Jackson had sent a map to Ewell with three words at the bottom: "Attack at dawn." Under the cover of darkness and fog, Ewell arranged his men in the early morning hours and readied them for an attack. When morning arrived, he sent out skirmishers, but the fog made progress impossible. They withdrew and waited for it to clear.

While the Confederates laid in damp fields waiting for visibility to improve, the mist had cleared faster on the western side of the pike. Jackson had set to work deploying his division, and had easily pushed Gordon's skirmishers off the field. General Winder's Brigade was put into battle line and two artillery pieces were placed well in front. They fired blindly into the fog, unable to see the Union regiments' positions.[5] George Brooks recalled the 46th Pennsylvania's early morning maneuvers:

At 4:25 the fight began by an attack on our left by a battery of rifled pieces; one of the first shells killing a man named Thoman of my company and wounding several in Company "F". Being directly in the range of their shells, we marched our position beyond a small rise in the ground, formed our regiment "close columns in mass" and patiently and anxiously awaited further orders.[6]

As Ewell listened to the sound of Jackson's artillery moving into place and opening fire, he moved his own artillery into position and instructed Colonel Kirkland of the 21st North Carolina to attack. At 5:40, Kirkland—a West Point graduate who should have known better—sloppily advanced his regiment without first deploying skirmishers or allowing his men to drop their knapsacks. They moved forward along the turnpike in columns of four, with the stone walls on either side of the roadway preventing any other form of deployment. The mist parted just long enough for

---

4. *Brooks Diary.* May 25, 1862.
5. Cozzens, *Shenandoah 1862*, 351-2.
6. *Brooks Diary.* May 25, 1862.

the 1st Maryland (CS) to observe the North Carolinians advancing. Blinded by the fog, the Tar Heel men were headed straight toward the 28th New York, which was lying behind a stone wall on a rise in the terrain. With no way to warn their comrades, all the 1st Maryland (CS) could do was watch.[7] "Oh, it was a sickening sight to see them thus marching into the jaws of death," recalled a veteran of the regiment.[8]

Marching straight into the 28th New York was bad enough, but neither Confederate regiment could see the 5th Connecticut and 46th Pennsylvania hidden in a hollow between the turnpike and the 28th New York. The 21st North Carolina was completely taken by surprise when they advanced further and looked over the fence to their left and saw the 46th Pennsylvania, with George Brooks' Company at the head, not fifty yards away.

The 46th Pennsylvania sprung into action, equally surprised, but struggled to deploy into battle line from columns under such circumstances. Kirkland's North Carolinians, four abreast, were able to more easily deploy and opened fire. A first and then second volley rained into the Pennsylvanians, some bullets finding their marks as Colonel Knipe frantically ran about trying to get his men into line with profanity-laced commands. Bullets grazed his uniform and a ricochet off his pistol holster cut his leg, but the Colonel pressed on.

Captain Brooks pulled together Company D and the color guard and rushed forward half the distance to the Confederates. To the Pennsylvanians' left, the 5th Connecticut was also coming into line, and started firing into the Rebels' right flank.[9] "We answered the fire gallantly," remembered George Brooks, "and though volley after volley was poured into their ranks with fearful effect, the Fifth Connecticut upon our left, meanwhile giving [the 21st North Carolina] a galling cross fire, they still doggedly maintained their position."[10]

The North Carolinians were suffering for it, though. Men were falling, and their predicament was growing worse. The 28th New York moved down from its elevated position to the left of the 5th Connecticut and opened fire, while the 46th Pennsylvania fixed bayonets.[11] "Finding all other attempts to dislodge them useless,"

---

7. Cozzens, *Shenandoah 1862*, 353-4.
8. Washington Hands Civil War Notebook, 52-53. University of Virginia Library.
9. Bradley, *Surviving Stonewall*, 101-3.
10. *Pennsylvania Daily Telegraph.* May 27th, 1862.
11. Cozzens, *Shenandoah 1862*, 354.

recalled Captain Brooks, "a bayonet charge was resolved upon. Our boys came up to the work beautifully, and they were driven with terrible slaughter from their shelter."[12]

Colonel Kirkland finally gave way, his men taking shelter behind another stone wall about one hundred yards to his rear. They had sustained heavy casualties, but after a fifteen-minute pause, he tried to dislodge the Yankees again by sending his men forward in a futile bayonet charge. With a yell, they rushed forward, some of the more zealous fellows jumping onto the wall behind which Donnelly's men were sheltered. Colonel Kirkland was shot through the thigh, and his second in command was mortally wounded. Bloodied and without leadership, the North Carolinians soon broke and ran, leaving nearly one hundred of their comrades on the field behind them.

As the North Carolinians retreated, the 21st Georgia attempted to provide covering fire. The Georgia men opened fire on the left flank of the 28th New York, but the the New Yorkers held firm. The 21st Georgia was preparing to make a charge when the fog moved in again and, paired with gunsmoke, blocked their view. Both sides stopped firing and settled into a thirty minute silence, during which Colonel Donnelly counted the flags of at least nine Rebel regiments maneuvering in the distance. He knew he was outnumbered and that his three regiments couldn't hold against the next attack.[13] George Brooks wrote of the lull in activity:

> So heavy had been the firing that the smoke completely enshrouded the battlefield and for over twenty minutes hostilities were entirely suspended; our regiment in the meanwhile taking a new position on more advantageous ground. Soon the sun arose clear and beautifully and the firing of their artillery right and left began with redoubled firing; their guns being most elegantly served and our small, or rather, few pieces gallantly responding. Their shells falling with wonderful accuracy producing sad havoc in our ranks. Everybody having stood the first fire stood manfully and we anxiously awaited another infantry regiment to give us a show, throwing out skirmishers as a precautionary measure.[14]

West of the turnpike, Jackson's artillery had suffered early losses at the hands of Union skirmishers, and he had responded

---

12. *Pennsylvania Daily Telegraph.* May 27th, 1862.
13. Cozzens, *Shenandoah 1862*, 355.
14. *Brooks Diary.* May 25th, 1862.

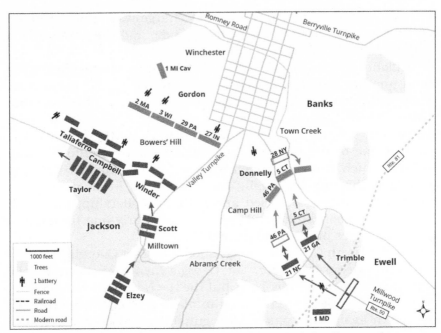

[First Winchester Battle Map 1.] 21st Georgia and 21st North Carolina attack.

by bringing up more. For nearly two hours, he hit Gordon's brigade, on the Union's right on Bower's Hill, with fire from sixteen cannons, to which they responded with their eight. Under the cover of the artillery, Jackson deployed his infantry in support. By 7:00 A.M., fifteen Confederate regiments had arrived on the western side of the pike.

Half an hour later, Jackson ordered forward Brigadier General Richard Taylor's Brigade of three thousand Louisianians. They advanced toward the 2nd Massachusetts Infantry while taking artillery fire. Taylor lead from the front of his brigade, riding steadily forward with sword drawn. After covering half of the distance between him and the Massachusetts regiment, and within earshot, Taylor gave the order to charge.

Taylor's men rushed forward just as the 29th Pennsylvania and 27th Indiana regiments were brought up for support. Seeing the wave of Confederates headed straight for them, the Indianians mostly broke formation and ran for a stone wall in front of them where they started firing into Taylor's tightly packed ranks. Their aim was accurate, and the Confederates started to fall. Simultaneously, the 29th Pennsylvania was maneuvering into position,

The charge on the stone wall at the First Battle of Winchester. (Source: Library of Congress.)

but before they could even fire their weapons Colonel Colgrove of the 27th Indiana noticed a Confederate regiment was trying to flank the Pennsylvanians while shielded from their view by the terrain.

Colgrove set a courier over to warn the 29th, and they fell back twenty paces in response. Colgrove then attempted to move his two right companies backward so they would line up with the 29th, but as he did so, the eight other companies started to fall back on the order of their Lieutenant Colonel who had conflicting orders from Gordon to retreat. After just three volleys, the 27th Indiana broke and ran. The 29th Pennsylvania followed and tried to maintain formation, but in the process accidentally maneuvered into a gully and came under heavy fire. They traded one or two volleys with Taylor's men as they tried to retreat, but about two hundred of the Pennsylvanians and their Colonel were surrounded and captured. The 2nd Massachusetts, left alone, had no choice but to withdraw, which they did in good order despite their comrades falling as they were shot in the backs trying to march off the hill. With the line disintegrating, the 3rd Wisconsin, which had been on the left of the 2nd Massachusetts, was ordered to fall back.[15]

George Brooks watched the right wing crumbling. "We could plainly see the position of the right wing and a terrible contest was going on there," he wrote, "but being overpowered by superior numbers they gave way slowly at first but ending in general retreat, the rebels pursuing them yelling like demons."[16] General Williams flew about the field attempting to rally some members of the 27th Indiana and 29th Pennsylvania, but the frightened soldiers wouldn't stay. By 9:30 that morning, all resistance west of the turnpike had ceased.

15. Cozzens, *Shenandoah 1862*, 355-366.
16. *Brooks Diary.* May 25th, 1862.

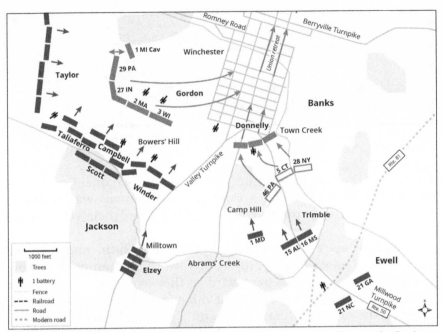

[First Winchester Battle Map 2.] Taylor's Brigade charges and the Union right flank gives way.

Donnelly's now exposed brigade was about to come under attack by Ewell again when Williams gave orders to fall back.[17] George Brooks remembered the route through town:

> The left wing . . . stood firm until a retreat was commanded, and fell back in perfect order, moving through the town amid the fire of round shot and shell—the deadly missiles falling all around us, and the rattle of musketry from windows of houses in which soldiers or citizens were concealed. The women also aided by throwing into our ranks hand grenades, and anything which would prove injurious. On reaching the end of town we met on our left a regiment of "Louisiana Tigers," who had pursued our right wing; but such was the order in which our regiment moved that they feared to advance too closely, and contented themselves with giving us a random volley or so, which from prudential motives we did not return.[18]

---

17. Cozzens, *Shenandoah 1862*, 367.
18. *Pennsylvania Daily Telegraph.* May 27th, 1862. His boast about the Tigers does not stand against their reputation, and it's more likely they didn't see the 46th or were heading elsewhere.

As the regiments fell back, the townswomen caused more harm than the Confederates, who were slow to follow. Women wounded and killed the Federal soldiers in cold blood as they moved through the city streets and did enough damage that, in some instances, soldiers returned fire. Corporal George C. Peoples of the 46th Pennsylvania and a soldier in Gordon's Brigade later testified that they had fired at civilians. Some members of the 3rd Wisconsin swore to avenge the civilian's hostility, saying that, "as the women of Winchester forgot on the day of our retreat that they were women, so shall we forget when we return."

South of town, Jackson ordered his men forward after the Yankees. The 3rd Wisconsin and 2nd Massachusetts found themselves facing fire down cross streets as they and the enemy advanced down parallel roads. The 29th Pennsylvania and 27th Indiana rushed through town as a mob while General Williams tried to reign in the frightened men.

Panic only grew when a building full of quartermaster supplies that couldn't be evacuated was set ablaze, and the flames quickly spread to adjacent warehouses and homes. Confederate soldiers broke ranks to fight the fire, while others turned to looting or dropped to the ground out of exhaustion. Others were caught up in the celebration of civilians who were unfurling Rebel flags and handing out food. By the time the Confederates reached the north side of town, some regiments only had a few men left.

Confederate regiments who made it through town mostly intact started after the retreating Yankees, but exhaustion was getting the better of them. After pursuing Banks' column for about five miles Jackson ordered a halt. He knew he stood a chance to destroy Banks then and there, but his men didn't have the energy to finish the task. At noon, the exhausted Confederates dropped to the ground and slept.

Banks continued his flight north, his only hope crossing the Potomac before Jackson could trap him there and crush him. Little did he know that his enemy had given up the chase. A few miles from town the infantry regained some order, with Gordon's Brigade moving on the turnpike, the 10th Maine guarding the left flank and Donnelly's Brigade marching east of the turnpike to guard the right flank. The artillery, cavalry, and civilians were less disciplined and pushed their way to the head of the column, sometimes knocking over infantrymen on their way.

Generals Banks rode along the column rallying his men, calming them as best he could. There were all aware of their precarious position. General Williams observed that their orderly retreat seemed fragile, and an aggressive cavalry attack or two by the enemy could throw the whole Union column into panic. But a serious attack never came. Confederate artillery and cavalry half-heartedly harassed the Union column, but did little damage, and so the Union line moved on.[19] George Brooks remembered the retreat:

> We then rapidly retreated keeping to the right of the road and passing through the fields, their artillery shelling us to within three miles of Martinsburg and then cavalry following, shooting and taking prisoners our stragglers. When about seven miles from Winchester our batteries were planted, our regiment drawn up in line of battle, three rousing cheers given and we began shelling them but soon moved on again. After that they pursued us with less rigor, evidently fearing reinforcements had arrived, which was quite a diversion in our favor. About 4 we reached Martinsburg . . .[20]

Upon reaching the Potomac at Williamsport, Banks had anticipated a traffic jam. The river, swollen from recent rain, was 300 feet wide and the ford was almost five feet deep. Only a single boat was available to ferry men across, and he immediately set it to work moving wounded and sick across the river. Wagons started to ford the river, but only the strongest horses could fight the current, and many weaker teams drowned. Still, Banks was encouraging, a Wisconsin officer commenting that, "General Banks was untiring in his efforts to bring our train safely over, even riding into the water to save mules that had lost their footing and were in danger of drowning."

The last of the exhausted infantry arrived on the muddy banks of the Potomac around 11:00 P.M. to find their regimental wagons either waiting to cross or lost, and so food and supplies were scarce. At 2:00 A.M., the regiments started to cross using the ferry.[21] George Brooks wrote of the 46th's arrival at the river:

> [At] about 9 reached the shore of the Potomac opposite Williamsport, finding the river too high to ford and no means of crossing save our ferry boat. This boat was reserved for ambulances to

---

19. Cozzens, *Shenandoah 1862*, 367-374.
20. *Brooks Diary*. May 25th, 1862.
21. Cozzens, *Shenandoah 1862*, 374-6.

carry over the sick, and fearing momentarily a descent upon the whole command, were ready clenched by fear. Teams hitched up and the horse teams endeavored to ford it, many getting across, and amid the wailing of women on the bank the swearing of drivers, the rushing of men etc it was a fearful night. Gen Banks moved among them encouraging everybody and by his influence greatly soothing the feelings and fears of all. Sending trunks along with an ambulance, I lay down under a wagon and went to sleep. Many of the men went to sleep out of sheer exhaustion, having made the unprecedented march of over 60 miles in two days had several skirmishes, fought one severe engagement, and remained without anything to eat from Friday evening at supper until Monday noon. Some however receiving supper on Sunday evening. It was a horrible day—a terrible night and never to be forgotten by those engaged in it.[22]

The next morning, Banks, far from demoralized, telegraphed the War Department to let them know his entire force was expected to cross in safety, and that the enemy had yet to appear. By midday, the last of his men crossed the Potomac. Brooks spent May 26th getting his men across the river:

MONDAY, MAY 26. Fine, clear morning. Crossing the river at daylight. I met Col Selfridge and went with him to town and after resting awhile went up the creek about a mile and finding a boat took it down to the shore and worked until noon ferrying my men across, after which giving the boat into other hands. Went to my good friends Mrs. Long's and received the first meal I had eaten since Friday evening and did not find myself half as hungry as I anticipated. By 3 o'clock nearly everything was across and our regiment was marched out to camp and the tents arriving in the evening were put up and we were again enjoying camp life being however somewhat deficient in clothing having lost our knapsacks, gum and wool blankets, in fact everything save the clothing on their backs and equipment, some even losing them. Took tea at Mrs. Long's and remained all night. Spent my evening pleasantly.

Total casualties sustained are hard to estimate due to conflicting and inaccurate reports. Official casualty reports lumped

---

22. *Brooks Diary.* May 25th, 1862.

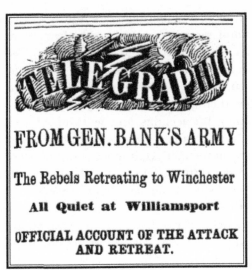

(Source: Pennsylvania Daily Telegraph
[Harrisburg, PA], May 27, 1862.)

the casualties from May 23rd to 25th together, making it unclear when casualties actually occurred. Some men later died from their wounds, while others who were missing or prisoners eventually returned.[23] George Brooks wrote home to the newspaper with an initial casualty report estimating five killed, forty-five wounded, and sixty missing:

> Our regiment is now lying in camp near Williamsport, having lost everything save their equipments, and not yet being able to procure clothing. The loss of our regiment is about five killed, forty-five wounded, many mortally, and sixty missing, many of whom countless fell out and were murdered. Our whole loss will be known in a few days and officially published.
>
> The loss of Company D, (Verbeke Rifles,) is as follows:
>
> Sergeant Philip Chubb, of Halifax, wounded and missing, at Winchester.
>
> Corporal Samuel O. Nace, of Halifax, slightly wounded.
>
> Private Samuel Thoman, of Georgetown, mortally wounded and left at Winchester.
>
> Private Thomas Lyne, of Carlisle, slightly wounded.
>
> Private Peter Flickner, of Wilkes Barre, missing and reported to be killed.

---

23. Cozzens, *Shenandoah 1862*, 377.

Private John Shelly, of New Buffalo, in hospital at Strasburg, missing.

Private Matthew Taylor, of Halifax, missing.[24]

❄ ❄ ❄

Chubb, Taylor, and Shelly, all missing, returned to the regiment. Nace and Lyne, slightly wounded, remained with the regiment. Peter Flickner had been captured on May 24th at Front Royal and spent thirteen months in Confederate hands before he was paroled and rejoined the regiment.[25] Samuel Thoman, a forty-eight year old miller, was the only casualty in Company D. His arm was shattered by an artillery shell, and he died of his wounds in Winchester the following day.[26]

Of the 879 men present in the 46th when their retreat began on May 24th, six were killed or never seen again. Seventy-eight were wounded, nine of whom died from their wounds. Thirteen were discharged due to the severity of their wounds. Twenty-one wounded were captured, and forty-eight others dropped out during the retreat because they weren't physically able to continue. Most who weren't able to complete the retreat were captured and would spend the next four to five months as prisoners, where three of them would die. Others, many of them the older men Colonel Knipe had accepted to quickly fill his regiment, were broken down by the physical demands placed on them and 26 were discharged. That meant that as an immediate result of the battle, the regiment's ranks reduced by 18 percent. After men returned from the hospital and imprisonment, that number decreased to a permanent loss of 6.5 percent.[27]

General Banks officially, and no doubt inaccurately, reported a loss of 71 killed, 243 wounded, and about 1,700 missing. Most of the missing were due to the capture of the 1st Maryland (U.S.) at Front Royal. Although many would eventually return, in the three days of retreat, Banks had lost approximately a third of his men, along with almost 10,000 small arms, half a million rounds of ammunition, about 17 tons worth of food and rations, and about $125,000 worth of quartermaster supplies. The massive loss of stores, and their subsequent capture by the Confederates, led to Banks' unfortunate nickname: "Commissary Banks."

24. *Pennsylvania Daily Telegraph.* May 27th, 1862.
25. Bates, *History of Pennsylvania Volunteers*, 382-410.
26. *Brooks Diary.* June 16, 1862.
27. Bradley, *Surviving Stonewall*, 115.

Official Report of General Banks.

WASHINGTON, May 26.—The following was received at the War Department at 11 o'clock to-night:

WILLIAMSPORT, May 26—4 P. M.

To the President:—I have the honor to report the safe arrival of my command last evening at this place at 10 o'clock, and the passage of the Fifth Corps across the river to-day with comparatively but little loss.

The loss of men killed, wounded and missing in the different combats in which my command has participated since the march from Strasburg, on the morning of the 24th instant, I am unable now to report, but I have great gratification in being able to represent that, although serious, it is much less than might have been anticipated, considering the great disparity of the forces engaged, and the long matured plans of the enemy, which aimed at nothing less than the entire capture of our force.

A detailed statement will be forwarded as soon as possible.

My command encountered the enemy in a constant succession of attacks, and in the well contested engagements at Strasburg, Middletown, Newton, at a point also between these places and at Winchester, the force of the enemy was estimated at about 15,000 men, with very strong artillery and cavalry supports, while my own force consisted of two brigades, less than 4000 strong all told, 15,000 cavalry, 10 Parrott guns and 6 smooth bores.

The substantial preservation of the entire supply train is a source of gratification. It numbered about five hundred wagons. On a forced march of fifty-three miles, thirty-five of which were performed in one day, subject to constant attack in front rear and flank, according to its position, by the enemy in full force, notwithstanding the panic of teamsters and the mischances of a river passage of more than three hundred yards, with slender preparations for ford and ferry, and more than fifty wagons were lost.

(Source: Pennsylvania Daily Telegraph [Harrisburg, PA], May 27, 1862.)

Jackson and Ewell suffered fewer casualties, reporting a combined loss of 68 killed, 329 wounded, and only three captured or missing. Jackson had missed the opportunity to destroy Banks entirely, but over the course of two days had provided his army with ample supplies and permanently changed Union strategy against Richmond. For the Union, in the months to come, the effects would be disastrous.[28]

---

28. Cozzens, *Shenandoah 1862*, 377.

CHAPTER NINE

Hope Delayed Maketh the Heart Sick

May 27–July 1, 1862

THE PANIC IN the Shenandoah Valley on May 25th was also felt by the War Department in Washington, D.C. At 7:00 A.M., General Banks had telegraphed that he was retreating from Winchester, but after hours had passed there was no further update. Failing to indicate where he was retreating to, President Lincoln and Secretary Stanton assumed Banks' destination was Harpers Ferry. Worried Jackson would strike there, a nervous Lincoln continued to direct the Corps of McDowell and Frémont toward the Shenandoah Valley in the hopes of placing them behind Jackson's advanced position and thus cutting him off.

Still, nerves in Washington didn't fully fray until General Geary, commanding a brigade in Virginia about fifty miles from the capital, unexpectedly telegraphed around 10:00 A.M. that he was surrounded on three sides. He said he had gathered the information from runaway slaves who weren't sure what Confederate command was approaching or how many they numbered. No Confederate forces of significant number were known to be in the area, so over the next few hours, Geary and the War Department exchanged telegraphs as they tried to determine exactly what was going on. If Geary was actually about to be attacked, it meant Washington was in danger. By mid afternoon, still without any word from Banks, Secretary Stanton lost his composure and telegraphed state governors asking for them to immediately send as many militia and volunteers to Washington as they could muster.

It wasn't until 2:40 P.M., and then with an update at 5:30 P.M., that Banks sent telegraphs informing Stanton and Lincoln that although he was retreating and expected Jackson to attack at Harpers Ferry, he thought his men and their wagons would

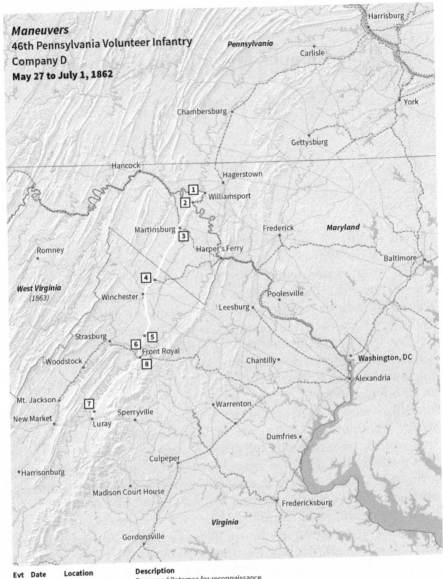

Maneuvers
46th Pennsylvania Volunteer Infantry
Company D
May 27 to July 1, 1862

Evt	Date	Location	Description
1	28-May	Williamsport	Recrossed Potomac for reconnaissance
2	31-May	Falling Waters	Crossed Potomac; bivouacked at Falling Waters
3	1-Jun	Martinsburg	Encamped
4	9-Jun	Stephenson's Depot	Bivouacked
5	10-Jun	Front Royal	Passed through Winchester; bivouacked seven miles from Front Royal
6	11-Jun	Front Royal	Camped one mile from Front Royal
7	29-Jun	Luray	Marched towards Luray, stopping after twenty-two miles
8	30-Jun	Front Royal	Expedition to Luray; returned to camp in Front Royal

cross the river safely at Williamsport. Knowing that Banks' army wouldn't be destroyed sufficiently calmed Stanton and the president's nerves, and by mid-evening they had also determined that Geary's claims seemed near impossible. Ensuring him that reinforcements were on the way, they told him to stay put. Still, lamps at the War Department burned late into the night as news continued to trickle in from Banks as he endeavored to ferry his men to the safety of Maryland.

For all of the panic on the 24th and 25th, the press was mostly calm in the following days. The majority of papers acknowledged Banks' movement back to Williamsport, but few called for alarm and reasoned that the damage to the Union effort was little. *The New York Times* of May 26th buried the story of the retreat on page eight, and the streets of Washington were quiet.

Banks' exhausted men, now resting in Williamsport, were proud of how they and their commander had handled the retreat and directed their anger over the need for it at Washington. Many felt that by ordering Banks' forces elsewhere, the War Department had placed them in an untenable situation. Banks, however, remained optimistic. In a letter home, he told his wife, "The escape of my command was a miracle. No victory could have produced so profound an impression upon the soldiers or the country. I am very glad that it was well done." The War Department agreed that Banks had done his duty.

From the Journal of Capt. George A. Brooks

TUESDAY, MAY 27. Glorious morning. Slept soundly with Captain Griffith and on going to camp was requested by the Col to give Mr. Donelson, one of the associate editors of the "Enquirer," a detailed statement of the battle and such scenes and incidents as transpired under my notice, which kept me keenly engaged all morning and did not reach the camp until after noon. Got there, pretty comfortably fixed in our tent and began making out my report of goods etc lost in action which occupied me all evening. Did not go to bed until late.

WEDNESDAY, MAY 28. Fine morning, day very warm. Was in town last before dark. Saw Billy Bell, George and Buch. Stayed all day with me. Went with Lieut Augustine to General Banks' on business. Got furlough for James O'Donnell and he went home to Harrisburg with the Col this morning. Would like to have gone myself but on account of so many desiring laid aside my claims. Whilst busy writing in the afternoon our regiment received orders to cross the river and were soon again in Dixie taking a position in the woods at the top of the hill—our trip considered somewhat of a dangerous one and everybody in doubt a kind of fearful feeling permeating the whole regiment. We are, I believe, to act as a reserve for the main body of pickets to rally on, but I cannot see the idea of placing infantry on such a position cut off as we are from all retreat if too sorely pressed. About 8 o'clock we received an order from General Williams to fall back and were just in the act of doing so when Col Selfridge rode up very much excited ordering "take arms left face march" so rapidly that his actions almost created a panic and I had some difficulty in having my men fall properly into their places. Came back to river very much frightened—that is the men were—and taking position along the bank prepared to give them a volley or two, our regiment meantime passing in the boat. Reached the Maryland [side] safely and went a mile to camp, the regiment under my command, Col, Lt Col and Major being absent.

❊ ❊ ❊

While Banks' men scouted into Maryland and recovered from their recent hard service and waited to re equip—many of them having lost everything on the retreat—McDowell and Frémont were in motion. Lincoln's plan to use their corps to trap Jackson was complicated and required maneuvering both corps from afar in a short period of time. The plan was altered from the start when Frémont, because of poor road conditions, moved north instead of east toward Harrisonburg as Lincoln had ordered.[1]

On May 28th, intelligence had indicated that Jackson had halted between Charlestown and Winchester, and an attack on Harpers Ferry seemed unlikely. General Shields' Division had made good progress on their return to the Valley, and by May 29th were located within a hard day's march of Front Royal. Their orders were to move toward Winchester, and Jackson, with all haste.

Stonewall Jackson was thankful for his success at Winchester. The victory solidified his reputation in the South as a hero. He let

---

1. Cozzens, *Shenandoah 1862*, 378-87.

his men rest on the 26th and 27th, and they took the opportunity to stuff themselves with captured food and refit their uniforms and equipment with abandoned Yankee stores. Spirits were high for Jackson's soldiers, and also for the pro-Southern residents of Winchester.

Jackson still had a job to do, though, and his May 16th orders from General Lee still stood. Lee had instructed that if Jackson were to defeat Banks in battle, he should then "drive him back toward the Potomac and create the impression, as far as practicable, that you design threatening that line." With that in mind, Jackson sent a brigade of troops toward Harpers Ferry on the evening of May 27th. There, they would demonstrate in the hopes of tricking Washington into thinking an attack on the critical railroad town—and then perhaps the capital—was imminent.

The following day, while Jackson moved his men around the hills outside Harpers Ferry, a messenger arrived with word that McDowell had left Fredericksburg and Shields was nearing Front Royal. Jackson was skeptical, but ordered his chief quartermaster to hasten the removal of Federal stores from Winchester and Front Royal.

Jackson's ruse outside of Harpers Ferry still wasn't having much effect by the evening of May 29th when a more reliable source indicated Frémont seemed to be moving toward Strasburg and Shields was indeed back in the Valley. In a jarring change of circumstance, the tables had turned, and Jackson was suddenly surrounded from all sides. 52,400 Federal soldiers from four commands—Shields, Frémont, Banks, and the garrison at Harpers Ferry—were poised to converge on Jackson's 16,000.

The morning of Friday, May 30th was clear and cool as Jackson found himself overwhelmed by the situation before him. Utterly outnumbered, and with his presence at Harpers Ferry failing to cause alarm, he started his men back toward Winchester in the mid-afternoon. A few hours earlier, General Shields' men had arrived at Front Royal and overwhelmed the Confederate garrison located there with ease. Simultaneously, Frémont was making good progress and covered twenty-eight miles in twelve hours. Jackson knew that by mid-morning on May 31st, Frémont and Shields would be able to converge on him at Strasburg. With overwhelming numbers, they could completely destroy his army.

But the 31st, clear and warm, passed without Shields or Frémont taking the opportunity. Shields had grown cautious after convincing himself that Confederate reinforcements were on the way to join Jackson, despite there being no intelligence substantiating his worries. He feared that if he turned his back to an approaching Confederate force to attack Strasburg, the results would be disastrous. He deliberated all day and had the luxury of doing so since his commander, McDowell, neglected to send him any orders to attack.

Continuing toward Strasburg, Frémont was stymied by poor roads caused by heavy rains, and after struggling all day to cross the Big North Mountain, he ended the day after midnight with his advance forces still five miles from his destination. The pause gave Jackson a full day to retreat, and after a somber and tiring march, his men spent the night of the 31st just north of Strasburg.[2]

Jackson had survived another day, but his situation was still dire, and the Confederate war effort outside of the Valley was seemingly about to crumble. Many thought the war would soon be over. On May 29th Confederate forces had started evacuating the important railroad junction of Cornith, Mississippi, leaving it to the approaching Union forces. Simultaneously, McClellan, set into motion by Lincoln after the defeat at Winchester, had pushed Joe Johnston's Confederates back to the suburbs of Richmond. On the 31st, Johnston was wounded in the Battle of Fair Oaks, and command was assumed by General Robert E. Lee, who had already been advising strategy.[3]

From the Journal of Capt. George A. Brooks

THURSDAY, MAY 29. Another beautiful day. Engaged all morning in writing. Wrote to "Telegraph"—Wm Sayford, A G Keet, Emily, Frank and Sarah Bridges informing them of our safe arrival from Winchester and some other business. In evening after dress parade went to town with Adjutant, took a glass of ale, roamed about the town, went to Col Donnelly's quarters in search of Witman, and with him arranged some business and affairs. Stopped at Mrs. Long's and in evening or about 9 o'clock returned to camp. Mr. Care, father of Sgt John Care, came to town today. Also Mr. Simmons, both from Harrisburg.

---

2. Cozzens, *Shenandoah 1862*, 389-415.
3. Wagner, *Desk Reference*, 19, 256.

FRIDAY, MAY 30. Fine morning. Spent it in fixing up my diary and arranging books etc. Have never yet received a letter from home or from anyone since April 14 save a few business letters. Col Knipe not yet back from Harrisburg. No news of any account stirring. Mr. Care left at noon preparatory to going home. Heavy cannonading in direction of Harpers Ferry and presume an engagement is going on.

Letter from Capt. George A. Brooks to Emily Brooks

46th Regt P.V.

Williamsport May 30

My Dear Emily,

In my last written on the 20th a day or so before we left our old camp near Strasburg, I averred my intention of never writing to you again, as I had already sent you five letters and not received one in reply since April 14. The recent stirring events of the past few days, and the severe engagement through which we have passed have however induced me to allay your fears, by assuring you of my safety and my passing through engagement unharmed, save a bullet hole in my coat, being thankful it is not in my skin. We are now lying in camp near Williamsport, very near home, but am unable to get there.

I do not know how long we may live here or remain in camp, but if we should stay very long I may get a chance to see you.

I have written to your father once and Frank twice, to neither of which I have received an answer. Yesterday I again wrote to Frank making inquiry as to whether you were alive or not and whether you were at home or in Coalmont [with my parents]. If they see proper to answer I may [get] an answer.

With my love to Willie and all I remain, in haste until I hear from you,

Your affectionate husband,

George

From the Journal of Capt. George A. Brooks

SATURDAY, MAY 31. Rained all night and morning very wet and despicable. Great surprise in camp over the reported intention of the Confederates invading Maryland at this point. Heavy firing this morning in direction of Harpers Ferry. Paymaster arrived. Had pay rolls soon squared and ready for pay. In afternoon received orders to march and about 5 o'clock started from camp in a drenching shower. On way to the ferry met Oliver Sees, now Mayor Sees, who came by order of Governor Curtin to take charge of our wounded and have them safely transported to Harrisburg and placed in hospital. Pennsylvania makes better provision for her wounded soldiers than any state in the Union. Whilst waiting on the shore for our boats, there being some delay, went in company with the Adjutant to Mrs. Long's. My good friends had a few moments chat, and in the meantime getting us a "bite." Did not get over river till after dark, when it began raining. Marched as far as Falling Waters, turned into a woods as dark as Ebony and lay down without covering on the bare ground no fires being allowed.

SUNDAY, JUNE 1. Rained hard all night, though I managed to secure some sleep but was wet to the skin. Such a muddy, wet and dusty set of men I never saw as our regiment. The Tenth Maine looked far more dejected and did not bear it half so patiently as our boys, it being the first night they have endured any hardship since entering the service. Still cloudy. Lay around camp all morning and by noon received orders to move forward, reaching Martinsburg about 2 o'clock. Never since entering the service have we received such a cordial greeting as was extended to us by the ladies of the town. Our march through the place was amidst one continued ovation, the waving of handkerchiefs and cheers of ladies gratefully acknowledged by the smiles and cheers of our boys. Martinsburg having felt the reigns of both sides can appreciate the superior of Union rule. Quartered in Catholic church, the same one we had occupied on a previous occasion. Securing it again however under protest. Very fine quarters. On our march through town saw Estelle, a lady friend with whom I have corresponded occasionally, having found in her a brave and devoted Union girl. In evening called on Estelle who was glad to see me, hearing I had been left behind.

✳✳✳

On June 1st, General Banks started his men back into Virginia and encamped that evening in Martinsburg. General Jackson continued his southward movement while he did his best to harass and slow Frémont's advance, but Frémont himself was more effective at slowing his own pace. By noon he had his men in line of battle, ready to attack Jackson, but paused. Perhaps the knowledge that Jackson had just badly whipped Banks entered into his mind. Whatever the cause for his reservations, nature soon took control when a violent thunderstorm let loose with lightning, wind, and hail. The mandated pause seemed to give Frémont time to gather his thoughts, and toward the end of the storm he sent out cavalry to enter Strasburg. They found that Jackson's men were already gone.

Meanwhile, at 3:00 P.M., Shields' Division finally started out. With the blessing of McDowell, Shields would execute his own plan to cut Jackson off once and for all by moving his men down Page Valley, parallel to the Shenandoah Valley, and burn the bridge near Conrad's Store. Jackson had used the bridge to cross the Shenandoah during his last retreat, and Shields reckoned that he would repeat the action this time, too.

The plan was doomed from the start. Not only did Shields make slow progress on the rain-soaked and inferior roads of Page Valley, but Jackson easily discerned Shields' intentions. Making exhausting but good time on the Valley Pike, Jackson's "foot cavalry" continued southward, repelling Frémont and outrunning Shields. Jackson burned the bridges across the Shenandoah, including the one at Conrad's Store, as he drew southward, preventing Shields from even attempting to join forces with Frémont and forcing him to continue south through Page Valley.

Jackson's evasion was successful, but it didn't come without a price. Jackson's army was on the verge of collapse as his footsore and hungry troops started succumbing to the rigors and mental strain of their retreat. Stragglers were captured by the score and men discarded equipment by the roadside as they attempted to keep up. Shoes fell apart and off the feet of soldiers without bias— Northerner and Southerner alike found themselves barefoot.

As Jackson's men fought just to continue on their dogged march, many wondered just how far south they were going. The answer would soon reveal itself. On the evening of June 5th, Jackson committed to a plan he had been considering for a few days. He would gather his forces at Port Republic, which was just northwest of Brown's Gap, and offered an excellent route through the Blue Ridge mountains should he want to leave the Valley. From Port Republic, Jackson could also attack Frémont's flank or rear should Frémont attempt to move on Staunton. Furthermore, the bridge over the North River at Port Republic was the only remaining means of communication and consolidation for Frémont and Shields. It wasn't a position Jackson could hold indefinitely, but that prospect didn't bother him. Having successfully tied up a large number of the enemy in the Valley, he considered his mission successful, and telegraphed Lee that perhaps he could be of help outside Richmond.[4]

From the Journal of Capt. George A. Brooks

MONDAY, JUNE 2. Rained hard all night and some indications of rain today. At 10 o'clock company were ordered out on picket duty, one fourth being sent out on Tuscarora pike under Sgt Wolf, one fourth out Harpers Ferry road under Lt Geiger and the balance of the company under my command on the Charlestown pike.[5] Borrowing horse from Major made rounds, after which remained in town, the most central position between pickets. Spent evening in company with Miss Dubbs, three very interesting very sociable and elegant singers, and having a fine mandolin we had some fine singing and passed a very pleasant evening. Did not go back out to picket station but remained in town, and roaming around went to bed about 10 o'clock. Raining very hard when we went to bed.

TUESDAY, JUNE 3. Rained all night. Relieved by Company "F". Had company in town by 10. News of the taking of Richmond by McClellan came last night and every body in a glorious mood.[6] In afternoon our baggage came up and we received our trunks and were enabled to dress up. Had a very fine dress parade in company with the NY Twenty-Eighth. Very fine effect for just as the band returned on "beat off" Gen Banks and staff rode after them, the regiment presenting arms whilst they rode by. Had a very fine effect. After our parade listened to music of Maine band. Very large, making most magnificent music. "Sounds from Home" was played with brilliant effect. In evening about 9 and 1/2 visited Estelle, spending very pleasant evening, she being very talkative and a strong, very patriotic Union girl. Col Knipe

---

4. Cozzens, *Shenandoah 1862*, 418-19, 421, 424, 431-2.
5. Samuel Wolf enlisted as 1st Sgt of Co D. Promoted to 2nd Lieutenant, he was killed in the Battle of Peach Tree Creek.
6. This, of course, was a rumor, and didn't actually happen.

returned from home bringing along a watch for Bernheisel and a long welcome letter from my dear Emily whom I have not heard from for so long.[7] What a joyous messenger. Before dusk saw Col Kenly, the hero of Front Royal, gave him a hearty shake and had a few moments conversation with him. Would give one half my existence could I exchange places with him—claim so justly the honors—and glory he has so nobly won.

WEDNESDAY, JUNE 4. Raining all day. Received long letter from Helen and Tuttie. Just like them, warm, friendly, lively and gay but strong in secession sentiments. Sat down and answered them sending picture of "Willie", "Emily", and self as a slight token of affection. If we ever retreat again—and God grant we may not—I think I will wind my way to the Potomac at Hancock and see my good friends there. In afternoon wrote to Mrs. Long, sending photograph album containing my picture in return for the many kindnesses I have experienced at her hands. Spent evening at Headquarters until 12 o'clock having no quarters of my own which I find very inconvenient.

THURSDAY, JUNE 5. Still raining. Have received no newspapers since our arrival here and the men are still without clothing and blankets. The Potomac was too high for train to cross, and ours is lying on the other side in Williamsport. As soon as our clothing comes we will probably move. Our new brigadier is running the machine with a rush. Spent most of day in and around Headquarters talking and making love to girls.[8] In evening called on Estelle but did not find her at home after which Lt Witman and I went on a skylarking expedition around town. At 10 went to General Crawford's and leaving "Ned" there, spent til 12 at Headquarters.

FRIDAY, JUNE 6. Cloudy morning, no rain. Forgot on Tuesday to mention the visit of P. K. Boyd, Hachuler and Geo Ball, three of our Harrisburg friends who returned next day. Have orders to march tomorrow morning but do not think it probable we will go. At noon received an elegant bouquet, tastefully arranged and beautifully decked in "red white and blue" with a note accompanying it from Estelle. Received it more as an evidence of her love for the cause than from any partiality for myself. Visited her in

---

7. First Sgt. Samuel Bernheisel. Died September 26, 1862 of wounds received in the Battle of Cedar Mountain.

8. "making love" in the 19th Century indicated courtship—slightly different from the modern usage.

evening as she requested and passed my time very pleasantly, finding her very intelligent and witty, with a beautiful eye but not very pretty. Before going had answered her note, thanking her in polite terms for her favor.

————•◦•————

Letter from Capt. George A. Brooks to Emily Brooks
Martinsburg Va. June 6

My Dear Emily,

Your letter brought by Col Knipe was the first one I have received since I was home, as you may well imagine how anxious I was.

Since our great retreat we have been very busy. On Saturday last we came to this place and tomorrow will move to Winchester, the scene of our old battle, memorable for two battles fought there. We have been so very busy, and will be until we reach Winchester, that I will have scarcely any time to write to you, but will answer you more fully tomorrow, or as soon as we get in camp where I will have an opportunity of writing. We have not been in camp for several days in fact since we left Williamsport. I am very well and we are all in the best of spirits hoping soon to have another brush at the rebels. The war is now drawing to a close and we will all soon be home. Give my love to all and believe me in great haste

Your affectionate husband,
George

I am in a great hurry merely writing a line

————•◦•————

From the Journal of Capt. George A. Brooks

SATURDAY, JUNE 7. Cloudy morning. Paymaster arrived last night and began paying us off which prevented our moving this morning, as a result boys all in high glee. Quartermaster arrived, says our train would be up by 12½, we would receive some of our clothing, but not all as a full supply could not be procured. Spent portion of evening at Estelle's, other company present. Find her married sister Mrs Baker a lively woman and her father and mother very pleasant. Letter from Sayford stating box containing clothing from officer which I had ordered had been sent and would soon reach us. Nothing stirring in the way of news, save reports of the taking or rather evacuation of Cornith by Beauregard and its occupation by Helleck. Frémont still closely pursuing Jackson.

✳ ✳ ✳

On June 6th Frémont and Jackson continued to spar as Jackson retreated south. In a small skirmish outside of Harrisonburg that otherwise would've been much like the other engagements during the retreat, Turner Ashby was killed while commanding some infantry. A Virginia soldier summed up his death, writing, "we had lost more by his fall than we had gained during the whole campaign."

Frémont did some reconnaissance on June 7th, sending forces within a half mile of Cross Keys. That night he called a council of war. Despite the ragged state of his men and the worry that Jackson outnumbered him, Frémont took an aggressive stance and decided to attack the following day.

Unfortunately, unknown to Frémont, the War Department also considered the Valley Campaign at an end, well aware that trying to catch Jackson before he was able to slip through the Blue Ridge mountains was useless. On June 8th, while Frémont was starting his men toward Jackson at Port Republic, Secretary of War Stanton was dictating orders that would keep Frémont at Harrisonburg and return Shields to McDowell's Corps at Fredericksburg. Neither corps commander received their new orders before it was too late. Referred to by Lincoln's private secretaries as "two unfortunate engagements," the fighting at Cross Keys on June 8th and Port Republic on the 9th resulted in a victory for Jackson that left 816 Confederate casualties and 1,002 Union. There was no tactical gain for either side.

On rainy June 10th, General Banks was on the way to Front Royal and Frémont's soggy, chilled troops turned their backs on Jackson and returned to Harrisonburg. The next day Jackson sent out his cavalry to harass Frémont. Combined with spreading rumors that Jackson was following with a large force, Frémont needed no further prodding, and continued to Middletown, where Banks had also arrived, on June 14. Shields took the week to move to Front Royal, where he remained until June 21st when he left to rejoin McDowell near Fredericksburg.

Pleased with how far he had pushed Union forces up the Valley, Jackson moved the main of his force a few miles south of

Port Republic, made camp, and let his men recuperate. Despite Jackson's request for more troops and to do more in the Valley and perhaps even attack northward, pushing the war into Pennsylvania and lessening pressure on Richmond, Lee was aware that the Union forces in the Valley posed little threat. He ordered Jackson to join him in Richmond on June 16th, needing every man possible to counterattack McClellan. Jackson's departure meant Banks and Frémont were now without an enemy.[9]

Banks' Corps spent all of June in camp, moving slowly south, and waiting to get new equipment. Languishing in the Valley, they were wet, hot, bored, and had grown tired of soldiering. Drunkenness and desertions were common, and about a dozen men slipped from the ranks of the 46th that month.[10]

While they waited, their division, still commanded by General Williams, was reorganized. The 3rd Brigade, commanded by Colonel Dudley Donnelly of the 28th New York, was re-designated the 1st Brigade and placed under the command of Brigadier General Samuel W. Crawford. The brigade officially consisted of the 5th Connecticut, 28th New York, 10th Maine, and 46th Pennsylvania.[11]

Crawford had been an army surgeon prior to the war and was the surgeon on duty at the time of the firing on Fort Sumter. He had no experience in the field or commanding troops, and he immediately started garnering a bad reputation. Following the command of General Williams, a fatherly figure, and Colonel Donnelly, a volunteer, Crawford's regular army discipline was unexpected and unwelcome to the volunteers serving under him.[12]

The 2nd Brigade was commanded by Brigadier-General George S. Greene, and the 3rd Brigade was led by Brigadier-General George S. Gordon.

From the Journal of Capt. George A. Brooks

SUNDAY, JUNE 8. Very fine morning. Dressed up and prepared for inspection. At 9 received orders to march. Occupied all morning in issuing clothing, though we did not receive any knapsacks or haversacks, both of which we need badly. Spent remainder

9. Cozzens, *Shenandoah 1862*, 439-42, 499, 502-7.
10. Bradley, *Surviving Stonewall*, 121.
11. Williams, *From the Cannon's Mouth*, 99.
12. Bradley, *Surviving Stonewall*, 120.

Brevent Major General Samuel Wylie Crawford. (Source: Library of Congress.)

of day in receiving money preparatory to sending it away. Sent home to Emily $250, besides a large quantity for my boys with Captain Morgan, who visits home. Towards evening in company of Lieut Caldwell took a walk around the town, many of the men under the influence of liquor. Had to put one of my own in the guard house. Had dress parade, after which marched two miles into the country and fired off our guns. Saw Oliver Sees of Harrisburg. In evening, after parade, went to Estelle's and came in early. Bade her goodbye, probably never to see her again until chance should throw us together, but ever will I remember her kindness and vivacity which relieved and cheered many moments for an oftentimes weary soldier. "May the snowy wings of innocence and love protect her" and God's choicest blessings be vouchsafed.

MONDAY, JUNE 9. Regular April day. Started at 7 o'clock and marching out of town, halted, and sent back guard for stragglers.

Again started at 9 and reached Stephenson's station—18 miles by 4 o'clock—camping on the ground on which our first or second skirmish took place, and which had been formerly occupied by our rebel friends. In evening at dress parade had McFarland and Orth reduced to the ranks.[13] Received papers containing Bank's official account. Sent one away. Pitched our tents, thinking we may stay a few days. Began raining about dark.

TUESDAY, JUNE 10. Rained nearly all night. Received orders to march and at 9 started in a drenching shower which continued nearly all day. Passed through Winchester, from which we had emerged over two weeks previous under very different circumstances. The town was nearly deserted by citizens but full of soldiers. Taking Front Royal road, passed our old battlefield where for over four hours death held her court and glutted herself with blood. It recalled many pleasant and very many unpleasant associations. The heavy rain had swollen the streams very much and we were compelled to wade two streams over knee deep, all the bridges being swept away. When within about seven miles of Front Royal we began quartering by companies in barns as we passed along the road and were soon all snugly bunked, everybody though being wet to the skin, and having no change of clothing save pantaloons which was all save shoes and blankets that we drew—built large fires to dry clothing—but many went to bed wet. It is strange what we can endure when forced to. Got good supper at dwelling house and took bed on floor. Farmer named Mr. Seech.

WEDNESDAY, JUNE 11. Cloudy morning but indications of a clear up. About 9 sun came out beautifully and at noon we again moved out, reaching Front Royal, or rather the river this side about 3 o'clock. Found bridge down and about faced marched one mile back and encamped. Field very muddy caused by the constant rains we have had. A large portion of McDowell's force lying at Front Royal. Do not know how long we will remain here. Saw the positions in which the brave Kenly made such a desperate stand against such heavy odds himself and regiment "never surrendering" and fighting to the last. In evening wrote busily until 10 o'clock.

---

13. "reduced to ranks" indicated demotion to Private, usually for disciplinary reasons. The cause was never given, but was probably related to the drinking mentioned on June 8th.

General Banks' forces camping outside of Front Royal. (Source: Library of Congress.)

THURSDAY, JUNE 12. Beautiful morning. Slept soundly and up early. No news of any account stirring. Anticipate moving tomorrow but in afternoon Lt Matthews, Lt Wm Caldwell and myself laid out a new camp. In evening wrote to Emily, sending home $320 and several small items. Also wrote to Wm Sayford, A. G. Keet, Estelle. Went to bed very late.

Letter from Capt. George A. Brooks to Emily Brooks
Camp near Front Royal, Va.
June 12, 1862

My Own Dear Emily,

We have been so hurried of late, constantly marching, and seldom waiting in one place long enough to allow us to get up an impromptu writing desk, that you really must excuse my delay.

I have twice written to you since I received your note from the Col though in a great hurry and this evening I know not how soon my [letter] may be interrupted by orders to "march" on the "long roll" sending its ominous sound out upon the night air. But I will write at any rate and stop when I <u>must</u>.

It is strange, very strange none of your letters have reached me, as you say you have answered every one. I have not received any from you since I left home except the one the Colonel brought along when he returned. I am sorry, however, that I laid all the blame upon you, but it is very provoking to wait two months for long looked for letters and one is apt to say what upon reflection he might regret. Will you pardon me? "To err is human" etc.

I am very much pleased to know that you spent such a happy time in the mountains after all the fears you had concerning what you so much dreaded—a visit to Huntingdon County, and will cheerfully consent to you going back whenever you please. It must have been an admirable place for Willie and he no doubt enjoyed himself very much running after geese, turkeys, etc. Such a life would be the <u>life</u> of him and I only wish I could behold his capers.

Father is a queer soul and I am glad you paid so much attention to Annie—she is a good girl, but has never had any advantages and father is so impatient. When I get home we will have her spend some time with us.

About the last of April I sent "Dixie" to your father, with George Hoffman, also a letter desiring him to take care of the horse and get him in pastures. By letting him run another year I could have got about $250 for him, and though I only used two or three times a week, yet I was afraid of spoiling him. Your father nor Frank have never yet answered a word though I have written three times concerning him. From some who came on from Harrisburg, I learn he is now kept as a regular riding horse, used by your pap, Frank, and whoever they choose to lend him to, never having made an effort to carry out my request. I sent him home merely to prevent his being used, but find he receives far more than I gave him, and so many riding a young horse will spoil him. I know Frank's disposition, and how he will use him, and consequently know I have already lost at least $100 by my foolishness in sending home at all. But so it goes. My absence is taken advantage of in every way, till I scarcely know who to trust with the few little business matters I have at home, and from present indications I will be poorer than when I started. Besides this month I was pretty well strapped having lost my overcoat etc on our retreat.

I intended making enough on my horse to pay Sen Kinnard the debt I owe him but am afraid the jig is up. How much money have you on hand of mine—laid by—including that which I last sent you. That is all we have so far saved and I do not know how soon the war may end. Trust the termination is not far off as we have passed through some pretty rough scenes and seen war in all its forms. I suppose you saw my letter in the "Telegraph." I had written it to you, but after it was done changed heading and sent it to the paper having no time to write another one—consequently you were cheated out of your treat but had as much as though you had read my hand.

From the Journal of Capt. George A. Brooks

FRIDAY, JUNE 13. Another fine morning. Did not move. Some indication of our staying here sometime but are patiently awaiting orders. Yesterday afternoon went down to river on Major's horse to cross but the float had been taken out. Consequently must postpone my visit. Very warm day. Received letter from Brumbaugh asking for descriptive list as he is discharged.[14] Rumors of a severe fight between Jackson and General Shield's forces, or rather Carroll's Brigade, which was severely cut up and had to retreat.[15]

Letter from Capt. George A. Brooks to Emily Brooks
Camp near Front Royal
June 13, 1862

Dear Emily,

This morning I sent you by Express a package containing $321. $16 of which is in envelopes, direct; $85 put up separately, which you will send to Samuel Wolf, Duncannon, Perry Co. Pa, and the other amounts you are to pay out of it I designated in my letter. The balance you will have put some place where I can draw it when I want it as it belongs to some of my boys who gave it to me for safekeeping.

I also send you a small box containing some articles I value very highly, and some clothing. You will please put away the most valuable things carefully. There is also a piece of shell

---

14. Private James A. Brumbaugh was discharged on July 3rd for disability.
15. This was the fighting at Cross Keys and Port Republic.

found on our battlefield, also a scabbard and powder flask. I merely send them as curiosities and to fill up the box.

Last night I received the box from Mr Sayford containing the articles you sent me or rather Frank from the store and also a letter containing pictures for Keet. I will write them in a few days.

I write in haste. Give my love to all.

Yours only

George

————◆◆◆————

From the Journal of Capt. George A. Brooks

SATURDAY, JUNE 14. Another fine morning. Knowing or judging from indications that we may stay here sometime the Major, Caldwell and self laid off the camp again. Very warm work. Eleven tents were struck and by noon we had a very fine looking camp comfortably located, so soon was confusion brought to order. In evening had dress parade, something very unusual on Saturday, after which wrote to Lew. Got signatures of most of the men to clothing book. Sat up reading until late.

SUNDAY, JUNE 15. Another glorious morning. At 4½ went to Shenandoah river and took a fine bath. After inspection took a ride in company with the Adjutant, crossing the river and visiting the village of Front Royal, also the different camps, about six or seven regiments being there. Front Royal is a small but shady pleasant little place situated near the foot of the mountain, the railroad to Manassas passing through it. Warm Springs, a summer resort, is not far from it. Since the beginning of the war it has been generally occupied by the rebels who have two fine large hospitals erected near the edge of the town. It is also famous as the position which Col Kenly of the Maryland First so desperately defended. Made a few purchases at the Sutlers and afterwards saw the famous Belle Boyd who has become so notorious.[16] She is not pretty but possesses a fine figure and splendid conversation powers. She is, take her all in all, quite a character. Visited the Eleventh Pennsylvania and saw Captain Wm Sees, a Harrisburgian who is looking remarkably well. Returned to camp by 4. Our own Sutler arrived with a large supply of goods.

---

16. Belle Boyd became famous for providing General Jackson with information regarding General Shields' forces in the area of Front Royal. She was imprisoned in late July of 1862, shortly after Brooks met her.

Belle Boyd, who spied for the Confederacy. (Source: Library of Congress.)

Had dress parade, after which religious service which I attended. Spent evening in conversation among friends and in sauntering around the camp. How I long to be in Harrisburg once more to enjoy the comforts of home and the sweet converse of my wife and prattling boy. Went to bed early.

MONDAY MORNING, JUNE 16. Very cool night and heavy dew. Received last evening a note from Surgeon Seland at Winchester giving me official information of Samuel Thoman, who died from a shattered arm, received by a shell in the engagement at Winchester May 25. He died on the 26th. Samuel was a good soldier, unusually dearly, and we are all very sorry to lose [him]. Received a note from my friend Small stating he would try and give me a pop call today. On Friday received a box from home containing clothing for Capt's Griffith and Mills and Lt Greatsake and also a photograph album and some other knick knacks from home for me. Also received in it a package of photographs of Willie, Emily and self which are very fine ones. No mail came today but sent a very heavy one off. Our mail arrangements very poor. Spent portion of evening in reading and remainder in "Vantoon."[17]

TUESDAY, JUNE 17. Very cool night and pleasant morning. Wrote Captain McCormick sending my photograph. Nothing unusual today. In afternoon Lt Taylor of the 84th P.V. from Harrisburg called to see me and stayed for tea. Did not go out on company drill leaving Lt Geiger exercise his bones. Had a very fine dress parade and after reading a while the Colonel sent for me to play "Vantoon" in which very foolish amusement I spent the remainder of my evening going to bed at 12.

WEDNESDAY, JUNE 18. Another glorious morning. Up before sunrise as usual. Received today a large bundle of papers and letter from Surgeon Md Vols. Sutler came up today with large supply. Day cool. In afternoon rain. Dr. Coover joined regiment today after two months absence on detached service.[18] Still no letter from home. In afternoon Witman spent a portion of his time with me—on Company drill—after dress parade. Spent a few hours in reading Byron and after tattoo wrote long letter to my dear Emily, Frank, Lew, and Dr McKee. By this time just as I am writing up my diary to date it is 12 o'clock—time to be in bed. With fervent prayer that God will shield and protect my dear wife and babe, I close the labors of another day.

Letter from Capt. George A. Brooks to Emily Brooks
Camp Near Front Royal, Va.
June 18, 1862

My own Dear Emily,

Since you have quit writing to me or at least since the mails have quit bringing your letters I scarcely know what to say, as if it exhausts one stock of ideas very much to write nearly a dozen without receiving any answers at all. However, I will write a few lines from which you may know something about my whereabouts and health.

We are now lying on the western side of the Shenandoah river, near Front Royal on the ground which the 1st Maryland under the brave Col Kenly so gallantly contested inch by inch against an overwhelming force of the rebels. The command of General

17. The Americanized name for "vingt-et-une," a French card game now known as Twenty-One or Blackjack.
18. Assistant Surgeon John B. Coover.

Shield's and a portion of General McDowell's are now lying opposite us but will move in a day or so. The day we arrived here the regiment in which Theodore is was lying on the other side of the river but left the next morning before I found it out. I should have liked to have seen him, but his regiment is now lying at Cattlet's Station, seventy-five miles from here near Manassas Junction. If I can will slip down.

We are snugly encamped, have everything comfortable fixed since our late disastrous retreat—tomorrow will receive our knapsacks etc, and will then be ready and eager to give our rebel friends another brush. I suppose, however, you would prefer our keeping out of one, though you need to be afraid of "your Georgie" coming home for secession bullets have yet been made for him, though he has made some narrow escapes.

You will laugh Emily when you see my diary and read of my adventures among the girls through the country we have traveled. Being young I readily pass for single and have had some rich fun. Have several notes I will show you when I return to show what a good looking, attractive husband you have, and what a siege has been laid by some fair southern damsels against your peace. But they didn't know I had a dear little wife and boy and I enjoying fun, didn't tell them. We must have some sport and while others drink I amuse myself in that way. Which surely is not very wrong, is it? I am <u>faithful</u>, <u>true</u> -

Enclosed I send you $15 which you will have <u>expressed</u> to "Mrs. Nancy Griffin, Care of Geo. W. Brubaker, Millersburg. Dauphin County, Pa," as soon as you can as she may need it. Please send me an account of how you transacted the business I have entrusted to you. If Mrs. Noonan has received her money or her husband did, do not give her $26.

How is Maggie Etter and when did you hear from her. Remember me kindly.

Write to me very often my dear for I am very lonesome and long to see and hear from you and our dear boy. It seems so long until this horrid war will end. But trust and pray.

Give my love to pap and mom and all the boys etc. Remember me very kindly to Dr. Hay and family, Valle Hummel and family, and all friends, and believe me as ever

Your affectionate husband,
George

THURSDAY, JUNE 19. Nothing very strange today. Rumors of Shields moving away and Jackson advancing from Luray but not very reliable. Our quartermaster detailed to act as Brigade Q.M. and to receive all the stores in Front Royal and transport them at once to this side of the river. No mail.

FRIDAY, JUNE 20. Fine morning. Day very warm. Nothing beyond the usual routine today. Gen. Shields' command leaving Front Royal today for Catlett Station. Gen. McDowell's two brigades which had been lying there having moved yesterday. Loaned Caddie my belt and pistol. Rumors of a change in staff and instructions by Col that I would be promoted to the position of Adjutant General of the Brigade. Trust it may not be as I would be sorry to leave the regiment to go under a man whom I did not like, and who is so very unpopular as General Crawford. There are many however who would gladly embrace the chance. Just before going to bed Col sent for me to select a man for recruiting service but would not allow me to go for a few days.

SATURDAY, JUNE 21. Glorious morning. Col offered me position of A.A.G on Gen Crawford's staff which was certainly a compliment but which I very respectfully declined. Promotion to such a position would be very credible and speak volumes at home, but to leave a company in which I have such a deep interest a regiment like the Forty-Sixth and the many friends I have bound to me by those social ties which camp life renders so valuable for a position under a man so very unpopular, is more than I am at present desirous of doing. I may be wrong, may have neglected an opportunity, but have carefully counted the cost and accordingly refuse. There are plenty, however, who would cheerfully embrace the chance. In afternoon rode with Major to Front Royal and spent a few hours there. Considerable excitement and fear of an attack, our signal corps having been fired upon and driven in. All soon quieted, it being the work of guerrillas. Nobody hurt. Came back by 5 o'clock having had a pleasant jaunt and spent some time with "Caddie." Went to bed early.

SUNDAY, JUNE 22. Another fine morning. A small billet-doux from my duck [sic] brought by Sutler. Officer of the day. Lt Care starting home, wrote to Emily with him and sent word to many friends. Spent afternoon in reading Byron, evening in reading Bible and Mrs. Norton's poems.

MONDAY, JUNE 23. Fine morning. Nothing stirring, strange or startling. Spent morning in reading. In afternoon a terrible thunder gust came up and the rain came down in torrents drowning many of the boys out and giving our camp quite a jolly appearance. Our own tent pretty dry but some of our neighbors fared badly. Chaplain started for our mail this morning, not having any for over a week but it did not come this evening. Wrote to Emily. Spent evening at Col's quarters. Wrote our charges against several men who had become drunk on guard whilst I was officer of the day. All quiet along the Shenandoah.

TUESDAY, JUNE 24. Rained very hard all night and some of the most terrific thunder I have ever heard. So close was it that the concussion threw down and scattered around the gun stacks of the guard and on picking them up, many of them were shocked until their hair stood up, and so frightened were they that some even refused to go on guard. Still raining hard and continued until afternoon. Chaplain arrived bringing mail, but no letters for me, save one from an anxious brother for information relative to Philip Chubb.[19] Twas strange, very strange, I have none from home though I know they are sent. Wrote again to Emily determined to persevere and also wrote to Jeremiah Chubb. This afternoon Best's battery was placed in position on the hills commanding the passage of the river located in front of our camp, which looks like war, although everything is apparently quiet. As war, however, is a very uncertain vocation, we may very soon have livelier times than we anticipate. A calm generally precedes a storm and as there is such a dearth in news throughout the whole country it may only be the precursor of grand and glorious victories which will give a death blow to the hydra of secession and virtually end the war, that we may return to our homes and once more enjoy the swirl of pleasures and contentment of peace.

19. Private Philip Chubb served in Co. D from muster in to muster out in July of 1865.

Letter from Capt. George A. Brooks to Emily Brooks
Near Front Royal, Va
Tuesday evening June 24, 1862

My Dear Emily,

This afternoon we received another mail, but no little "messenger of love" did it contain for me—no news from home of my precious dear ones. Truly Emily if "hope delayed maketh the heart sick," I would indeed be beyond recovery. For over two months, though writing to you every few days, I have not received <u>from</u> you a single word save the letter which Col. Knipe brought, and though I do not blame you, yet I must complain to you of the manner in which Uncle Sam manages his <u>mail</u> arrangements. They are conducted in a way highly prejudicial to my <u>female</u> consolations, but I trust your energy and perseverance will overcome all. Continue to write and one will soon reach me some way or other. Patience and perseverance are good traits.

Since writing to you on Sunday nothing on any particular account has transpired worth noting. We are still lying here in camp awaiting the arrival of our friend Jackson, but are afraid he will not give us a call.

A few days, on Saturday I believe, the position of assistant adjutant General on Gen. Crawford's staff became vacant, and through Col. Knipe it was tendered to me. This was very flattering, a high compliment, as to be attached to a staff in such a capacity is a high and important position—but after a days consideration I declined and another one has not been selected. I had many reasons for declining. In the first place, Gen Crawford is becoming very unpopular on account of his ridiculous orders, show, flourish, etc and secondly because I did not wish to leave a company who have been true to me as the needle to the pole, men in whom I have every confidence who have been tried and not found wanting and because I did not wish to leave the gallant old 46th and the many friends I have among its officers and men. Perhaps I may have done wrong, perhaps when such a promotion offered I should have accepted it, but I have simply done my best, and trust I may have done right.

Really, Emily, I am tired of the war, or I may better say tired of being away from Willie and you so long. Tis true we are in a holy, glorious cause, and I have no wish to leave the service of my country while young willing hearts are needed, but none would more gladly than myself hail the termination of this horrible contest. I confidently trust, however, the end is not far distant, that our gallant McClellan, with the aid of God, may succeed in scattering to the winds the upholders of so unholy a rebellion, and the wand of peace may soon again hold universal, sway throughout the length and breadth of old America.

Today I sent an order to Jeremiah Chubb (brother of Philip Chubb in my company who was taken prisoner), for thirty-four dollars ($34) which you will please pay when he presents it. Keeping the order. We will make a business woman of you somehow.

Give my love to pap, mom, and boys. Remember me very kindly to all our friends. Tell them to write to me. You write soon, very soon. With love for Willie and yourself and a thousand kisses for each I remain

Truly Yours
George

Write to me very often my dear. Some of them will come and I expect them in a burst.

———•◆•———

From the Journal of Capt. George A. Brooks

WEDNESDAY, JUNE 25. Bright and clear morning but air cool. Hailed during night. Ground very muddy and stream much swollen. Boys catching fish in abundance. Took a walk with Lieutenant Alex Caldwell to the heights on which our artillery is planted, and having a Marine glass along had a fine view of the country. No indications of an enemy. Returned before noon. After dinner took a nap and on wakening found a letter from Wm Reigle, one of my boys sick in Frederick Md.[20] Wm Swayer, one of my men, a steady fellow, has been missing since Tuesday noon and no one can account for him.[21] Greatly fear that he has been accidentally drowned. Lt Geiger, being officer of the guard, went on dress parade alone.

THURSDAY, JUNE 26. Another fine morning and very warm day. This morning procured clothing etc for men, and after dinner

---

20. Private William Reigle returned to the company and served until muster out.
21. Private William Swayer is listed on the muster rolls as having deserted June 27, 1862 at Front Royal.

issued it. All in good spirits at idea of getting knapsacks, canteens etc. This afternoon mail came bringing me no word from home. Received however a letter from Reigle asking for his descriptive list etc, preparatory to a discharge. Sent it to him. In afternoon, all the field officers being absent, was placed in command of regiment. In evening was not on dress parade but took ride with Dr Rodgers, trying the muscle of his new mare. She trots well and will make a very fine animal. In evening, feeling tired, went to bed late or I mean early. How I long for home.

FRIDAY, JUNE 27. Formed under arms at daybreak and marched down to river followed by Twenty-eighth NY. Ascertained that whole division had been ordered out. After a few minutes marching came back to camp. Very fine morning. This afternoon again in command of camp. Dr. Wilson of Hancock came on a visit. Will stay till tomorrow. All very glad to see him. In evening wrote to Bridges at Hancock and will send letter by Dr. Wilson in morning. Nothing stirring along the border. Gen Pope who made himself so famous in the west and is a progressive man has been assigned the command of all the forces in the valley of Virginia, embracing the commands of Franz Sigel and Banks' infantry, cavalry and artillery and we are confident in trust this will be productive of beneficial results.

SATURDAY, JUNE 28. Glorious morning. Called to arms at daylight and with the Twenty-eighth NY marched to General Williams' Headquarters. Our band gave him a serenade before he was up. It was quite a surprise. Officer of the day. Wrote to Emily. No mail and no news by papers of stirring importance, save the anticipated attack on Richmond by McClellan. What a terrible loss of life must ensue. The Confederates fight with a determination worthy of a bitter cause, but must yield, our old government must be sustained, but at what an awful loss of life. How many hearts will bleed, how many homes will be made desolate, war especially civil war is terrible, and when the basic passions of men become excited, they are worse than brutes. How gladly I would go home, if I could only do so honorably.

SUNDAY MORNING, JUNE 29. Last evening received orders to cook two days and be ready to march by daylight. At daybreak fell in under arms with haversacks and were soon on our way towards Luray. The Tenth Maine and Twenty-eighth New York went the regular road whilst the Fifth Connecticut our own regiment, two pieces of artillery—Hampton's—and a squadron of cavalry took a back road, very rough and rugged, near the mountain. Progress very slow having skirmishers out all the way. At noon it began raining and rained very hard all afternoon. Marched about 22 miles, not stopping till after dark, and having to grope our way among pines and made a bed in the mud. Wet to the skin everybody and "muttered curses loud and deep" went on record against our Brigade Commander for making such an outrageous, ridiculous move, and marching men so rapidly so great a distance for nothing. But a war sometimes places men in positions God never intended them to adorn. Took a good drink of whiskey—something very unusual, and being badly galled, did not sleep very sound until after midnight when I snoozed as comfortably as though I was at home in a feather bed.

MONDAY, JUNE 30. Did not rain much last night. Indications of a clear up this morning. Boys hard to get up and everybody greatly incensed at the idea of advancing. Many were unable to proceed further—in fact yesterday was one of the most fatiguing marches we have ever made. Marched towards Luray and when within five miles halted in a woods our cavalry going ahead alone with battery. Charged into town and through Luray finding three companies of rebel cavalry and taking four prisoners. One of the Vermont cavalry was instantly killed and another badly wounded. While we were lying in the woods the 1st Sergeant of Company "K" Tenth Maine was killed by the accidental discharge of his piece. Poor fellow. At noon the wonderful reconnaissance had been made. A whole brigade of infantry accompanied by artillery and several regiments of cavalry had marched over twenty-five miles and found three small companies of cavalry, the mountain labored and brought forth a mouse, and General Crawford was satisfied. We started on our return and after a very hard march—feetsore [sic] and weary, reached camp by 11 o'clock with nearly all our regiment. Brought all my own company in camp save four men. Had supper ready and after a good cup of coffee all the men gladly went to bed.

TUESDAY, JULY 1. Slept after sunrise this morning which I have not done for a long time. Boys very tired but inspection being ordered this afternoon began cleaning guns etc. Mail came bringing letter from Emily written June 7, the first I have received by mail since April 13 1862. Very glad to hear from home. In afternoon

A rougher looking Captain Brooks posed for this photo, likely during the summer of 1862. (Source: Author's Collection.)

at 5 o'clock were mustered for pay. In evening wrote to Valentine Hummel and pass remainder of time in reading until Adjutant came who gave a terrible account of things near Richmond.[22] He seemed very much discouraged but I think without cause. I have every confidence in our little Mac and believe he will win a decisive victory.

✳ ✳ ✳

"Terrible" was an accurate word for describing news from Richmond. McClellan was heavily engaged with Lee and Jackson in what would come to be known as the Seven Days' Battles. None of the battles around Richmond resulted in a stunning victory for Lee, but his ruthless fighting succeeded in intimidating McClellan.

---

22. Valentine Hummel was a friend of Brooks' and a prominent citizen of Harrisburg.

Still fearing he was outnumbered, McClellan started withdrawing troops from the Peninsula, effectively ending the threat to Richmond, the Peninsula Campaign, and also the North's hopes that the war would soon be over.[23]

McClellan's failure showed the true cost of Stonewall Jackson's campaigning in the Shenandoah Valley. Prior to the Battle of Winchester, Jackson's victories had only served to boost Southern morale, but Banks' retreat triggered a reaction that proved Jackson's efforts in the Valley a success. Lincoln's decision to divert McDowell's 40,000 men from supporting McClellan outside of Richmond had significantly hindered McClellan's ability to attack, and had given Lee precious time to strengthen fortifications. Jackson's small force, which would have been inconsequential had Lincoln concentrated all of his available forces and taken Richmond, had prevented that very circumstance. Lincoln realized his error in early June, but by then it was already too late. With Crawford's late June reconnaissance having proved there were no Confederates within striking distance in the Shenandoah Valley, the Union army remained idle in the summer heat while the cavalry scouted south and kept an eye on Richmond and Gordonsville, waiting for Stonewall Jackson's return.[24]

23. Wagner, *Desk Reference*, 256-8.
24. Cozzens, *Shenandoah 1862*, 508-9.

CHAPTER TEN

Our Course is Just

July 2–29, 1862

-------◦•◎•◦-------

T AKING THE CONFEDERATE capital of Richmond had seemed all but certain in June, but when McClellan's advance stalled late in the month, hopes for a quick victory sank. Although General Lee had successfully beaten the Federals back from the suburbs of Richmond, his army was pinned there with fewer than 70,000 men. McClellan, with his 100,000 soldiers, and 42,000 more Federal troops available a few days' march away in the Valley, was still a formidable opponent. If McClellan renewed his advance, Lee would find himself surrounded by a force that outnumbered his two to one.[1]

Disappointment over McClellan's latest failure was shared by civilian, common soldier, and commander alike. Even before the discouraging news from Richmond arrived, President Lincoln was already reassessing his strategy. Commanding Banks, Frémont, and McDowell, as well as some smaller scattered organizations in the Shenandoah Valley, had proven too difficult. In late June, Lincoln organized all of the separate commands into a new army called the Army of Virginia. Major General John Pope, a career officer who had gained accolades for his accomplishments in the Western theater earlier in the year, assumed command of the 42,000 man organization.

General Frémont's Corps was designated the 1st Corps of Pope's army, but Frémont refused to serve under Pope, who was technically his junior, and resigned. General Franz Sigel took his place. Sigel lacked a stellar military record but immediately gained the favor of his mostly German-American soldiers. The 46th

---

1. Catton, Bruce. *The centennial history of the Civil War: Terrible Swift Sword.* Doubleday, 1963. 389.

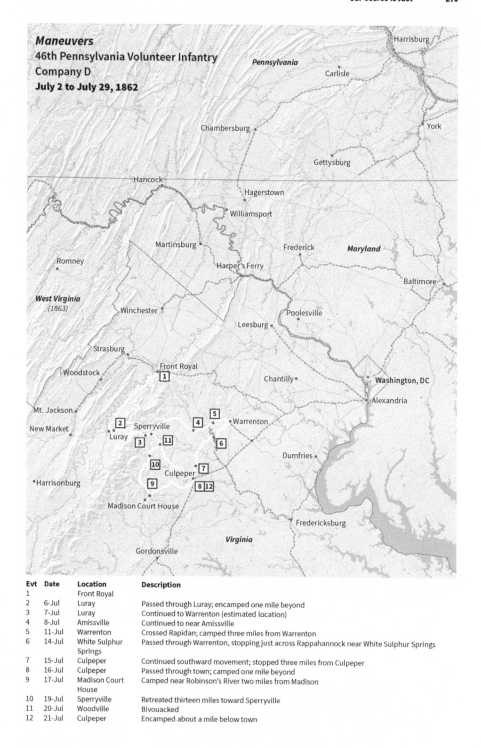

Maneuvers
46th Pennsylvania Volunteer Infantry
Company D
July 2 to July 29, 1862

Evt	Date	Location	Description
1		Front Royal	
2	6-Jul	Luray	Passed through Luray; encamped one mile beyond
3	7-Jul	Luray	Continued to Warrenton (estimated location)
4	8-Jul	Amissville	Continued to near Amissville
5	11-Jul	Warrenton	Crossed Rapidan; camped three miles from Warrenton
6	14-Jul	White Sulphur Springs	Passed through Warrenton, stopping just across Rappahannock near White Sulphur Springs
7	15-Jul	Culpeper	Continued southward movement; stopped three miles from Culpeper
8	16-Jul	Culpeper	Passed through town; camped one mile beyond
9	17-Jul	Madison Court House	Camped near Robinson's River two miles from Madison
10	19-Jul	Sperryville	Retreated thirteen miles toward Sperryville
11	20-Jul	Woodville	Bivouacked
12	21-Jul	Culpeper	Encamped about a mile below town

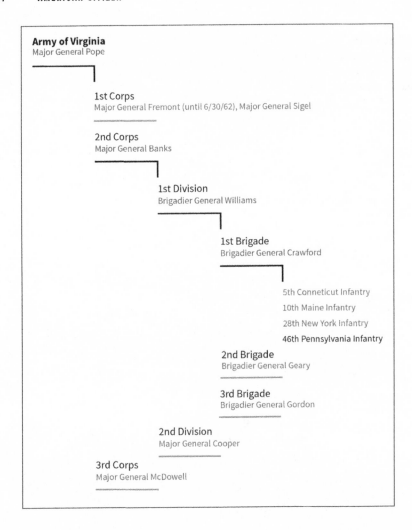

Army of Virginia
Major General Pope

1st Corps
Major General Fremont (until 6/30/62), Major General Sigel

2nd Corps
Major General Banks

1st Division
Brigadier General Williams

1st Brigade
Brigadier General Crawford

5th Conneticut Infantry
10th Maine Infantry
28th New York Infantry
46th Pennsylvania Infantry

2nd Brigade
Brigadier General Geary

3rd Brigade
Brigadier General Gordon

2nd Division
Major General Cooper

3rd Corps
Major General McDowell

Pennsylvania's brigade remained the 1st Brigade (Crawford's) of the 1st Division (Williams') of Banks' Corps, which was now designated as the 2nd Corps. McDowell's Corps was now the 3rd.

General Pope was brought east by Lincoln not only to better command the troops north of Richmond and hopefully pair with McClellan in Lee's destruction, but also to wage a new kind of war. Until Pope's arrival, the war in the east had been conducted on civil terms, under which the civilian population of Virginia had been mostly protected from the hardships of war. Union soldiers had been barred from taking private property or food, owners of property destroyed by the army were refunded, and guerrilla

Major General John Pope. (Source: National Archives and Records Adminsitration.)

attacks by civilians were mostly unpunished. By the summer of 1862, however, with victory nowhere in sight, northern Republicans and President Lincoln felt a harder strategy had to be put in place to make the citizens of Virginia feel the results of their support of the rebellion. The notion that the north could win the war without creating deep and lasting scars on the south had finally subsided.

After assuming command, Pope issued a series of orders that outlined the new conduct of his army. Citizens in occupied territory were now to be held responsible for any damage done by guerrillas, and captured guerrillas were to be executed along with everyone who aided them. Shots fired at Union soldiers from private homes, a phenomenon witnessed first hand by the 46th Pennsylvania at Winchester, would result in the inhabitants being arrested and the house destroyed. Disloyal citizens would be driven from Union territory and executed without trial if they returned. Citizens in Union territory who stayed would have to take an oath of allegiance and violators would be shot. Finally, and most pertinent to the rank and file soldier, the army was given permission to forage and confiscate food from the surrounding countryside.

By the end of the war, the conduct of Pope's army was more or less normal operating procedure for an army campaigning in enemy territory, but in the summer of 1862, Southerners were aghast and declared John Pope a monster. In truth, the policies had more of a mental effect than a physical one, and were never fully implemented. Innocent noncombatants were never shot, though the threat was often made.

Paused in the Shenandoah Valley in early July, George Brooks and the 46th Pennsylvania, impatient and homesick, would soon experience the aggression and ambition of their new commander and put his policies into practice. In early July, General Pope had written General McClellan to strategize how best to defeat Lee's outnumbered army which lay squarely between the two Union commands. McClellan's response indicated that Pope should concentrate his army and attempt to divert Lee's attention from the Peninsula. However, McClellan had no intention of taking the offense against Richmond. Saying he was unsure if Lee would attack on the Peninsula or instead move on Washington, McClellan intended to stay put and "carefully watch for any fault committed by the enemy and take advantage of it." Lee would get to make the first move.

Coordination between two isolated armies would have been difficult enough, but doing so for Pope and McClellan was impossible. The two commanders disliked and distrusted each other passionately. McClellan expected Pope to fail, and Pope expected that McClellan would let him. Soon, they would prove one another correct.[2]

From the Journal of Capt. George A. Brooks

WEDNESDAY, JULY 2. Raining. This morning Saml Deafenbaugh returned from "desertion" and looks very much reduced.[3] Had him sent to guardhouse by order of Col, and must prefer charges against him. In afternoon Lieut Care, Major Matthews, Billy Bell, and James Gowan came, Care bringing me a small bundle and

---

2. Catton, *Terrible Swift Sword*, 383-4, 386.
3. Private Samuel A. Deafenbaugh. Charges were never pressed and it's unclear what "desertion" in quotes means. He served until Muster Out in 1865.

several letters from Emily. Was very glad to hear from her and all the folks in Harrisburg. The albums Frank sent came very opportunely as they were all wanted save one and the Handkerchiefs were just the things I needed. How much I felt like going home on reading Emily's letters. Glad to see Billy and Gowan. Care brought no recruits along save one, my old three month's friend John C Major, who came to join my company. In evening wrote to Frank, long letter and also to Emily: wrote a short letter to my old friend Jennings. After 1 o'clock when I got to bed.

———◆•◆•◆———

Letter from Capt. George A. Brooks to Emily Brooks
Camp near Front Royal, Va.
July 2, 1862

My Own Dear Emily,

I was glad, very glad to receive from you, by Lieutenant Care, who came today at noon, two cheering letters, and although on Sunday morning we started at 4 o'clock, marched to Luray and back again on Monday night by 11 o'clock, a distance of over fifty miles, since which I have been writing steadily getting my pay rolls ready, and though it is now twenty minutes after 11 o'clock still, having an opportunity of sending a note by Mr. Bell, who goes home tomorrow, I write tonight. It is strange I do not receive your letters, but we suppose all our mail matter is still lying in the P.O. at Washington and wrote yesterday requesting them to send it on at once, so we soon expect to receive a large batch.

I am sorry you accuse me of writing such <u>unfeeling</u> letters, saying I have no <u>confidence</u> in you, etc, merely because I state from time to time that I do not receive them and wonder why. Oh, Emily, if you had to live away from home enduring all kinds of hardships, sleeping on the hard ground night after night with only the sky for a covering, and no Emily or Willie to cheer my loneliness, and if I do become somewhat impatient when only hearing from you in three months <u>once</u>, surely you ought to excuse me. I am also very sorry I so wounded your father's feelings. I may have written hastily but I wrote to Frank so often and he did not answer, and had no information in reference to what had been done with "Dixie" or to contradict the stories I heard, that I was inclined to believe he had been badly treated. If I did a wrong I of course will cheerfully apologize. I am glad to hear by Mr. Bell that he is so well treated and looks so finely. Lt. Care also spoke of him and consequently I may make something of him yet as he is a [young] blooded horse.

In reference to renting the rooms I would give you the same advice I did in the Spring—that is—to do so by all means if you have a chance. I do not want you to live alone—would prefer to have you spend your time between my home and your own until my return when we will permanently settle somewhere, very soon, well if we must go to the "far West." You could also go and see Grandma Brooks, Mrs. Matea and many more of my relatives who would give you a more cordial reception than they did me, or would, though it is a long time since I have troubled any of them. Misfortunes have made me too proud. Do by all means break up housekeeping, and if you do stay at home, do not work hard but pay your boarding—you are able. Go and see my good old Grandmother at once, and cultivate the acquaintance of my friends, and they will be pleased.

I will do as you say, order no more pictures. I got mine for distribution among my friends many of whom want them here—and have received some in return. I will not however, in the future be so extravagant. On July 15 I want you to give Sen. some money. I will write to you how much and want you to give it to him yourself, not through the hands of other persons. He will do what is right. I want to pay him as soon as I can but we must keep some ahead. Please inform me by <u>return mail</u> or get Frank to do it of <u>how much we have</u>. Just have him send a statement of my account. I am glad to hear Lew is going into business and must help him all I can. Trust he may be more lucky than I was. However my day will come, we will yet prosper. Will you please send me M. M. Strickler's letter inquiring my address. He is an old friend of my boyhood days of whom you have frequently heard me speak, but which some differences estranged. I wonder what he wants, as I owe <u>him</u> nothing.

I am sorry to hear of your health being so poor and wish you would consult the doctor at once. Do not delay such matters as they might result seriously and I would lose you for the world. When you next write I want to know if you have seen him.

But I must close, and write an answer the remainder of your letter tomorrow or next day—yes I will celebrate part of my 4th in such an appropriate way. Write to me often, never less than three times a week, and I will answer as often as I can.

Love to pap, mom and boys—a thousand kisses to Willie and Emily. Believe me as ever

Your affectionate husband,
George
Direct
Capt Geo A Brooks
Co. "D" 46th Regt P.V.
Banks Corps, Army of Virginia
Washington, D.C.

From the Journal of Capt. George A. Brooks

THURSDAY, JULY 3. Fine morning. Cleared up beautifully. On taking my letters up to Bill found he did not intend going. In afternoon Lt. Ned came and informed me that he was going home. Accordingly sent my letters along with him and word to all my friends. Spent portion of afternoon in Colonel's quarters with Bill and Gowan. Discouraging news from Richmond and fears of McClellan's defeat has made a great movement. In afternoon charged all my issues of clothing and finished my pay rolls, on which I have worked hard for two days. Had a fine dress parade then inspection. Several of Pope's Corps witnessing it and having come to inspect our Regiment. Greatly pleased our appearance. Spent evening sociably. Field books and chair came. Went to bed early.

FRIDAY, JULY 4. A fine morning. Up by day break and shortly after a national salute was fired by our battery. Band played "Star Spangled Banner," colors were raised and a round fired by Corps. Very discouraging news from Richmond, McClellan has undoubtedly been defeated and it has caused somewhat of a damper upon our fourth. Spent day in social converse. Had Billy Bell for dinner—who spent afternoon with us. In evening staff all went on a visit to General Williams and returned in a glorious mood. Two or three baskets of mail matter came this evening and all the boys got a good supply of letters. Received fifteen as my share—many from Emily—one from Scheffer—Kinard, my own Captain McCormick, Estelle, James O'Donnell, Deafenbaugh, and several others. Sat up til one reading them in fine spirit.

SATURDAY, JULY 5. Very fine morning. Reread all my letters and distributed mail to our boys, all in good spirits. Wrote long letter of 8 pages to Emily also wrote to Capt McCormick and Valle Hummel. A call having been issued for 300,000 more men, have some notion for applying for a field position and have met with every encouragement from Col and all my friends. Col intends giving me a strong letter to Governor Curtin, and if properly worked the thing can be put through. It would be quite an advance, as I am tired of a Captain's duties and anxious to go into a new field of operations. Billy Bell has steadfastly urged me to push the matter, and if we only keep the ball moving, can surely help but succeed. This evening took a bath with Caddie, Gowan, Rogers and Bill, and on our return found we had marching orders. Sat down and concluded Emily's letter and fixed up diary to present.

SUNDAY MORNING, JULY 6. Fine morning. At 7 o'clock were on our way. Sad so the fortune of war. It really seems as though the quiet calm of the holy Sabbath was purposely selected for every important movement. Until an urgent necessity requires it we should rest on Sunday. Marched through the village of Luray and a mile or two beyond it before halting. Passed some of Frémont's old division who had passed our camp during the night and were resting. Day excessively warm. Some of the men had sun stroke or coup de soleil [sunburn]. At noon, reaching a small stream, took a rest of nearly three hours and started much revived, but only went a few miles when we went into a beautiful woods and bivouacked for the night. Moon shining brightly and evening cool and pleasant. Did not go to sleep, lying on my back reflecting until I fell into a dreamy and refreshing slumber.

MONDAY, JULY 7. Awakened at 2 o'clock, got cooks up and again laid down and got up again at 4 o'clock, starting soon after marched into a large field where, after our brigade forming, we marched in regular order. One of the warmest, most severe days I ever saw. Over half of some regiments dropped by the wayside. Human flesh couldn't stand it. About noon whole brigade gave out and were compelled to stop in a hollow where water was plenty. Many cases of sunstroke. Have never suffered from heat so much. In afternoon I went in bathing. News of taking Fort Darling. In afternoon or towards evening it began raining quite briskly.

TUESDAY, JULY 8. Rained nearly all night. Slept in hammock suspended between trees quite comfortably. Did not move this morning as anticipated though we were kept on the que vere momentarily awaiting orders. Nothing stirring, no mail, no papers—no news. No anything.

WEDNESDAY, JULY 9. Very pleasant morning. Ned Witman came this morning and brought letter from Emily. If afternoon mail came for company, none for me save from "Telegraph." Leebrick today received a furlough under very urgent circumstances.[4] Wrote letter and sent by him to Emily. Also got letter to Gov C[urtin] from Col. and one from him to P. Allabach, both of which I sent to Billy Bell also writing. News from McClellan, issued a spirited address to his troops. Spent afternoon in reading "Shanandale," a funny novel. In evening Lieut Ned called to see me in company with Lieut. Crawford. Witman had all kinds of news from him. Spent an hour pleasantly. Read very late and went to bed.

----------◄●►----------

Letter from Capt. George A. Brooks to Emily Brooks
Camp near Amissville Va
Thursday evening July 9, 1862

My Own Dear Emily:

Yesterday afternoon I received your long and very pleasant letter. At once penciled an answer, to send by Tom Leebrick who had received a furlough which I did [all] the more promptly because your letter was such an improvement on the ones you have for two months past sent me. It was so jovial, so good natured, cheering and free from the fault finding which characterized the ones I spoke of. Will you not always write so. It will please me so much and I shall answer more promptly. Now Emily is not that inducement enough. I answered Frank's letter as soon as I received it but will answer your Pap's as soon as I again get in camp as we move tomorrow morning with two day's rations. Where we will go or how soon stop I know not but as soon as we do you will hear from me.

When I wrote for an account in order to see how much ready money we had on hand I had not the remotest idea of inquiring what disposition you had made of that which you spent, but only a general account. You surely misunderstood my letter, as I had no such intention of giving it such a meaning. Of course, spend all necessary to make Willy and yourself perfectly comfortable.

---

4. Private George Thomas Leebrick. Discharged September 2nd 1862.

Why neglect to do so when we have it—at the same time do not be extravagant as you say I am—surely one in the family is enough and you should not seek to emulate my vices. What say you dear? Am I not right.

I have several times began writing to Dr. Hay but something always interferes. As soon as we again get into camp I will again make another attempt and promise you I will succeed. Give both him and Mrs. H my very kind regards. I must also write to several other good old friends whom I owe letters to. Today I wrote to Senator Kinard from whom a letter a few days since in which he informed me that he had opened a hat and cap store in Market Street with every prospect of doing well. I sincerely trust he may succeed, he has my earnest wishes for his prosperity. If you have $50 to spare, without unaccommodating your ready charge, walk down there someday yourself and give it to him, taking a receipt only. I will arrange it with him hereafter. I wrote to him stating if you had it to spare you would give it to him, but do not draw on the money on interest in bank or you would thereby lose the interest. Besides I do not want that touched.

So, you have seen my maiden Aunt Sue and are pleased with her, and I am very glad. Though I have not seen her for many years, yet she has been very kind to me. You will find her a warm-hearted woman and she is a pleasant and entertaining and agreeable companion. When you visit her and I would be pleased to hear of your taking a trip to my old grandmother. I know she would be glad to see you. Would extend you a cordial welcome and whilst I am away from home—now is the time for Willy and his little mother to see all your relatives for when I come home after being away so long I shall be so very selfish as not to let you go anywhere for a long, long time. Be very careful of Willy's health though, I do not think you need apprehend any trouble from brain fever or any disease of the brain as it only results from a disordered stomach. He being so very fat the warm weather will be very severe on him. And besides, my dear, do not have so many fears for my safety. You are too apt to look on the dark side of the cloud without seeing the silver lining or the sunshine struggling to peek through. I admit war is a terrible thing we carry as it were our lives in our hands but "he who tempteth the wind to the shorn lamb" will protect me. Though a brave patriot heart has already been offered on our country's altar, and though many will yet bleed and die for those preambles which our fathers gave us and will render themselves immortal, yet I have few fears of my own safety. Already I have stood amidst the battle roar, already rushed madly forward cheering my men, in face of a terrible iron hail, yet I have remained unscathed, untouched and yet have come out of the fiery ordeal. More fully convinced that I shall, even should we again get into an engagement (and I ordinately hope I may be at the taking of Richmond), that I will still come out safely. But if I should fall, if my body should be required as a sacrifice to aid in restoring peace to our once happy country, it is in the hands of "he who gave and can take away" and know, my Dear Emily, it would be hard to part from Willy and you whom I love so devotedly, just when hope is brightly guiding our future, yet I would cheerfully yield to my fate, knowing that my memory would ever be cherished green in the hearts of those that love me most, and history would do justice to our cause and the men who bravely died for it. But Emily your uneasiness has led me farther than I intended. Rest safely tho heaven shall be reached at last, the battle shall be won, and I will return to find thee waiting with a fond embrace, and our boy grown to a mischievous size, gazing with indignation at the privilege a stranger will take with his Mother for I am away so much he will scarcely know who I am. Won't it be happy times when we can reach home, safe and sound from the war. What rejoicings there will be over our whole country when peace is declared. But Emily, forget me not in your prayers to the throne of grace. God I know will answer them—trust in him and he will comfort thee.

I am sorry Sue Crunkle acted so strangely after so many adventures on your part. She has scarcely seen enough of adversity to teach her the inconvenience of selfishness and now, when a widow young and childless and thrown without any provision upon the world, she should not refuse the consolations of those who were her friends in earlier days. Do not give up, persevere and she will yet yield. She has been in Baltimore since the sale of Harry's effects and does she intend staying there?

You did write and pay my order to Jeremiah Chubb for $34. I will only send you two more of $26 each but how soon I know not. That then will finish the fund I last sent you, belonging to some of my boys.

In my trunk, if I send it home, you will find all the letters I have received from ladies since I have been in service which you are perfectly at liberty to read. They were merely answered to while away a passing hour but some of them through the purest of friendly feelings. In traveling through this country we sometimes find warm-hearted Union girls who are glad to meet those congenial natures which sympathize with them, and it is very cheering after we pass, for them to embrace such a privilege—the privilege of replying to a few friendly lines. If I chance here and there among the crowd to have one of them, it is quite a compliment and you should so consider it to one whom you so dearly love. Remember Emily I can be admired without admiring, can even admire without loving or violating any of the solemn pledges I made on the evening of our marriage, and which I hold sacred and inviolate. I know you are not jealous, you have no cause, but I merely write to assure you of my faithfulness. Emily, dear, tell me if there is anything wrong in it?

I received M. M. Strickler's letter and was of course greatly surprised. What prompted him to write after so long an estrangement I can only imagine, and of course await with anxiety a letter from him, judging from the inquiry he made that he intends writing.

The handkerchiefs and geranium bouquet which you sent me were safely received, and of course I am greatly obliged. I shall use the handkerchiefs and cherish the bouquet.

The concluding paragraph of my letter I do not understand or is it rather your "P.S." You speak of some mistake Frank made in sending a letter by Ned Witman. I only received one, and I can see no mistake in it or that it was intended for another person.

But I must bring my long letter to a close, as I have written nearly all afternoon and must post my company books tonight yet. I wish you would write to me oftener, as in moving about the way we are now, I have very little opportunity of writing unless I do it on my knee with a pencil and even then I have not always paper. So of course you will excuse me.

I sent with Leebrick to Billy Bell a strong letter from Col. Knipe urging me for a majorship in one of the new regiments about forming, and my chances for the position are very good if my friends at home only urge it promptly. Col. Knipe also wrote a letter to Peter Allabach who anticipates a Colonelcy, urging him to place me in his regiment. Have your father stir up some of his friends. It is the only way I can get home before the close of the war, as I would scorn feigning sickness to gain a furlough, and sick ones are the only ones which can be secured except in extraordinary cases. If I don't get [promoted], however, I will stick to good old Company "D" which I would sorely dislike to leave at any rate, and come home with it at the close of the war.

Give my very kind regard to all my friends. Same to pap, mom, and all the boys. When did you hear from father and how are they at my home? How soon do you intend going again etc etc. Write me a long careful letter like this one—not a nasty scrawl.

With a thousand kisses for yourself and Willie

I remain

Your affectionate husband

George

Direct until I change, and have all writing to the company do the same to:

Co "D" 46th Regt PV

Banks Corps Army of Virginia

Washington, D.C.

Have Frank get my Telegraph directed as above. Did you get a cartridge box of things I sent you.

———————◆•◆•◆———————

From the Journal of Capt. George A. Brooks

THURSDAY, JULY 10. Awakened very quietly at three o'clock this morning with orders to form the company at once without noise. Had them soon on the pike, every heart beating anxiously and eagerly awaiting an order to move. After standing in the rain until 6 o'clock found it was a false alarm and went into a large orchard where we put up tents and went into camp. Wrote to O'Donnell, Sen. K., AGK, and a long eight page letter to Emily. Also made out several descriptive lists, posted diary and did all kinds of writing generally. Capt Matthews from battery came this afternoon. Heard from Godbald and Ricketts. His battery is lying at Warrenton. In evening received orders to move at daylight, two days cooked rations. Wrote till late in the evening—nothing new. Had paper of yesterday.

FRIDAY, JULY 11. Reveille at usual hour, awakened cooks at 3 o'clock to prepare breakfast. Cloudy morning and pleasant and cool for marching. Did not start until nearly 8 o'clock. Our regiment on the left. Marched through a fine country but land worn out and very poorly cultivated. Crossed the Rapidan river about 4 o'clock at the point at which a large mill was engaged in the manufacture of cloth for the Southern army. A few days before a body of our cavalry secured a large quantity of clothing. Reached a point about three miles from Warrenton and encamped for the night, in fact pitched our tents in regular order, not a man out, everyone standing the marching admirably and all in good spirits.

SATURDAY, JULY 12. Very fine morning and very pleasant. Fixed our camp in "ship shape" order. Received from Col, Lt Col and Major a very strong letter recommending me to the position of Lt Col or Major in one of the new regiments about being formed in Pennsylvania and gave it to Col K who goes to Washington and will represent my claim in person. Do not know how I may succeed but have every hope. It is the first position I ever asked for and will be quite a "push up" if I succeed. Saw several friends [from] home who visited me from other regiments during the day. No stirring news by paper, which we now receive on the evening of the day on which they are published. In evening wrote to Wm Bell and Emily after which went to bed.

SUNDAY, JULY 13. Very fine morning. After inspection started in company with Major M. S. Weber and Caldwell and Adjutant to town of Warrenton which is one of the finest and most beautiful little places I have ever seen in Virginia or anywhere else. Neatly constructed houses are embowered [sic] in nicely shaded groves and everything has such a cozy home like appearance. Rode through the town and went to the camp of the One Hundred-Seventh PV, met Dr Carman 1st Lt Co "E." Afterward saw Theo. F. 1st Lieut Co "A." Both are hearty and looking remarkably fine. Spent over an hour with them. Theo gave me picture of his mother. Started to Winchester and rode from thence two miles out to Towers Brigade, then returned and dined at "Warren Green." After a siesta started for camp of Eleventh PV finding my old friend and comrade, A. F. Small, and several other friends with whom I passed a pleasant time. From thence rode to Battery of Capt Matthews and making a short call started for home arriving in camp at 5 o'clock. Nearly whole regiment on extra detail, consequently had very small dress parade. In evening an order came reducing

Fauquier White Sulphur Springs, a popular rest and recuperation destination, was burned in August of 1862 during the Second Manassas Campaign. (Source: John J. Moorman, The Virginia Springs, 1857.)

our baggage to one volume each. Very short allowance but have no choice. Must show some important move anticipated.

MONDAY, JULY 14. Fine morning. Every five minutes or so an order round in reference to tents, baggage, etc. Committee to inspect baggage round. Only reduced us to mess chest and one trunk. Packed up such articles as we cared for without and sent them home or rather got them ready. Presented Col. Selfridge with a fine photograph album. Left us two Sibley tents for company and wall tent for ourselves. In afternoon received orders to cook two days rations and by 5 o'clock struck balance of our tents, packed up traps and started. After considerable delay reached Warrenton about dusk and taking the Culpeper road jogged along rapidly the night air being cool and pleasant, passing a number of camps. About 10 o'clock the moon rose beautifully the sky was clear and her mild rays shed a genial glow over nature. It was too dark however when we passed the famous "White Sulphur Springs" with its marble fountains, shady groves, and large airy buildings, to give us a fair view of the place and it surroundings. Beyond the "Springs" a mile we all had to wade quite a river and after crossing it about a mile, by which time it was 1 o'clock, we then bivouacked for the night. Not unloading the wagons, slept without blankets.

❋ ❋ ❋

General Pope's movements in early July alarmed Lee, who thought it likely that McClellan was readying to renew his attack on Richmond with help from Pope from the north. Badly outnumbered, Lee felt his only hope was attacking first and putting Pope's army, now almost 50,000 strong, out of action before McClellan could move. Then, Lee would turn and concentrate on McClellan. On July 13th, Lee detached Stonewall Jackson's 12,000 men to Gordonsville, an important railroad junction sixty miles north of Richmond. It was a risky move, because if McClellan attacked while Jackson was gone, Jackson would be too far away to aid Lee. Still, there was little else Lee could do, and so he took the risk.[5]

While Jackson marched northward, Pope was consolidating his forces near Sperryville. In addition to his orders involving civilians and foraging, Pope also made his army more mobile by instructing that surplus equipment, baggage, and commissary stores be sent off to Alexandria. Officers and enlisted men were limited in what they were allowed to keep with them, and two days cooked rations were to be kept on each man at all times so he could move at a moment's notice. With a lightened load, on July 14th, the 46th Pennsylvania and the 28th New York were instructed to accompany a cavalry expedition to Culpeper, fifteen miles south.[6]

From the Journal of Capt. George A. Brooks

TUESDAY, JULY 15. Clear morn. Started at 5. Was up early and before regiment started assorted mail. Long and very pleasant letter for me from Hancock. Marched slowly, the day being very warm. At noon halted an hour or two on the banks of the Rapidan river, which at this point becomes quite a large stream. Nearly the whole regiment went in bathing, and it was one of the most interesting sights I ever saw, worthy of the pencil of a Staguith[sic] or the descriptive powers of a Headley.[7] Went in myself and was much refreshed. Continued on marching to within

---

5. Catton, *Terrible Swift Sword*, 389-90.
6. Bradley, *Surviving Stonewall*, 122.
7. J.T. Headley, one of the most popular historians of the mid- to late-nineteenth century. The Staguith reference couldn't be identified.

Culpeper, Virginia, in August of 1862. (Source: Library of Congress.)

about six miles of Culpeper and got tents up just before a heavy thunder gust came upon us. Took tea at the house of a lady whose "better half" or "worse half" was in the rebel army—she was however quite pleasant. Returned to tent and read "Taylor's Central Africa" until I fell asleep. Went in swimming today [and] skinned my face severely.

WEDNESDAY, JULY 16. Clear morning cool and pleasant. Reveille at 4. Took breakfast at place I received supper and by 5 were on our march again. Road almost the whole way to Culpeper though a shady wood making our march very pleasant. Entered the town of Culpeper C. H. with the music of bands, colors saucily flying and the sullen gloomy looks of the residents. We were not by any means welcome visitors. The sympathies of the inhabitants are all with the South, though I saw more able bodied men here than anyplace I have yet been in Virginia. Passed beyond the place about a mile and went into camp in a woods. Towards evening received orders to cook one day's rations. In evening closed diary to date.

THURSDAY, JULY 17. Rained nearly all night. Reveille at 3 o'clock. Still cloudy. At 5 started for Madison Court House over the muddiest and worst road I ever traveled. Rained all day. Reached a point on Robinson's river about two miles from Madison, but being too high to cross had to go in camp or rather in the mud, awaiting another order to move at any moment. Horrible march and evening chill.

FRIDAY, JULY 18. Still raining and rained all night. Slept cold and uncomfortable in wet clothing, our wagons not coming up, being unable to do so on account of mud. Men out of rations and gone to foraging on their own account. Our position considered somewhat dangerous, the rebels being in strong force at Gordonsville and advancing toward us. Roads too bad however for our trains to move, consequently we could not get out of the way. Our cavalry, about 3000 strong, sent out to make a demonstration and present an attack. The First Penna and First New Jersey cavalry, both excellent regiments, joined us. Orders to clean guns and get everything ready for immediate use issued about 4 o'clock. At 5 o'clock my company were ordered out on picket. Orders to shoot etc very positive. Had in addition to my company nineteen cavalrymen whom I used as videttes. Made a reconnaissance nearly two miles beyond our outpost on my own look, accompanied by an orderly. An attack anticipated before morning, consequently on the alert but do not see any indications for immediate alarm. Posted pickets myself. Prospect of a rainy night.

SATURDAY, JULY 19. Still cloudy but has ceased raining. Only one alarm during night. Horses of videttes became frightened and, throwing riders, rushed in past reserve. No indications of the immediate presence of the enemy though he is at the Rapidan seven miles off. About 9 o'clock the field officer of the day ordered us to join our regiment at once and bringing in my pickets, reached the regiment just as it was crossing, or about to cross, the river. Had barely reached there when orders were countermanded; the enemy were so close we could not reach Madison Court House and accordingly had to take a mountain road under the guidance of a negro. Everybody somewhat scared but all hoped to reach Sigel at Sperryville. Not starting till 12 o'clock as we covered the retreat, we only marched about thirteen miles and went into camp feeling secure from pursuit.

SUNDAY, JULY 20. Beautiful morning. Did not anticipate a move today but at 9 received orders to march at 11 o'clock and starting reached a small place called Woodville by evening, camping in an orchard. Here we met all our cavalry. Our route lay through a Union locality—one brigade of Sigel command at this point. Rations scarce and boys foraged on their "own look." Took bath, being considerably chafed, and went to bed late.

MONDAY, JULY 21. Reveille at 3 o'clock. Rained some during night. At 6 o'clock started and marching on an excellent pike, reached Culpeper, a distance of fourteen miles, by 3 o'clock. Here we met the Colonel, from whom we have been separated since leaving Warrenton. All very glad to see him. Found all Hatch's command at Culpeper, went into camp about a mile from town. No very stirring news from the world, from which we have been cut off over a week, save the effort of the abolitionists in Congress to make the war an abolition crusade. Strong efforts being made to supplant McClellan, in which case many of the best officers in the army will resign and leave the army in disgust. I am now heartily tired of the subject.

✳✳✳

The expedition to Madison Court House had abruptly ended when federal cavalry had captured some Confederates north of Gordonsville and learned that Jackson had arrived there on the 19th. Upon learning of Jackson's position, General Pope immediately recalled Banks and returned the men to the safety of camp life near Culpeper, where they resumed sweltering in the summer heat. The only change their movement had brought them was shoelessness—after a week of marching over rough roads and fording rivers, many found themselves barefoot.[8]

It wasn't just the army that was tired of war—so were Northern citizens, and Lincoln's call for 300,000 more volunteers in early July went largely unanswered. A correspondent of the London *Times* wrote that "the first bloom of war excitement is over" and that the harrowing stories of soldiers back from war, paired with the wounded returning to civilian life, proved that soldiering wasn't all glory. "They were ready for a short, sharp and decisive conflict," the *Times* continued, "They were not ready for an obstinate struggle, to last for years."[9]

In the face of waning enthusiasm, numerous military defeats, and the threat of the Confederacy gaining the support of foreign

---

8. Bradley, *Surviving Stonewall*, 124.
9. Catton, *Terrible Swift Sword*, 403.

powers like England and France, the Lincoln administration grappled with what to do. Lincoln became convinced only emancipating the slaves could offer the war effort new hope. Transforming the war's moral message would not only help to cripple the South's war economy, but it was also send a message abroad for which countries and citizens were waiting.[10]

Since the war's outbreak, the Union's stance on slavery (or lack thereof) had immense international implications. Both the United States and the Confederacy had been waging an international public relations battle in an era before the term *public relations* had even been coined. The Confederacy, fully aware that defeating the Union without international assistance would be difficult if not impossible, attempted to gain recognition by foreign powers as a sovereign nation worthy of assistance. Simultaneously, the United States attempted to prevent the South from gaining the recognition it so desired, all while tip-toeing around the issue of slavery to avoid its eradication. President Lincoln, though he personally did not agree with slavery, felt his Constitutional powers did not allow him to address the issue, and that his true duty as President was to preserve the nation and throw down an illegal rebellion.

But to citizens of the world, watching Union and Confederate diplomats play out the American struggle with words, it seemed clear enough that the war was indeed about slavery, and so the war would have to determine its fate. The Confederacy, after all, had included a clause in its Constitution to preserve the institution forever. America's problem with slavery, which existed decades after most other European powers had abolished the institution, was intertwined in the very idea of America and a government for and by the people.

Starting with the American and French revolutions in the late 1700s, the radical new idea of personal freedoms and rights had sprung to life and unsettled the age old governments of hereditary, aristocratic power. Though some small instances of progress were made, all nations who had seen revolution or a cry for elected government had ultimately failed by the late 1840s—except in America. When war broke out thousands of miles across the sea, European revolutionaries saw the war as a new contest for freedom. Their struggle was now being perpetuated, and the war's outcome would determine whether a democratic government,

---

10. Doyle, *Cause of All Nations*, 211, 216.

represented by popularly chosen leaders, and based on at-will labor and inalienable rights could indeed exist. Should America fail, so would the idea of Republican government and personal freedom.[11]

Though Lincoln knew his war was about more than *just* restoring the Union, the complexities of politics within the United States had caused him to remain silent on slavery until doing so seemed a necessity to win the war. Not only would foreign powers be much more unlikely to support the South should the Union come out against slavery, but doing so would also serve to cripple the South's economy since slaves both enabled white Southern men to go fight and continued the production of goods crucial to the war effort.

Although Lincoln couldn't free slaves physically in Confederate states, he could give them the option to flee north to freedom. Escaped slaves and those who found themselves in Union occupied territory could also join the fight themselves, and by war's end ten percent of the Union army would be composed of black soldiers.

The first step toward emancipation came on July 17th when Congress passed and Lincoln signed a new confiscation act that enacted higher penalties for secession. The law granted freedom to slaves of secessionists in areas under Union control. It also declared slaves seeking refuge behind Union lines free, but did not give them any civil rights. In an attempt to maintain the favor of border states, loyal Union slave owners were allowed to keep their slaves. Finally, the government could use freed slaves for the war effort.[12] While the legislation's implementation was unclear, didn't provide emancipation, and still regarded slaves as property, it moved Congress closer to true emancipation.

Later in the month, Lincoln called a cabinet meeting to present his preliminary draft of a document which, once issued, would give freedom to enslaved persons in the South and permanently entwine Union victory with emancipation. On the suggestion of his cabinet, Lincoln would wait for a military success to issue the document which we now know as the Emancipation Proclamation. For the time being, its existence was kept secret.

While Lincoln set about linking Union victory with the cause of freedom, Congress acted on the lack of response to his call for

---

11. Doyle, *Cause of All Nations*, 1-11, 85, 86.
12. Wagner, *Desk Reference*, 150, 210-1.

300,000 volunteers. Without bolstering the ranks the war would surely be lost, and so they enacted a practice the Confederacy had already embraced earlier that spring: conscription. The army was no longer composed of just patriotic volunteers.[13]

From the Journal of Capt. George A. Brooks

TUESDAY, JULY 22. Still cloudy, in fact we seem to have a constant supply of wet weather. Nothing stirring today. In afternoon, in company with Adjutant, took a ride to Culpeper, passing through the town, and from thence rode into the country several miles in search of butter etc, but found none; the country all round having been completely ransacked by soldiers. The village of Culpeper is a very desolate place, perhaps the more so on account of the absence of so many of her citizens in the rebel army. In the evening wrote long letter to Telegraph and one to Emily. In bed by 11 o'clock.

Letter from Capt. George A. Brooks to Emily Brooks
46th Regt P.V. near Culpeper Va
Tuesday July 22, 1862

My Dear Emily,

I have just finished a letter to the "Telegraph" from which you will readily perceive why I have not written sooner, and from which you can glean an idea of our marches etc without my repeating it here.

Since leaving Warrenton on last Monday week we have not received a mail or even a newspaper, and I had not up to that time heard from you. We, however, expect one tomorrow, and I will be greatly disappointed if it does not contain one from you. Only write to me often. Did you receive the letter sent you by Leebrick, also the long one I wrote on the day following? Tell me when you write.

Col. Knipe was in Washington for several days and I believe Mrs. Knipe came on to see him. I suppose you are aware of it. I only wish we were in such a place that Willie and you could come on and see me. I am tired, very tired of being away from you,

---

13. Catton, *Terrible Swift Sword*, 365-7, 404.

and were it not for the name of the thing would resign and come home. But then I have no business at which I could readily jump into, and perhaps I had better stay awhile. A furlough is not to be had at all now, and my only hope of seeing you is by resigning, or securing a position in one of the new regiments. However, wait patiently. Something may turn up that we may soon meet.

How is Willie getting along and how is Frank and all the family. Has your father got in a good humor at me yet.

But Emily I have no news to write and no letter to answer consequently I will now close as it is very late and write again in a day or so, tomorrow if I receive one to answer. It is growing very late so good night. May God protect you and our dear boy.

Give my kind regards to all friends. Love to pop, mom, and the boys. A thousand kisses for Willie and yourself, and believe me as ever

Your affectionate husband
George

Pennsylvania Daily Telegraph
46th Regiment P.V., Near Culpeper, Va.,
Tuesday evening, July 22, 1862.
From Capt. G. A. Brooks

MR. EDITOR : – So rapid have been our movements of late, and so constantly have we been on the march, that I have been unable to write earlier, and will therefore briefly related our progress during the past few weeks.

On Sunday morning, July 6th, the command of Gen. Banks left their camps in the vicinity of Front Royal and moved towards Warrenton, arriving there after very tedious marches on Friday evening, July 11th. The heat, which during our march was exceedingly oppressive, rendered our progress very slow, and during an experience of over fourteen months in the service, I have never seen men so completely worn out—strong, robust systems, inured to hardship and fatigue, so utterly prostrated.

Locating our camp about three miles from the town, we were soon snugly ensconced in our tents, and made every preparation for a season of rest, but were not destined long to enjoy it. On Monday afternoon, in connection with the New York Twenty-Eighth, we received orders to join General Hatch's Cavalry Brigade at

Culpeper, and starting about 6 o'clock passed through the pretty little village of Warrenton just before dusk. In all our wanderings through the States we have never yet seen a place in which the private residences were so neatly and tastefully arranged, or surrounded by so many cozy comforts and conveniences, and the genial glow of a calm summer evening seemed to spread a home-like influence o'er it which gave additional beauty. How mournful that a people so happily and pleasantly situated should have been so misled by the siren songs of ambitious and designing men.

Continuing our march, the lengthening shadows of evening dimly fading away, gave us the bright stars, radiantly shining from the clear blue sky, and the air being cool and balmy, we moved along in fine spirits. About ten o'clock the fair moon rose beautifully, just as we were passing the famous "White Sulphur Springs," with their marble fountains, delicious baths, shady groves and rustic bowers; and the large, airy buildings, which in peaceful times, daily and nightly resounded to the jocund laugh of youth and beauty, or the merry sounds of voluptuous music, whilst the gay votaries of pleasure "chased the glowing hours with flying feet"—were now all lonely and deserted and echoed only to the heavy tread and lively jests of armed men. Marching on, in the pale moonlight, we waded a fork of the Rapidan river—the bridge having been destroyed by the rebels—and at one o'clock halted, bivouacked, rose by four o'clock, and were off again, and passing through a poorly cultivated country, without anything unusually attractive to break the monotony of our march, entered the town of Culpeper on Wednesday morning, our colors saucily flung to the breeze in response to sullen looks which greeted our arrival, we being the first Federal infantry which had ever *invaded* this portion of Virginia. Passing a mile beyond the town we encamped, and before daylight on Thursday morning started again, marching in a terrible storm and over one of the very worst roads I have ever traveled, towards Madison Court House, halting, however, two miles this side of the town, unable to reach it on account of Robinson's river being so high as to prevent our crossing. The train containing our tents, knapsacks, provisions, &c., did not reach us till late next day, and we consequently laid our weary limbs on the wet grass, exposed to a drenching rain all night. Our destination was Gordonsville, but the storm continuing, we had to remain in our position, unable to move any way, and the Confederates receiving information of our proposed occupation of that place, hastily threw a large force, by rail from Richmond, under command of the energetic Jackson, and they knowing our exposed condition, made every arrangement, and began placing their forces in a position to surround and capture us. On Friday evening we became painfully aware of our danger, and on Saturday morning took a mountain road leading to Sperryville, twenty-five miles distant, to reach Sigel's command, which laid at that point, the 46th covering the retreat. Our route was through the most forsaken country I ever saw, but we safely reached Woodville, a small place, five miles from Sperryville, and from thence were immediately ordered to Culpeper, which we again reached on yesterday (Monday) evening. During the last seven days we have marched over one hundred miles, but our boys stood it bravely. Our force here consists of about fifteen hundred infantry, three thousand cavalry and four pieces of artillery, and our men being greatly fatigued, and badly off for shoes, we will probably remain in camp a week or so, unless our friend Jackson should interfere with our comfort.

The timely proclamation of President Lincoln, calling upon the loyal freemen of our country for three hundred thousand more men, has awakened a feeling of renewed confidence and revived the drooping spirits of our soldiers. It is a mournful face, notwithstanding our boasted army of seven hundred thousand, that we have now, and scarcely ever have had three hundred thousand *effectual fighting men*, and conscious therefore, of our weakness, the energies of our Generals crippled and the movements harassed by the unwise legislation of grave Senators who sit in the easy arm chairs of the Government, surrounded by every luxury, knowing nothing of the practical operations of war, and yet criticizing and censuring those who are braving danger and death, and bearing the trials and hardships of the field, is it to be wondered that our armies have apparently accomplished so little, or can successfully carry on an offensive warfare in an enemy's [territory] against so wary, skillful and energetic a foe, where their forces far outnumber our own! The truth is, our strength has been vastly overestimated, theirs correspondingly underrated. The people of the north are scarcely yet alive to the magnitude of this rebellion. Coining money on the incentive which this war has given trade, or wrapped up in the giddy wheel of fashion and folly, they seem to have forgotten—save by an occasional contribution to the wounded and suffering, which is ostentatiously paraded in the public press—that their fellow men are enduring untold hardships and dying upon the bloody battlefields of the south, whilst they sit in comfort and security at home; and that we are fighting for the very protection of those who are most loudly denouncing our inactivity without knowing the causes which compel it. Come face the danger with us, put your shoulder to the wheel, spill some of your patriotic blood, or show your willingness to do so, and you will find the war will terminate much sooner. We have an abundance of means; we have able, skillful and experienced Generals. Our gallant M'Clellan, the idol of American soldiery, is a host in himself; but we want *men*, and we know Pennsylvania will cheerfully and promptly respond to the calls. In every important battle which has taken place the gallant sons of the Old Keystone State have borne a conspicuous part, crowning themselves with imperishable glory, and we know the heroic deed of those she will send will add renewed luster and renown to her arms. Move with us "on to Richmond," and aid our noble leader in reducing the stronghold of rebellion, till, like the ancient temple of Jerusalem, "not one stone shall be left standing upon another." True, it will cost immense amounts of treasure and blood; many noble lives will be sacrificed, but the great principles of liberty must be perpetuated; our government, in all its original purity, must be preserved. Let Pennsylvanians then rally around the old standard, support our noble Governor in the pledges he has made in behalf of the State of which he is justly proud, respond promptly to his call, and before the festive days of Christmas make the annual round you will have returned to your homes with the consciousness of having performed a sacred duty, and earned the glorious title of an "American citizen."

SOLDIER.

--------◆◆◆--------

From the Journal of Capt. George A. Brooks

WEDNESDAY, JULY 23. Raining this morning. Officer of the day. Still no papers or mail. Painful rumors of the superseding of McClellan but trust they are not correct. Spent greater portion of day in reading Taylor's Travels in Africa. In evening wrote to Dr. Hay and Sayford. Our Brigade will join us tomorrow.

Letter from Capt. George A. Brooks to Reverend Charles A. Hay

Write to me soon and whenever at leisure you may think of me
46th Regt Penna Vols
Culpeper Va, July 23 1862

Rev. C. A. Hay -
Dear Friend -
Do not chide me for negligence in not sooner answering your very welcome favor received so long ago. Emily has frequently reminded me, and I have often thought of it myself, but generally at times when least prepared to write. Besides we have of late been constantly on the move, seldom resting long enough in camp to become at home, and you scarcely know what disadvantages a soldier has to contend with in writing, our facilities not being such as are most convenient and our mails very irregular. For twelve days past we have been entirely shut off from the world, not having received a mail or newspaper during that time. This is a great deprivation, for ever our life becomes monotonous without the news.

On Monday Col. Knipe rejoined the regiment having been absent for a week on business in Washington. He brings us the pleasing information of early adjournment of Congress and you may soon expect more energetic movements in the Army. To no other cause can be attributed the prolongation of the war, than the constant interference of Congress in its operations, and the unwise policy they have pursued—one mind—one supreme head has long been needed to control our movements, concentration of our forces is imperatively demanded, and the strengthening of McClellan sufficiently to enable him successfully to "advance on Richmond"—in fact more men are wanted.

There are painful rumors afloat in camp today, concerning the removal of our "young Napoleon" and should such a suicidal course be pursued, it will give the whole Federal army a severer [sic] blow than all the defeats we have thus far experienced. He is beloved, fairly idolized, even in the "Army of Virginia," and not a man, no odds how humble his position, but will deeply feel any act which will imply a censure upon his conduct—many of our best and bravest officers will resign—and such a triumph of the

Abolition element, even should Halleck supersede him, will have a more ruinous effect on our cause than any which can be pursued. We sincerely trust the rumor is without any foundation.

Before this reaches you, you will probably hear of a dashing exploit of our cavalry. Yesterday about 3000 moved towards Louisa Court House, in the rear of Gordonsville for the purpose of destroying several railroad bridges thereby breaking the railroad connection between that place and Richmond. During their absence our infantry about 1500 strong are left here unprotected with Jackson's force of 20,000 directly in our front.

The spiritual condition of our regiment is sadly suffering. True, we have a Chaplain, but like nine-tenths of the others in the field his position is a mere sinecure—occasionally we have a formal sermon on Sunday afternoon, and that is the full extent of his labors. No prayer meetings through the week, no association with the men, no apparent effort to check by presence and influence the evils and temptations with which one is peculiarly surrounded in camp. Truly there is a great reformation needed; either the position should be abolished or some measures taken to render it effective and beneficial. As you are well aware, I am no professing Christian, yet I sorely miss those influences which were thrown around me at home.

How heartily tired I am of this war; how I wish it was over and how I long once more to enjoy the comforts of home, and the society of my wife and boy, now just at an age when most interesting. Fourteen months I have been in the service and yet nearly two more years loom up with every prospect of remaining until their expiration. Recent orders have entirely abolished furloughs, unless in cases of severe sickness, and when I think of home, of the trials and hardships I am enduring, and of the many young men in our own city who are free from which ties and should be in the service taking no interest in the war, I feel like returning. So badly has it been managed thus far that we are all discouraged, a position like mine is so pregnant with care, trouble and suspense—and my mind is so much harassed that the salary we receive will not begin to remunerate for the sacrifices we are making—and were it not for the little love of country I possess I should have resigned long ago. If some modification of the order in reference to furlough is not made within the next few months, or some prospect of a speedy termination of the war, many, very many officers will resign.

Give my kind regards to Mrs. H and family—well wishes to friends—remember me in your supplications at the Throne of Grace—and believe me as ever

Your Friend
George

I have written hurriedly intending to copy, but as the mail is just starting I have not time.

From the Journal of Capt. George A. Brooks

THURSDAY, JULY 24. Fine morning. Nothing unusual occurring. In afternoon again went to town and in evening visited a new acquaintance in Culpeper in company with Major Matthews. Rode in evening out to camp only staying a short time. Wrote to Wm Sayford.

FRIDAY, JULY 25. No news of any importance. Rumors float through camp every day of the nearness of the enemy and their approach, but we have become so accustomed to danger that we never mind it. Officer of the day. In the evening paymaster arrived and we will be paid tomorrow. Had my rolls signed and in first, after which went to town in company with Major. Did not come home until nearly 12 o'clock on account of a severe storm. Have an unusual amount of wet weather.

Letter from Capt. George A. Brooks to Emily Brooks
Culpeper Va July 25, 1862

My Dear Emily,

A large mail arrived a day or so ago—none from you although I received two from Leebrick who was in Halifax. Please have Frank direct you some letters or envelopes, as I direct on the last page of this, and put your letters in them.

Enclosed I send you $275 which you will please take care of. Out of it you will pay as follows; when the persons present themselves—James O'Donnell $26—Isabella Deafenbaugh $25—Beattie M Carroll $40. Perhaps you had better send for them and give them the money at once as they may need it. It will keep you doing something too to help along the cause. Have you sent the money I desired to Mrs. Nancy Griffin [of] Millersburg. I am now in a great hurry putting up money package in order to send it off. Must be brief as this is merely a business letter. I will in my next send you some further directions. I must also write to your pap or Frank in regard to what I send them—as I will send him the whole package

Love to you and Willie
Very affectionately
Your husband
George

O'Donnell $26
Carroll 40
Houser 18
Expense Trunk 2.50

———————◆•●•◆———————

From the Journal of Capt. George A. Brooks

SATURDAY, JULY 26. Fine clear morning. Have neglected my diary several days and consequently it is somewhat defective. This morning paymaster Major Sherman began paying off my company being first. Very briskly occupied all day in settling up sutler accounts and other claims in company. Considerable trouble. All paid in my company which is more than any company in the regiment has been. In evening rode to town on Dixie in company with Major M. and Surgeon Rodgers.[14] Spent portion of evening with Miss Setchel. Came to camp late, it being very dark.

SUNDAY, JULY 27. Fine morning. Had regular inspection. Received a large company mail. Got letters from my old friend and Captain McCormick, Bill Dodge, Mrs. H inquiring for her Lieut Jennings, enclosing his picture and a long one from my dear Emily. In afternoon read some. Leebrick came bringing no letter. Last night the whole brigade were under arms about 2 o'clock expecting an attack but the alarm was a false one and we again went to bed. Intended writing but too warm. In evening went into town and came out about 10 o'clock. Have kept my diary very carelessly for several days past, in fact have not kept it at all and (must) be more attentive in future. Have had the blues at the bad management of our course. Hope however brightly holds

---

14. Brooks' horse, Dixie, had returned from Harrisburg, probably brought to him by a friend or member of the regiment.

the future and providence will provide for our defenses when our course is just.

MONDAY, JULY 28. Very fine, cool, windy morning. Our sutler, H.C. Randle, a very prince of good fellows, having some misunderstanding with our Colonel, left this morning and we are now without a sutler. Sent with express from Warrenton my trunk so that between Lt Geiger and myself we have now only one left. Saw Colonel Knipe, Selfridge and Maj [Mathews] in reference to my appointment who all heartily unite in urging it and I mean to push the matter forward at once to a conclusion trusting that I may be successful. Wrote a long letter to Emily. Made out several descriptive lists after which accompanied Col Selfridge to town on horseback to attend a Masonic meeting. Received letter from Val Hummel. Wrote to Capt Dodge. Saw Miss Kate in afternoon. Lodge did not adjourn until after 10. Reached camp by 11. Firing among pickets.

TUESDAY, JULY 29. Very cool and pleasant morning. Made out descriptive list and wrote to Beddleyoung, also to Capt Dodge concerning arrest of William Swayer.[15] Feel very unwell and have for several days past. In afternoon a very strange recommendation for a position as Lieutenant Colonel reached me from Capt Wilkins which was most hastily approved by General Williams and Brig General Crawford. Could have procured very high recommendations from Colonel Donnelley but considered them unnecessary. In afternoon went to town with Col Selfridge, but being no meeting we returned to camp for supper, after which we again went to town. Did not however go to Masonic meeting, but went to see Miss Kate, playing afterwards one of the greatest tricks I have ever did on one of my friends which I shall always remember, after which went to lodge. After it dismissed went to Provost Marshall's and from thence to camp.

✳ ✳ ✳

On July 23rd, General Henry Helleck was given the position of General in Chief by President Lincoln. He immediately departed for McClellan's headquarters on the Peninsula hoping to get the Army of the Potomac back in action. McClellan, miffed over Helleck's appointment without being consulted, informed his new

---

15. Private William Beddleyoung, discharged November 18, 1862 by Surgeon's Certificate.

commander that he was badly outnumbered with 100,000 present for duty to face Lee's minimum of 200,000 troops. Helleck, new to the eastern theater, hadn't even an inkling of McClellan's overestimation and agreed that attacking such a force would be disastrous. McClellan reasoned that he could advance on Richmond if strongly reinforced, and until that point he should remain on the Peninsula, from which point he could ensure Washington's defense. Helleck informed the timid commander that reinforcements were not easily at hand and if he didn't attack soon he would have to be removed from the Peninsula. Helleck returned to Washington to ponder the best course of action with the War Department, leaving McClellan idle.

McClellan and Pope hadn't taken any action after learning of Jackson's arrival in Gordonsville. With the Yankees remaining quiet after Jackson's movement, Lee took the next step in his plan and sent General A. P. Hill's Division to join Jackson on July 27th. Combined, their soldiers numbered 30,000 of Lee's finest. McClellan had never before had such an advantage over Lee, yet he did nothing.[16]

Even with the addition of Hill's Division, Jackson would still be outnumbered two to one. He planned to use tactics he had used before with varying success—a hard, offensive attack that would surprise Pope and delay whatever plans he had in mind. On July 29th, while George Brooks busied himself with paperwork, socializing, and practical jokes, Jackson started his men north. The Confederates had been given the time to take the initiative, and they hadn't let it go to waste.[17]

16. Catton, *Terrible Swift Sword*, 388-390.
17. Krick, Robert K. *Stonewall Jackson at Cedar Mountain*. Univ of North Carolina Press, 2000. 7.

CHAPTER ELEVEN

Glory, Cripple, or Death
July 30–August 9, 1862

———•❖•———

BY THE END of July, George Brooks had seen his fair share of war. The grand spectacle he had marched off to during the patriotic spring of 1861 had faded into a harsh reality of boredom, defeat, and homesickness. He, and most Northerners, were finally accepting that the war would be neither short or glorious.

With no end to the conflict in sight, and no way to return home honorably, Brooks decided that perhaps it was time to leave his beloved Company D after all. Inquiring about a promotion, he hoped another regiment would take him to a more active theater of operations, like outside of Richmond, instead of languishing in the Shenandoah Valley. Having proved himself a capable officer, his promotion seemed almost a sure thing, with only paperwork slowing his advancement.

However, as July gave way to a sweltering August, the lull in the Shenandoah Valley was about to end. On August 2nd, twenty miles south of Culpeper, in the streets of Orange Court House, a fierce little skirmish erupted between some advance cavalry of Jackson and Banks' forces. After at first taking the upper hand but then running into reinforcements, the Yankee troopers decided it best to fall back behind the safety of the Rapidan.

The next day, Sunday, Jackson's men spent the sabbath in camp near Green Springs, Virginia.[1] The hot, sleepy day passed with neither Jackson or Pope knowing that on the Peninsula McClellan had received orders recalling his army. General Helleck had realized McClellan had no plans of renewing the offense on Richmond, and, risking his own reputation, instructed McClellan

———

1. Krick, *Cedar Mountain*, 8-10.

to return to Washington and prepare his army to assist Pope in Northern Virginia. The Peninsula Campaign had failed.[2]

* • ◆ • *

From the Journal of Capt. George A. Brooks

WEDNESDAY, JULY 30. Fine morning. Regiment out under arms at reveille and the Colonel designed having battalion drill but so badly are we off for shoes and so were our duties. Coming as we do on guard every other day that we were sent to quarters after only having roll call was our company drill. No stirring news. Mail from headquarters bringing me letter from Sen Kennard, JM Rutherford and Mrs S.S. Mac in reference to her husband. Fixed up my papers preparatory to sending them by Capt McCormick and wrote him a long letter. Also wrote to Wm H Bell and went to bed very late.

THURSDAY JULY 31. Cloudy morning. Cool and pleasant. Sent off letters by mail and my own documents by the Chaplain who goes to Harrisburg. No very important movements on front that we know of, but trust something may soon turn up as we are tired of remaining idle, preferring more activity. Pope made large glowing promise and surely must do something. Wrote to Val Hummel Jr. In evening took command of regiment and "turned off" dress parade. My first attempt in acting as field officer on dress parade, though I have on the march commanded. Got along middling well, though felt somewhat timid and shaky. Practice necessary to give one confidence. In evening went to town and visited Katy, a sweet confiding innocent, having every confidence. Had I better not retain it during our stay here, even though married and thoroughly disappoint the efforts of those whose intentions in seeking her socially are anything but honorable. I will try and save her, believing my advice and presence will do so by unrelenting good precepts. The ends will justify the means.

FRIDAY, AUGUST 1. Glorious morning, cool and pleasant. Wrote long letter to my friend Estelle to whom I have not written for two months. At 10 o'clock had dress parade at which the orders of President Lincoln in reference to death of Ex President Martin Van Buren were read. Early in morning a Salute of 13 guns were

---

2. Catton, *Terrible Swift Sword*, 388.

fired and continue to fire at regular intervals till now. But Van Buren is dead and no greater eulogy could be given than that he died a patriot—one of the mighty links which binds us to the past has been broken—a great man has fallen in Israel. Firing continued at intervals all day and in evening thirty-four guns were fired at a closing salute. Detailed as officer of the picket but returned.

SATURDAY, AUGUST 2. Cool, pleasant morning. Officer of the day; after guard mounting went to town on "Dixie" after milk. Purchased quart of whiskey for Major. Called at Katy's and secured a canteen of milk. After a few moments conversation, started for camp. On way out stopped at farm house. Men were on guard, got canteen of sweet milk and small bucket of buttermilk. Day very warm. Consumed time in reading Cookers "Story" and finished it towards evening. Went over to see Witman at Col Donnelly's quarters. Witnessed dress parade of 10th Maine. Spent evening in social converse with friends. Have been and am still quite unwell. Very severe attack of diarrhea, the first time I have ever had it, feel much weakened. Everybody greatly discouraged at the conduct of the war but must keep our spirits cheerful. Wrote cheering and encouraging letter home, but if our new troops do not come into the field very soon we will be badly off. Can make no forward movement and will be scarcely able to retain our present position. God speed the right.

SUNDAY, AUGUST 3. Fine morning. Very unwell all night and am quite sick this morning. Too unwell to have inspection. After inspection laid around all day. Towards evening, feeling somewhat better, rode to town with Major and with him called on Miss Kate who was dressed quite neatly and indeed looked pretty. Spent portion of the evening with her and returned to camp. Before retiring took dose of castor oil. In afternoon had a pleasant shower which cut the excessive heat.

MONDAY, AUGUST 4. Up quite early. Cloudy and indications of rain. Last night received no letter but several "Telegraphs". Letter in Telegraph of July 30 1862. No news stirring. Very unwell all day. Took five blue mass pills and another dose castor oil which made me quite sick.[3] Towards evening mail came bringing no letter from home.

---

3. Blue mass pills were prescribed for a variety of maladies and contained mercury, liquorice root, rose water, honey, sugar, and dead rose petals. Mercury, of course, is now a commonly recognized poison.

TUESDAY, AUGUST 5. Passed sleepless night and feel very warm. Day unusually hot. Took dose of salt. No operation. Passed afternoon at headquarters. In evening went with Col. Selfridge and Major M. to Fifth Connecticut. Spent evening with Col. Chapman.[4] Do not like the man. He has soared higher than his wings will carry him and "overtop the bounds of intelligence." He is besides utterly stupefied with liquor or opium, though I think the latter, and can only find engagement when under the influence of some powerful stimulant. Returned by 10 o'clock and went to bed, the ride doing me some good but still feel very weak and medicine has been ineffectual.

WEDNESDAY, AUGUST 6. Up nearly all night. Feel somewhat better this morning. Rode to town bringing in return two bottles fine Madeira wine, a lot of biscuits and some milk. Had long talk with Katie, who was very pleasant. Will visit town this evening. At noon took grain Calomel[5] and have three more to take at proper intervals. Had dumpling's apple for dinner.[6] Very imprudent to indulge when in my condition but could not resist the temptation. About noon Rickett's Brigade arrived, which is an indication of the concentration of our troops and a forward movement by Pope. Glad to see some indications of a move as our inactivity is becoming very irksome and we are all anxious for some glory, cripple or death, the former of course being preferred.

❉ ❉ ❉

Sick and bored, August 6th marked the end of Captain Brooks' diary. That day, Jackson's army relocated to four miles north of Gordonsville, about twenty-five miles from Banks' forces near Culpeper, so Jackson could attend a court martial. The legal proceedings were cut short the next day when scouts indicated that two of Banks' Divisions, Williams' and Augur's, were in camp near Culpeper and isolated from the rest of Banks' forces. The moment Jackson had been waiting for to deliver a disorienting attack on Pope had arrived. He postponed the court martial, never to return to it, and started his army on the road toward Culpeper.

On August 8th, as Jackson slowly continued north, his men struggling in the extraordinarily hot August heat, Banks was also

---

4. George Dunham Chapman commanded the 5th Connecticut during this period. Taken POW at Cedar Mountain, he resigned upon his return in early 1863.
5. Calomel was another mercury-based medicine.
6. apple dumplings - an apple stuffed with sugar and cinnamon wrapped in dough and baked

in motion.[7] Around noon that day, Crawford's Brigade headed south from their camp slightly north of Culpeper with two days' cooked rations to support General Bayard's cavalry which had been strongly pressed by Jackson's troopers along the Rapidan. Entering the town, rumors filled the streets of Jackson's approach, indicating some engagement was sure to be made. The men were taunted by the citizens with exclamations like "Old Jack will give you all you want!" and "You will come back tomorrow on the double quick if you come at all!" The men, however, were well used to the chatter of southerners and Charles W. Boyce, historian of the 28th New York, recalled that "The men were full of enthusiasm, never in better spirits or condition. Conscious of their strength, they proudly started out, expectant and ready to meet the enemy." A General on Banks' staff said "Crawford's brigade was moving to the front, with drums beating and colors flying . . . it was the most inspiring sight I ever beheld."

The brigade halted in the shady town square by the court house, where they took drinks and filled their canteens. Temperatures were high that day, near one hundred degrees, and within a mile men started to fall by the roadside in considerable numbers. Some were so badly affected they "lay by the roadside in almost a dying condition, as far as appearances could indicate, and it was a wonder that so few of them were really seriously affected."[8] General Gordon, commanding the 3rd brigade in Williams' Division, said his men were "more fatigued than if they had made a march of twice the distance."[9]

General Pope's other brigades also took to the march, following orders to converge on Culpeper. The remainder of Banks' Corps started near the Rappahannock River that morning and had reached Hazel River by night, while Rickett's Division of McDowell's Corps marched through Culpeper and headed towards Madison Court House in search of Confederate threats. Sigel's command, located in Sperryville, had the most unproductive day. Despite there only being one clear route, Sigel deliberated on which road to take, and didn't start for Culpeper until evening.[10]

Crawford's Brigade struggled along the Culpeper Road in the heat, moving along about a mile at a time before they had to pause to rest and allow those who had fallen out to catch up. This continued for about five miles, at which point they crossed

7. Krick, *Cedar Mountain*, 13-16.
8. Marvin, *Fifth Connecticut*, 35, 152.
9. Gordon, George Henry. *Brook Farm to Cedar Mountain*. JR Osgood, 1883. 279.
10. Krick, *Cedar Mountain*, 21-2.

Photograph of the Cedar Mountain battlefield with its namesake mountain in the distance. (Source: Library of Congress.)

Bayard's cavalry picket line. Leaving the road, they bivouacked in support of some artillery near a small stream known as Cedar Run at the foot of Cedar Mountain. Sometimes called Slaughter's Mountain because of the Slaughter family's residence on its slopes, the elevation offered a commanding view of the surrounding countryside. Facing the south-west, Captain Edwin E. Marvin, historian of the 5th Connecticut Infantry, described the topography near Cedar Mountain:

> To the left of the Orange (Culpeper) Road, which led off to the front, and in the direction a little to the right of Cedar Mountain, the country was open fields almost all of the distance to the mountain for a half a mile or more in width. In the midst of this open land on the left, there was a large field of standing corn fully grown, beyond which the land ascended to a slight ridge, then further on fell into a valley and beyond this rose again towards the mountain. At the right of the road the country, within view, was wooded, with the exception of one open field stretching off into the woods on either side, to what extent could not be determined from that point. Up the northeastern slope of it, about halfway, the forest land commenced and from that point to the top it was wooded.

By evening, stragglers caught up to their regiments. Dinner was prepared and tired bodies laid out on the ground in the hopes of a restful night's sleep. Most of Jackson's forces stopped and encamped about a mile north of Orange. Exhausted from their toilsome march in the summer heat, they were given little chance to recuperate due to a Federal cavalry probe around 3:00 A.M. that woke just about everyone. By daylight on August 9th, Jackson's sleepy soldiers were back in their ranks and on the march.[11]

Crawford's Brigade woke at dawn to find the heat still in full force; by 7:00 A.M. it was already 84°. Fixing coffee and a "hasty breakfast" of pork and hardtack, 40 additional rounds of ammunition were passed out per man. Around 11:00 in the morning, Crawford's men noticed movement on the heights of the mountain, and assumed it must be Confederate cavalry or Union officers scouting the area. When some artillery shells rained down, they were soon sure of the identity of those on the mountain, and Crawford's batteries replied.[12]

The Federal infantry rested in a clover field with their rifles stacked nearby until mid-day, when General Williams arrived to join Crawford's Brigade. Soon after, the first artillery duel quieted, and General Banks, Gordon's Brigade, and Augur's Division reached the field.[13] Assuming command, Banks deployed Augur's Division to the left of the road and placed Gordon's Brigade behind Crawford's on the right.[14] Banks' 9,000 men, probably at this point more concerned with the heat than anything else, didn't know they were lining up to make a stand against 15,000 of the Confederacy's finest soldiers.[15]

General Banks waited for orders from Pope, and while the field was mostly silent, General Williams took the chance to invite some of the officers from his old brigade, Crawford's, to lunch. A letter home recounts the experience:

> After my brigades were put in position, our cook got us up a good lunch of coffee, ham, etc., and I invited many field officers of my old brigade to join me. After lunching, we all lay down under a shade tree and talked over the events of the ten months we had been together, and everybody seemed as unconcerned and careless as if he was on the lawn of a watering place instead of the front of a vastly superior enemy. Col. Donnelly of the 28th New York, a great joke[r] and full of humor, was in excellent

11. Marvin, *Fifth Connecticut*, 152-54. Krick, *Cedar Mountain*, 34, 39-42.
12. Bradley, *Surviving Stonewall*, 129.
13. Williams, *From the Cannon's Mouth*, 100.
14. Bradley, *Surviving Stonewall*, 132.
15. Krick, *Cedar Mountain*, 45.

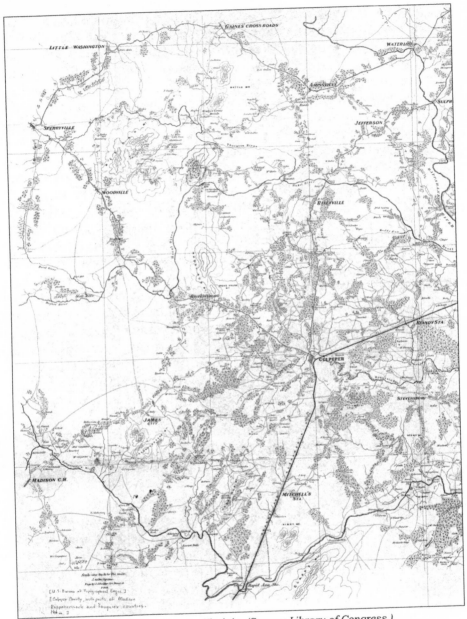

Circa 1863 map of Culpeper County, Virginia. (Source: Library of Congress.)

spirits and cracked his jokes as joyously as ever. Sorrow and misfortune seemed far away and yet of all the field officers of these three regiments (mine) not one, five hours afterwards, was unhurt. Everyone was either killed or wounded.[16]

16. Williams, *From the Cannon's Mouth*, 100.

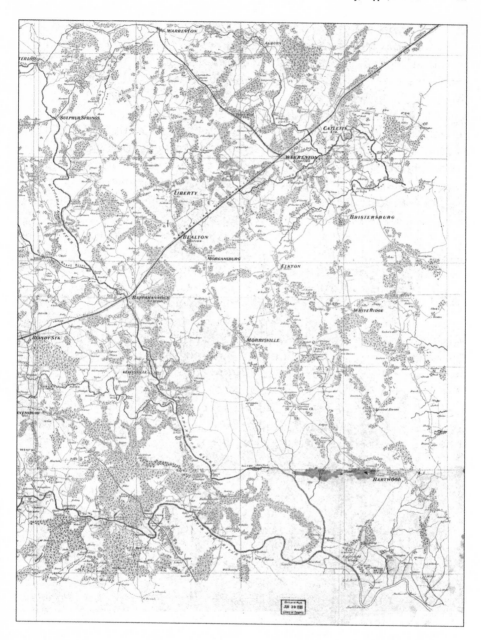

While the Union officers dined, Jackson's men were deploying under the hot summer sun, their movements hidden by the Virginia hills. General Jubal Early's Brigade, the vanguard of Jackson's army, stopped by a schoolhouse less than a mile south of what would soon be the battlefield. There they waited until orders arrived indicating that Early should advance with the support of General Winder's Brigade. As Early waited for Winder's arrival, artillery took position near the Major house. Around 2:00, the batteries opened fire and cavalry, which had been sparring in the open fields with little effect, was called in.

By that time temperatures had reached 98° with no breeze. Edmund Brown of the 27th Indiana, a part of Gordon's Brigade, said of the weather: "Our bodies seemed to be a furnace on fire" and described "many" men "lying on the ground frothing at the mouth, rolling their eyeballs and writhing in painful contortions."

As General Ewell was deploying two brigades on the slopes of Cedar Mountain, Early advanced onto the field below and took a position along the Crittenden lane, advancing forward until his brigade crested a ridge before them. Union artillery opened fire and he pulled his soldiers back behind the safety of the ridge.

In response to the Federal artillery fire, Early ordered up his guns. At 4:00 P.M., Confederate artillery opened from two locations near Early's Brigade—one to his right on a knoll covered in cedar trees that came to be known as the "Cedars," and another location to his left. Batteries joined in from the heights of Cedar Mountain, lobbing shells onto the Yankees from an elevation of about one hundred feet. Around the same time, General Winder's Division of Southerners reached the field and rushed artillery forward to a position near the Crittenden family's gate. By 4:30, they joined in the hot artillery duel and attracted the attention of the Union gunners.

The Crittenden Gate was bordered on both sides by heavy forest and fences, and would soon prove to be a bottleneck for Confederate troops moving onto the field. Winder's first brigade, commanded by Colonel Thomas Garnett, was the first to arrive at the gate just as Union artillery shells started raining in earnest. Pausing to allow some artillery to pass to the front, a Federal shell exploded in Garnett's ranks, killing five instantly and wounding six others.

Garnett ordered his brigade off the road and into the shelter of the woods. Artillery shrieked and exploded overhead as the Rebels made their way into the foliage. The physical damage to the soldiers was minimal and was much more devastating psychologically. Garnett laid his men down in the woods for a period of time, and to his soldiers the wait under fire seemed excruciating. One terrified man recounted that they waited in the woods for two hours. In truth, it was about a half an hour until they were placed in line of battle at the edge of the woods. Due in part to the denseness of the brush and trees, they lined up in a somewhat L-shape, with two of the regiments facing forward toward a wheatfield and the other two perpendicular to them, facing Cedar Mountain. Still ducking from the concussion of shells and the splintering of trees, the soldiers' eyes scanned the fields before them, but the swells in the terrain prevented them from seeing the Union lines forming in the distance.

As Garnett maneuvered in the woods, more Southern troops had arrived on the field. General W. B. Taliaferro's Brigade, sweltering in the heat and having had almost no sleep the night before, passed through the artillery melee at the Crittenden Gate and took position on Early's left, creating a loose tie into Garnett's right.

By this point, the artillery fight consisted of twenty-three Confederate guns exchanging fire with Union pieces that enjoyed a slight advantage in number.[17] The batteries of large guns positioned at the Crittenden Gate between Garnett and Taliaferro were immediately recognized as especially problematic by Banks' men, and shortly a "great anxiety was manifested to capture the battery that was constantly firing from a position near [the] woods. This fire was directed to the forces of the Second [Augur's] Division on the left."[18] Appearing to only be lightly supported by infantry, Colonel Knipe of the 46th Pennsylvania suggested charging the batteries and taking the guns. General Banks, never accused of lacking aggression, agreed.[19]

Around the same time Banks was in consult with his officers, a battalion of U.S. Regulars advanced and deployed as skirmishers into the cornfield in front of Augur's Division. Hidden amidst the corn stalks, they started picking off Early's soldiers and came very close to a Confederate battery before their presence was realized. A regiment of Georgians was rushed up to protect the guns.[20]

Crawford moved his brigade—the 46th Pennsylvania, 5th Connecticut, 28th New York and some detached companies of the 3rd Wisconsin (the 10th Maine was left behind to guard artillery)— forward through the woods at about five o'clock.[21] Edwin Marvin of the 5th Connecticut remembered his brigade's deployment:

17. Krick, *Cedar Mountain*, 48-9, 50-3, 56, 60-1, 68, 77-81, 87, 92.
18. Boyce, *Twenty-eighth New York*, 35.
19. Bradley, *Surviving Stonewall*, 133.
20. Krick, *Cedar Mountain*, 92.
21. Boyce, *Twenty-eighth New York*, 36.

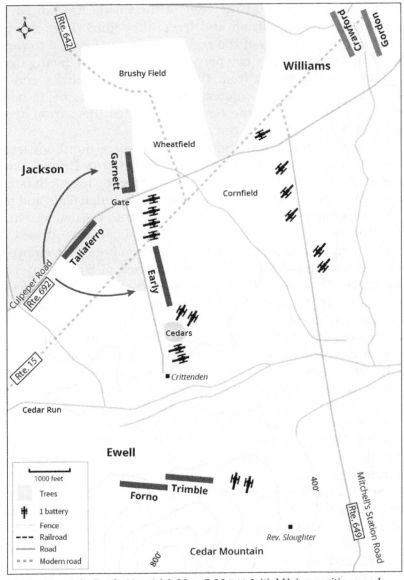

[Cedar Mountain Battle Map 1.] 3:30 to 5:00 P.M. Initial Union positions and Confederate infantry takes place during the artillery duel.

These woods were thick with weeds, briars and underbrush, and almost impassable, and one could see but a little way to the right or left and could not tell whether any of the other regiments of the brigade were advancing in the same line of battle or not, till the line came near the open field, where the woods became somewhat thinner. A high log fence ran along the edge of the woods, in front of the line of the brigade and between it and the open field. Over the fence, and covering more than the whole of the brigade front, was the open field. In front of the right of the line, the 46th Pennsylvania, were low shrub oaks and brush of a couple of years' growth, rising to the height of a man's shoulders, and to the right of this, heavy timber.[22]

As Crawford's men struggled through the foliage, the mostly ineffectual fire of the Union artillery found a target. While shouting orders to artillery near the Crittenden Gate, General Winder was mortally wounded by a cannonball. As the terribly wounded general who had "a tremendous hole . . . torn in his side" was carried from the field, General Taliaferro assumed command of the division. Jackson had imparted little knowledge of his plans on his subordinates, and Winder hadn't bothered to do so, either. Taliaferro found himself facing a battle with little idea of what he was supposed to do.

Taliaferro hastened off to examine the position of Garnett's men in the woods. Unable to see any significant Federal force across the wheatfield, Taliaferro warned Garnett that perhaps the hills were hiding the enemy. Skirmishers were sent out and quickly determined that there was indeed a Yankee force—Crawford's—on the other side of the wheat, and their battle line extended two to three hundred yards past the end of Garnett's line. If Crawford attacked, Garnett would be easily flanked.

To remedy the situation, Taliaferro detached the 10th Virginia Infantry and sent them to attach to Garnett's left, and also ordered the Stonewall Brigade, under the command of underqualified Colonel Charles Ronald, to form on the left of Garnett's line. Ronald's battle hardened veterans also ran into trouble maintaining their ranks in the thick woods, and Ronald became frazzled as he tried to maneuver the men forward. Finally, after about a half an hour, they reached the edge of the woods and faced a "brushy" unkempt field which occupied the northern edge of the wheatfield. Unfortunately, they had ended up nowhere close to the end of Garnett's dangling line. Leveling a fence before them and laying down, the Stonewall Brigade waited for about twenty minutes as Ronald sent off a messenger to get instructions from Garnett, the reason for which is unknown. As the brigade waited

---

22. Marvin, *Fifth Connecticut*, 154-5.

for the courier to return, Garnett's leftmost regiment, the 1st Virginia Battalion, remained exposed.

At this point, three Union brigades stood opposite four Confederate. The Union left consisted of two brigades, commanded by Generals Prince and Geary, of Augur's Division, who were preparing to advance through the cornfield in front of them at two Confederate brigades (Early and Taliaferro) and four batteries, while four more Rebel batteries loomed on the mountain side. On the Union right, Crawford's single brigade stood ready to charge on the Confederate battery at the Crittenden Gate, with Garnett directly in their path and Ronald's Brigade to their right. In their current position, neither Crawford, Garnett, or Ronald could see one another as they hid in the thick woods of the rolling Virginia countryside. Union reserves on the right consisted of Gordon's Brigade (2nd Massachusetts, 27th Indiana and a portion of the 3rd Wisconsin not attached to Crawford) and the 10th Maine. On the left, Greene's tiny brigade—numbering only 372 men—stood in support of artillery on the Union extreme left. More Union reserves were in route from Culpeper, and more Confederate from Orange. At 5:45 P.M., Augur's two brigades started their assault and stepped into the corn.[23]

Advancing forward toward the Confederate lines, the Union soldiers did their best to maintain ranks. The tall corn provided a visual shelter from the Confederate infantry, but it also disoriented the sweating and nervous soldiers. Passing over rises in the ground and fences, artillery shells rained in from their front and the heights of Cedar Mountain. After noticing Augur's presence, Early and Taliaferro moved forward slightly from their position along the Crittenden lane and opened fire. Artillery exploded overhead as Prince's Brigade took fire from Early, while Geary tangled with Taliaferro to the front and took fire from the 21st Virginia straight into his right flank.

The Union regiments took heavy casualties, a soldier in the 29th Ohio remembering that the dead and wounded were "left thick around . . . It was scarce possible to tell the living from the dead" amidst the stalks of corn. Volleys of rifle and artillery fire cut through the corn as the two lines of opposing infantry doggedly stood their ground, and eventually Taliaferro and Early's ranks started to tire. A member of Jackson's staff noticed the General "looking anxiously to the rear." Jackson soon passed a

---

23. Krick, *Cedar Mountain*, 96-7, 111-2, 114-6, 123.

message to Early that General Hill's Division would soon be arriving and to stand firm.

Upon Hill's arrival, Thomas' Brigade of Georgians were deployed where needed amidst Early and Taliaferro's troops, including dispatching the 12th Georgia to the right of the Cedars where Early feared being flanked. Coming into line at a right angle to the rest of the Confederate troops, the Georgians opened fire on the flank of Pierce's line, which consisted of the 102nd New York. An officer of the regiment recalled the Georgians "took every company till they got to the third from the right."

Crawford's Brigade stood in line and listened to the maelstrom to their left for about fifteen minutes. Lined up from left to right stood the 5th Connecticut, the 28th New York, and the 46th Pennsylvania. In addition, six companies of the 3rd Wisconsin came up on the right of the brigade and went into action with it, but their movement was uncoordinated with the main of the brigade. Due to the terrain, they could see nothing to their front but the ground before them. A soldier would later recall the terrain they faced: "There is a swell of the ground, which falls off gently toward the enemy's side, and becomes a marsh; but as it approaches the enemy's wood, it rises again rather suddenly, and the hillside thus made is densely wooded." In total, the field was about 300 yards wide and although most of the wheat had already been removed from the field, some shocks remained, interspersed with piles of rock from clearing the fields. Unsure of the ground before him, General Crawford sent forward a small scouting party to determine the location of the enemy.[24]

While the scouts moved forward, the men waited in their ranks, hearing the fury of Augur's advance and seeing the smoke of rifles and cannon as sweat continued to roll off of their bodies, only to be absorbed by their already soaked uniforms. Brows were wiped in an attempt to keep the salty liquid from falling into their eyes. George Brooks, still weakened from his illness, sweltered in the heat as he stood at the far left of the regiment, with fifty-nine of his men who were present for duty. Behind them, Brooks' friend Major Matthews surveyed the field from the back of his horse. To the right, near the center of the regiment, flew the national and state colors, draped still around their staffs in the breezeless summer heat. Behind them waited Colonel Knipe on his horse, his 5'1" frame anxiously waiting to advance. Off to his

24. Krick, *Cedar Mountain*, 123-4, 128, 131, 135-7, 144-7.

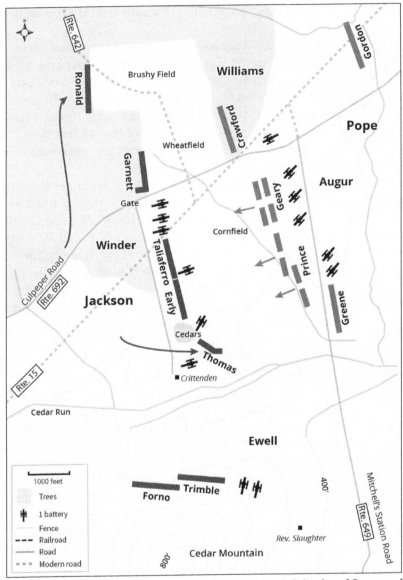

[Cedar Mountain Battle Map 2.] 5:46 to 6:00 P.M. Augur's brigades of Geary and Prince attack as Crawford takes position.

left, Colonel Donnelly, who had just hours prior been cracking jokes at lunch, shepherded over the 28th New York.[25]

The scouting party returned and reported their findings to Crawford, having come very close to the Confederate ranks.

25. Bradley, *Surviving Stonewall*, 134-7.

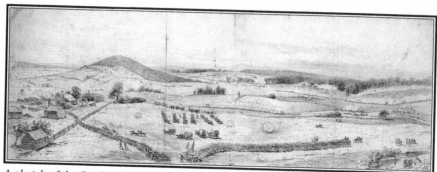

A sketch of the Battle of Cedar Mountain. (Source: Library of Congress.)

Banks had silenced the artillery in preparation for Crawford's assault, and Crawford hastily sent back a note asking for some close artillery support. It was too late, though, and Williams sent orders to attack. Knowing he would have to advance without artillery support, Crawford carried out his orders and sent an aide to dispatch instructions to his regiments. The 5th Connecticut received the orders first and eagerly jumped the fence in front of them and rushed into the field. Since the rest of the regiments weren't ready, the zealous 5th was rounded up and put back in place. The brigade line was straightened, rifles were loaded, and the call to fix bayonets rang out.

At about 6:00 P.M., the brigade moved past the fence, some jumping over and others pushing down sections so they could more easily pass through.[26] Reforming and straightening ranks on the other side, they started into the wheatfield at a double quick, the officers yelling "Charge, charge and yell."[27] General Gordon, who watched from his reserve position, said the brigade "burst with loud cries from the woods, swept like a torrent across the wheat-field."[28]

The Confederate gunners up on Cedar Mountain also noticed Crawford's wave across the wheat, and immediately opened an accurate fire. Blue-clad men started to fall. Next to Company D, a shell fell into Company F, leaving Charlie Pettiford with a minor head wound and fracturing Samuel Cupps' scull. For the rest of his life, he suffered from epilepsy and memory lapses. Another projectile found Company I, leaving a man almost deaf, and Company B, where Michael Higman's right foot was almost blown off.

26. Krick, *Cedar Mountain*, 144-8.
27. Marvin, *Fifth Connecticut*, 158.
28. Gordon, *Brook Farm*, 294.

Colonel Knipe, riding forward behind the regiment, was struck by a shell fragment which cut a gash above his right eye and ripped loose a large flap of his scalp. Another shell struck the palm of his right hand, cutting skin and muscles. In terrible pain, he was forced to leave the field early in the assault, leaving Lt. Colonel Selfridge in command.[29]

The brigade pushed onward, and upon reaching the midpoint of the field came under rifle fire from the Confederate line. The volleys were heavy and continuous and "became a steady roar."[30] Colonel George Andrews remembered the volume of the rifle fire, commenting that it was "the heaviest and most continuous sound of musketry that I ever heard." Captain Owen Luchenbach of Company C fell to the ground, a musket ball having shattered the bones of his right calf. Colonel Donnelly of the 28th New York fell mortally wounded, and the Lieutenant Colonel of the regiment fell shortly afterward with a shattered arm.[31]

Garnett's Brigade threw unrelenting volleys into Crawford's ranks, their fire focused on the 5th Connecticut and 28th New York based on their position. Color bearers fell in succession in the 5th, and afterward they realized seven had fallen in the initial charge.

As they swept forward, the right of the 46th Pennsylvania had fallen slightly behind the main line due to the rugged terrain, and even further to their right the 3rd Wisconsin had struggled through briars and saplings into an isolated position in the brushy field. Moments after Garnett opened fire on the left of Crawford's line, the Stonewall Brigade opened on the right, focusing volleys into the 46th Pennsylvania and 3rd Wisconsin.[32]

Pausing at the base of a small ravine a short distance from a fence that bordered the woods, Crawford's men fired into the Confederate ranks before them. The Rebel regiments, still poorly placed and all smaller than Crawford's, were growing anxious as the overwhelming force approached. Still, they laid down heavy fire. Lt. William Caldwell of Company K of the 46th Pennsylvania rushed in front of his men and waved his sword yelling "Follow me in the charge!" Moments later he fell, shot through the head. Around the same time, Adjutant George Boyd was knocked to the ground by a musket ball that found his left thigh.

---

29. Bradley, *Surviving Stonewall*, 139-40.
30. Krick, *Cedar Mountain*, 149.
31. Bradley, *Surviving Stonewall*, 140.
32. Krick, *Cedar Mountain*, 149-151.

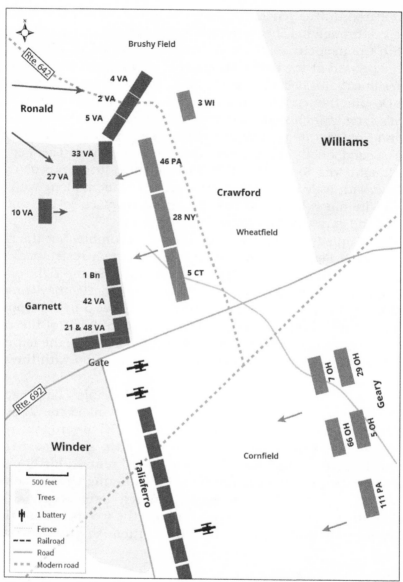

[Cedar Mountain Battle Map 3.] 6:00 P.M. Crawford charges into the woods.

On the left side of the 46th, Lt. Robert Wilson, now in command after the wounding of his Captain, ran toward the woodline yelling "Company C! Get over the fence and after them!" All along Crawford's line, men obeyed their officers' cries and moved forward to the fence, some pushing it down and others trying to go over it. Nineteen year old George Hoffmaster of Company E clambered up the fence but fell back to the earth when a bullet passed through his chest, shattering his rib as it exited his back.[33] A 5th Connecticut soldier was struck and killed by nine bullets as he paused at the fence. So many soldiers were slain along the fence line that it became hard to pass without stepping on a body.

Despite the terrible slaughter at the edge of the woods, Crawford's men launched themselves into the foliage, in some places found Confederate ranks three deep—the first rank laying down, the second on its knees, and the third standing. The Federal onslaught was too much, though, and after firing two or three volleys with little effect, the 1st Virginia Battalion, along with the 10th Virginia (which was trying to get into place in the woods) broke and ran within minutes.[34]

The Confederate line was beginning to crumble, but the right of the 46th Pennsylvania had run into staunch resistance. The seasoned 27th and 33rd Virginia, who stood on the right of the Stonewall Brigade, directly faced the advancing Pennsylvanians and poured a steady fire into their ranks. Slowed by the opposition, the 46th broke in two, with roughly two-thirds of the regiment remaining to fight the Stonewall Brigade while the leftmost third, including Brooks' Company D, continued on with the rest of the brigade.[35]

The right of the 46th exploited the 27th Virginia's failure to tie in with the 1st Virginia Battalion and fully flanked the 27th, at which point the 27th started to dissolve and fell towards the rear. However, the 33rd Virginia, next to the 27th, stood fast. Their Colonel, upon hearing the 27th "was gone," refused his line and started pouring merciless fire into the withering Union ranks.[36] Here the right of the 46th would remain in a perilous fight as the rest of their brigade arced away through the woods toward their objective: the artillery placed near the Crittenden gate.

---

33. Bradley, *Surviving Stonewall*, 141-3.
34. Krick, *Cedar Mountain*, 151.
35. Bradley, *Surviving Stonewall*, 145. Bradley, George C. "Re: 46th Pennsylvania Volunteer Inft." Received by Ben Myers, 26 July 2012. There is no account of which companies went where, except for Company K which was on the extreme right that day. By George Bradley's astute reasoning, this is consistent with army regulations of the time to order companies in line by their Captain's seniority. If the 46th followed the regulation that day, as the second most senior, Captain Brooks and Company D would've then been on the left flank of the regiment. This is reinforced by an article on September 18th, 1862 in the *Pennsylvania Telegraph* which states "command of the regiment fell upon Capt. Brooks in fact he found himself in command of the entire right wing [of the Union line]" which indicates to the author that Brooks remained with the main body of Crawford's Brigade and helped lead the main charge instead of remaining in the woods.
36. "Refusing" the line involves placing companies on the threatened flank back at an angle to the rest of the regiment. In this position, the regiment isn't as exposed to enemy fire from the rear.

Further to their right, back in the Brushy field, six companies of the 3rd Wisconsin—about 250 men total—were brought to a standstill by the other three regiments of the Stonewall Brigade. After moving slightly forward into the Brushy field, the 5th, 2nd, and 4th Virginia fired from an angle into the badly outnumbered Wisconsians' right flank, and despite a brave stand, they were forced to retreat.

While the 3rd Wisconsin and the right part of the 46th Pennsylvania were taking a beating from the Stonewall Brigade, the 28th New York, 5th Connecticut and the left three companies of the 46th Pennsylvania, including George Brooks and Company D, continued to roll up Garnett's Brigade. The 1st Virginia Battalion's departure had completely exposed the flank of the 42nd Virginia. The 42nd Virginia had seen action earlier that year during the Shenandoah Valley campaign, and cooly unleashed heavy fire into the 5th Connecticut's charging ranks to their front.[37] The 42nd paid for their coolness under fire in casualties. Within minutes, the Virginians realized the 28th New York and 46th Pennsylvania were on their flank and wrapping around behind their ranks.[38] Trying to fight from three directions, men started to fall in great number, and the fighting turned savage. Ammunition was plentiful—few volleys had been fired—but there was no time to load weapons. Soldiers turned to bayonets, rifle stocks and butts turned into clubs, fists, stones, and any other available object as they struggled to kill before being killed. A staggering third of the 42nd Virginia was killed, a statistic almost beyond comprehension in comparison to other major battles of the war. Historian Robert Krick concluded in his extensive analysis of the battle that Crawford's fight with the 42nd was "unsurpassed for ferocity by any other engagement during the war."[39]

Blue-clad soldiers fell too. George Brooks pressed forward, perhaps seeing his friend Major Matthews fall from his horse. Three bullets struck Matthews in the knee, forearm, and sliced his scalp. Another felled his horse, and as he tumbled to the ground his sword broke in two, the jagged edge slicing through his groin, creating a wound that would still be open ten years later. Lt. Col Selfridge also fell to the ground after his horse was shot, but despite a uniform, hat, and saddle riddled with bullets, he remained

---

37. Krick, *Cedar Mountain*, 154, 170-4.
38. Bradley, *Surviving Stonewall*, 145-6.
39. Krick, *Cedar Mountain*, 159.

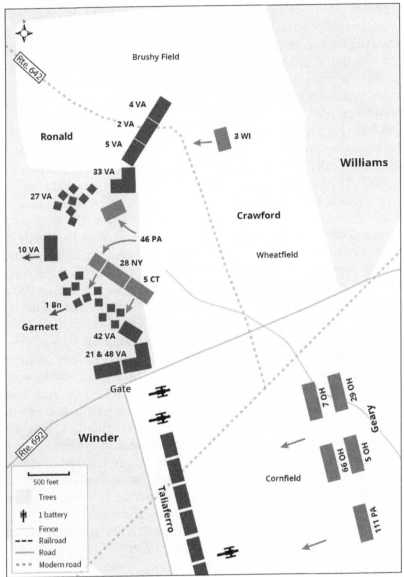

[Cedar Mountain Battle Map 4.] 6:05 P.M. Garnett's left gives way.

unscathed except for bruises. The men would later nickname him "Old Ironclad" in honor of his good luck.

Sergeant Oliver Simmons of Company D found himself surrounded and was nearly knocked senseless by a blow from a rifle butt, but still managed to bayonet two Rebels and club a third to death. Crawford's soldiers fell shot, sometimes more than once, in every location of the body imaginable. Bones were broken by the impact of bullets and handheld weapons. Snipers in trees picked off blue-clad soldiers.[40] Officers were falling quickly, and somewhere in the melee George Brooks was struck in the left foot and arm. The wounds were minor enough to continue forward, and so he pressed on.[41]

As casualties mounted, some Virginians attempted to surrender, but by this time confusion and frenzy were paramount in the hot, smoke filled woods, with men scattered and fighting for their own survival. Veterans on both sides of the fight would go on to claim that they watched comrades being murdered as they tried to surrender. In the confused and desperate fighting where no time existed to distinguish friend from foe, this solemn occurrence was probably unavoidable.

After delaying the Federal onslaught for perhaps ten minutes, the overwhelmed 42nd Virginia was forced to fall back in disorder. Their departure meant the remainder of Garnett's line—the 48th and 21st Virginia—were in serious trouble. Not only were they all that remained of their brigade, but half of the 48th and all of the 21st unknowingly stood with their backs to the storm of advancing Federals. The remainder of the 48th, which had faced the wheatfield during the fight, had fallen back with the 42nd Virginia.

Despite the mayhem and ferocity of the fight in the woods, Crawford's Brigade maintained some cohesion and advanced on the backs of the unsuspecting Virginians in some form of battle line. As the 21st and 48th Virginia continued firing upon Augur's men to their front in the field, they were utterly surprised when Crawford's men fired a volley at their backs from a distance of only thirty paces. Within minutes, the fight again went hand to hand. One soldier of the 1st Virginia who witnessed the fight commented on the ferocity, saying that "when the bayonet failed to do its work, or was broken or lost, with clubbed guns the contest was continued." James Binford of the 21st was one of the six survivors out of the eighteen his company took into the fight because he collapsed from the heat before something worse happened. He wrote of his regiment's experience: "We were literally butchered . . ."

Lieutenant Colonel Cunningham, acting commander of the 21st, was attempting to move his men out of their death trap in the woods when he was struck by a bullet and killed. The 21st

---

40. Bradley, *Surviving Stonewall*, 145-8.
41. *Pennsylvania Daily Telegraph*. August 14th, 1862.

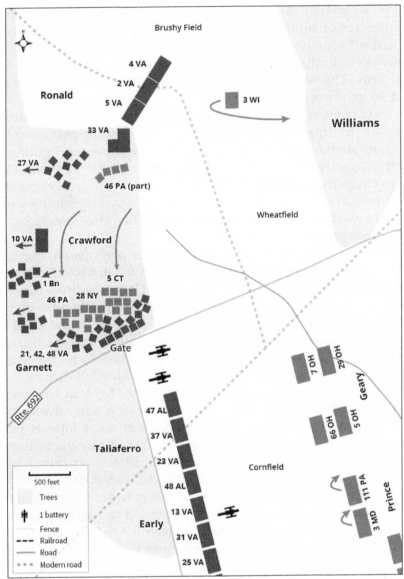

[Cedar Mountain Battle Map 5.] 6:15 P.M. Crawford shatters the 48th and 21st Virginia.

lost all order and stampeded for the rear. In the confusion, many of them fell prisoner. Portions of the 48th Virginia followed the 21st in their race away from the battle, while other remnants of both units remained on the field in small clusters, the Federal tide having missed their location.[42]

42. Krick, *Cedar Mountain*, 160-1, 177-8, 183-4.

Casualties in the 21st and parts of the 48th were daunting, but still fewer in comparison to Crawford's ranks. The brigade paid a steep price to scatter the Virginians from the woods, but the job still wasn't done. They continued onward, bursting out of the woods and into the road that led to the Crittenden Gate. General Jackson himself was in that area, and while the Federals had been tearing up his line he had looked in the direction of the firing acting slightly nervous. He commented that "some hard work" was soon to come.

Riding closer to the Crittenden Gate, Jackson paused momentarily until the first few Federals ran out of the woods. He immediately leaped his horse over an adjacent fence and rode into the woods. Coming across some of Garnett's men who were running away from the front in disorder, he realized the peril in which his line had been placed and rode for the rear in search of more of A.P. Hill's reinforcements.

Jackson had also ordered back the artillery at the Crittenden Gate, and the artillerists dutifully ceased fire and limbered up. A few pieces were drawn off, but soon the remaining guns were surrounding by panicked Confederate infantry fleeing the woods. The guns couldn't be withdrawn or fired without hitting friendly troops, and so they sat silently in place.

While Crawford's Brigade had been busy destroying the left of the Confederate line, Augur's Division had been pounding the right for around a half hour. Although Augur hadn't made considerable progress, he had occupied the Confederate brigades of Taliaferro, Early and Thomas. As Crawford's men spilled out of the woods where they had just destroyed Garnett's Brigade, they moved directly for Taliaferro's Brigade's left flank. Unfortunately for Taliaferro, the regiment that stood there was the green and shaky 47th Alabama. The Federals immediately started firing volleys straight into the Alabamians, and the outmatched, inexperienced Southerners began to panic and fell back in chaos. On the other side of the brigade, their sister regiment, the 48th Alabama, crumbled and ran, too.

With half of Taliaferro's Brigade gone, the veteran 37th Virginia regiment was the new left flank, but they too proved no match. Now, the 23rd Virginia was the only regiment of Taliaferro's Brigade that remained. Their Colonel, George Curtis, held them in place until they were ordered to fall back. Curtis paid for the stand with his life; he was mortally wounded during their retreat.

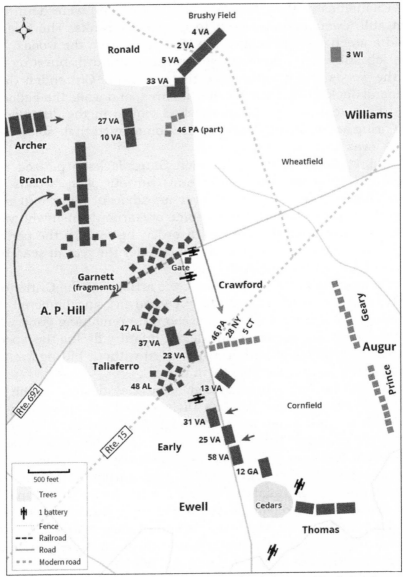

[Cedar Mountain Battle Map 6.] 6:15 to 6:30 P.M. Taliaferro and Early break as reinforcements arrive.

By this point, well over half of the Confederate line had ceased to exist. With Taliaferro gone, Crawford's men continued onward toward Early's now exposed left, forcing the removal of Pegram and Hardy's batteries from the field for fear of capture. Early's leftmost regiment, the 13th Virginia, was a veteran regiment that had started its service under the command of A.P. Hill, and at

Cedar Mountain they were commanded by the capable Colonel James A. Walker (nine months after the battle Walker would be promoted to command of the Stonewall Brigade). Coming under flank fire from Crawford, the 13th stood firm even though regiments to its right started to waver and break. As pressure increased on the regiment, Walker maneuvered them to help an artillery piece escape the field before retreating in good order.

Moments earlier, General Early, who had been off to his brigade's right positioning Thomas' men, returned to his line to find it wasn't there. While absent, the rolls in the terrain had blocked his view and he had no knowledge of his brigade's plight. With his men already scattered, Early had only Thomas' Brigade and the 12th Georgia, a regiment from his own brigade that had been detached. He immediately turned and rode back to their position, resolving to hold onto what was left of Jackson's line with all of his will.

As Crawford's Brigade came into sight of the 12th Georgia and Thomas' Brigade, the 12th grew uncomfortable with the numbers of enemy soldiers approaching. Early silenced their fears, reminding them that Thomas' Brigade stood near and reinforcements were imminent. Owing partially to a strong strategic position on a hill and some heavy artillery fire from the Cedars, the 12th held just long enough to slow Crawford's momentum, which had already far exceeded expectations. Having lost about a third of their strength, running low on ammunition, and under heavy artillery fire from the base of Cedar Mountain, Crawford ground to a stop just north of the Cedars.[43]

Crawford's men must've known they were spent, but with the Confederate line in shambles they stood and fought in the hope reinforcements would arrive. Tragically, due to a delay in bringing up Gordon's fresh brigade, none appeared. With A.P. Hill's reinforcements arriving and the urging of Stonewall himself, Confederate regiments that had retreated moved back up into the fight. Facing fire from several angles and an overwhelming number of fresh Confederate reinforcements, Crawford's shattered brigade gave way. In the woods, the remaining pockets of the 46th Pennsylvania still facing off against the Stonewall Brigade and Branch's fresh North Carolina Brigade were also overwhelmed.

Retreating back over the wheatfield which they had just fought so hard to capture, Crawford's men still resisted, stopping

---

43. Krick, *Cedar Mountain*, 185, 187-193, 194-201.

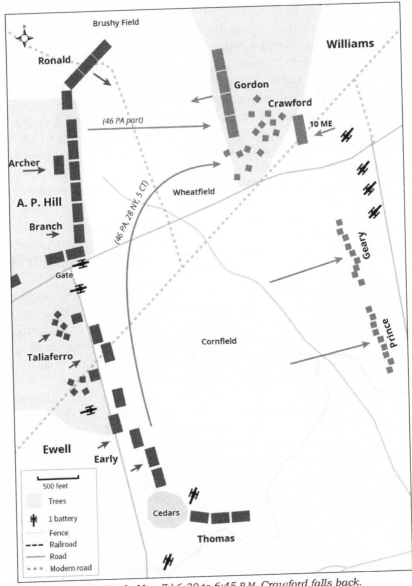

[Cedar Mountain Battle Map 7.] 6:30 to 6:45 P.M. Crawford falls back.

to fire as bullets rained in from the front, side, and rear. Corporal
Jonathan Morgan of the 46th Pennsylvania was shot in the back
as he made his way across the open expanse. The bullet passed
through his ribs and through his upper arm, but he kept on running. Two comrades who fled, Daniel Bobb and David Snyder of
Company K, fell prisoner when Bobb was struck in the spine with

buckshot and Snyder stayed with his fallen friend. John Crosby of Company H, one of the last on the field, fired his rifle one last time, and then turned to retreat, but was hit by a bullet in the back of his thigh. The state and regimental colors only made it off of the field because of the bravery of their bearers, one of whom died from wounds that evening.[44]

Moments before, as Crawford's Brigade passed the midway point of their retreat, the 10th Maine had advanced into the wheatfield and opened fire on the Confederates, but proved no match. Two fresh Confederate brigades commanded by Generals Archer and Branch leveled a harrowing fire on the Maine men, many of whom were certain their fight lasted over thirty minutes, when in truth it could not have lasted more than five. With casualties mounting and the Stonewall Brigade nearing from the right, the 10th Maine retreated from the field. At the same time, Gordon's Brigade finally came into place at the edge of the woodline before the wheatfield in preparation for their own advance.

It was now 6:45 P.M., and the infantry battle had been raging for about an hour. Crawford's remnants escaped into the woods as the 10th Maine retreated. Simultaneously, 164 cavalrymen of the 1st Pennsylvania Cavalry raced onto the field in a desperate charge. Both artillery and musketry paused momentarily in expectation as the troopers ran headlong toward Branch's North Carolinians. The Confederates, surrounding the 1st Pennsylvania on three sides, sent multiple volleys into the easy targets to their front, and the Pennsylvanians and their mounts began falling to the ground. After coming within a few hundred feet of Branch, the troopers veered to their right, passing parallel to the Confederate line. The results were disastrous as the Confederates poured fire into the riders' sides. Forced to retreat, the cavalrymen turned to the rear and headed back toward the direction they had come. Forty-three men were lost in the useless charge. With so many Confederate reinforcements having arrived, one might have thought the battle was at an end, but more blood was about to be needlessly spilled.

General Gordon's small brigade had been waiting about a mile from the battlefield under occasional long range artillery fire as Crawford's Brigade made their futile charge. After a hurried and strenuous march at the double quick, they arrived in time to

44. Bradley, *Surviving Stonewall*, 148-152.

watch Crawford's survivors retire from the field.[45] General Gordon commented upon reaching the woods: "When I gained the timber I looked for Crawford's regiments, but so broken had they been by their repulse that I could find, of all, only what remained of the six Wisconsin companies. Of the 28th New York, the Fifth Connecticut, or the 46th Pennsylvania, not a vestige met my eyes. The slaughter had indeed been fearful." He continued, "But there was, however, one relic of Crawford's Brigade, and that was Crawford himself. I saw him back in the woods sitting quietly on his horse, with a musket across his saddle . . ." Surely by this time Crawford realized the terrible plight which had befallen his men.[46]

Gordon lined up his brigade and moved out of the woods and onto the darkening, smoke enveloped wheatfield that was covered with the wounded and dead of Crawford's Brigade and the 1st Pennsylvania Calvary. Soon they came under fire from Archer, Branch, and Ronald's Brigades. Taking heavy casualties and facing vastly superior numbers, Gordon's men managed to halt Archer's progress and seriously disrupt his ranks, but the Confederates rallied as General Pender's Brigade arrived with more reinforcements. Under steady fire from two angles, Gordon's men faltered and started to break for the rear. The fractions of each regiment that held in place were soon rushed by Pender's North Carolinians who demanded surrender. Gordon's Brigade was done.

In the dark, Banks' defeated men retreated as Jackson's Brigades swept across the battlefield and Archer and Pender's Brigades pushed forward in pursuit of the Union route. After couriers arrived with news of Banks' crushing defeat, General Pope rushed to the front, and arrived there around nightfall along with Ricketts and McDowell's Corps. All were too late to be of any use.[47]

Stonewall Jackson had hoped to exploit the Federal collapse and capture Culpeper Court House that night. In preparation, he paused his advance after Banks about a half mile from the battlefield to reorganize his men. Exhausted and still facing 86 degree temperatures at 8:00 P.M., the soldiers were happy for the respite. Artillery was moved forward and opened fire on the Federals. Union guns responded and a "flaming pyrotechnic display" lit up the night. After about an hour's time, the artillery fell silent,

45. Krick, *Cedar Mountain*, 230, 232-6, 238-9.
46. Gordon, *Brook Farm*, 305.
47. Krick, *Cedar Mountain*, 264-6, 268, 271, 274-6, 291-2, 294.

and other than some cavalry roaming the field and light skirmishing, the Confederates ceased their advance. Having received intelligence that Banks had been strongly reinforced, Jackson knew pursuit by his exhausted men was pointless.

As soldiers on both sides dropped to the ground for sleep, the sounds of gunfire were replaced with the moans and cries of more than 2,000 wounded men. A full moon illuminated the fresh battlefield and its horrors. While most of Jackson's army slept, some remained awake and moved about the battlefield helping wounded friends and carrying off the bodies of those who weren't so fortunate. Others occupied their time stripping shoes, clothing, and food from their dead foes, leaving some of them naked. With the battlefield entirely in Confederate control, the much better equipped Union medical personnel were of little use to the thousands of wounded and dying Federal soldiers who spent the night pleading for help.[48]

---

48. Krick, *Cedar Mountain*, 299, 301, 311-3, 319, 323-5.

CHAPTER TWELVE

The Good Die First

August 10–September 14, 1862

ON THE MORNING of August 10th, the rising sun illuminated the bodies of dead and wounded soldiers covering the Virginia countryside beside Cedar Mountain. Men who had escaped harm and hadn't been able to find their regiments the night before got up from their impromptu beds on the ground to continue their search. Others, like Joseph Matchette of the 46th Pennsylvania, hadn't rested at all that night, and had spent it tending to the wounds of comrades.[1]

Daylight made it plainly apparent how terrible the prior day's fighting had been. Although bigger and bloodier fights would occur in the future, at that point in the war the close-quarters slaughter at Cedar Mountain was ghastly. Portions of roads were impassable with dead men and horses. Saplings four to six inches in diameter had been cut in two by rifle fire. The Crittenden farm house was riddled with bullets and stuffed with wounded who had soaked the floors with blood. The front yard was torn up from artillery shells, and a fresh grave rested beside the front steps of the house.

Shortly after dawn, skirmish fire rang out and continued throughout the morning, and it seemed probable that the battle would continue. Stonewall Jackson's men spent the morning moving Confederate and Federal wounded to hospitals in the rear. The day was just as hot as those preceding it, and despite working diligently to tend to the fallen, the exposed soldiers suffered considerably in the hot summer sun. Everyone was unbearably thirsty and resorted to drinking water out of muddy and bloody puddles and hoofprints. Late in the afternoon, relief finally came in the form of a thunderstorm that drenched the countryside.

---

1. Bradley, *Surviving Stonewall*, 154.

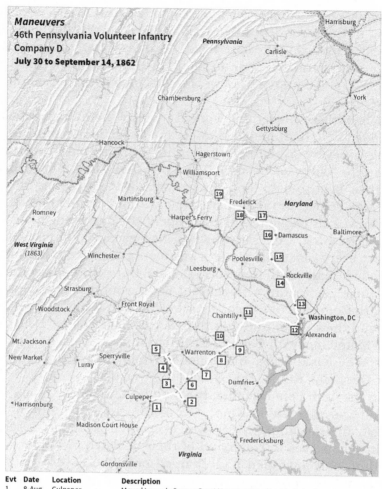

Maneuvers
46th Pennsylvania Volunteer Infantry
Company D
July 30 to September 14, 1862

Evt	Date	Location	Description
1	8-Aug	Culpeper	Moved towards Orange Court House; camped beside Cedar Run
	9-Aug	Culpeper	Battle of Cedar Mountain
	19-Aug	Culpeper	Left Culpeper
2	20-Aug	Kellys Ford	Arrived in Kelly's Ford
3	22-Aug	Beverly Ford	Maneuvers in support of Sigel
4	23-Aug		Marched toward Sulphur Springs
5	25-Aug	Waterloo Bridge	Marched toward Waterloo, then Warrenton, back to Sulphur Springs, then Warrenton, then Bealton; camped two miles outside of Waterloo
6	26-Aug	Bealton	Moved towards Bealton
7	27-Aug	Warrenton Junction	Moved through Bealton; bivouaced within one mile of Warrenton Junction
8	28-Aug	Bristow Station	Moved through Catlett and Bristow Station toward Manassas Junction
9	29-Aug	Manassas Junction	Moved through Manassas Junction, then east along the railroad back toward Bristow and guarded railroad
10	30-Aug	Broad Run	Guarded railroad near Broad Run
	31-Aug	Broad Run	Burned rail cars and stores; left for Brentsville
11	1-Sep	Chantilly	Bivouacked at the intersection of West Ox Road and Little River Turnpike
12	2-Sep	Arlington	Moved through Annandale to Arlington; arrived at Ft. Richardson at 1:30am on the 3rd
13	4-Sep	Tenleytown	Moved through Georgetown to Tenleytown
14	5-Sep	Rockville	Encamped
15	8-Sep	Middlebrook	Encamped
16	10-Sep	Damascus	Encamped two miles below
	11-Sep	Damascus	Moved closer to Damascus
17	12-Sep	Ijamsville	Encamped
18	13-Sep	Frederick	Encamped outside Frederick
19	14-Sep	Spoolsville	Moved through Frederick, camping in Spoolsville

While some Confederates worked in earnest to relieve the suffering of the wounded, others had different priorities and spent the day scavenging the battlefield. Food, especially delicacies like coffee that were near non-existent in the South by that point, weapons, and equipment were popular finds. Others searched for souvenirs.

While the Confederates worked to clear the battlefield, Union wounded who had managed to escape Confederate capture were filling up every available building in Culpeper and turning the town into "one vast hospital." The pro-Confederate townspeople did their best to help tend the wounds of the suffering soldiers, although sometimes their help came with an earful of politics.[2]

Crawford's decimated brigade spent the day trying to account for the missing. General Crawford had escaped unharmed, but almost every officer in his four regiments was dead, missing, or wounded. In the 28th New York, Colonel Donnelly had been killed, and their Lieutenant Colonel had been wounded and captured. The 5th Connecticut's Colonel and Lieutenant Colonel were missing, and their Major and Adjutant were killed. Colonel Beal of the 10th Maine met with General Crawford and broke into tears, sobbing "Where is my splendid brigade? Where are my brave fellows? Poor Donnelly, Knipe and Blake!"

In the 46th Pennsylvania, the pain from Colonel Knipe's scalp wound was unbearable. Knipe, George Brooks, and Adjutant Boyd all left for Harrisburg to recover from their wounds. Sergeants found themselves in command of their depleted companies. Five hundred and four men had charged onto the battlefield twelve hours earlier—now ninety-two responded at roll call. Comrades tried to remember and confirm who had been killed, wounded, and who was unaccounted for, but with the battlefield in Confederate control, they often could only guess.[3]

Other than the light skirmish fire and some cavalry scouting, Jackson and Pope did little on August 10th other than tend to their wounded and dead. The next morning the task continued, and Jackson accepted a truce to allow the Federals to tend to their wounded and bury the corpses still on the field. Groups of soldiers from regiments went about the battlefield taking stock of the carnage. A Massachusetts soldier couldn't find words for

---

2. Krick, *Cedar Mountain*, 326, 334-5, 338-40.
3. Bradley, *Surviving Stonewall*, 152-3. *Pennsylvania Telegraph*, August 14, 1862. Wagner, Richard. *For Honor, Flag, and Family*. White Mane Books, 2005. 123.

what he saw, writing that the scene was "too awful to attempt to describe." Friends searching for dead comrades were often unsuccessful—the sun had blackened and bloated many corpses beyond recognition. Federal soldiers soon resorted to the same shallow mass graves as the Confederates had the day prior, placing their friends in "a long ditch for a grave and a blanket for a coffin."

Surprisingly, the truce produced the opportunity for some new friendships, and Federal and Confederate soldiers met on the neutral ground between them, striking up cordial conversations. Even the higher ranking officers on the field—including Confederate Generals Jeb Stuart and Jubal Early and Union Generals Bayard and Crawford, sat together, joking and eating. The strange juxtaposition of the enemies cordially chatting on the battlefield where they had so brutally butchered each other two days prior wasn't lost on the participants.

The truce ended about 5:00 P.M. and Jackson started his army southward, aware that Pope now had far superior numbers in the Culpeper area. With Pope massed north of the Rapidan River, Jackson could safely return to Gordonsville and absorb reinforcements from Lee in preparation for another movement.

In the following days, press on both sides claimed victory at Cedar Mountain, yet in truth there was no real tactical gain for either side. In the South, morale soared and Stonewall Jackson was hailed for his victory. Until his death, he was exceedingly proud of his participation in the battle.

Most northern papers also reported victory and that Jackson had been defeated, but those in the ranks knew the truth and extent of Pope's failure at Cedar Mountain.[4] Crawford's Brigade had achieved a mighty feat, but without the proper reinforcements, the opportunity to truly defeat Stonewall had been squandered. Days later, General Williams wrote home that "if [reinforcements] had arrived an hour before sundown we should have thrashed Jackson badly and taken a host of his artillery."[5]

General Pope's failings came with a steep price tag. Over 600 Union and Confederate soldiers lay dead beside the mountain's slopes, while nearly 3,000 more suffered wounds. Almost 1,000 Federals, some wounded, headed for prison camps.[6] Of total Federal casualties, Crawford's Brigade bore an immense 36 percent.

---

4. Krick, *Cedar Mountain*, 344-8, 351, 358-9.
5. Williams, *From the Cannon's Mouth*, 101.
6. Krick, *Cedar Mountain*, 372-3, 376.

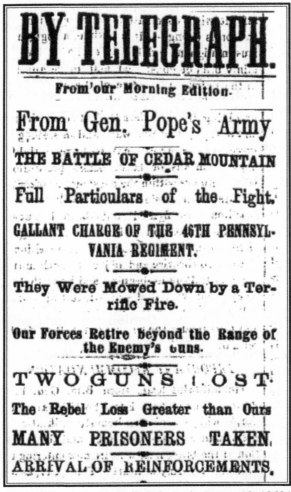

BY TELEGRAPH.

From our Morning Edition.

From Gen. Pope's Army

THE BATTLE OF CEDAR MOUNTAIN

Full Particulars of the Fight.

GALLANT CHARGE OF THE 46TH PENNSYLVANIA REGIMENT.

They Were Mowed Down by a Terrific Fire.

Our Forces Retire beyond the Range of the Enemy's Guns.

TWO GUNS LOST

The Rebel Loss Greater than Ours

MANY PRISONERS TAKEN,

ARRIVAL OF REINFORCEMENTS.

(Source: Pennsylvania Daily Telegraph, August 12, 1862.)

Fifty-two percent of the brigade was killed, wounded, or missing. While some of the missing returned after spending a period of time as prisoners of war, others were never found. Time would show that 29 percent of the brigade had been killed or died. To put this in perspective, an average of 4.7 percent of Union soldiers were killed or died of wounds during the war.

"It is customary at the close of a report like this to mention those whose conduct has merited commendation," General Crawford wrote in his after action report, "but I point the general commanding to the vacant places of my officers and the skeleton

COMMAND.	Killed.		Wounded.		Missing.		Present in Engagement.	
	Officers.	Enlisted Men.	Officers.	Enlisted Men.	Officers.	Enlisted Men.	Officers.	Enlisted Men.
5th Connecticut,........	3	18	8	63	2	143	21	424
10th Maine,............	2	22	5	140	1	3	26	435
28th New York,........	1	20	6	73	10	103	18	339
46th Pennsylvania,.....	2	28	8	94	8	104	23	481
Total,.................	8	88	27	370	21	353	88	1,679

Brigadier General Samuel W. Crawford's after action casualty report. These numbers give an idea of the devestation of his brigade, but are generally inaccurate since men later returned from capture, were otherwise accounted for, or died of wounds. (Source: The war of the rebellion: a compilation of the official records of the Union and Confederate armies. Volume 12, part 2, page 153.)

regiments of my brigade to speak more earnestly than I can do of the part they played in that day's contest."[7]

After a long, hot, and miserable five day journey home, George Brooks, Adjutant Boyd, and Colonel Knipe made what must've been a bittersweet return to Harrisburg. George Brooks, who had thus far carefully penned remembrances in his diary and written letters to the families of the men who had died under his command, was suddenly faced with the loss of over half of them, along with many of his close friends who served as officers. Though some of the wounded and missing would return in time, the regiment was still a shadow of its former self. Shortly after their return, Brooks and George Boyd (Colonel Knipe was still suffering terribly from his wound) were visited by the *Pennsylvania Telegraph*. Harrisburg residents were eager for news of how their sons and husbands had fared in the battle, and Brooks and Boyd had to recount that the regiment was shot to pieces and many men were missing.

---

7. Official Records Volume XII, Part 2, Page 152. Fox, William. *Regimental Losses in the American Civil War*. 1889. 48.

———•·◆·•———

Pennsylvania Daily Telegraph
August 14, 1862

The Forty-Sixth Pennsylvania. – *The Verbeke Rifles-List of killed and wounded.*

Adjutant George W. Boyd and Capt. George A. Brooks, of company D, (Verbeke Rifles) both of the Forty-Sixth Pennsylvania Regiment, arrived at their respective residences in this city at noon to-day, direct from Culpepper Court House. Col. Joseph F. Knipe, of the same regiment, has also arrived in the city, but we have not had an opportunity to see him.

Adjutant Boyd and Capt. Brooks were both wounded in the recent battle with the rebels near Culpepper Court House, Va., the former in the fleshy part of the left thigh by a minnie rifle ball, which has not yet been extracted, though the wound has been several times probed, and the latter in the left foot and one of his arms. Neither of the wounds are considered dangerous, and with the proper care and attention there is no doubt of their ultimate recovery. In every other respect, both seem to be in the enjoyment of excellent health.

The gentlemen state that Col. Knipe was slightly wounded in the side of his head by the explosion of a bomb shell directly in front of his face. A portion of the shell struck him in the head, tearing away the skin without breaking the skull bone, but by its concussion rendering the Colonel delirious for several hours.

Capt. Brooks went into the battle with sixty men of his company, and came out with only nineteen, the remainder having been either killed, wounded or missing.[8] He was the only commissioned officer of his company in the action, the others having been detailed on other duty.

The following is a list of casualties in the "Rifles", furnished by Capt. Brooks himself:

AUTHOR'S NOTE: The following list and the wounds suffered by each man were recorded by Captain Brooks and confirmed by muster rolls. Each man's fate due to his wound was added by the author for the reader's benefit. Some of the men listed were wounded or killed in later engagements.

---

8. After recovering from wounds and/or being returned via the prisoner exchange, twelve of Brooks' men died or were discharged due to wounds. That means a 20 percent casualty rate, or one in five men, which was still very high.

Name	Wound
Captain George Brooks	Wounded in left foot and arm
1st Sergeant Samuel Bernheisel	Died September 26 1862 of wounds
Sergeant Samuel Pottiger	Wounded in ankle. Discharged November 10 1862 for disability
Sergeant George Durell	Killed
Sergeant Luther R. Witman	Prisoner, returned
Corporal Thomas Novinger	Wounded in thigh and taken prisoner. Returned
Corporal John Yeager	Wounded in ankle. Returned
Private John Hoak	Prisoner, returned
Private Elias Early	Missing, returned
Private Edward Rhoades	Prisoner, returned
Private Thomas Lyne	Wounded in thigh. Died August 12, 1862
Private John Houser	Prisoner, returned
Private Simon Powley	Seriously wounded in side. Returned to duty
Private Matthew Taylor	Wounded in right knee. Returned to duty
Private Archibald Griffin	Wounded in leg and taken prisoner. Returned
Private Joseph Albert	Left leg amputated; discharged for disability
Private Benjamin Douney	Killed
Private Jacob Killinger	Wounded in leg and shoulder. Discharged
Private James Shannon	Wounded in thigh. Spent remainder of enlistment in hospital
Private William Baughman	Missing, returned
Private William Mease	Missing, returned
Private Samuel Geiger	Missing, returned
Private Frank Martin	Shot through upper chest. Discharged for disability
Private Alexander Rhoades	Prisoner, returned
Private Levi Ney	Prisoner, returned
Private William Martz	Wounded slightly on head, returned
Private William Ensigner	Missing and never found
Private Joseph Smith	Wounded and prisoner. Discharged for disability
Private Joseph Sullenberger	Prisoner, returned
Private Alexander Orth	Wounded in knee. Returned to duty
Private Jacob Good	Wounded in shoulder and leg, returned
Private William Seyfert	Wounded severely in body and taken prisoner, returned
Private Henry A Weidensaul	Prisoner, returned
Private Solomon Tromblee	Prisoner, returned
Private Samuel O Nace	Missing and never found
Private Cyrus Liddick	Prisoner, returned
Private Hugh McCarroll	Prisoner, returned

Soldiers stand at fresh graves on the Cedar Mountain battlefield days after the fighting. (Source: Library of Congress.)

For the next few days, Pope's defeated army remained near Culpeper, and the survivors of Crawford's Brigade found themselves struggling to continue with their duties. While some helped with tending the wounded, after the strains of battle and still feeling the brunt of the summer's heat, many of the men were so exhausted they found it impossible to do much of anything. Private William T. Shimp of the regiment wrote home that, although he was unhurt in the battle, he was so drained that he could barely write, let alone help someone else.[9]

Hoping to lift the spirits of his men, General Crawford ordered a review of the brigade on August 13th. The men cleaned up as much as possible and drew new equipment to replace what they had lost. With the brigade lined up, all could clearly see that they occupied about half of the space of a full regiment. Crawford praised their heroics and "did not deem it unsoldierly nor unmanly to shed tears, in speaking of the dead."[10] Unfortunately, the whole affair just served to exhaust the men further and remind them of how many of their comrades were gone. Each day more men reported for sick call, too exhausted and ill to continue.[11]

While Pope was languishing near Culpeper, Generals Lee and Jackson were assessing strategy. Lee's gamble to detach Jackson and send him north to attack Pope had worked, and now

9. Bradley, *Surviving Stonewall*, 163.
10. Boyce, *Twenty-eighth New York*, 44.
11. Bradley, *Surviving Stonewall*, 164.

he executed the next—and more risky—step. On August 13th, he sent General James Longstreet with 25,000 men to Gordonsville, and two days later departed for Gordonsville himself. Fewer than 25,000 Confederate troops remained to guard Richmond. With 55,000 soldiers in the newly dubbed Army of Northern Virginia, Lee planned to smash Pope before McClellan could move his men off of the Peninsula. Lee could then push the war up into Maryland where a decisive victory on Union soil would surely end the war.

General Pope had been ordered to hold his current position until McClellan could withdraw from the Peninsula and join him, but the arrival of Lee's army upended that plan. After scouting on August 18th indicated Lee was on the move, Pope put his men on the road and withdrew to behind the Rappahannock river and carefully guarded the ford points. Unable to cross, Lee spent the next two days skirmishing with Pope across the river. With each passing day, McClellan's reinforcements grew closer. On August 20th the Fifth Corps landed ten miles northeast of Fredericksburg, and on August 22nd the Third Corps landed at Alexandria and started marching southward.[12]

Williams' Division had started their retreat on the morning of August 19th. Rain had softened the roads, and poor footing paired with frequent and useless starts and stops in the march made their progress slow and miserable. Spirits sank lower because all were aware that they were retreating and that McClellan's grand attack on Richmond was a failure. After reaching the temporary safety of the Rappahannock, the weather worsened, and with tents packed in the wagon train far to the rear, the men found themselves drenched to the skin on the night of the 21st. The rain did serve to flood the river and further slowed Lee's pursuit.

In the following days, Williams' men were ordered to-and-fro along the Rappahannock to guard various locations, often retracing their prior steps. Frustration was soon usurped by another problem—they were out of food. Haversacks were empty, and food stores, along with the tents, were miles away with the wagon train.[13] The men were given an insufficient diet of what was available: coffee, sugar, salt, green corn and fruit.[14]

By August 25th, the arrival of McClellan's reinforcements meant 70,000 Federal troops were available north of the

12. Catton, *Terrible Swift Sword*, 391-2, 417-9.
13. Bradley, *Surviving Stonewall*, 166-7.
14. Marvin, *Fifth Connecticut*, 230-31.

Rappahannock. Lee was already outnumbered and could wait no longer to attack without facing sure defeat. That day, he sent Stonewall Jackson with 24,000 men off to the northwest in a flanking movement. They would march away from Pope's front, circling around the Bull Run mountains and then coming east through Thoroughfare Gap and strike Pope's army from behind. Lee and Longstreet would remain to Pope's front to trick him into thinking the whole Confederate force was located there, giving Jackson time to surprise Pope. With Pope defeated, Lee could then turn his attention to McClellan's army.

Pope's scouts noticed Jackson's movement that day and reported it to their commander, but Pope incorrectly assumed that Jackson was heading for the Shenandoah Valley. It wasn't until the next day that his suspicions rose, but it was too late. That evening, Jackson's footsore and exhausted men, having covered fifty miles in forty hours, swept through Thoroughfare Gap and hit the Orange & Alexandria Railroad at Bristoe Station. Then they took the Federal supply base at Manassas Junction. In one blow Jackson had cut off Pope's supply line and cut telegraph communication with Washington.

In dividing their forces, Lee and Jackson had assumed a large risk, and because of the overwhelming number of Federals, could potentially be destroyed. With his flanking movement a success, Jackson would now have to strike Pope's 75,000 men with enough force to pin them down so Lee could attack from the south, but not with so much force that Jackson's own small command would be destroyed before Lee arrived. For the plan to be successful, Pope would have to make mistakes. Unsurprisingly, as Union commanders repeatedly did during the early years of the war, he did just that.

On the 27th, while Jackson was leisurely burning massive amounts of Union supplies and equipment at Manassas Junction, Pope fully realized he was in trouble, and sent off a telegram to Washington that never arrived because of the cut cables. Without guidance, Pope dispatched orders for his men to trap Jackson at Manassas Junction, but by the time they arrived Jackson was gone and his location was a mystery. Preoccupied with catching Stonewall, Pope seemingly lost sight of Lee and Longstreet's presence and left Thoroughfare Gap unguarded, effectively opening a door through which Lee and Longstreet could freely pass.

It wasn't until the 28th that Jackson made his true position known by opening fire on some unsuspecting Federals on the

Warrenton Pike, not far from the Bull Run battlefield where Union forces had been defeated the prior summer. The fighting lasted until darkness fell, but no tactical gains were made. 2,300 soldiers fell wounded or dead, the only outcome being that there was sure to be a larger battle the next day.[15]

General Pope continued to err. The next day, convinced that he had trapped Jackson, Pope concentrated his army against him in a series of assaults. From a strong defensive position, Stonewall's men repulsed the Federal soldiers with high casualties. Midday, General Longstreet arrived on Jackson's flank without Pope noticing. The next day Pope renewed his attacks, but his left flank was crushed when Longstreet counterattacked with 28,000 troops. A complete route was only avoided because of an effective Union rearguard. Almost 14,000 Union soldiers and 8,000 Confederates were wounded or dead.[16]

Crawford's Brigade and a majority of Banks' Corps were not ordered into the fight partially because they had been so badly cut up at Cedar Mountain and partially because Pope struggled to effectively deploy his army. Instead, they remained in the rear, guarding various locations along the line of retreat. During the second day of the battle, they moved through Manassas Junction and viewed the damage wrought by Jackson on the supply depot. No news or orders arrived—in fact General Williams, temporarily in command of the corps, was unsure where General Banks was. The men waited, watching a mile long train filled with supplies that had been cut off because Jackson had burned the railroad bridge to Washington. Food and water remained scarce.

In the early morning of the 31st, General Banks arrived with news of Pope's defeat and orders to burn all public property at Manassas Junction. The entire train Williams' men had been guarding was set on fire as the men watched. The ground shook as cars full of ammunition exploded and filled the sky with smoke. More than one million dollars worth of equipment (almost 23 million in today's dollars) and ammunition were burned in an attempt to keep them from enemy hands. By 9:00 A.M. the work was completed, and the brigade headed off toward Brentsville. Receiving jeers from the townspeople there, they continued northward "as fast as we could go all day long" and by that evening had reached Centerville and the main of Pope's retreating army.[17]

---

15. Catton, *Terrible Swift Sword*, 418, 423-27.
16. Wagner, *Desk Reference*, 264-5.
17. Marvin, *Fifth Connecticut*, 233.

General Pope's soldiers overlook the remains of a burned train near Manassas Junction on the Orange & Alexandria railroad during the Second Manassas campaign. (Source: Library of Congress.)

Outside of Chantilly on September 1st Banks' Corps stood in reserve, listening to the sounds of battle as Jackson attempted to cut off Pope's line of retreat toward the safety of Washington. The fighting continued until a fearsome thunderstorm struck, making visibility impossible and drenching everyone to the skin. Banks' men stood in place through the downpour and shivered in their ragged and filthy uniforms with aching stomachs.[18]

By September 2nd, the Army of Northern Virginia was 9,000 fewer in number after suffering casualties in battle and exposure to the same hardships as Pope's men. Lee and Jackson stayed put that day, allowing their men some time to recover, while Pope withdrew further toward the strong defensive line of forts around Washington.[19] At 1:30 in the morning on September 3rd, Crawford's Brigade stumbled up to the barricades of Fort Richardson in Arlington, stacked arms, and out of exhaustion dropped to the ground "as if shot."[20]

Pope had successfully evaded Lee for now—the defenses around Washington were too strong for Lee to attack. Knowing that time was of the essence, Lee pivoted his plan quickly and set

---

18. Bradley, *Surviving Stonewall*, 174.
19. Catton, *Terrible Swift Sword*, 435-6.
20. Bradley, *Surviving Stonewall*, 174.

his sights on Maryland where he could requip his troops, recruit pro-Southern residents, and make the North feel the brunt of the war. Although his men were exhausted, and many shoeless, he wasted no time turning them northward.

Upon the arrival of Pope's men in Washington, President Lincoln effectively transferred them to the command of General McClellan. A few days later, Pope was dismissed for his follies at Cedar Mountain and Manassas. Despite McClellan's questionable record, he was the best option available at the time to command the army. He had trained the Army of the Potomac and Pope's men from civilians into soldiers, and their affections ran deep for one another. With the army ill-equipped, worn out, and demoralized, Lincoln knew he needed McClellan if the army was to fight at all. With Lee already on the move, there was no time to waste.[21]

After a short break in Arlington and Tennallytown (modern-day Tenleytown), Banks' Corps camped near Rockville, Maryland on September 6th. The day before, supply wagons had finally caught up to the men for the first time in three weeks, and after being reunited with their knapsacks, they were able to change clothes for the first time since leaving Culpeper.[22]

After the war, a 28th New York soldier attempted to describe what they had endured during their retreat from Culpeper. "The men experienced on this retreat more of the hardships of a soldier's life than ever before," he began. "It would be difficult to describe their sufferings. Often they were destitute of rations, subsisting entirely on green corn. Much of the water to drink or for coffee was obtained from stagnant puddles. The men were forced to sleep on the ground, without covering. Most of the time they were under arms, doing the same duty as large regiments."[23] The physical strain and demoralization had been too much for many men, and many broke down for good. One of them was twenty-five year old Jerome Stewart, the 1st Sergeant in Company G, who was so weakened by a chest cold and rheumatism that his one leg simply wouldn't work anymore. The young man's joints were ruined, and he wrote home telling his family "I rite an awful looking letter for my nerves move my hand just as it please."[24]

General Williams took stock of his old brigade while they were camped at Rockville. He had taken command of them not far from

---

21. Catton, *Terrible Swift Sword*, 436, 446-7.
22. Bradley, *Surviving Stonewall*, 177.
23. Boyce, *Twenty-eighth New York*, 45.
24. Bradley, *Surviving Stonewall*, 175.

that location a year prior, at which point there were 3,000 men in the ranks. Now, there were fewer than 400, and not a single field officer was among them. "Instead of hopeful and confident feelings we are all depressed with losses and disasters," he wrote.[25]

As a surgeon by profession, General Crawford, although unpopular with his men, was also concerned with their condition. He wrote to his superiors:

> Since Cedar Mountain where my brigade was well nigh destroyed, the service has been such as to threaten the reduction of its shattered state. I fear for its very existence. Every day adds to the report of the medical officers. The men suffer from exposure, the deprivation of proper food and the want of rest. The marches are long, done in the heat of the sun, and when we arrive at camp at night the men without regard to weather or hunger throw themselves on the ground to seek rest . . . the depression of spirits adds significantly to the induction of our camp disease . . . the organization trembles in the balance. The men feel the want of officers and nothing keeps them together but common interest and association. I urge to have my command placed where they may do useful service and at the same time have an opportunity to reorganize and recruit the health and the spirits as well as men.[26]

No rest was granted, but resupply did occur, and provided the tired men a new feeling of confidence and started restoring some order to the ranks. "The time ought never to come to humanity when clean whole clothes and shoes afford the infinite luxury which these, which we have now received, do to us," recalled Captain Marvin of the 5th Connecticut.[27]

Pope's army was also reorganized. General Banks, who had led the 46th Pennsylvania's Corps through the failures in the Shenandoah Valley campaign and the retreat from Culpeper, was transferred to the command of the forts surrounding Washington. He switched places with his replacement, white-haired Joseph Mansfield, a West Point graduate who had commanded Washington's forts since the spring of 1861. Banks' Corps, now designated the Twelfth Corps, was his first combat assignment.

---

25. Williams, *From the Cannon's Mouth*, 111.
26. Wagner, *Home, Flag, and Family*, 130.
27. Marvin, *Fifth Connecticut*, 237.

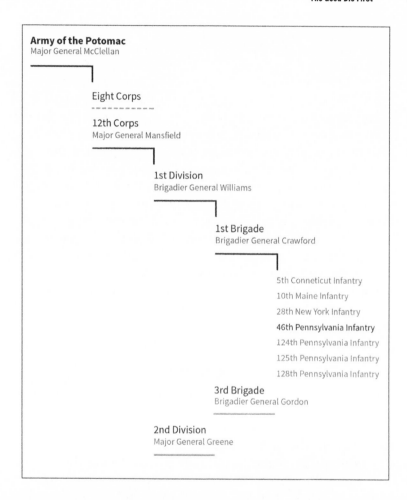

Army of the Potomac
Major General McClellan

Eight Corps

12th Corps
Major General Mansfield

1st Division
Brigadier General Williams

1st Brigade
Brigadier General Crawford

5th Conneticut Infantry
10th Maine Infantry
28th New York Infantry
46th Pennsylvania Infantry
124th Pennsylvania Infantry
125th Pennsylvania Infantry
128th Pennsylvania Infantry

3rd Brigade
Brigadier General Gordon

2nd Division
Major General Greene

Williams' Division was also reinforced to nearly 8,000 troops by the addition of fourteen new regiments, six of which consisted of green recruits. The 124th, 125th, and 128th Pennsylvania were added to Crawford's Brigade. The 124th had been in service since August 12th, and the 124th and 128th had mustered in on August 16th. They hadn't even had time to gain proficiency in basic drill.[28]

While convalescing in Harrisburg, George Brooks had been doing his best to help his shattered regiment by recruiting new men for his Company. Posting in the newspaper and talking with townspeople, a few men responded to Brooks' proposition.

---

28. Bradley, *Surviving Stonewall*, 182-3.

———◆•◉•◆———

Pennsylvania Daily Telegraph
August 30, 1862

Young Men, Attention! - Captain Geo. A. Brooks, of the gallant
Forty-sixth, which suffered so severely in the late battle at Cedar
Mountain, August 9, expects to rejoin his regiment in the early
part of next week, and is desirous of securing before his departure as many able-bodied, sober young men as possible; either
for his own company from this county, or any other company
they may select. The usual bounties will be given, and those con-
necting themselves with this regiment will share the glory it has
already achieved in more than one well fought engagement, and
receive the care and attention which only experienced officers
can give men in active service, where they require so much.

Capt. Brooks can be found at the store of Bell & Bro., corner of
Second and Chestnut streets.

❋ ❋ ❋

With news of Pope's defeat and Lee's northward advance, George
Brooks decided to end his all too short visit on September 3rd.
His son was turning two in less than a week, but if ever Brooks
was needed at the front, it was now. Lee's invasion meant a
battle—perhaps even the battle that would decide the fate of the
Union—would be waged, and with the 46th lacking in both men
and officers, Brooks felt he needed to return. As he had done far
too many times before, he bid farewell to his friends and family
and started the journey south, joining the regiment a couple of
days later.[29]

While McClellan was refitting his army, General Lee's was fording the Potomac near Leesburg on September 5th. Lee planned to
move his army north behind South Mountain where he could maneuver out of McClellan's sight. Then, Jackson could sweep down
to capture the only Union outpost that posed a threat west of
Washington—10,000 troops at Harpers Ferry. With that done, Lee
and Jackson would reunite and smash McClellan. It was another
risky plan. McClellan was moving slowly, as expected, but when
the armies did meet Lee would be outnumbered and out supplied.

---

29. *Pennsylvania Daily Telegraph.* September 18th, 1862.

His troops were tired, and he was banking on their morale (and, conversely, McClellan's men's low spirits) to gain victory.

By the time Lee's men marched into Frederick on September 9th, the North was in full panic. Never before had Confederate feet trod on Union soil. McClellan's army moved slowly in pursuit, sweeping north toward Frederick. It was there, on September 13th, that two Federal soldiers found a piece of paper that had carelessly been dropped by an unknown Confederate officer. On it were Lee's campaign orders. When the paper was placed in front of General McClellan he knew the power of the information before him—now he knew where Lee was, and where he was going. The opportunity to defeat Lee had never been greater.

His spirits lifted, McClellan set to work on September 14th and sent his army forward to cross South Mountain and strike Lee.[30] The Twelfth Corps (formerly Banks') marched through Frederick on a harrowing forced march. Elated to have Union troops back in force, the people of Frederick flooded the streets. Flags lined the way, and handkerchiefs waved as the infantry marched through town. Colonel Knipe returned to the 46th Pennsylvania that day, further bolstering the men's spirits.[31]

Moving west, the infantry marched on both sides of the road in columns of four while ammunition and artillery traveled down the center. The men trampled through corn, sweet potatoes and wheat. Although they were under strict orders not to forage, as the saying goes, "an army marches on its stomach," and this army was no exception. Along the way, the men managed what foraging they could and paid for that they couldn't sneak.

The day was hot and the wheels of the artillery and ammunition trains, along with the hoofs of horses and the boots of men, stirred up huge, choking dust clouds. Cannons boomed in the distance and the men longed for water. Crossing the peak of Elk Mountain, the soldiers could look across the valley below. A soldier in the 125th Pennsylvania remembered the sight years later:

> . . . we could look down and across Middletown Valley—through the shimmering heat waves we could see lines of infantry—which looked like ribbons of blue—being rushed to the front; the rays of sun glinted from musket barrel and bayonet and polished brass cannon; batteries in position—in the fields in the valley—firing over the heads of the advancing line of battle; smoke of shells

30. Catton, *Terrible Swift Sword*, 447-50.
31. Bradley, *Surviving Stonewall*, 177-9.

Union soldiers march through Middletown, Maryland in pursuit of General Lee during his invasion of Maryland. (Source: Library of Congress.)

bursting in air at Crampton and Turner's Gaps, and could see lines of smoke in the woods near the summit of South Mountain—where the infantry boys were fighting in the brush among the rocks. It was a panoramic moving picture.

Crawford's men were not called upon to fight, and after waiting in reserve all day, they ascended South Mountain in the darkness. At times they were stopped to let ambulances pass, and the green new Pennsylvania regiments assigned to Crawford's Brigade saw their first ghastly sights of battle.[32]

That night, as the soldiers were halted and allowed to fall out of ranks, the 46th Pennsylvania had been in service for almost a year. There were barely one hundred men present—the size of a full-strength company—to throw ground cloths and blankets to the earth and collapse upon them in exhaustion. Company I had nine men present, and Company C only eight. Perhaps only those who fell asleep instantly avoided reflection on all of the friends lost over the past year, and the unavoidable truth that more were soon to fall.[33]

32. Huyette, Miles C. *The Maryland Campaign and The Battle of Antietam.* Buffalo, NY, 1915. 13-26.
33. Bradley, *Surviving Stonewall*, 183-4.

CHAPTER THIRTEEN

If I Should Fall

September 15–17, 1862

O N THE NIGHT of September 14th General McClellan had never had a better opportunity to destroy General Lee's army and end the war. After a bloody and grueling summer, fraught with embarrassments and mistakes, McClellan could finally redeem himself and prove true the convictions of his men who fought for him so devotedly. That day, McClellan had put Lee's army within reach when his soldiers had spilled their blood to capture two gaps in South Mountain and opened the roads leading directly to Lee's position. If they had pushed forward that night, he could have robbed Lee of precious time to maneuver, and could have slowed or stopped Stonewall Jackson's advance on the garrison at Harpers Ferry. As in the past, though, McClellan failed to seize the advantage, and let his weary men drop to the ground and sleep. Lee now had the time to gather his troops and fight. He issued orders indicating that his army should converge near a small town called Sharpsburg.

Located on high ground that overlooked Antietam Creek and close to the Potomac River, sleepy Sharpsburg soon was overwhelmed with ragged, barefooted, and hungry Confederates who had been consuming green corn and apples as their primary sustenance. On September 15th, when General Lee placed them in position sheltered by the hills overlooking the Antietam, they weren't really in any physical or moral shape to be facing the overwhelming number of blue-clad soldiers who tramped toward them. They were, however, veterans, and knew well how to use the weapons they had lugged the whole way from Virginia.

When McClellan's scouts arrived within sight of the Confederate lines outside Sharpsburg, the cautious General again called his army to a halt. He surveyed Lee's line and maneuvered almost 90,000 troops into position, and then told them to wait. In the lull, more of Lee's forces continued to arrive in Sharpsburg and then more good news arrived—Stonewall Jackson had captured Harpers Ferry and the 10,000 Union soldiers garrisoned there. Now Jackson could join Lee. McClellan was making mistakes in Lee's favor, but even if all of Lee's forces were able to converge in time, the Southern army could still only muster only about 40,000 strong.

Lee's decision to stand and fight at Sharpsburg has long been debated. His position was strong but not impenetrable, and his back was to the Potomac river with only one ford through which his army could escape if routed. With McClellan dragging his feet, Lee could have slipped across the river and left Maryland without any bloodshed. Instead, he stayed in the face of total destruction because he wanted an absolute victory and believed his army could win it.[1]

September 16th dawned foggy and it was difficult for McClellan's scouts to assess the enemy before them. The strong positions on the right and center of Lee's line were visible, but the left was hidden from view by the topography of the countryside. Even after the fog had lifted little was done to determine much of use about the Confederate line.

Despite the lack of information, McClellan decided to attack the left of Lee's line first. That afternoon he ordered Major General Joseph Hooker's First Corps, formerly commanded by McDowell, to continue its march in the direction of Sharpsburg. Then pickets and artillery were moved up to advantageous locations, and shelling and small skirmishes broke out as the Union soldiers secured the three available bridges spanning the Antietam Creek.

As Hooker approached Sharpsburg from the North, his men became engaged with elements of Brigadier General John Bell Hood's Division. Rifle shots and artillery shells were exchanged, but a small number of troops were involved and casualties were light. No strategic gains were made, and by the end of the day Hooker had failed to gain more knowledge of the enemy's position or turn Lee's flank as McClellan had hoped. The action had only served to alert Lee that McClellan was planning an attack on his left.[2] Lee immediately started reinforcing his line and when

1. Catton, *Terrible Swift Sword*, 448-452.
2. Carman, Ezra A. and Thomas Clemens. *The Maryland Campaign of September 1862*. Volume 2: Antietam. Savas Beatie, 2012. 22-4, 33-42.

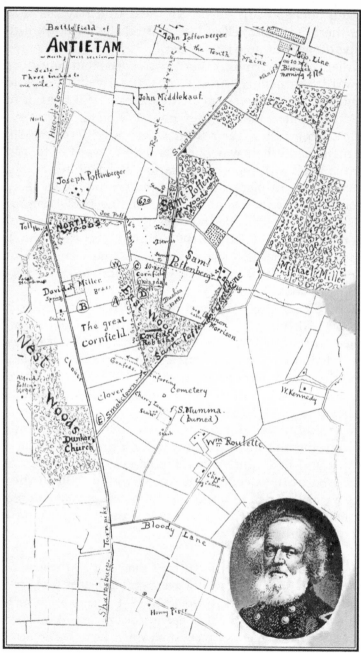

Veteran John Mead Gould of the 10th Maine hand drew notations on a map by the U.S. Engineers showing the general vacitinity of the Antietam battlefield. (Source: Gould, John Mead. Joseph K. F. Mansfield, brigadier general of the U.S. Army. A narrative of events connected with his mortal wounding at Antietam, Sharpsburg, Maryland, September 17, 1862, 1895.)

Stonewall Jackson arrived on the field that day his men were placed there, too. McClellan had started the day with a three to one advantage, but now it was lost.[3]

Earlier in the morning, other Union corps had continued moving toward Sharpsburg. At 8:00 A.M. the Twelfth Corps fell into line and left their bivouac near Nicodemus' Mill west of Keedysville. After a mile's march, they halted, watching artillery shells explode atop a hill to their front where a battery was situated. Some men made their way about a mile forward of this location and came back with reports of infantry skirmishing.

They waited in place until dark, when the order was passed to pitch tents for the evening. "Beef on the hoof," live animals, were issued to the brigade to be slaughtered. Some of the newer regiments had trouble killing their dinner, and the animals tried to make an escape. Soldiers gave chase, and General Mansfield shouted at his scurrying troops: "Let them go, boys, you won't have time to cook them!"

After a dinner that was more successful for some than others, the corps laid out in full equipment with their cartridge boxes strapped to their sides. Those who managed to fall asleep were awakened after a short while when orders arrived around 10:30 to resume the march toward Sharpsburg. The entire Twelfth Corps moved through the night under strict orders against talking, and after they passed over the upper bridge across the Antietam, they held anything metal—including cups, coffee boilers, and frying pans—to avoid alerting the enemy to their presence.[4] Rain started to fall around midnight, and the soldiers were wet by the time they arrived at the George Line farm around 2:30 in the morning.[5] Crawford's Brigade settled down in columns of companies in a cornfield. Miles Huyette, a veteran of the 125th Pennsylvania, recalled the night well:

> . . . the night was close, air heavy, some fog and smoke from the skirmish firing of the late evening and picket firing of the night and from stragglers' bivouac fires—to the rear—hung low; the only lights the twinkling flashes of fire-flies—kept in motion by the movement of men, mules and horses. The air was perfumed with a mixture of crushed green cornstalks, ragweed

---

3. Catton, *Terrible Swift Sword*, 451.
4. Huyette, *Battle of Antietam*, 26-7.
5. Carman, *Maryland Campaign*, 43. Priest, John M. *Antietam: The Soldiers' Battle*. White Mane Publishing, 1989. 29.

and clover. We made our beds between the rows of corn and did not unbuckle or remove accouterments. The night sounds—the scattered firing and occasional rattle of musketry on the picket lines—to the front; the mingled low-toned conversation of the men, occasional neighing of horses, barking of dogs—at the farm houses, crowing of roosters—disturbed at an unusual hour, and the chirping of crickets; Katy-dids joined in the night chorus with high pitch and speed. Slowly the morning came on.[6]

Ol' Pap Williams also found that night worthy of mention, recalling a few days later: "I shall not soon forget that night; so dark, so obscure, so mysterious, so uncertain; with the occasional rapid volleys of pickets and outposts, the low, solemn sound of the command as troops came into position, and withal so sleepy that there was a half-dreamy sensation about it all; but with a certain impression that the morrow was to be great with the future fate of our country. So much responsibility, so much intense, future anxiety! And yet I slept as soundly as though nothing was before me."[7]

What lay before McClellan's army arrived quickly, and dawn soon illuminated the horizon. McClellan's plan was effectively simple and relied on the three available bridges to cross the Antietam creek: via the upper bridge, he would attack Lee's left with Hooker and Mansfield's Corps, with support from Major General Edwin V. Sumner's and Major General William B. Franklin's Corps if needed. As soon as headway was made on the left, he would deploy Major General Ambrose Burnside's Corps against Lee's right, situated near the southernmost bridge. After one of Lee's flanks gave way, McClellan would push across the center bridge and flood the field with as many troops as possible. The day's events would soon show his plan to be feasible in nature but completely flawed in execution.[8]

The Twelfth Corps rose from their fitful slumber at the Line farm at about 5:00 A.M. Moments after their waking, a single shot rang out and a green soldier in the 124th Pennsylvania, surely still half asleep, remarked that "Some fellow is out shooting squirrels this morning." More shots soon followed and the man realized his mistake.

---

6. Huyette, *Battle of Antietam*, 27-8.
7. Williams, *From the Cannon's Mouth*, 122-32.
8. Carman, *Maryland Campaign*, 26

Damp and stiff, the men broke rifle stacks and got into ranks and waited.[9] There was no time for breakfast, and most of them were too nervous to eat anyway. "Breakfast was not to be thought of, although we had scarcely eaten anything for the last two days," remembered Private Frederick Crouse of the newly arrived 128th Pennsylvania.[10]

The new regiments had bolstered Crawford's Brigade to about 2,500 men. Hot marches over the past few days had reduced the green regiments of some of their strength, and consequently they all averaged about 700 men per regiment. Despite their reduction in size, they still greatly outnumbered the experienced, veteran regiments. The entire 46th Pennsylvania was slightly larger than the size of a full company, the 28th New York was barely three-fourths of a company, and the 10th Maine numbered about 300 men. Together, the three veteran regiments were barely the size of one full regiment.[11]

General Crawford began delivering orders as more rifle volleys and artillery fire sounded in the distance, and even the inexperienced Pennsylvanians could tell they were in for it.[12] A soldier in the 124th Pennsylvania remembered years later that their wait to advance that morning was "the most trying time of my three years experience as a soldier."[13] General Crawford seemed equally aware of what his men faced, commenting as he rode about, "There is work to do up there." Each man was issued twenty more rounds of ammunition to add to the forty they already carried.[14]

The brigade moved forward toward the sound of battle, crossing the Smoketown Road and moving west for a while before turning left and moving southward. The advance was slow and cautious, and Mansfield ordered frequent halts. Regiments were detached to occupy woods on the flanks of the column, then brought back into line and again detached as the corps crawled forward. They could hear the firing in front of them, but were unsure what was going on. Each time they halted, the men would start boiling some water to make coffee, but before the were finished they were ordered back into ranks and moved forward. Some started letters home, but were unable to finish them.

---

9. Priest, *Soldiers' Battle*, 30.
10. Wagner, *Honor, Flag, And Family*, 136.
11. Carman, *Maryland Campaign*, 583. Bradley, *Surviving Stonewall*, 183-4.
12. Gould, *History of the First - Tenth - Twenty-ninth*, 233.
13. Bradley, *Surviving Stonewall*, 187.
14. Wagner, *Honor, Flag, And Family*, 136.

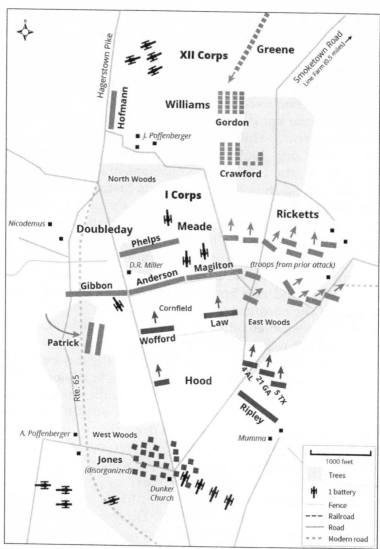

[Antietam Battle Map 1.] The XII Corps' advance.

Finally, around 6:30 A.M. the frustrating advance came to an end. After covering roughly a mile, the corps came to a halt west of Samuel Poffenberger's woods, and General Mansfield rode forward to consult with General Hooker. Artillery fire started raining in on the men as they waited in an open field without shelter. The newer regiments found their first experience under fire unnerving, and as the shells screamed by a member of the 125th Pennsylvania remembered, "most men ducked and then would straighten up with a sickly kind of grin." Even more disconcerting was the steady stream of wounded making their way past the Twelfth Corps to the rear. Some yelled encouragement, but others were terribly maimed. An artilleryman was carried by them with both of his legs badly mangled, shrieking for someone to just kill him.[15]

Mansfield's men were starting to get an idea of what they were in for, but no one knew the extent of the horror occurring before them. At daybreak, while the stars were still showing, General Hooker's First Corps had advanced against Lee's left flank on familiar enemies—the Confederate divisions of Ewell and Jackson. Assessing the field from a body of woods just north (now referred to as the North Woods) of a cornfield (the Cornfield) owned by D. R. Miller, Hooker had set his objective on a small white church (Dunker Church) located on top of a rise in the terrain. If he could collapse Lee's left and take that position, he would have a chance of winning the day. As he surveyed the high ground (Cemetery Ridge), artillery and rifle fire broke out in another body of woods to the east of the cornfield (the East Woods).

Hooker's assessment showed that the positions of Confederate forces on the left were not as expected (and they were really just an expectation, since scouting had been lax the day before). Lee's men were positioned so the left of his line was almost at a right angle to the main of his forces, and so the flank was protected. In some areas, the terrain offered the Confederates natural shelter from their enemies.[16] But orders had been given, and Hooker had to try. For unknown reasons, Hooker made no plans for coordinating his attack with Mansfield's Corps, who were just beginning their sluggish advance a mile to the rear.

Hooker's skirmishers moved forward into Miller's head-high corn through a gray, damp daybreak. Three dozen cannons were moved up to occupy a low ridge north of the Cornfield. Then, Hooker's first brigade moved straight into the corn, advancing to its southern edge and breaking out. Immediately, a brigade of Georgians rose to their feet before them and opened fire. The two lines stood 250 yards apart, neglecting to take any cover, and threw volleys into each other's ranks. Reinforcements arrived for both sides and casualties mounted. As the 12th Georgia Infantry tried to flank the left of the Federal line in the corn, a harrowing

---

15. Williams, *From the Cannon's Mouth*, 125. Carman, *Maryland Campaign*, 113-4. Sears, Stephen W. *Landscape Turned Red: The Battle of Antietam*. Mariner Books, 1993. 203-4.
16. Carman, *Maryland Campaign*, 51-6.

Knapp's Battery, which was attached to the Twelfth Corps, was captured in this image two days after the battle. Behind them lies the Cornfield and East (right) and North Woods. (Source: Library of Congress.)

flank fire poured in from the East Woods. When the Georgians' Colonel ordered his veterans forward from their position sheltered by a rock ledge, most of them stayed in place. Riding up to them to urge them forward, he realized they were all dead. Of the one hundred men he had taken onto the field, only about forty were still fighting.

The Federals weren't fairing much better, and with ammunition low and promised reinforcements nowhere to be found, they were forced to fall back through the corn. A third of them remained on the field, wounded and dying. It had only been about half an hour.

Finally, after some confusion in their deployment, Union reinforcements arrived and pushed forward into the hellish scene before them. "I do not see how any of us got out alive," recalled a Massachusetts soldier. General Law's fresh brigade of Confederates arrived and rushed forward, intensifying the contest. Federal artillery moved into the corn and cut down stalks and soldiers alike. Confederate case shot (fused shells filled with marble sized balls) from the plateau near the Dunker Church poured in on the Yankees.[17]

Bullets and shrapnel cut its way through flesh in every way imaginable. Men were disemboweled, others had feet and hands and limbs shorn off, others lay choking to death in their own blood.

---

17. Sears, *Landscape Turned Red*, 185-90.

The Dunker Church served as the focal point for much of the fighting on the northern part of the battlefield. (Source: Library of Congress.)

Limbs flew through the air, and wounded were trampled where they lay. Those who still stood loaded and fired, some yelling while others did their best to steel their nerves as tears ran down their cheeks. Color bearers fell with rapidity and others quickly picked up the banner and took their place, only to be mowed down soon after. "Never have I seen men fall as fast and thick," recalled a Confederate soldier. Ammunition started to run low and rifles started to foul on both sides and men bent to take unused rounds and weapons from fallen comrades. Amidst the smoke of rifle fire entire regiments dissolved, but more arrived just in time to be thrown into the meat grinder.[18] By the time the clock was nearing 7:00 A.M., some regiments had been more than halved and two ferocious waves of fighting had surged across the Cornfield. Though no tactical gain had been made, it seemed as if the Confederates were gaining the upper hand. Hooker's men were trying desperately to hold on, but they were getting shot to pieces and needed help.[19]

After waiting in place for about an hour with artillery shrieking overhead and the wounded staggering past, the Twelfth Corps and the 46th Pennsylvania noticed a change in the sound of the battle. Many correctly deduced that things were not going well to their front. They noticed the direction of artillery fire had changed, indicating lines had shifted, and the wounded streamed out of the

18. Priest, *Soldiers' Battle*, 49, 60, 65.
19. Carman, *Maryland Campaign*, 87.

woods at a much faster pace. No one needed to say it—everyone knew their turn was coming.

The corps had advanced to their current position in "columns of battalions in mass," and General Williams noticed that deploying intervals (the space required to march the troops into line of battle when desired) hadn't been maintained. Sensing they would be called into action soon, Williams started deploying Crawford's Brigade when Mansfield returned from his visit to General Hooker and countermanded the order. "I begged him (General Mansfield) to let me deploy in line of battle in which the men present but *two* ranks or rows instead of *twenty*, as we were marching, but I could not move him." General Williams recalled, "He was positive all the new regiments would run away." Williams quickly gathered the commanders of his old regiments under a large tree and instructed them that when the time came to deploy, the old regiments would cover the new ones so they could deploy out of the direct line of fire. With hasty plans in place, at about 7:15, Crawford's Brigade started forward.

Feeling the urgency of getting his men into action, white-haired General Mansfield, in his first combat command, ordered his regiments, still massed in columns of divisions, forward at the oblique (diagonally). Not only was it difficult to deploy men at the oblique, but it was near impossible with them in columns of divisions and with green recruits. The 124th Pennsylvania was detached and started toward the right under the guidance of General Williams, and the remainder of the brigade started to the left under the direction of General Mansfield.[20]

The 10th Maine, still in columns of divisions, moved through a small cornfield in front of the East Woods and crossed over the Smoketown Road. Still obliquing toward the left as a few bullets zipped by them, they marched down and up a gentle slope when a picket line of the enemy came into view behind a fence at the edge of the East Woods.[21] Skirmish fire from the woodline started to drop the Maine men as they slowly advanced forward, and Adjutant John Gould remembered that they were "almost as good a target as a barn . . . it is terrible to march slowly into danger, and see and feel each second your chance of death is surer than it was the second before."

---

20. Williams, *From the Cannon's Mouth*, 125. Carman, *Maryland Campaign*, 115-6.
21. Gould, *History of the First - Tenth - Twenty-ninth*, 235-36.

*An illustration of the formation of "double column at half distance"
or "columns of divisions." The positioning of the exact companies
illustrates the 10th Maine as they advanced into battle. This
formation was rarely used during the war for an attack, since
eight of the regiment's companies were blocked from firing by the
two front companies. (Source: Gould,* History of the First - Tenth -
Twenty-ninth, *pg. 233.)*

Aware of his men's precarious formation, Colonel Beal of the
10th Maine, still without orders to deploy from General Mansfield,
did so himself and got his veteran men into line of battle. Their
brief pause to do so allowed the Confederates in the woods—some
outnumbered Texans low on ammunition—to pull back from the
fence line and take shelter behind trees closer to two other Confederate regiments. The New Englanders advanced to the fence
and part of the regiment jumped over it before the Rebels opened
fire. Men fell from the ranks and the regiment stopped, taking
shelter behind trees on the right and a limestone ledge on the
left, and started to return fire. Bullets whizzed through the air
from their front and also from concealed snipers who targeted
officers who were trying to get their commands into line. Within
minutes Colonel Beal's horse was mortally wounded. As the horse
reeled from its wounds it spun about, and at the same time the
colonel was shot in both legs. Then, the Lieutenant Colonel took
two kicks from the horse to his chest and stomach. The regiment,
on the extreme left flank of the Union line, was now under the
command of their major.[22]

---

22. Priest, *Soldiers' Battle*, 73-4.

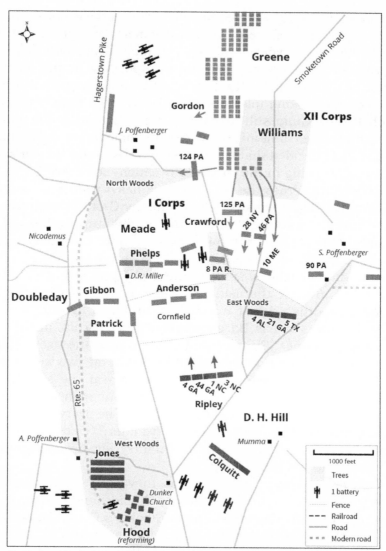

[Antietam Battle Map 2.] Crawford's Brigade deploys.

Fire was also coming in from the pasture south of the Cornfield where Ripley's Brigade of Confederates had taken position. The 46th Pennsylvania and 28th New York were moving off at the double quick toward the Cornfield.[23] Lieutenant Colonel Selfridge, Old Ironsides, of the 46th rode forward with them as a bullet—probably from a sniper—streaked by his temple and raised a welt. He had escaped other close calls at Winchester and Cedar

---

23. Carman, *Maryland Campaign*, 117.

Mountain, and today seemed no different. George Brooks, the only captain with the regiment, guided the men forward on foot with sword in hand, his voice straining to communicate with them over the rifle and artillery fire. Moving into position at the northern corner of the Cornfield, the two small regiments opened a brisk and accurate fire on Ripley's line. Paired with the sight of the large 125th Pennsylvania still massed in columns and visible behind them in reserve, some of the worn out Confederate regiments in the Cornfield decided that it was best to retreat, and Hooker's regiments still fighting in the corn finally caught some relief.

Enemy fire across the corn was still heavy, and bullets found their marks. Noah Armstrong in Company G of the 46th was hit in the chest by a round that cut through his lung and exited out his back. One of George Brooks' boys, Leonard Long of Company D, was hit in the left ankle, and another, Anthony Helmerick, who was standing nearby, was hit in the fleshy part of his left elbow. He refused to leave the field, the same as he had when he was wounded months prior at Winchester, and kept fighting. Further down the line, Francis Baronowski was also struck in the arm, breaking the bones. Surgeons later amputated the useless limb. Charlie Brant was hit in the torso—he would die two weeks later.

Company I, consisting of just nine men at the start of the battle, took a direct artillery hit, leaving four men standing. In Company G, James Cole loaded and fired. The overwhelming din of the battle would ring in his ears days later.[24] General Williams recalled later that, "The roar of the infantry was beyond anything conceivable to the uninitiated."[25]

Ripley's men were falling too as they fired across the decimated, bloody corn into Crawford's Brigade and, to the right, what remained of some regiments of Hooker's Corps. Handfuls of Georgians and North Carolinians fell to the ground, some rising up and staggering to the rear for help, others never to rise again. Veterans fired skillfully at veterans across the field, both sides unwilling to yield.[26]

Back in the East Woods, General Mansfield was still trying to deploy Crawford's Brigade. Bullets hissed by men's ears and artillery rained in as Mansfield left the 10th Maine and hurried off to get the large 128th Pennsylvania into position. He ordered

24. Bradley, *Surviving Stonewall*, 194-6. Sears, *Landscape Turned Red*, 205.
25. Williams, *From the Cannon's Mouth*, 126.
26. Priest, *Soldiers' Battle*, 77.

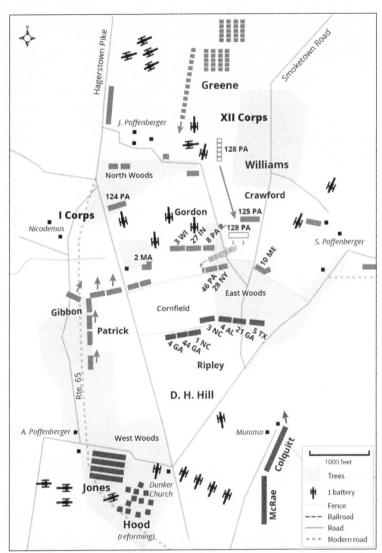

[Antietam Battle Map 3.] Deploying the 128th Pennsylvania.

the regiment to form to the right of the 46th Pennsylvania and 28th New York in the Cornfield.[27] Not having time to deploy, they moved forward in columns of divisions through a slight ravine in the woods, but as they funneled through, their lead companies came under the fire. The Pennsylvanians were immediately frightened, and Private Frederick Crouse remembered, "We heard the whistle of the Minnie ball and we all began to duck and I got a

---

27. Carman, *Maryland Campaign*, 118-22. Bradley, *Surviving Stonewall*, 190.

little weak in the knees." The Rebel fire was accurate, and within moments the 128th's Colonel was killed and their Lieutenant Colonel wounded, throwing the shaky regiment into panic.[28]

Most of the regiment rushed over to the right of the 46th Pennsylvania in a mob. Officers of the 28th New York and 46th Pennsylvania, along with General Williams, went over to try to align the 128th into a line of battle along the northern side of the Cornfield. Bullets rained in and men struggled to gain a foothold without stepping on the dead or wounded. Voices went hoarse, and acrid smoke clung to the ground. Bullets hit their mark with a sickening frequency.

About thirty minutes had elapsed since the 46th Pennsylvania and 28th New York had moved into the East Woods and the 128th Pennsylvania had finally somewhat settled into place beside them. In the chaos and confusion, with lead flying through the air and wounded screaming for mercy, no one recalled the exact moment when George Brooks fell to the blood-stained ground with a bullet through his right forehead. He died instantly.[29]

---

28. Wagner, *Honor, Flag, And Family,* 138.
29. *Pension File, Captain George A. Brooks.*

CHAPTER FOURTEEN

From the Dead the Living Should Learn a Lesson

September 18, 1862–Present

JOHN W. BROWN'S wagon rattled through Frederick, Maryland on Thursday the 18th of September, and then turned and continued up the pike toward Harrisburg. His job that day was a somber one—in the back of the wagon was the body of a twenty-eight year old captain, still wearing his uniform and draped with a blanket. George Brooks was finally going home for good.

News of the battle that had raged all of the day prior reached Harrisburg quickly, along with word that Captain Brooks had been killed. He would receive a proper burial with his family and friends in attendance unlike thousands of young soldiers who were being unceremoniously dropped into mass graves in the decimated fields surrounding Sharpsburg.

Pennsylvania Daily Telegraph
September 18, 1862
Thursday Afternoon

Capt George A Brooks–

A report reached this city today to the effect that Capt. George A Brooks, company D, Forty sixth P.V., was killed. His body will arrive here this afternoon.

Capt. Brooks was a private in Capt. M'Cormick's company, the Lochiel Greys, in the three months service, and immediately after his return, recruited a company, the Verbeke Rifles, attached it to Col Knipe's 46th regiment, in which position he served until he met his death. He was with the company in all the important battles in which his regiment engaged—participated in the first assault at Winchester—was at Front Royal to repel the attack of Jackson, and covered the rear of General Banks' masterly retreat through the Shenandoah Valley. After that retreat he again marched over the valley to Culpeper Court House, and at the battle of Slaughter [Cedar] Mountain, in consequence of the absence of his First Lieutenant on other duty and the illness of his second, Capt Brooks himself left a sick bed, to lead his men into the field, resolved that they should not go without the direction of an officer with whom they were acquainted. In this bloody encounter, the field officers of the 46th were all disabled, when the command of the regiment fell upon Capt. Brooks in fact he found himself in command of the entire right wing, in which position, by the coolness of his direction and the gallantry of his daring, he won the applause of all who followed his leading. In this engagement he was himself wounded, while only sixteen of his company escaped with their lives, the others having all fallen into the jaws of death.

In this connection, it is not out of place to mention that Capt Brooks, from time to time corresponded with the TELEGRAPH. His letters from the army were always read with interest, and as a writer, (with the advantage of being a practical printer,) was very popular with our readers.

Just two weeks ago Captain Brooks left his home, his wife and his only child, and hastened forward to the head of his shattered yet undaunted command. He had scarcely recovered from his wounds—he was yet weak and weary from the effects of the brunt of battle, but with a mind glowing with ardor and a heart full of hope, he hurried from his precious loved ones to join his gallant companions, and once more bear his arm in the glorious fight for liberty, for law, and for government. In that fight he fell—in the defense of liberty he perished—and while liberty survives may his name be remembered with gratitude.

Pennsylvania Daily Telegraph
Friday Afternoon, September 19th

Arrival of the Body of Capt George A Brooks—The body of the gallant George A Brooks, of the immortal Forty-Six'h Regiment, Pennsylvania Volunteers, arrived in this city to-day, and is now in the charge of his immediate friends. It was brought from the battlefield to this city by John W. Brown. Of course due notice of the interment of the remains of Capt. Brooks will be given, so that the public may pay their last respect to the memory of a brave and true man.

His funeral will take place this evening at six o'clock, from the residence of his father-in-law, Mr. Theodore F. Scheffer, in Locust Street, near Front, to which his relatives and friends are invited to attend.

———————•◦•◦•———————

Pennsylvania Daily Telegraph
Saturday, September 20th

The Funeral of Capt. Brooks– The remains of Capt. Brooks were buried last evening in the family lot at Mt. Kalma Cemetery.

At the request of the relations of the deceased, the funeral was entirely private, or at least it was divested of all military pageantry and display. He was buried from the residence of his father in law, Theodore F. Scheffer, in Locust street, below Front. The military escort that accompanies the body from the battlefield to this city, followed it to the grave, and this was all that distinguished the funeral from that of the burial of a civilian.

By the time the funeral procession reached the cemetery, the dark clouds of night had gathered over the earth, thus rendering the scene and the occasion, solemn, impressive and even melancholy. Rev. Dr. Hay officiated, and with the most touching and pathetic eloquence, alluded to the virtues of the deceased, the noble cause in which he had died, and the reward which was surely his in that Heaven where battles do not rage, nor death enter to disturb its peace. He spoke to those who mourned a hero, and reminded them that he who was now in the grave, had won other victories than those which crimson the garments with blood in their achievement. The hero of war, had also been the hero of peace. He who had covered himself with laurels in the defense of his country, and laid down his life that freedom might live, had also crowned himself with laurels that would bloom in other scenes, and shed their fragrance to perfume the atmosphere of the divine. He spoke to her who mourned a husband, and reminded her of the presence of Him who had promised to be a husband to the widowed—Tears could not call back the dead. Lamentation would not break the chain of his sleep. Let him rest, then, in his grave and his glory. Such at least, were Dr. Hay's thoughts on the occasion, but far more eloquently expressed than we can attempt to sketch. From our pen, no tribute would be too glowing in memory of Capt Brooks. We honored him while he lived, because he was brave, courteous and frank. We now deplore his death, because had he lived, he might have risen to the eminence which his noble qualities ever indicated that he should occupy. And yet we bow to the inscrutable decrees of Providence, and beseech in fervent sincerity, *for peace to the ashes of George A. Brooks.*

❋ ❋ ❋

The fighting on September 17th had consisted of a savagery and scale that is still regarded by historians as the bloodiest day in American military history. After a single day of battle, almost 23,000 men lay wounded, dead, and dying. After losing even more men from their depleted ranks, the 46th Pennsylvania had left the field as reinforcements from Sumner's Corps arrived. Almost twenty men in the regiment were wounded, five of whom would die of their injuries in the coming months. General Mansfield had fallen mortally wounded around the same time as Captain Brooks, leaving Ol' Pap Williams back in command of the corps. Twenty-five percent of McClellan's committed troops had fallen dead or wounded, and about 31 percent of Lee's.[1] In some places, General Williams remembered the dead lay "as thick as autumn leaves . . . In one place, in front of the position of my corps, apparently a whole regiment had been cut down in line. They lay in two ranks, as straightly aligned as on a dress parade."[2]

As desperately as both sides had struggled, there was no real tactical gain. Lee's bloodied and exhausted army remained in place on September 18th, and McClellan made no attempt to crush him at his most vulnerable. By the end of the year, McClellan's inaction would leave Lincoln with no choice but to dismiss the once promising young general.

Lee and Jackson considered a counterattack of their own, but the toll the campaign had taken on their army was enormous. Their soldiers were in no shape to fight, and were still badly

1. Bradley, *Surviving Stonewall*, 199-201. Sears, *Landscape Turned Red*, 295-6.
2. Williams, *From the Cannon's Mouth*, 130-2.

Confederate casualties awaiting burial line the Hagerstown Turnpike. The fence borders the western edge of the Cornfield where the 46th PA fought. (Source: Library of Congress.)

outnumbered. By evening on the 18th, Lee started his defeated army across the Potomac and headed back into Virginia. Though no one had won the battle, Lee had clearly lost the campaign and his chance for a decisive confrontation that would win the war.

Lee's repulsion was victory enough for Lincoln to revisit his plans for addressing slavery. On September 22nd, he called his cabinet together to read to them the final draft of the preliminary Proclamation of Emancipation. Though Lincoln had long avoided answering both domestically and internationally whether the war was about slavery, it was now unavoidable. The patriotic fervor of 1861 that had inspired northerners to send their sons and husbands off to restore the Union had been extinguished by the realities of war. To win, there would have to be a greater meaning. When the Emancipation Proclamation was released to a weary northern public, the freedom of three million enslaved people was permanently entwined with the fate of the United States of America.[3] To the world, America's war was now about freedom and the survival of the idea of democratic government. As Lincoln so eloquently phrased it in his address to Congress that December, the

---

3. Catton, *Terrible Swift Sword*, 456, 461, 477.

United States was the "last best hope of earth." If America failed, so too would freedom.[4]

And so, as 1862 gave way to a new year, the armies marched on, leaving behind comrades in fresh graves. George Brooks had died a tactically needless death at a time when everything about the country he had volunteered to defend was changing forever. Militarily, the valor and patriotism of service had been bloodied beyond recognition. Modern weapons and a hostility that first made itself known on early-war battlefields like Cedar Mountain and Antietam would send hundreds of thousands more to their graves and leave a psychological wound on a generation. Politically, socially, and diplomatically, the war was now going to answer the question of freedom.

✳ ✳ ✳

The 46th Pennsylvania spent the fall shivering on the steep elevation of Maryland Heights overlooking Harpers Ferry before moving south to winter quarters in Fairfax, Virginia.[5] Hard service returned soon, though, and by spring they were back on campaign. They served meritoriously at Chancellorsville and Gettysburg before transferring west and participating in the Atlanta Campaign, Sherman's March to the Sea, and the Carolinas Campaign. After a long four years, when peace finally arrived, the civilians that George Brooks had helped turned into soldiers were exactly that, and they were among the finest in the army. After one last long march to Washington, they participated in the Grand Review of the Armies in May and were mustered out in July.[6]

George Brooks' men in Company D who had started the war with him had felt its full brunt. Sixty-three percent of them were wounded at least once, and thirty-three percent were prisoners of war at least once. Eleven percent of them were killed or died of their wounds. Another ten percent died of disease, accidents, or were missing in action. Eight percent were discharged for their wounds. Forty-five of Brooks' original volunteers stood in rank in July when the regiment was mustered out.[7]

---

4. Doyle, *Cause of all nations*, 7-11.
5. Bradley, *Surviving Stonewall*, 204-5.
6. Bates, *History of Pennsylvania Volunteers*, 1111-7.
7. Statistics compiled by the author using Muster Rolls, the personal correspondence of Captain George A. Brooks, and George C. Bradley's pension file database for the 46th Pennsylvania. Infantry.

Regiments of Sherman's 20th Army Corps parade down Pennsylvania Avenue in Washington, D.C. (Source: Library of Congress.)

They returned home and tried to resume the lives they had left four years prior, but in the same way the nation they had preserved had changed, so had they. Some had become strangers to their own families and found their long awaited return awkward and fraught with loneliness. Others struggled to find work, with some employers refusing to hire veterans because they feared they could "do nothing hereafter for a living but fight." Things were even worse for the permanently disabled, who had no choice but to rely on family, pensions, or their comrades for help. Almost all found themselves struggling to accept what they had seen and done during the war. During a time before the medical community recognized what we now call Post-traumatic Stress Disorder, soldiers were left to their own devices to deal with the horrors of war.[8]

---

8. Jordan, Brian Matthew. *Marching Home: Union Veterans and Their Unending Civil War.* WW Norton & Company, 2015. 40, 50, 54, 56, 73.

Brooks' friends were no exception as they resumed their lives as civilians. Lieutenant Witman (or "Lieut Ned" as Brooks referred to him) had led the company from the time of Brooks' death until September of 1864 through some of the hardest fighting the regiment experienced. In July of 1864, at the Battle of Peach Tree Creek, Witman's older brother, Luther, Adjutant of the regiment, was mortally wounded.[9] A month later, Witman was promoted to Lieutenant Colonel of the 210th Pennsylvania Infantry and was later promoted to Colonel. After the war, he resumed his occupation as a druggist in Harrisburg, and later worked as a civil engineer for the railroad. He never married. He died in 1912 and is buried in the Harrisburg Cemetery not far from Captain Brooks.[10]

Valentine Hummel, who was a Harrisburg friend of Brooks' and served in a cavalry regiment, mustered out as a Captain. He eventually moved west to Illinois where he worked in various occupations. At the age of forty-six, he checked into a Soldier's Home, which provided aging and permanently disabled veterans with a place to live and medical care. His young age was not unique—thousands of veterans were permanently "prematurely broken down" by their service. He lived in soldier's homes on and off until his death in 1916. He never married or had children, and is buried in Peoria State Hospital Cemetery in Illinois.[11]

Another Harrisburg friend, John Wesley Awl, served in various Pennsylvania regiments and attained the rank of Lieutenant Colonel. After the war he resumed his profession as an attorney. He never married and died suddenly while at work in 1894, his obituary indicating that his health had been poor ever since his military service thirty years prior.[12]

Estelle Hughes, Brooks' Williamsport friend who clearly took a liking to the young Captain, married after the war and had two children. Her husband died in 1876 and she never remarried, dying in 1924 at the age of eighty-one. She is buried in Morgantown, West Virginia.[13]

Many of Brooks' friends in the 46th left by various means shortly after his death. Captain Benjamin Morgan of Company F,

---

9. National Cemetery Administration. *U.S. Veterans Gravesites*, ca.1775-2006.
10. *General Index to Pension Files, 1861-1934.* Washington, D.C.: National Archives and Records Administration. T288, 546 rolls. *Harrisburg Cemetery Records,* Harrisburg, Pennsylvania. Plot: Section H-2, Lot 106.
11. Jordan, *Marching Home,* 127. "Capt Valentine B Hummel." Find A Grave. Accessed July 17, 2016. www.findagrave.com.
12. HC Cooper, *The Twentieth Century Bench and Bar of Pennsylvania,* Volume 2. 1902. 769.
13. "Estelle Hughes Wallace." Find A Grave. Accessed May 30, 2016. www.findagrave.com

with whom Brooks had spent much of his leisure time, had seen his fair share of war by early 1863 and resigned. He returned home to Pittsburgh and married in 1865. He and his wife didn't have children, and he died in 1907. Adjutant George Boyd was discharged in October of 1862 for the wounds he received at Cedar Mountain. He, too, married, and died in 1900. Major Cyrus Strouse died in May of 1863 of wounds received at Chancellorsville. Major Joseph A. Matthews was promoted to command the 128th Pennsylvania who had lost their Colonel at Antietam. He served in various commands until the end of the war and returned to Harrisburg where he died in 1873 at the age of forty-seven.[14]

Captain Owen Lukenbach of Company C was discharged in November of 1862 for the leg he lost at Cedar Mountain. He had a successful life after the war, serving as Postmaster of Bethlehem, PA, for a number of years and running a hardware business. He married and had four children who survived to adulthood. Active with veterans affairs and his community, he died at age fifty-six in 1890.[15]

Quartermaster George Cadwalader transferred in mid 1863 to serve as assistant quartermaster to the US Volunteers. Captain Griffith of Company I eventually served as the regiment's fourth Major until their muster out.[16]

Colonel Joseph F. Knipe took command of the 46th's brigade after Antietam. He was promoted to Brigadier General in early 1863 and served until shortly after the battle of Gettysburg when he was forced to return to Harrisburg from complications of wounds and malaria. For the remainder of the war he occupied a few different commands, including returning to his brigade for a short time. After the war he was appointed Postmaster in Harrisburg and served in various political roles at the state and Federal level, including Postmaster of The House of Representatives. He died August 18th, 1901 at the age of seventy-eight and was also interred at the Harrisburg Cemetery.[17]

Lt. Colonel James L. Selfridge was promoted to command of the 46th Regiment after Antietam. He led them through the remainder of the war until the Atlanta Campaign when he took

---

14. Pension files for Morgan (P#1095938), Boyd (A#567489), Strouse (SP#35687), and Matthews (P#115751).
15. Jordan, John W. *Historic homes and institutions and genealogical and personal memoirs of the Lehigh Valley, Pennsylvania*, Volume 2. Lewis Publishing Co., 1905. 250.
16. Bates, *History of Pennsylvania Volunteers*, 1117.
17. "The Bugle." *Quarterly Journal of the Camp Curtin Historical Society and Civil War Round Table, Inc.* Vol. 17, No. 2. 2007.

command of the brigade. He was breveted to Brigadier General for bravery during the campaigns that followed. The end of the war did not bring peace to Selfridge's life—in April of 1865 his only child, Annie, died at age ten of spotted fever and in 1866, a little over a year after returning home, his wife passed away. He remarried the next year. In 1868, he was elected Chief Clerk of the House of Representatives of Pennsylvania, serving until 1873. He then became proprietor of the Lehigh Hydraulic Cement Company and served as Major-General of the Seventh Division of the National Guard of Pennsylvania.[18] He died May 19th, 1887 at only sixty-two years of age, his death certificate indicating he committed suicide while "temporarily insane." He is buried in the Nisky Hill Cemetery in Bethlehem, Pennsylvania.[19]

Major General Alpheus S. Williams, Old Pap, who had successively commanded the 46th Pennsylvania's brigade, division, and corps, always remained fond of his "old brigade." After muster out, he stayed in the service and was assigned to administrate southern Arkansas. Retiring from the army in early January of 1866, he returned to his home in Michigan. There he assumed a post as the U.S. Minister in San Salvador, where he stayed until 1869. After a failed run for Governor of Michigan in 1870, he took a short respite from public life, but unable to remain docile, he ran and was elected as a Democrat in the 45th Congress. While serving in that post, he suffered a stroke on December 21st, 1878 and perished in the Capitol Building. He is buried in Detroit at Elmwood Cemetery.[20]

George and Emily's only son, William, married during the 1880s. He and his wife had two daughters, Helen and Emily. By the early 1900s, William had located the family in High Point, North Carolina, where he worked as the manager of a glass factory. He lived in North Carolina until his death in August 1927 at the age of sixty-six.[21] His daughter Helen had three children and a large number of descendents still live in the High Point area and throughout North Carolina.[22]

18. Blanchard, Charles. *The progressive men of the Commonwealth of Pennsylvania*. 1900. 572-73.
19. "Pennsylvania, Philadelphia City Death Certificates, 1803–1915." Index. FamilySearch, Salt Lake City, Utah, 2008, 2010. From originals housed at the Philadelphia City Archives. "Death Records." Pennsylvania Historical and Museum Commission; Harrisburg, Pennsylvania. *Pennsylvania Veterans Burial Cards, 1929-1990*; Archive Collection Number: *Series 1-11*; Folder Number: *439*.
20. Williams, *From the Cannon's Mouth*, 10-11.
21. North Carolina State Board of Health, Bureau of Vital Statistics. *North Carolina Death Certificates*. Microfilm S.123. Rolls 19-242, 280, 313-682, 1040-1297. North Carolina State Archives, Raleigh, North Carolina.
22. Year: *1930*; Census Place: *High Point, Guilford, North Carolina*; Roll: *1695*; Page: *3A*; Enumeration District: *49*; Image: *631.0*; FHL microfilm: *2341429*.

William D. Brooks, bearing a striking resemblance to his father, and his wife, Lenay. (Source: Brooks Family Collection.)

After a marriage of only three years that was overshadowed by George's long absences from home, Emily Brooks never remarried. With the help of her father who had so disliked George, she applied and was granted a pension backdated to September 17th, 1862.[23]

Emily and several of her unmarried brothers and sisters ran their father's print shop and book bindery until they retired. Emily died on September 15th, 1907, almost forty-five years to the day after her husband's death. She was buried with George at Harrisburg (Mount Kalma) Cemetery.[24] Forty-eight years prior, on a spring morning in 1859, George had started a letter to his future wife:

Had a long and very pleasant walk again this morning, and would gladly have had my own dear Em by my side, never mind, we will soon have rambles together. Won't you go to the Cemetery some pretty afternoon? I had a pleasant saunter through it myself

23. Widow's Certificate No. WC12134, Brooks, George A., Captain.
24. Harrisburg *Patriot* Newspaper, September 16, 1907.

this morning. Oh, how I love to muse o'er the graves of those who were once as gay and happy as your own George, but who now alas "sleep the sleep that knows no waking" in the "silent city of the dead," Mount Kalma, where the weeping willow gently kisses the tomb of the slumbered who rests beneath, and flowers—those bright emblems of mortality on which the kind hand of affection has planted o'er the grave of some dearly loved one, fill the air with fragrance. How sorrowful, to read the tributes of love, engraven upon the marble tablets, but how much more sorrowful would it be could we read the thoughts and feelings which are engraven upon the tablets of the heart of those who have lost some near and dear friend. From the dead the living should learn a lesson, for we know not how soon we may rest among them.

BEN MYERS was born and raised just outside of Harrisburg, PA, where an interest in local and family Civil War history found him at a young age. His research on the 46th Pennsylvania Volunteer Infantry has appeared in *The Civil War Times* and *Military Images* magazines, as well as online at fortysixthregiment. org. He holds a B.S. in Computer Science from American University and works as a web designer and developer in Washington, D.C. *American Citizen* is his first book.

Made in the USA
Monee, IL
15 July 2021